The Gold Rush Diary of Ramón Gil Navarro

The Gold Rush Diary
of
Ramón Gil Navarro

Ramón Gil Navarro

EDITED AND TRANSLATED BY
MARÍA DEL CARMEN FERREYRA
AND DAVID S. REHER

University of Nebraska Press
Lincoln and London

Library of Congress Cataloging-in-Publication Data

Navarro, Ramón Gil, d. 1883.
The gold rush diary of Ramón Gil Navarro / Ramón Gil Navarro ; edited and translated
by María del Carmen Ferreyra and David S. Reher.
p.   cm.
Includes bibliographical references (p.) and index.
ISBN 0-8032-3343-4 (cloth : alk. paper)
1. Navarro, Ramón Gil, d. 1883—Diaries.   2. California—Gold discoveries—Social
aspects.   3. Gold mines and mining—Social aspects—California.   4. Argentines—
California—Diaries.   5. California—Social conditions—19th century.   6. California—
Race relations.   7. Mexican Americans—California—Social conditions—19th
century.   I. Ferreyra, María del Carmen.   II. Reher, David Sven.   III. Title.
F865.N38   2000
979.4'04'092—dc21   00-020988

Contents

Illustrations

Acknowledgments

Any worthwhile project invariably ends up becoming a kind of obsession if it is ever going to be a true success. The story of this project is the story of an interest in a fascinating historical and family figure that grew into an obsession with the man, his diary, and the historical period in which he wrote. The editors of this book, both practicing historians working on different continents, originally approached this initiative from divergent perspectives. One of them, the great-granddaughter of Ramón Gil Navarro and the person who undertook the original transcription of the diary many years ago, was drawn to the project because of family interests and pride and an awareness of the originality of the author at a key juncture in Argentine history. The other, a specialist in Spanish (and only secondarily in Latin American) history and a native of California, was attracted by the uniqueness of the diary, by the chance to bring to light new sources on the history of South America and especially of California, and by the friendship and common interests he shared with his coauthor. Once the team started its work, however, the diary and its author sucked them into a whirlpool of fascination and became a never-ending subject of conversation for those around them, often depriving them of the desire to do anything but work on its completion. In this way, the project became an obsession, as well as an enduring source of joy, for both authors. Whether this obsession has given rise to a truly successful initiative can only be judged by the readers and by the extent to which they too are swept up in the excitement of the diary and its author.

Any intellectual adventure creates innumerable debts of gratitude. This diary is no exception. A book of this nature would never be possible without the support of major research libraries and archives. In the course of our research, we were able to make ample use of the collections held at the Hispanic Division of the Library of Congress and at the Biblioteca Hispánica in Madrid. The Bancroft Library at the University of California at Berkeley deserves special mention not only for having granted us permission to publish the diary and a number of the illustrations in this book but also for facilitating access to their own magnificent collection of documents.

Over the past several years, we have been fortunate enough to have colleagues and friends who have generously offered us their assistance and encouragement in many different ways. René Navarro Ocampo (†) was the person who first gave us access to the diary many years ago, Enrique Capdevila(†) read the original transcription of the diary back in 1977, and Fernando Allende Navarro(†) graciously gave us the family picture included in this text of Samuel Navarro with William Perkins and his wife, Parmenia Navarro Ocampo, and shared many intimate details about the Navarro family in Chile. All of them deserve to be remembered here. Juan Bautista Yofre allowed us the unrestricted use of his personal library. Father Carlos Heredia, Efraín Bischoff, and Ariel de la Fuente facilitated pertinent bibliographical material. Rudecinda Lobuglio, Mimi Lozano, and Carmen Boone de Aguilar provided valuable information on a number of persons mentioned in the text and gave us many other useful suggestions. Carlos M. De Ferrari, Joan Gorsuch, and Santa Maria Marrone were instrumental in helping us locate some of the original mining sites. Suzanne Pazstor and Seth Meisel provided useful archival assistance, and Alejandra Araya Espinosa, Eduardo Cavieres, Deborah Mastel, Mary Dufour, and Patrick Galloway helped us secure copies of pertinent publications or assisted in other aspects of this project. Susan Socolow was an ongoing source of encouragement and helped put us in touch with the University of Nebraska Press. Charis Anne Baz-Takaro helped us invaluably by putting together the set of illustrations from the collection of the Bancroft Library used in this edition. Guillermo Reher helped design all the maps. José Sánchez Bretón, Valentina Tikoff, Charis Baz-Takaro, Kathie Strafaci, José Moya, and Paula Moya read parts or all of the text and gave us many useful suggestions. We are especially grateful to the two readers for the University of Nebraska Press for their helpful comments, to copyeditor Anne Taylor for her gracious and efficient help in getting the manuscript ready for publication, and to the staff at the University of Nebraska Press.

Numerous friends and colleagues have been kind enough to listen to our unending tales about the diary, its author, and this entire intellectual adventure. Their encouragement of and suggestions for the project proved to be extremely helpful. Finally, special mention is due to Dolores Moyano Martin, another great-granddaughter of Navarro, whose enthusiasm, suggestions, and insight have been essential at every stage of this project. We owe a great debt of gratitude to all of these people, which can only be repaid, and then only in part, if they too end up thinking that, indeed, this project has been a successful one.

Introduction

~~~♪~~~

I am going to California! Everyone has heard about California. This entire society, from the wisest of the wise to the most rustic hillbilly, has been talking about California. The friars at church talk about its gold, and on walks, in drawing rooms, and even while praying people ask the Lord for a safe trip up there. I believe that for centuries there has not been anything that has obsessed everyone all over the world as much as California. They say so much about that far-off land that my diary, even if it were to be completely filled, could never contain all the news that reaches us all the time from that remote land. Summing it up, they say that everyone who gets there can make his fortune. Then fine, that is where I am going.

Navarro, diary entry for 15 February 1849

Ramón Gil Navarro's diary contains the intimate confessions of a young man during one of the most important periods in any man's life, his late adolescence and young adulthood. It is a diary written by an Argentinean political exile who first took refuge in Chile, just beyond the reach of the Argentinean political hatreds, disputes, reprisals, and singular lack of political tolerance. From there, he, like thousands of people from all over the world, heard the call of California, the California where gold had been discovered. Heading up a Chilean mining company, he set sail in search of his own personal fortune and destiny.

Navarro's intensely personal account is about California and about gold, of course, but it is also about life, love, success, and frustration. A stunning tale of his own experience as a forty-niner, the diary is also an often intensely lyrical exploration into our human condition. Navarro was a keen but seldom dispassionate observer of life with a penchant for literary description. He was strongly Argentinean in his education, outlook, and temperament, but he was also a man enthusiastically caught up in the maelstrom of life that took place in California during the gold rush.

Navarro began his diary several years before his departure for California. It opens with the author, only eighteen years of age, leaving his beloved Catamarca as a political refugee in September 1845 with his mother and his siblings. A caravan of refugees on horseback, they set out to cross the implacable deserts of La Rioja and San Juan and the Andes Mountains in search of freedom. They left behind a silent, empty house, where time seemed to have ceased and only echoes remained. Only Tirano, the family dog, remained behind. In his still childish script, Ramón Gil Navarro says, "I made signs to him to follow me, but he lowered his head and lay down where I had left him. I tried to get him going by calling him, but he never budged. Then a sad idea came to my mind. It seemed to me that he was reproaching us all for having abandoned the roof that had protected us for so many years and that he alone would stay behind, keeping a watch on that isolated and lonely home. That thought brought tears to my eyes." The banished family was heading for Chile, where the father had gone some years earlier for political reasons, which never seemed to be lacking in the turbulent lands of South America.

Argentina began its movement toward independence from Spain in 1810, but by mid-century, it is safe to say, it still had not found its way. It was a period dominated by the long shadow of the tyrant Juan Manuel Rosas, who originally came to power in 1829 and remained there until 1852, despite political instability and civil war. Navarro's kin were fierce enemies of Rosas and his regime, and they were to pay for their dissent with a prolonged period of exile in Chile.

The Provinces of Catamarca and La Rioja, a remote region of semibarbaric Argentina that bordered on Chile, were the homes of the ancestors of the Navarro exiles. Living off the beaten commercial path gave rise to a special society and attitude in those provinces. A harsh and vast countryside made up of deserts, mountains, and deep blue skies, where time seemed to have stopped, or at least where it seemed to repeat itself over and over again, could not help but leave an imprint on its people.

This family of exiles was one of the most important in Argentina. On the Navarro side, Ramón's family had descended from the conquistador Juan Ramírez de Velasco; on the Ocampo side, they had descended from the Bazán de Pedraza, the Herrera y Guzmán, and the Villafañe. All of these names are linked to the most illustrious Argentinean lineages, dating back to the sixteenth and seventeenth centuries, who had come to Argentina from upper Peru either as conquistadors or as settlers. The legends of their past glories, transmitted from generation to generation, were always present in the family lore and ended up conditioning their actions, marking their lives with a special sign.

The Ocampo side of Navarro's family included "governors, military figures, politicians, jurists, churchmen, writers and pioneers, all of whom were intimately united by a pervasive spirit of cast and of clan."[1] This spirit was reflected in their often endogamous marriage strategies. The tendency to marry within the family group was prevalent among the exiles: Ramón Gil, the author of the diary, ended up marrying his second cousin; his brother Samuel married his aunt; his uncle Domingo Ocampo married twice, both times with his nieces; and his brother Darío married his first cousin.

One of the Navarro family descendants, Fernando Allende Navarro, a respected genealogist, points out one of the most salient traits of his father's side of the family, the Navarro de Velasco: the almost pathological pride of its members. This same writer, who was able to trace the lives of a number of the people mentioned in this book, sent us a copy of a letter by Ramón Gil's older brother Mardoqueo that offers us a bruising portrait of his own personality and the traits he saw in his siblings. In the letter, he warns his younger brother Darío against "that never exaggerated or sufficiently maligned pride of all of the persons who make up our family." He continues, "I must plead with you for a promise, based on your word of honor, that you will fight in yourself that infernal quality which has overwhelmed me my entire life."

This somber panorama gives way to a brighter side, as Allende Navarro explains: "Even if they were victims of some of the characteristics I have mentioned, I would also like to say that they had very important good qualities as well. Agile, quick, and intuitive intelligence, along with great sensitivity and capacity for affection, they were capable of any sacrifice, no matter how great, in order to help out a friend. Yet much of this talent, legitimately inherited from their parents, was often diminished by the affective volubility so typical in them. What is more, they were extremely affectionate, very pleasant in society, and capable of very elegant and sparkling conversation. They were cultured beyond what was typical in their times, and, in addition, they were all very good looking."[2] Throughout his diary, the young Ramón Gil will display many of these same qualities and defects that had always characterized his lineage.

Navarro's refugee family arrived in the southern Chilean town of Concepción in early 1846. There Ramón Gil, no longer able to continue his studies, was a simple employee, an exile, a stranger to the conservative society of Concepción. His decision to join a Chilean mining company in 1849 to prospect for gold in California would change his life forever.

Map 1. Chile and Argentina

Upon arriving in California, where his brother Samuel awaited him, he resided briefly in Stockton before leaving for the mines in Calaveras. After more than a year in the mines, he returned to Stockton and resided at his brother's home. Melones, the Stanislaus River, Sonora, Mokelumne, Sacramento, Marysville, and, of course, San Francisco all became essential parts of Navarro's personal history.

In California he met his future brother-in-law, William Perkins, a Canadian, who had the following opinion of the conflictive relationship between North Americans and South Americans: "To the South American, the arrogance or rather the quiet contempt of the North American must be very galling. The Yankee has in a preeminent degree the Saxon vice of looking down, as upon an inferior, on all those who may happen not to be able to converse with him in his own native tongue." Regarding the Argentineans, he says:

> The immigration from the Argentine Republic is composed almost exclusively of men of education and family. . . . Those Argentinos in California then, are almost without exception the exiles from Chile and Perú. They are proud, clean in their habits, fast friends and fonder generally of the guitar and poetry than of hard work, but never meddle with any one, shun brawls and drinking saloons, and do not gamble as much as other South Americans. They are ostentatious in dress, and are generally honorable in their mercantile transactions. Once a friend, an Argentino knows no bounds to his disinterestedness. . . . These people are very reserved, mixing little with other Spaniards. They are proud yet very good fellows, when one becomes intimate with them. They hold in contempt the Peruvians, Chilians and Mexicans, to all of whom, at least those we have here, they are in truth vastly superior."[3]

Navarro's experience in California changed him greatly, and by the time he returned to Chile he had acquired a great admiration for American society. The love-hate relationship that characterized his first contacts in California turned into one of respect and admiration, which can be seen in the many letters he sent from Chile to his relatives in Catamarca. The letters are filled with projects of how to improve the living conditions and the economy in his homeland: "Manuel, you cannot imagine how much you can learn about action itself in the United States. There you think, then you act. If not, it is as though you have not been thinking. . . . In all of South America, people see things, they know them, they see their usefulness, yet they do nothing to make them happen. They do not make necessary improvements because they are afraid of making a mistake. Who knows what is behind that willingness to always be content with the same thing and never to improve anything, no matter how necessary it might be."[4] When he published his story "Los Chilenos en California en 1849 y 50" in 1853, Navarro said: "Far from having any personal hostility toward the Yankees, the author of these notes has left perhaps some of his very best friends in California. He feels himself to be a Yankee in ideas regarding freedom, trade, improvements, and innovations. Far from hating the Americans, he has only respect and admiration for them."

After their father's death in Chile, pressure increased on both Samuel and Ramón to return home to take care of the family's affairs. By the time Ramón finally left California, Rosas had been overthrown, and a new future was dawning for Argentina and for Argentinean exiles. Upon his return to Valparaiso, he joined the Club Constitucional Argentino, a group of Argentinean exiles promoting the quick approval of a constitution based on the ideas of one of their members, Juan Bautista Alberdi. The progress he witnessed in California had a profound effect on him. During his remaining years in Chile, the backwardness of his native Catamarca overwhelmed him, and with his youthful ardor he would dream up all kinds of projects: creating primary schools, teaching languages, creating newspapers, building hospitals, increasing commerce, implementing cotton farming, facilitating immigration, and so forth.[5]

A number of years went by before Ramón was able to return to Argentina. In Chile he prepared himself for journalism by writing, which is what he did best. Writing was his passion, and he spent many hours doing just that. When he was finally able to return to Argentina in 1855, his entry into politics signified another important change in his life. From then until his death, politics and journalism were his passions.

Back in Argentina, he lived first in the town of La Rioja and later in Paraná in the Province of Entre Ríos, where he combined his political obligations as a representative in the national congress with his work as a journalist. He finally took up residence in Córdoba after marrying his second cousin, and he lived there for the final twenty-three years of his life. It was in Córdoba that, thanks to the help of President Urquiza, in 1867 he was able to found the newspaper *El Progreso*. As had happened with many other projects in his life, the newspaper was at the service of an ideal, an ideal that had his country en route to peace, progress, and prosperity.

In a real sense, Ramón Gil Navarro and Argentina grew into adulthood together. His life encompasses the evolution of the country, from the polit-ical and social chaos that followed the War of Independence against Spain, through the turbulent years dominated by Rosas, through its consolidation as a constitutional republic, to its final emergence in the 1870s and 1880s as one of the most prosperous and advanced nations in the hemisphere.[6]

Shortly after Ramón Gil Navarro's death in July 1883, Joaquín González, an eminent politician and a man of letters from La Rioja, recalled Navarro and his experience in California in the following terms: "The most florid and delightful part of his youth was spent in Stockton, where, imitating the troubadours of the Middle Ages, he delighted social gatherings with his poetry and his traditional guitar. . . . As a man, he had defects, but all of them paled in the light of his great heart. He loved life, his family, his fellow men, his country, and his youth, and he was always willing to give of his time and energy to promote these sentiments."[7]

Navarro's diary contains an account of life during the gold rush rendered from the perspective of an Argentinean refugee who reached California through Chile. It is an account written by an astute, cultured, yet impassioned, observer. The line separating historical actor from observer appears to be a thin one for Navarro. Any true diary exudes a certain immediacy, and Navarro's is no exception. Even so, it is apparent that in his daily life and in his diary he made every effort to be both actor and observer. This was a central aspect of his personality, and it is one of the key characteristics of his diary.

The twenty-two-year-old Argentinean forty-niner experienced California life and wrote about it from a perspective colored by his own background and temperament. Tolerant by nature and belief yet traditional in his upbringing, Navarro continually struggled to assimilate, to categorize, to understand, and to judge a world that was anything but traditional. Having been raised a Catholic in Argentina, he was, at the very least, a formally religious person, and he continually contrasted his childhood experience of religion in traditional, Catholic Argentina with the unorthodox, makeshift, and mostly non-Catholic religiosity he experienced in California. His diary is filled with invocations to God to guide his steps and to help deliver him from the constant dangers and evils of life in the mines. While at times this religious sense of life appears to be a mere formality, almost a figure of speech, at other times there is reason to believe that his faith was a source of support and comfort in a bewildering world.

Living as a political refugee during the Rosas regime and dedicating his life to political causes after his return to Argentina attest to the depth of Navarro's staunchly liberal political beliefs. His encounter with California is continually filtered through these political ideals, which he used both to criticize and to praise the society he observed. His account is laced with an ongoing preoccupation of the anti-Rosas, liberal political cause in Argentina as well as with a strong sense of patriotism. Diary entries on this subject are frequent and often reveal his hopes of returning to his homeland someday and playing an active role in the establishment of a liberal, democratic society. For Navarro, all of life was, in one way or another, related to his political ideals.

Family ties and loyalties were central to Navarro's system of values. In California, Ramón and his brother Samuel formed a team and were continually on the lookout for each other's welfare. Loyalties, however, went far beyond his brother Samuel or even his immediate family, encompassing his entire extended kin group. Though he suffered from bouts with homesickness, Navarro's family was one of his main sources of inner strength during his California days and doubtless during the rest of his life. Whenever Navarro mentions his strategies about California or Chile, he speaks in terms of his family group rather than of just himself. Intrafamily marital ties, family companies, family solidarities, or memorials to deceased kin are all recurrent subjects. The depth of these kin group ties, visible both in California and later in his life, is a characteristic trait of traditional Hispanic cultures and contrasts sharply with the sturdy individualism prevalent among the American miners and typical of most Anglo-Saxon cultures.

Ramón Gil Navarro had an enviable educational background, one not uncommon during the nineteenth century for young men from well-to-do families in South America. Knowledgeable in philosophy, theology, history, and literature, he was also conversant in a number of languages. French was his preferred second language, though he was also able to speak and write English and Latin. Sections written in these different languages can be found throughout his diary, and he frequently put to use his understanding of both classical and contemporary literature. Navarro continually read books about history, geography, and literature, and had set for himself a very strict regimen to improve and deepen his own education. His ambitious and often inquisitive intelligence served him well in the fairly uncultured California of the gold rush and is a telltale indicator of the highly disciplined and demanding attitude he had toward learning and toward life.

The author was always a Latin American, always an Argentinean, which constitutes perhaps the most important filter of perception during his time in California. Comparisons between Argentina or Chile and California are present throughout his account. These range from his musings on the similarities and differences in the weather in the Northern and Southern Hemispheres to his observations on plant and animal life in both contexts. The same inquisitive curiosity leads him to plant wheat near his tent at the mines of Calaveras in order to compare the quality of California wheat with that grown in Argentina or Chile. His comments on different aspects of California society and life in comparison with those of the Southern Hemisphere are recurrent. They include cultural comparisons and considerations regarding the major flaws or qualities of the spirit of North Americans and Latin Americans. His tone is mostly comparative and seldom negative or judgmental. In Navarro's diary neither society is perfect or beyond criticism, though in his heart and, to a certain extent, in his temperament he is decidedly Latin.

Navarro's account of the gold rush touches on many key themes of that era: gold rush fever, a get-rich-quick attitude, total success and clamorous failure, the influx of migrants by the thousands, life at the mines, ostentatious wealth, fantastic growth of cities and towns, societies with few women and practically no elderly, arbitrary and often inefficient justice with ambiguous limits to the reach of the law, a society based on the preeminence of the resourcefulness of individuals, a multicultural society, and a world in which hostilities exist between different ethnic groups or between individuals.[8] As the author experienced these aspects of mid-nineteenth-century California, he consigned his observations almost daily to his diary. His descriptions are insightful, even brilliant, yet they are always given from his own cultural perspective, that of an astute, cultured, critical, and appreciative observer.

This diary, however, is more than a straightforward account of the gold rush in California. It is also a profoundly personal, even introspective, look at the author's own life, his ideals, his feelings, and his experiences. There is much in it about the meaning of such universal subjects as life, love, honesty, ambition, fulfillment, and sentiment. One of the reasons for this is that Navarro's account is a true diary, written at night, day after day, rather than a tale about the gold rush based on a diary but prepared at a later date. Had this not been the case, Navarro would have certainly edited out the personal aspects of the diary in favor of those strictly related to his experiences at the mines or in mining society. Most of the diary was never made public; what we have here is, for the most part, the unedited and personal reflections of the author.[9]

Herein lies one of the most fascinating aspects of this often impassioned testimony of life. When we set out to edit Navarro's diary, we were convinced that it would become a valuable historical testimony about life during the gold rush in California. In the end, however, this perception has changed substantially, as the diary has proven to be more than just a historical record. There are many occasions in which the most riveting situations described by Navarro have nothing specifically historical about them, except for the fact that the events he describes take place during the gold rush days of California. These descriptions are often wonderful in the depth of human perception, in the feeling, and even in the emotion they are able to transmit to the reader. In other words, the author and his personal quest have become an integral part of the historical reality contained in these pages.

A product of his historical epoch, Navarro is intensely romantic both in his political sentiments and in his attitude toward life. Though prone to exaggeration, he has an ability to describe persons, events, and situations in a striking, almost literary, fashion. He is a man of contradictions, far from perfect in any way. He is extremely proud and filled with his own sense of self-worth. His sense of humor, or at least of irony, is far-reaching and can be seen best when he is speaking of business matters or of human foibles. He has an uncanny, often even disconcerting, way of changing the rhythm of his discourse, mixing seemingly unrelated matters in the same passage. This is not just a literary device but a characteristic of his personality. He is able to describe the winter weather of Stockton in a most poetic way or can find solace for his own feelings of guilt in the execution of an Irish criminal without so much as blinking an eye. He is a freethinker, against slavery and those who oppress freedom, yet he is keenly aware of the fact that the underlying order in California must be defended at all costs. He is misogynous and yet idealizes women. He is a religious man whose religious sentiments never seem to enter into conflict with his personal life. He loves to play the guitar and to write, and he is an excellent conversationalist. He also has a tendency to dress like a dandy, and, especially later in life, he becomes quite a ladies' man.[10] He is a man of great virtues and great defects, a man of intense contradictions; he is a man who is human in every way.

Navarro's diary is as much a faithful mirror of himself as it is a representation of California during those heady days of the gold rush. It has violence, romantic interest, disappointments and hopes, and it has perceptive observations about California, about mining society, about life, about men and women, about violence, and about ingenuity. All diaries tend to be self-serving in some way, and this one is not an exception, but its almost daily entries make it refreshingly spontaneous. There are times, however, when there is such an intensity of spirit that it seems more like a work of literature than a diary written at night by the light of a candle or a lantern. All of these elements should make this book a source of pleasure for readers willing to be transported to another era. They will enter into a fascinating moment of history and into the life and experiences of an equally fascinating man.

The Manuscript Diary and the English Edition

Navarro's original diary remained family property until it was purchased by the Bancroft Library at the University of California at Berkeley in the 1970s. It is currently in their collection.[11] The diary is contained in two volumes, handsomely bound in red leather with gold trim, and is written with an exceedingly careful and elegant script. Most entries were made in the diary at night and were based on notes Navarro kept during the day in small notebooks bound in black leather.[12] Most of these notebooks have been lost; the only remaining one we know of continues to belong to the family.

The initial entry in the diary is dated 6 September 1845 in Catamarca, Argentina, and is headed with the following title: "Diary that contains the itinerary undertaken by my family from Catamarca to Concepción [Chile] and the duration of my stay in Chile from the 24th of March when I arrived in San Felipe, alias Aconcagua.[13] Ramón Gil Navarro y Ocampo." The final entry in the diary is dated 19 July 1856 in Paraná, Argentina. It is impossible to know whether Navarro continued his diary later in life, though it would not be surprising had he done so. Nevertheless, there is no trace of any later volumes. The diary itself is voluminous, a fitting testimony to the fact that Navarro was an avid writer. Prior to his arrival in California in April 1849 the diary contains approximately 140,000–150,000 words; the California segment, from April 1849 to June 1852, has between 310,000 and 320,000 words; and the final part in Chile and Argentina contains a little more than 150,000 words.

This English-language edition of the diary is based almost entirely on Navarro's stay in California, representing somewhat over half of the entire diary. Even so, less than 50 percent of the California text has been retained in the present edition. The following criteria have been used in the selection of texts: all descriptions of California life, personal experiences of the author, sections referring to his economic activities, and texts in which he gives his viewpoint on life and on people. We have chosen to minimize references to Argentina and Chile as well as to his family back home. Excessively repetitious parts of the diary have also been excluded.

During approximately the last year of Navarro's stay in California, his diary becomes much less consistent. Instead of the almost daily or at least thrice weekly entries of the first two years, periods of two weeks or longer go by without any entry. Even then, the text tends to return to Navarro's unsettled "affairs of the heart." This is clearly a period of his life in which his personal and sentimental affairs have altered his basic attitude toward his life and his diary. We have attempted to compensate for this lack of information in his diary by including a selection of letters he wrote to different persons in California, Argentina, and Chile during that time. These letters contain more information and provide a useful counterbalance to the tone taken on by the diary itself. These letters are also held at the Bancroft Library at Berkeley.

By and large we have preferred a liberal translation of the original text, one designed to convey a ready understanding of the text in up-to-date English rather than one that attempts to reflect in any exact way the author's literary style, his specific use of metaphors, and his nineteenth-century vocabulary. The resulting text conveys quite accurately the intensity of the original as well as the author's style and his sense of rhythm and timing in the way he describes California and his own experiences there. Much of the translation has been based on a transcription of the original diary undertaken several years ago by one of the coeditors of this edition, when the diary was still at the family home in Córdoba, Argentina. Whenever difficulties have arisen, the transcription has been compared with the microfilm of the original diary, which was kindly facilitated by the Bancroft Library at Berkeley. Grammatical and spelling inaccuracies in the way Navarro rendered texts in English, French, and Latin have not, for the most part, been altered.

The chronological organization of the diary has been respected, and a subject index is located at the end of this volume. Notes have been kept to a minimum in the main body of the text to facilitate easy reading. They are designed to explain certain aspects of the original diary to render a more ready understanding of the text. They also contain the translations of aspects of the text in other languages, or they briefly identify certain characters, places, or things mentioned. This edition also contains a glossary (appendix 2), where fuller identifications of persons who appear in the diary have been given, along with reference to their origin and, whenever possible, the main events in their lives. The glossary includes references to almost everyone mentioned in the text, though in a small number of instances we have not been able to find any further information. This edition includes a fairly complete chronological biography of the author (appendix 1), plus a bibliography containing works cited in the book, works by the author, and works about the author.

María del Carmen Ferreyra
David S. Reher

The Gold Rush Diary of Ramón Gil Navarro

The Diary of Ramón Gil Navarro

CONCEPCIÓN [CHILE], 15 FEBRUARY 1849. *On my way to California*

Several days ago Don Ignacio Palma, Don Manuel Zerrano, Liljebalch, and Juan Alemparte were attempting to arrange an expedition to California. Four people were appointed directors of a company that is supposed to take thirty workers plus a ship full of supplies up to California for a two-year stay to work the gold mines there. I am one of the four who is supposed to direct this venture. A ship called the *Carmen* has been bought for 10,000 pesos, and it is being loaded. It will leave as soon as possible. Don Manuel Santamaría, Don Tomás Rioseco, and Don Borjas Fernandes are my fellow directors. I have been signing up men, and we are all part owners. The expedition will cost 30,000 pesos, but this investment will also eventually be ours. I have given my word, and I cannot back off now. I do not know what Lady Luck will do for me. . . . For the past three years I have had no real place to call my own, though during this period I have progressed a great deal, always in the right direction. Who knows if Lady Luck wants me to get rich as well? Anyway I am going to go six thousand miles from here. God, what will it be like? Well, my thoughts are pure, and God will be with me. And if I am to die at sea or up there where the life of an adventurer is fraught with so many perils, so what? But no, God will not want this. I have a poor family that deserves to be happy. I am searching for that and nothing else. My God, help me and stay with me!

28 FEBRUARY 1849

New decisions have been made regarding our company. The partners have rightfully reached the conclusion that having four persons heading up the company would lead to total disorder, rendering it difficult to make decisions. They have decided that I should go along with Dr. MacKay, who, being English, will be able to help me. Besides, he is a doctor by profession, and this might be useful as well. Actually I don't normally get on very well with the English, but this decision seems like a good one to me. Everything is almost ready. The *Carmen* will be carrying 150 passengers, including the crew. It looks as though the total cost will be more than 30,000 pesos. There are hardly any young men left in Concepción. The ones not going with us are going to be aboard the *General Rivera,* which is ready to leave, or the *Holland,* which is to leave in another fifteen days. The *Freire* should be coming soon from Valparaíso to get ready for the voyage to California, and the *Oballe* left about twenty days ago. This place is almost empty.

ON THE MERIDIAN, 11 DEGREES NORTH, 4 APRIL 1849. *Another storm*

Today around ten o'clock a horrible storm of funneling wind struck us. The entire crew was in a fix, but the ship finally was able to smooth its sails, and now the strength of the storm is a little less fearful. We are heading into the wind, but at least we are able to advance a bit.

I feel sorry for the young men in the crew who have to climb to the top of the masts on the captain's orders to reef the sails. How appalling it would be for the mothers of these lads to see them swinging at the end of a pole only held by their chests, with the rest of their bodies flailing wildly in the air. This would not be so bad if the wind were not blowing hard, but now, when the sails and the masts are creaking with great force, it is really frightening to behold how these poor devils are so close to real danger. And despite the fact that storms have often thrown sailors into the sea, for them, one of these storms is not dangerous at all. They are jumping up and down now with joy because it is pouring rain and they can finally wash their clothes.

On deck you can hear shouts and exclamations of joy as each one washes his clothes. They make one of their comrades slip on deck and that way he gets a bath, and everyone laughs all the time. The carpenter has tied a rope around his waist and has jumped overboard just for fun. The ship is moving as fast as lightening now, and he is towed alongside. It looks like mountains of water rise and come to gobble him up, but he and the ship pass over the waves like a feather. It would not be surprising either if a shark just slipped up and made a nice sandwich out of his leg. The captain says there are many sharks in these waters.

SAN FRANCISCO, CALIFORNIA, 30 APRIL. *The anchor went down in the bay!*

It is half past two in the afternoon, and we have just put the anchor out in this port. I am hardly able to write because I am trembling all over with excitement. . . . Thank the good Lord, who has protected us so well and has granted us the most felicitous voyage imaginable. We arrived before many other ships that set out twenty or thirty days before us. Yet even this most fortunate of ships arrived here with no mast and while taking on water. The port was filled with warships and merchant marine vessels, almost one hundred of them. It is hard to imagine a more impressive and beautiful port. The bay is the most beautiful and secure bay of all the Americas, and possibly of Europe as well. It is entirely protected on all sides. The hills are completely green as befits the springtime at hand, though it is as cold as can be. . . . The wealth of the mines is beyond doubt, but it might be very costly to get there. There are warships and an established government here, but laws do not seem to be respected, and there are no police officers around to make sure they are obeyed or to establish a semblance of public order. There are murders and robberies, but nobody protests, and nobody pursues the murderer or the thief. Everyone carries his own weapons, living and sleeping with them, defending himself as best he can. In other words, this is even more than a Babylon because there is the greatest sort of confusion of languages, of religions, of laws, of taxes, etc., etc. We found out all of this thanks to some Chileans who just came abroad. I shall go ashore and will take it all in with my own eyes.

TUESDAY, 1 MAY 1849. *Back on board*

It is nine o'clock at night, and I have just come aboard the ship with the captain. All night yesterday and this morning I was writing and sending letters aboard a ship that left this midday. None of what they had told us about California is false. Everything, everything is completely true. There must be as much bustle and confusion in the port as there will be in the valley of Josaphat on the day of the Last Judgment, where, according to the prophets, all the nations of the world will come together.[1] Well, this could not be much less; there are people from all over the world, and loads of them. The houses are as lovely perhaps as those of Valparaíso. The luxury of the cafés is almost unbelievable, considering how expensive everything is because of all the gold. Their windows at night afford a view much like that of an enchanted palace. From the outside you can see the wonderful landscapes, portraits, and other paintings, the likes of which I have never seen. All of it is so alive and natural that it is as though you were touching them in reality. The rooms of these cafés are luxuriously appointed in the extreme, and their walls are filled with paintings of all types and subjects. I would call most of these paintings both very beautiful and very obscene.

Gambling tables are all over, and people gamble all the time, no matter

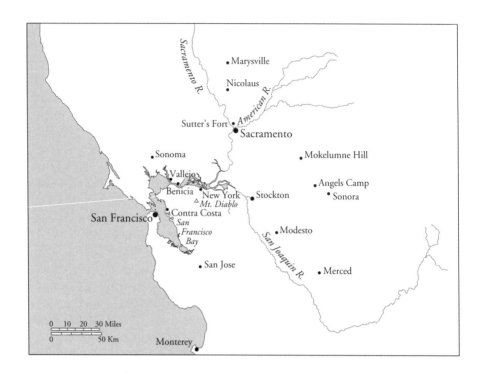

Map 2. California from Monterey to Marysville

whether they are laborers, artisans, public employees, military officers, Indians, or just about anyone else. The least they bet on a card is one or two ounces of gold, and each dealer has at least six, eight, or ten thousand pesos in front of him. In a saloon there are only six or eight types of games. There was one dealer who caught my eye more than the others. He was a Chilean with a straw hat pulled down over his eyebrows and who handled the cards with amazing dexterity. Around the table he had one man who was picking up his earnings and another paying what he had lost. I came up to the table almost at the same time as a Mexican with a poncho down practically to his heels, a sombrero so large that the brims went out past his shoulders, with hair down to his waist, and a beard to his chest. He took out a little sack, which I thought had tobacco but which in fact was filled with gold, and bet all of it on the first card dealt. Since another card won, with no sign of any emotion at all, he pinched about a peso's worth of the gold dust he had lost and said, "this is for a slug of rum and off to bed." I was in a state of shock because it was the first time in my life that I had ever seen anything like it.

At the end of a long corridor the captain and I saw a group of men playing darts, where the only thing flowing was gold. There was so much gold on the table that the entire top was covered and it looked as if the table itself was made of gold. As we were leaving we asked how much a cup of coffee cost, and we were told it was twelve *reales*.[2] At that price we figured it was better to have our coffee on board the ship, and so we left. The price was not surprising. Around here a new shirt costs $4 [pesos], and washing it costs another $2. It costs $4 to carry a single load from the docks to the warehouse and another $34 (without meals) to get a man to the staging areas near the mining country. It costs another $25 to get one arroba of goods from there to the mines, as long as there are wagons or carts, and if not, two ounces of gold.[3] A leg of meat costs $25 in the mines, and a pound of flour costs one peso and twelve reales. All of this may seem like a dream, but it is as real as the person writing in this diary.

WEDNESDAY, 2 MAY

It is such a shame to watch the multitude of young men whose hopes appear to have been dashed and who are obliged to load and unload the boats in order to make a living. They thought that over here it was only a question of arriving, getting their share of gold, and returning to Chile with their fortunes made in two or three months. How wrong they were! I have seen a lot of elegantly dressed young men who are carrying boxes around on their shoulders from the beach to the warehouse in order to earn four pesos a day, hardly enough for a square meal. When Samuel arrived here, he consigned his cargo to an Englishman and went to live in the tent at the house of a friend.[4] He too has had to wash clothes and to cook for himself and for other mates who were desperate and who seemed to prefer to die of hunger and without clothing rather than to serve themselves. Poor Samuel! He is probably the most elegant young man I know, the greatest friend of comfort, and yet the English tell me he is the only one to have remained strong throughout all the travails they have had to endure. Who knows what awaits me, a person who has, up until now, only had to observe the privations of others?

I am beginning to see that over here only big investments really work, and even though we have some and our company is fairly large, I fear that we too will be reduced eventually to God knows what. . . . I can see that Dr. MacKay is doing his best to sell the cargo and take us and all of the supplies to Stockton. This part will cost us five hundred or one thousand pesos, and after that on to the mines, which is the hardest part for most outfits. We could take on a loan against the ship or its cargo, but today we have seen the contract, which has an article directly prohibiting the doctor or myself from incurring any debts against the company. We can have all the money generated from selling the cargo or the ship, but neither of them can be sold for cash just to gain ready access to this money. Today I took samples of all the articles to E. Mikel and Co., who told me that if we could not find buyers we could put up the goods at auction, which is rather like burning them.[5] The workers are like caged animals. The doctor has told them they can flee if they want, but if they do they should be prepared to work in jail. Since they know that his threats cannot be backed up, they say that they will go whenever they want. It is strange that they did not leave the day we arrived, much as has happened to many companies who have come here. Oh well, may the Lord's will be done.

THURSDAY, 3 MAY. *Revolution*

Today I was speaking with the doctor, and he told me that he has decided to go his own way and leave everything in my charge. I pointed out to him that according to the contract he could not leave the company unless there were fewer than ten men remaining. He seems to have regretted talking to me about his own determination so clearly. Yet it seems that my observation has opened the way for him, because just now he has granted permission to the crew to go ashore, and I am almost certain that half of them will never return. Three have already left, saying clearly that they will not return. One man named Montiel deserted yesterday, but I found him in the main square and ordered him to follow me. At first he resisted, but when I showed him the pistols in my holster, knowing that California is not Chile and that shootings and knifings cause no excitement here at all, he followed me without saying a word. This morning, while taking some cargo ashore in our boat, after insults and fights with other sailors, he finally jumped out when it reached shore and fled. This time I do not think I will find him.

This morning I wrote to Samuel in Stockton, advising him of my arrival and my situation. It looks like I will end up carrying the weight of the entire company. If he were here next to me, I am sure there would not be any major problems like there were with the doctor. I think he could handle everything. I may be wrong, but it looks like he is much more capable here than either the doctor or I.

FRIDAY, 4 MAY. *A terrible situation!*

This morning I went off very early to see if there was any work for our men while some sort of decision was being made regarding our going to the mines. A number of proposals were made that I did not find very interesting, and finally we decided to settle on an agreement tonight with an Englishman who needs eight men to cut adobe bricks and to dig a trench. He offered me six pesos per day plus meals for each man, and I asked for eight pesos without meals, which I could provide. Tonight we are to close this deal in the central square at the Café del Encanto. It might be a bit difficult to find my man because this is the café where all of California meets at night. The doctor no longer seems to be involved at all with our company. I do not know his whereabouts or how to find him. Four or six of the men have fled, and I have no news about their whereabouts. This morning E. Mikel told me that earlier he had proposed to the doctor that twenty laborers work eight days on a street. But the doctor had not been interested. His lack of diligence has made us lose 1,300 pesos for reasons I cannot understand. I sure hope it wasn't to damage the company, because in doing so he would not be getting anything for himself. Not feeding the laborers or finding work for them leads to boredom, and that is why they leave. If only ten remain, then he is a free man. . . . *Ergo c'est vrai, il ne veut pas travailler pour la compagnie, il fait tout seul son affaire. . . .*[6]

The beach is completely filled with tents and shacks made of crates by the Chileans, who have nothing to do and spend their days mired in their misery and hoping to get to the mines. There are the young Aldunates,

Lucos, Martínez, etc., from Santiago, and the only thing you can see in their faces is the sense of abandonment of those who are carried along by misery perhaps to their death, for they cannot work nor are they used to the travails they are enduring. Poor devils! The wind is strong, cold, and humid, and the water comes up to the very entrance of their shacks. Who would have said that these young men who had departed from Chile, leaving behind their country, their families, their comforts and all, were only to come to this land to suffer the privations and miseries of a beggar. My Lord, what a horrible situation!

SATURDAY, 5 MAY. *Drowned in search of gold*

One of the young Martínez boys, after having made his fortune, was to travel once again to Sacramento on a great business deal. As he was leaving the bay the boat he was on developed a leak, took on water, and ended up sinking. He was able to grab his bedroll, which was floating on the water, but the current snatched it from him, and the waves swallowed him up amidst the shouts and cries he made for help, the last of which were destined for his family. His parents and his six brothers may have lost all of their hope and worldly possessions, but none of these would cause sorrow so great as losing a son and a brother.

Some men came from the mines today and said that the Indians have invaded the camps of the Chileans and, even though they were driven back, five or six compatriots perished, one of whom was a young man from Valparaíso. Another two or three young Chileans have just died of fever in Sacramento, and we still do not know who their families are. I am still waiting to see what God wants to do with me, though for now I am very happy.

SUNDAY, 6 MAY. *The first California mission*

I had hoped to go to mass today, but I am alone on board and cannot spend the entire day at mass without exposing the ship to some unforeseen danger. Here in San Francisco the Catholics do not have a church. A league from here there is a convent that they call the mission.[7] Even though the convent is now in ruins, it is clear from the order and the tastefulness of the building that it must have been built by the Jesuits.[8] At the mission there are a few Jesuit missionaries, who are the only Catholic priests you find occasionally around here, and that is where we have to go to hear mass. Since it is springtime now, vegetation and flowers of different types and colors cover the hills and plains you cross on your way there. In this way, the trip there is lovely. It is as though the God of the Catholics had lined the road to his temple with flowers and plants. I spent the entire day aboard ship, and the cannon shot sounding the nine o'clock hour at night from an American ship just rang out across the bay. What would I have been doing just now had I been in Concepción? I would have gone to listen to music with Juan, Mardoqueo, and Fabio!⁹ What sad thoughts have just come over me!

TUESDAY, 15 MAY. *The Chinese*

A ship from China just entered the bay, and it is quite unlike all of the other ships around. All of the crew are wearing red hats, and even the captain has one that folds and falls over his shoulders. Two additional American warships sailed into the bay, and they say another one that sunk six miles from here with 250 men on board belonged to the same fleet. A brigantine from the Canary Islands and another from the Sandwich Islands also came in, making five ships in only one day.¹⁰

Last night as I was walking with Rivero in front of the Café del Encanto, we heard them playing music and decided to enter. Inside there were two Mexicans playing the harp beautifully. We had a wonderful time inside listening to the music. It was the first time my heart has beaten softly to the rhythm of music since I arrived in California. They played pieces I knew and have played before. Parts of opera that I have sung together with Samuel, Mardoqueo, Juan, in those happy days before we decided to head for California. After they had finished playing, one of them came around with a tray in hand to collect whatever we might want to give him. Nobody there, I am sure, paid up with more pleasure than I.

WEDNESDAY, 16 MAY

It was ten o'clock at night by the time the captain came back after being away for a couple of days. The night is darker and colder than ever. The captain and his men were all wet and shivering from the cold. Fortunately, I was just having some tea and had saved them some ham and cake, which my *Chepe* had given me today. This wonderful black man idolizes me since I am the only one aboard who speaks French. With all his talent and capability, the poor guy cannot understand a word of Spanish or English. Let's leave Chepe for later. The captain found no trace of our lost boat, even though he went more than fifteen leagues down the coast. He found an old rancher who had been the local governor two years ago and now is not even the lowest soldier. He gave him lots of provisions, including four bottles of milk, bread, and meat. I am sorry I did not go with them.

THURSDAY, 17 MAY. *A death aboard!!*

This afternoon a terrible thing occurred. The captain of the *Roland,* anchored only twenty-five feet away from our *Carmen,* like all the other captains, has suffered from the tendency of his sailors to desert before unloading all of the cargo. Today the last two of them wanted to leave even before having finished a job they had begun this very morning. He was very upset and wanted to retain them by force, as is his right, according to the contract he has with them. They spoke to him impertinently, and he replied by saying that he was going to tie them up. At that point the most desperate of the two dared to grab him by the collar of his coat. The captain could not bear this sort of affront from one of his sailors, and, perhaps for the first time in his life, his French pride took over and he did not use his head. He took out a pistol he had brought from his cabin and ordered the sailor to let him go, lest he blow his brains out. Instead of letting him go, the sailor grabbed him and raised his fist to hit him. But there was no time because his fist stopped in midair as his brains were blown against the door of the cabin across the way, turning it into a tricolor door of white, red, and green. The captain immediately went to General Smith and told him what had happened. The general asked if there were any witnesses the captain had brought with him. The general replied "well done." Now two mates have just thrown the body of that poor devil overboard. One of them had him by the arms and the other by the legs, as they swayed the body back and forth to the rhythm of "one, two . . ." A terrible thing, but insolence and immorality were on the rise, and an exemplary punishment was necessary. It fell to this poor devil to be an example to all the others. May God receive this poor man, as he deserves.

FRIDAY, 18 MAY. *Samuel*

Samuel and I have just come aboard. While I was in the house of Nemecio Martínez I saw a young man arrive with hair to his shoulders and dark as a San Benito.[11] I hardly recognized him, but it was Samuel! He was carrying his bedding on his back, had a little yellow metal box under his arm, and was wearing a rich pair of pistols in an embroidered holster. He was a living bandit. He is fat and as healthy as ever. Thank God.

MONDAY, 21 MAY. *Preparations*

Today we got all of our equipment and cargo together, for we are to leave tomorrow. I am lucky because Samuel will accompany me to Stockton, where once again we will take leave of each other. Yesterday a North American friend of Samuel invited us to have lunch, and at two o'clock we were at the inn. I have never seen as much luxury, not even in the best inns of Valparaíso. The dining room was more than fifty yards long, and there were two lines of tables. At our table there were nearly 200 persons eating. It was a delight to see all the lavish decor in the room. All the dishes were made of Chinese porcelain, and the waiters were as facile and clean as the best of gentlemen. There were two Chinese servants with braids all the way down their backs and with the ugliest faces imaginable. Yet I was delighted to see the care with which they served each course.

TUESDAY, 22 MAY. *Our departure for the mines!*

Samuel and I have just gone aboard the boat that is taking us. It is noon, and we are just about to get under way with a very strong wind and a choppy bay. We are only going as far as Stockton, where the doctor will come to meet us in a few days. The captain has given me his berth, and the pilot has given his to Samuel. These are the only two berths on the boat; most boats navigating the river have no berths at all. Passengers going upriver have to sit close together and practically do not have room even to turn around. Our brigantine can carry eighty passengers plus the crew.

At six o'clock in the afternoon we arrived near Benicia. My eyes have seldom seen such beauty. We are navigating between two hills, and a velvet type of green covers the countryside, much as though it was a carpet. This placid scene is interrupted from time to time by immense pine trees, as lush as orange groves. On the next hill along the river there are lots of cows, bulls, and horses, all without any apparent owners, grazing in fields of grass so high that it looks like a wheat field just before it turns brown. The river is so filled with twists and turns that advancing is very slow, though always immensely beautiful. The flat area where Benicia is located is equally attractive and befits its name. Six ships are anchored in the port, and one of them is a warship. This Sacramento River could easily handle very large vessels such as the *Asia* or even larger ones in any of its bays.

We put down anchor at seven o'clock at night just past Benicia. It was not possible to navigate further because we would run aground, despite all the best practical knowledge of the people we have aboard. We shall raise our sails again at daybreak.

FRIDAY, 25 MAY. *In Stockton*

Dawn today was brilliant and peaceful, as it often is in my own Argentina.[12] You can see the radiant May sun on the horizon, whose glories have been sung by our poets Varela and Mármol. What happy men they must have been to be able to dedicate all their souls and thoughts to the memory of such days! I am not a poet like they are and cannot express in writing what my heart feels. Still, I greet the dawn in my country from the depths of California. You have a son who enthusiastically salutes your glory and sends you his best wishes from the beaches of the Sacramento River. May God allow this very son, who is now fleeing the knife of the Tyrant who oppresses and enslaves you, to one day be able to offer his life and his heart to you with utmost success!!

It is noon, and we are becalmed near a forest of roses and other flowers. All the plants are covered with flowers. I have never seen a lovelier garden with more beauty. I have in hand a bunch of roses and other flowers that I was able to cut from the very deck of the ship. What a notably beautiful contrast that comes from the ship, mixing its masts with the branches of the rose garden. We are all such ingrates because we see and enjoy this marvel without even thinking of the omnipotent hand that created it. It would be wonderful to be able to be in my country and give a lovely woman these wonderful and mysterious roses. I shall keep a bunch, and next May 25th I shall give the dry flowers to a beautiful patriotic damsel, who will be able to see them with my same enthusiasm for the glories of May.

It is six o'clock at night, and our ship has just docked. Just as we arrived, the bell at the Americana Inn called us to dinner. The Riosecos, Samuel, I went there, and we met up with two Argentinean friends. We toasted the glory of our own 25th of May. The food and service at this inn is as luxurious as at any in San Francisco.

SATURDAY, 26 MAY. *Drownings*

Yesterday, just before we arrived in Stockton, they fetched a drowned soldier out of the lake. Seeing that he was dead, they just returned him to the water from whence he had come with no further ceremony. The poor devil was drunk and fell into the lake without realizing that it was really a lake.

It is four o'clock, and something horrible just happened. While I was checking the cargo with the ship's manifest, five soldiers and an officer came around. They were pretty drunk. They took a launch that was nearby and started to cross the lake. We continued our work, though it was hard

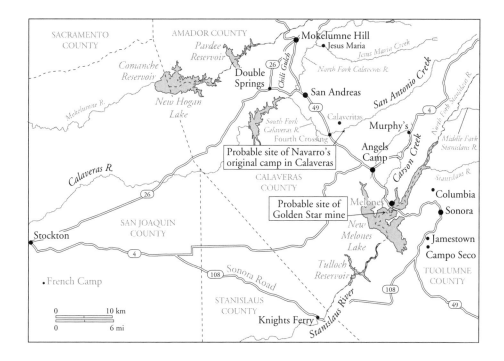

Map 3. California mining country

not to notice the way the launch was moving about on the lake. When it was halfway across we suddenly heard a terrible cry coming from the six men that startled us. What a terrible thing, my God! The only thing we could see was the keel of the launch sticking up out of the water. A thousand cries came from all the boats around the lake, and a thousand voices said to put boats into the lake to help these people, yet nobody really could do anything. Witnessing all of this, our captain cut the lines of one of the rowboats floating beside our boat and headed for the center of the lake by himself. While he rowed, the rest of us who were nearby shouted encouragement to the men who were splashing around their launch in the lake, telling them to try to swim to shore. By then the captain had reached them and grabbed the clothes of the first one he came upon and thrust him in his rowboat as though he only weighed a few pounds. Two others were still splashing around, and a third one, who was the officer, was trying to swim to shore. One of the two was able to climb aboard the rowboat, while the other was beginning to drown because despite all his splashing he was hardly able to raise his head above the water he was swallowing. By the time the captain reached him he was entirely underwater, but, faster than lightening, the captain put his oar in where he had gone down and to the amazement of all of us brought it up with the guy holding on to it gasping for air. Finally the captain grabbed him by his hair and lifted him out of the water and into the boat. By the time the captain got them all to shore, the officer had already made it. He embraced them briefly and jumped back into the water, swimming toward his launch. When he got there he put the rope between his teeth and crossed the entire lake to the other side. When he got there all of us gave him a round of applause. Four were saved, but the others . . . may God have mercy on them.

SUNDAY, 27 MAY. *The deer of California*

Today at noon some Mexicans brought a beautiful deer. Its size amazed us all because we had never seen anything like it before. It is nearly as big as a cow, and its antlers are nearly a yard and a half high with all kinds of branches and crosses. There was also something I did not really understand because they had loops around the antlers, and at one part the loop went right through one of them. There was lots of blood flowing from the hole in the antlers. I cannot understand why blood circulates, why there is life in those horns that seem so hard to us, as though they were the iron in the handles of silverware. Some Mexicans said that this one was a doe but that only the buck's antlers are good for knife handles. This again seems incredible to me. Nature sure seems to have odd ways of working out its designs. We went hunting today because they say there is much venison and deer nearby, but we ended up sleeping in the shade of some pine trees across from the beautiful forest of roses and other flowers. The fresh afternoon breezes brought us an exquisite fragrance and made us think it might be a good place to set up camp. We also saw a number of rabbits running in the same grove. They say there are a lot of these animals around here.

MONDAY, 28 MAY. *Our tent*

Today or tomorrow we plan to set out for the mines. Right now we are unloading the ship that yesterday brought the doctor here along with another two men who had deserted us in San Francisco. Samuel and I set up our tent, and it looks like a palace in comparison to all of the others around here. We receive visits almost all day long because our tent is as cool as it is comfortable. Across from the tent we can see the lovely roses and pine trees. We set it up right where the mineral enters town, and so a lot of people come by. We have made lots of Mexican friends, and even a lot of Americans come here to see us. Actually even two or three of them came in order to learn some expressions in Spanish.

FRIDAY, I JUNE 1849. *A town map*

Two governmental agents have just left my tent. They are drawing up a map of the city and have been working on it for five days. Their job should be finished in another three or four days. One of them will make 10,000 pesos for the job, and the other, 5,000 pesos. That is how the American government pays when it comes to any kind of public improvement or something of general usefulness. Lots around here are being sold very quickly and at extremely high prices. At present there are around 8,000 inhabitants here, and there really is only one wooden house. All the rest are tents; and nary a day goes by without another tent springing up. The location of Stockton is much more favorable than that of San Francisco, not only geographically but also because over here those furious winds do not blow, there are no glacial fogs, and everything—the vegetation, the temperature, the terrain—is better than it is in San Francisco.[13]

SATURDAY, 2 JUNE. *Horses at 200 pesos*

Today they came around to sell us a couple of ill-begotten horses: so skinny that they seemed bent by the wind, ugly, with their manes off to one side or the other, and almost without tails. It is the type of horse that in Chile would be worth five pesos at the very most. We asked their price and were told that neither of them would cost less than 200 pesos and might even reach 300. That sure made me think about my country and how at Carnival or Easter time you mount those wonderful horses used by the gauchos. What a marvel it would be to be able to gallop along the plain with all the fury of the horse but without worrying, like you do here, that the person who rented it to you was only concerned about making an ounce or two more or less with his horse. Oh my, that is certainly asking a lot, especially considering that I am in the California of Mexico and in Stockton. Here I could never mount one of those Carnival horses of my country at any price. To ride one of the best horses around here would cost me more than 1,000 pesos. Perhaps I have not properly understood the value of a horse here. One of these days I shall go back to my country and have a little of what I am missing here.

One of the things I had not noticed before is that around here there are no women. That is probably why I was not aware of the tremendous surprise the two women in my company caused for nearly everyone. People stopped to look at them as though they were smuggled goods. Darn if I had thought of any lasses, and much less of women, before today when I was invited to the home of the Sparrows to see a Mexican woman or miss for something special. She actually asked me to play the Aguado fandango for her, which is something as rare over here as the Carnival horses I mentioned earlier. It so happens that in this civilized and musical town, the only instrument capable of bringing good memories of past glories is my poor guitar! Well, I did not really want to go, and so I said I was busy. Good gracious, if supply means something, my guitar should be worth as much here as any girl, since with it my tent has as many visitors as the house where this woman lives.

STOCKTON, 6 JUNE. *The miseries of California*

Today I asked my laborer why he did not want to have lunch, and he answered that he had made a vow to fast on all Wednesdays for the rest of his life. I asked him why he took the vow, and he answered that it was when the boat was lost. In fact, the man speaking was Marcelo Camaño, who was one of the two men who almost drowned when that boat was lost. Today he told me that, every time he remembers that he was about to die without being able to bid a final farewell to his family, he could not help but burst into tears. That is, in fact, what happened. I have seldom seen a man of his standing so manly and honorable. While we are there alone, I show him how to keep accounts, and he is learning readily. He spends the entire day studying.

THURSDAY, 7 JUNE. *Corpus Christi in California*

Today is Corpus Christi, a holy day that is probably observed everywhere in the Christian world, except California. I must be the only one who even knows it is Corpus. It is eleven o'clock, and people rush to the eating house at the call of the bell. It is unbearably hot, kind of like the month of December in my country. Maybe right now, as I am writing, in my country they are justly celebrating Corpus Christi. On this date in the past I have been in the Province of Cuyo and in almost all of those in the south of Chile, but nowhere have I seen the solemnity with which it is celebrated in Catamarca.[14] What is going to happen to that nation and to its people? Soon it will have been two years since I last received any news from there.

It is midnight, and from my tent I can hear the oaths and cursing of the Englishmen and the Americans who are drunk in the gambling houses. The wind brings their voices and their coarse language here almost as loud as if they were shouting next door. A little while ago I heard the noise of a fight, but later it seemed like a gang of demons had attacked everyone, as the oaths and the noise of things breaking everywhere reached me. All of a sudden I heard two or three shots, one after another, and then all was silent. Now you can hear the bell ringing as though there was a fire. Who knows why there is so much noise? Camaño and the boy, meanwhile, are sleeping as though they were dead. Maybe right now the Manuelas of San Juan are dancing. . . .[15] What a difference!

FRIDAY, 8 JUNE. *Two ghosts! Sarapes*

Two Mexican or maybe California Indian women just left my tent and store. They are the first really native women I have seen so far in this country. But my diary, which knows everything I have seen around here, will be witness to the fact that until now I have never met more horrible looking women in my life. Their hair, as thick and stiff as a horse's tail, falls freely down their backs. A coarse dress that is little more than a sack and a cotton scarf is about all they wear. These women are the civilized ones, and that is why they dress this way, whereas others go around completely naked, just like their men. They speak a type of Spanish that is so corrupted that I could hardly understand anything at all. They mix a little Spanish with the national language of Mexico from before the conquest. The more civilized Indian men wear very baggy underwear, and over it they wear blue velveteen pants that are slit on the sides up to the waist in such a way that when they walk it looks like lightning, with flashes of light and darkness appearing with each step they take. You would believe that they would lose their leggings, but no, they are quite used to this type of clothing. Over the pants they wear a type of poncho called a sarape. Its width goes about three hands down their sides, and it is so long that it almost drags along the ground. This garment, which is what they spend most of their money on, is little more than a piece of embroidered blanket that costs between one ounce and twelve or even eighteen ounces, depending on the quality of the embroidery. Thinking to impress them, I allowed the Indian women to try on a silk dress made in Valparaíso I brought from Elisea. But they turned the tables on me by saying it was very poorly made. The problem, they said, was that the lining and all of the threads of the dress were *sacatados*.[16] Then they showed me the stitching of their own dress, and I realized that they were right. I have never seen anything so finely sewn and with thread they make themselves.

SATURDAY, 9 JUNE. *Rosas and his reputation*

Two Mexicans came in to buy some things today. As we were talking they thought I was Chilean, but when I said that I was Argentinean they asked:

"Where is that, in Buenos Aires?"

"Ah," one of them exclaimed, "there is a man there called Rosas, who they say is a very bad man."[17]

"Yes, that is right."

Right away they told some of the atrocious things Rosas had done and some of the most horrible deaths he had caused, and everything they had been told was true. They knew of the death of Dr. Masa and of those murders committed by Bárcena in Córdoba, who killed three young boys and presented their heads to their mothers on a platter. Curiosity led me to ask them what part of Mexico they came from, and they said they were from Tlascala. Good Lord! Just how far the voice of so many victims has traveled and the noise of the horrible atrocities of that monster! It looks as if the name of Rosas is going to become proverbial as a sign of Tyranny, replacing Nero along the way. People will say "you are as barbarous, as cruel, and as tyrannical as a Rosas." That is the way it will be pretty soon.

SUNDAY, 10 JUNE. *All kinds of memories*

It is nine o'clock on Sunday morning, a day that dawned as beautiful as a fall day in my country. There are eight bells ringing from different parts of town. It sure reminds me of Concepción. Yet these bells are not calling men like they do there. They are not calling for some religious service. None of that; quite the contrary! They are not calling Christians to mass, nor to a sermon or a rosary, even though the chimes sound just the same. Some are calling for lunch at one inn; others are calling men to a gambling table, where the cards are beckoning. Others are announcing to all corrupt men that the tavern is about to open and that all its corrupt functions, such as gambling, drunkenness, obscenities, etc., are about to commence. How much pain these bells would cause a true minister of Jesus Christ, seeing how the men of this town, even those of his religion, go down such a dangerous path without even thinking of what they were before coming here or what religion or sect they professed! There are no Christians here, nor Catholics, Protestants, Calvinists, Muslims, or anyone with any faith at all. All of the inhabitants in this California are men with no country, no God, no government, no laws, and perhaps without even passions. All have given themselves over to only one empire: that of greed. This is the only thing that shines here, and it compensates for everything that they are lacking. My God, what a horrible thing!

SATURDAY, 16 JUNE. *The first building block of our future*

Samuel was not able to leave today because of the wind, and I do not imagine he will be leaving before tomorrow. He and Mr. Sparrow have bought a warehouse, and he is going to bring a load of fresh supplies from San Francisco. It seems like a good idea all the way around, as he will have contacts with the places around here and the things we are expecting from Chile.

SUNDAY, 17 JUNE

Last night there was a great commotion here in Stockton because not a single person in town could remember the date. Some said it was Friday and others Saturday; some said it was the fifteenth and others the sixteenth. There was a big get-together of Americans, Englishmen, and Mexicans, and all were in disagreement. This is just proof of how completely everything that is not truly pressing is forgotten here, to such an extent that they cannot even remember the date. You know it seems rather odd, but hardly surprising in California, for an entire population to forget the date. I was the only person around who actually knew it, and that is because my diary does not deceive me. Of course my opinion on this count did not seem to matter more than that of the rest of them. They all must have known the real date this morning because nobody was up and moving about, and there were no merchants to be seen anywhere. It is as though yesterday everyone really knew it was Saturday and now is just fooling around. But no, they really did doubt. Evidently everywhere in the world the tradition of resting every seventh day is so strong that they know when to rest without knowing what day it is.

TUESDAY, 19 JUNE

Today Camaño arrived with news from Calaveras. The doctor is well, but some of the workers are sick with *la yedra*.[18] This damn weed is more abundant here than any other type of plant, and it ends up poisoning you even if you do not actually touch it. A man's body gets covered with sores, and his face swells enough to leave him practically blind, almost without a trace of eyes, and it makes his body terribly itchy. When he scratches, however, this leprosy spreads all over. Many men have been taken by it without having even touched it directly. The people it damages permanently are those who are already sick or those whose criminal parts are attacked in a frightening way.[19] When this happens, they can swell up to the size of a watermelon, and it is impossible for the poor man to walk. On the other hand, this poisonous plant must have exquisite use for botany. There are still no experiments on it at all. Thank goodness that I have touched it before and have not been hurt in the slightest.

The doctor says that if our work continues to go like it has up until now, we will make more than all of the other companies. In eight or ten days he has already mined 2,400 pesos' worth of unimaginably beautiful gold. Hopefully God will favor our efforts and recompense our labor.

WEDNESDAY, 20 JUNE

Today I bought the most beautiful gold nugget I have seen since arriving here. I was lucky because the *huaso* who had it showed it to me before anyone else.[20] It only took me a couple of minutes to make a deal with him. When I showed it to other people, they offered me twice what I had paid for it. It is a completely formed African lion with its haughty mane, its tail, feet, mouth, etc. I am going to keep this nugget as proof of volcanic eruption. How else could something as strange and prodigious as this have been formed? This type of jewel should be kept for life, never to be given away, sold, or even donated to anyone or anything, or, if it is, it should be donated to a museum or to a loved one who is really worth it. Every gram of gold I may eventually have, if indeed I get any, is going to cost me loads of troubles, privations, and work.

THURSDAY, 21 JUNE

It has been unbearably hot for the past three days. There is no place I can think of that could be compared to this, except perhaps the sandy deserts of Syria and a few December days in San Juan, Argentina. Down there, however, no matter how hot the day, there is always some breeze that helps you bear the heat. Not here. Not a single leaf on the tree is moving, and the thrushes and other birds do not sing in the shade of the trees like they do in Argentina. Rather, they open their beaks and move their wings as though oppressed by some horrible fatigue.

FRIDAY, 22 JUNE

Today an Argentinean friend, Zarabia, my young friend Araoz, and I set out for a dairy about two or three miles from here. I awoke before dawn and was able to enjoy the coming of the day being trumpeted at once by a thousand little birds. Dawns are wonderful here in California. You can feel their coolness and the fragrance of flowers wafting in the air. After washing up and taking a short walk in our private rose garden, I went to wake Zarabia up. As the first rays of sun were just showing over the horizon we set out on foot for the dairy. When we got there the cows were being milked, and so we helped the milkmaids tie down the cows and calves. The milkmaids included an old woman and her two daughters, sixteen and eighteen years of age. They were white, blond, had blue eyes, large firm breasts, and supple waists. They were lovely girls, as long as you did not look at their feet, because theirs were like the feet of the English women. None of them knew a jot of Spanish. I told them in English that we wanted to buy milk and that we would help them milk the animals because we knew how to do it. They thanked us very politely. We were there for an hour and paid twelve reales for a gallon of milk and another twelve for eight ounces of butter. We left in a good enough mood, and we would have preferred to stay there all day and even all night. . . . It is now six o'clock in the evening, and we just had marvelous tea with buttered toast.

SATURDAY, 23 JUNE

Since yesterday, another four ships filled with passengers have arrived here. About 200 men arrive in Stockton every day. It is fun to be down there at the docks. Some are waiting to board so as to return to San Francisco, and others are heading for the mines, and all of this happens at the same moment. The ones arriving are filled with laughs, hopes, and their eyes seem to be envisioning a future filled with fortune. Among those leaving you can see the bitterness of frustrated hope and the negative effects of a backbreaking job they were not used to, a job that can humble the toughest of men. Their faces reflect all the privations and even miseries they have had while here. Among those arriving you can see a gesture of contempt for that misery and ravage among those departing and a look of disdainful challenge.

MONDAY, 25 JUNE

At noon a cart stopped in front of my tent with a box containing the body of a man who had drowned in the San Joaquin River. He was an American who had a business in Valparaíso. They say he was a very good-looking young man, though now he is about as horrible as anyone I have ever seen in all my life. He is entirely dressed and even has rings on his fingers and spurs on his boots. He is as black as if he were from Guinea and so swollen that he looks like he is about to burst. They buried him beneath a tree about a half a block away from my tent. What a ridiculous ceremony! One of the Americans took the Bible, and while he was praying along with the others he repeatedly made the sign of the cross from right to left over the body of the dead man. Afterwards, every person threw in a fistful of dirt in the grave. Once this had been done, the fellow with the Bible began holding it out to the others so that they could kiss it, all the while they were making a funny type of genuflection and other ridiculous movements.

STOCKTON, TUESDAY, 26 JUNE. *What a dangerous life around here!!*

I would like to brand the events of last night in my diary with letters of fire so that they may never fade and may become a source of shame for all Americans who pride themselves on being as civilized as all the nations of

Europe. It was a little past eight in the evening. I was talking outside with Don José María Alvares, who was weeping and asking my advice about the position he was to take in his miserable situation. Just then we heard some horrible shouts and screams as though they were coming from desperate men. A moment later Araoz arrived, frightened to death and without his hat. He told us that what we had heard was in fact the desperate screams of Mexicans and Chileans who were being clubbed by a gang of Americans who were robbing them. A number of them had been injured, and Araoz had been struck and lost his hat. This happened around eight o'clock in the evening. You could hear the noise of breaking bottles and the howls these men made as though they were savages. The gang was in a French eating house.[21] After knocking out the innkeeper, they sacked everything and got drunk, all the while shouting hurrahs until they were hoarse.

By nine o'clock Araoz, Bargas, Trejo, Alvares, and my two helpers had gone to bed. I stayed up studying the guitar. It hadn't been long since they had gone to sleep when I heard a lot of noise in a nearby tent. I continued to practice so as not to frighten anyone. A moment later I saw fifteen men who were not more than twenty-five steps from my tent. They were speaking in hushed voices and were loading their pistols and rifles. I did not move. They came close enough to place us within range of their pistols. They must have been watching me the whole time they were out there, because I had the candle in front of me that lit up the music book I was studying. After a while they left.

I did not trust them, and a moment later I went out to see what they were doing. They reached the tree where yesterday the American had been buried. Later I heard curses, shouts, the noise of weapons and clubs, and the wails of some Mexicans. In fact, over in that direction there was a storage camp with sixty or seventy mules. The noises continued, and then I saw that they had started a fire and were throwing things on it. An explosion and wails of agony eventually accompanied all of this. . . . There was no doubt, I said to myself, that someone has died.[22] I entered the tent with a heavy heart but filled with a horrible desire for revenge. I woke everyone up, told them what had happened, and proposed that we go out and help those poor devils. No one wanted to. Just then five more Chileans arrived from a nearby tent. When there were twelve of us I once again proposed to them to go help, especially since we had good weapons and we could also count from the very beginning on the help of every Mexican in the area. Still, nobody wanted to go with me. Finally I touched the pride and humanity of Bargas, who I thought was the most capable of all, and he rose and said to me "Let's go." Each of us went out with a couple of pistols and with our knives. As soon as the rest saw us leave, they all rose and said "We're also coming." All of them were well armed with rifles, pistols, and knives.

As we went out we saw that the singing and jumping Americans were going toward the lake. We went straight toward the encampment where they had been, and when we arrived they were no longer nearby. What a horrible scene, my God, what destruction!! They had strewn all of the stored sacks of flour all around the ground so that it would be impossible to make any use of it; it looked as if white sheets were laid out here and there. They had also done the same with the supplies of crackers, frijoles, chickpeas, and wines and spirits. They had thrown all clothing, both for personal use and for sale, on the fire, and they had axed up all of the gear. In sum, they left no stone unturned. We called the owners, but nobody replied, and we found that their beds were empty. We shouted loudly so that the owners would recognize us and return, but no one answered. I was looking around the beds, close to where the gear had been, and suddenly I tripped over a body. . . . I jumped back and cried that I had found one of them. Since it was so dark and we could not distinguish anything at all, we explored the body with our hands. . . . It was completely bloodied. . . . "They have killed him" we all shouted together. As though these words had been a bullet, one of those who had come with us, Munita from Santiago, fainted. Yet another affliction!

Bargas put his hand on the chest of the man and said, "I think he is still alive." And in fact he was still alive. We struck a match and looked for the wound. The bullet had entered his thigh and had not come out. We covered him up with his own clothes and continued looking. We did not find anyone else. We did find two high-quality pairs of pistols with their Mexican holsters and used them to arm two or three of our own group who only had axes. We shouted again, and this time a man came out from behind a tree. We asked him if he was the owner of the grounds, and he said he was only a laborer. I could see that he was lying out of fear. I grabbed him by his coat and said:

"My friend, the time is slipping away, you are lying out of fear. Come and see a companion of yours they have either killed, or he might still be breathing. Then maybe something can be done. Do you still deny that you are the owner of the storage grounds?"

"I have a small part in the business," he said as a kind of reply.

We returned to the dead; our buddy Munita was still out cold, and the other one was much the same as before. We went to find other Mexicans who would come to help, because the man did not want to remain alone.

When we returned we lit a candle, and as soon as we called him he opened his eyes and mumbled: "Oh my God, *madrecita mía!*"

This last exclamation went straight to my heart, and my eyes filled with tears. At that moment I remembered my own mother . . . something not really difficult to do.

We attempted to console him first by whispering to him.

"They left me alone," he said as he looked over his shoulder at the man wearing the coat.

How ashamed that man (who was in fact one of the owners) must have felt. We attempted to bring the injured man to my tent, but he fainted from pain when we attempted to lift him. Finally we left two more men to care for him, along with the second owner, and returned to the tent. All night those bandits continued to do the same thing to others. We dug in and waited for them, but they were busy with the French inn and with other tents, where they did the same thing. . . . At dawn they took the wagon of the muleteers and raced past our tent toward the mines.

Our own Munita had finally come to by the time we returned to the tent. On the way back, we stumbled over the body of the American who had been buried the day before but who was only half-covered with dirt. I must have stepped on his stomach because it felt elastic. I jumped backward and went home another way. Four years ago, on the other side of the world in Argentina, I would not have been horrified, but since I have been in Chile, where you never see anyone dead, nowadays anything horrifies me.

It is now ten o'clock in the morning, and seven of those scoundrels have been arrested. They are aboard the boat of our comrade Sparrow. It is hard to believe what they did because they act like gentlemen from among the best Americans I have seen around here. Some of them are only between eighteen and twenty years old.

WEDNESDAY, 27 JUNE. *Some prisoners!*

Two more of those rascals from the other night have been taken prisoner. This afternoon a jury will be formed to judge them. We shall see what comes of it. They seem to be happy and are playing aboard the ship like little kids.

It was five in the afternoon when I returned from my bath. The jury has only made them post a bond of $1,000, so that they will not do anything like it again. And the poor man who was shot? He is left with a bullet in his leg. And they are able to go free on the streets of Stockton. The truth is that the jury was not able to find out who had shot him.

A number of people can be seen right now down below; they have brought in an Indian as a thief, and he has been sentenced to be hanged. The decision for that poor devil was sure fast! How can they possibly not punish those who shot a sleeping man and yet are willing to hang a man who stole probably because he was hungry?

THURSDAY, 28 JUNE. *Some poor Mexican girls*

On Sunday while I was taking a walk toward the other side of the mountain, I came upon two carts with some ladies in them. . . . One of these ladies is a woman with nine children who also seems to have come around these parts because of the gold. I was most interested in her situation. She has two little ones who are ill and another little girl who died in the mines. The only male with them is a little boy of twelve, all the rest are women. Three of them are girls between sixteen and eighteen, and two of them are quite pretty. I advised her not to go all the way into the town and to set up camp as far away from the center as possible. She finally chose a place about fifty paces from my tent. I sent my men to help her set up the tent, and I gave her what she needed for the time being.

On that famous night last Tuesday I went over to their tent as often as I could to cheer them up, as they were frightened to death. In fact, I am useful to them because I am really the only person they know around here, and so the mother and the girls are very grateful to me and await any chance they might have to show their gratitude. But there is really very little I have to ask of them, especially if you keep in mind my own guiding principles in life. For me to pay attention to a woman she must be pretty, well educated, and sensitive; otherwise it is just not worth it.

My tent has become the lodging house for everyone. Any Chilean who arrives in Stockton, whether or not I know him, with or without a pretext, invariably ends up coming by my tent so that I can get him whatever he needs. The same thing happens with those on their way back from the mines. Nobody bound for San Francisco passes through without staying here three or four days. Some leave and others arrive. Out of twenty days, there are only about four without visitors.

FRIDAY, 29 JUNE. *Life in California and my own life in Stockton*

When one recalls or thinks for only a moment about his past and present, when one stops being a savage for only an instant so as to think about his life, it is then that he sometimes feels as though he has been rudely awakened from a dream. The things that he sees happening to him seem almost unreal. It is this sudden and complete change that emigrants dream about at certain moments of their lives: beginning with the comforts of life and ending up with an abrupt halt of the tastes and pleasures of a society that we have been so accustomed to. For a person like me, whose well-being has not yet reached its zenith anywhere, I can, however, perceive an immense difference between my past and my present. I live under the roof of one of the best tents, and I am sheltered from all storms and cold weather. Yet the sun burns me in the course of the day with such force that I finally have to get out of its light and take refuge in the shade of some tree so that I can stop breathing flames. If it rains and there is no other way out, the tent ends up leaking, and I get wet, but not before my men and I have carried the twenty-five-pound sacks of flour out of the rain. Lunchtime comes, and there are more problems. Whether or not you consider it a meal is hard to tell, but it certainly is not well cooked, and there is no tablecloth to serve it on, nor any table for the tablecloth. And so if one is hungry he has to eat a few mouthfuls while he is standing up, as though he was just passing through. At night it is either fiercely hot or there is wind, and then you end up being covered with so much dirt and dust that it looks like you had a sack of dirt thrown on you.

The next day if you want to be a little clean, it is necessary to spend half the day washing up. And once your body is clean, you have to put on a shirt that has already gone four days without washing. Around here it would scandalize everyone if you were to change shirts more than every six or eight days. Since there is nobody to wash your clothes, no matter how much you are willing to pay, you have to make a shirt last at least six days before throwing it away.[23] And around here there are so many elegant people! Too bad for the poor people like us, who used to enjoy dressing properly! We do not know what vests are, or waistcoats, or suspenders, or leggings for trousers, or ties, or hats, or boots, or patent leather shoes. All of that, all of it, is gone. There is not so much as a trace of that taste for dressing, not with luxury, mind you, but at least properly. If a man combs his hair or his sideburns the day he works, mainly at the behest of his conscience, the other men make fun of him.

And after all, why dress well? There is nothing here that seems even remotely like a society of gentlemen or ladies. There is no one to meet with. One might even forget his language, because around here in order to make yourself understood you must speak a mixture of French, English, Spanish, and a kind of Mexican-Californian Spanish. Sundays, when you have your day off to rest a bit and amuse yourself as best you can, is when you suffer most. The bells begin ringing around six in the morning as though they were calling everyone to mass, but it is really the eating houses that are calling their residents. These bells ring the same way three times a day, at six, at twelve, and then again at seven, and every time they do it, it is a type of mortification for Catholics. It brings to their memories a time in which they had a religion and were called on Sundays by those same bells to the sacrifice of the mass or to the preaching of the gospel. There is none of that around here. It is as though the communion of men gathered together in California is a race damned by the Lord, condemned to wander over the globe without God, without a country, without a government, without law or religion. The night of a horribly hot working day comes at last, and then you want to relax, but even then it is not possible. You finally go to bed, saddened and filled with dark thoughts. In other words, it is then that a man thinks about his life and his condition, compares the present with the past, and the result is one of pain and suffering, though always mitigated by the hope of better days to come. Ay! How many have waited just like us for six months and have finally seen the illusion of it all, as when a man condemned to death sees the place where all of his hopes for life will come to an end!

Then add the diseases, the poison ivy, and the mosquitoes to all of this. The ivy drives you crazy, and when you happily escape from it you fall in among the mosquitoes, from whom nobody escapes. They turn your hands into a piece of flesh, they bite you through your jacket, and they bother you mostly at night just when you would like to sleep so as to forget your life here, just like Martin, who got drunk to forget that he was a slave!! The most important of all these little discomforts and dangers are the Yankees, who constitute the danger that most affects the life of all immigrants. The day they feel like it, they simply start a big fight just like the other night, no matter how frivolous the pretext may be, and go around shooting at us just like that poor devil the other night. Had they hit him in any other place of his body than in his leg, he would have been done for.

Today has been the most beautiful day I have seen for at least four months. It is completely cloudy just like in my country. Big and thick clouds are rolling about as if announcing a real summer storm. It is as cool as a July day in the south of Chile. It looks like the loveliness of the day has infected us all, and everyone seems to be happy, and it is as though the rigors of summer have passed.

I received two letters from Samuel in San Francisco. He is sending some things we need for our store, which are the only ones he was able to embark on the *Golondrina*. He said he will use three or four thousand pesos to send for another boat.[24]

He also says that there have been more than just shots. Some Italian friars, from some sort of religion, started a tavern, where they made a lot of money in just a few days. Some Americans used to go there to get drunk, and for whatever reason—maybe to scandalize people—the friars dressed up as lay persons. Things were that way for eight days, after which there was a fight with a lot of Americans, one of whom was shot to death. The friars fled right away, and the Americans tore up the tavern and sold everything piece by piece to the highest bidder. They are desperately looking for the friars right now. The burial of the American was done with military honors, with all kinds of military salutes, even though he may not have been more than a bandit.

STOCKTON, SUNDAY, 1 JULY 1849. *It looks like we are being threatened . . .*

More dangers and disorder! On the fourth of this month they are preparing a revolution that will be almost simultaneous everywhere. Using the pretext that the 4th of July is Independence Day for the United States, great riots have been prepared in San Francisco and in all of the mines. The Yankees have a secret association of forty bandits, called "The Forty," that has no rival. These people, as honorable Americans tell us themselves, have spread everywhere to rally people to the cry of extermination and death for all Chileans, Mexicans, or Peruvians. We have found out that the assault committed the other night was in fact ordered by one of "The Forty," who left for Stanislaus after having preached and planted here the flag of his sect. Everyday you can hear threats of Americans against all foreigners on the 4th of July, even in front of the mayor. All of the Mexicans have left Stockton, and you can see others getting ready to abandon their place. Those of us who must stay will soon find out how we can escape this difficult situation.

TUESDAY, 3 JULY. *An unexpected friend!*

A few days ago on his way to San Francisco, a German friend of mine left me two yoke of oxen, asking me to have my men take care of them and offering me their use if the occasion arose. With all this commotion I had almost forgotten about them. All morning I looked for a cart I could rent, but none appeared. As I was returning to my tent, I met Mr. Stockton, who is one of the richest men around here and who gave his name to this town.[25] Since he saw me coming out of one of his inns, he asked me what I was seeking. I told him what I wanted. In an instant he told an Indian to bring one of his carts, and in the meantime he invited me to have a drink with him. I accepted, and he very politely clinked my glass and said "To your health." He offered me the use of his house anytime I needed. This was certainly a singular occurrence, and it was made still more singular by chance. In Samuel's package there was a letter addressed to Mr. Stockton that he had asked me to deliver. I had not done so because I did not know who he was. After our drink I ran home to get the letter and gave it to him. He was very grateful.

It is ten o'clock in the morning, and Camaño is leaving for Calaveras with a loaded wagon. He has twenty-something *quintales* of cargo.[26] That is sure called saving by sheer luck. I could not find anyone to take two wagons for me, or even one, even if I had offered him an ounce of gold per hundredweight, and now all of this cargo is going for free. We have saved at least $340 because the Lord is great and Mr. Stockton is a good man, and that's that.

WEDNESDAY, 4 JULY. *Fiesta*

Today is the much feared 4th of July. There is going to be an immense meal at one of the inns that is costing them close to 4,000 pesos. This meal is being put on by the principal merchants around here in honor of the commander of the troops, stationed fourteen leagues from here. Today a bunch of Americans, who had gone out to invite him, arrived back in town. They are two blocks away, but you can hear the boisterous hurrahs of more than 200 men. Who knows where all this champagne is going to end up? Since last night there have been constant fireworks and gunfire. Let's hope things are quieter tonight.

THURSDAY, 5 JULY. *The calm returns*

Last night was a lot better than the night before. You could not even hear the shouts of the drunks or anything else indicating disorder. It was a lovely night. The moon lit things up as though it was daytime, and there was a cool breeze blowing. Zarabia, the young lad Elordi, and I spent part of the night rowing on the lake. The fireworks were exploding all the time. Entire boxes of fireworks were burned, and this made enough noise to shake the ground. They sang a lot of songs and played some lovely opera arias on a cornet. Some American guy was playing, and he did so beautifully.

STOCKTON, 6 JULY. *Cupertino Ocampo*

My cousin Cupertino Ocampo just arrived this afternoon. I was not expecting him at all and was delighted to see him, at least until I found out why he had undertaken this sudden trip. The Zonoreños' land burned before anything on it had been sold.[27] The little house Cupertino and Samuel had there also went up in flames. They lost only $1,000, but, more important, they lost all hope of making money after all that sacrifice of getting the investment set up. Things evidently are moving fast for us. These blows come one after another in rapid succession, leaving little opportunity to make up for the losses of one blow before another graver one comes along. The fire was started on Monday afternoon by an old lady who was making meat pies when her tent caught fire, which then spread to the entire field. Why do women like Helen always have to be the cause of fires and other misfortunes?[28] She was probably the only woman in that field at that time, yet she was able to ruin more than four people by burning up three hundred thousand pesos in less than an hour. Besides, since she was old she was also ugly, and this adds insult to injury. Every time a man suffers at the hands of a beautiful woman, after his first impression of pain, his suffering is mitigated by the beauty of that same woman, because he can see the tenderness sparked by his own suffering in her beautiful eyes. She helps give him fortitude and serenity amid his ruin, as though she was an angel or some greater divinity. But an old and ugly woman, what consolation can she give to a person she has undone? None!

STOCKTON, SUNDAY, 8 JULY. *A serenade*

Last night around 10, Cupertino, Mr. Thibault, and I went to serenade the young Digson girls. We had two guitars with us. First we sang, and later we played some duos that fortunately turned out very well. We received lots of applause, often coming straight from the girls' beds, and pretty soon Mr. Digson came out practically undressed and made us enter the courtyard with no more light than that of the moon, which was shining straight on the doorway and bathing the entire building. We could not see any of them, and the curtains around each bed stayed drawn. But we could hear the murmurs of the girls and the sound of little hands lifting the sides of bed curtains just enough to look out, and then you could see just a little white thing, like a shirt. . . . They gave us champagne twice, and, after having sung for about a half an hour, we left around half past eleven at night. We sang another song at the door of the house of the widow of Stockton and later went aboard the *Susana*, where for a half an hour we sang and played opera pieces with some friends of Mr. Thibault. We were singing a war march as we left there. While we were doing this in front of Mr. Thibault's boat and were about ready to turn in, more than twenty Americans joined us, enthusiastically jumping and clapping. A moment later Sparrow showed up with four more, and he took all of us to his tent. The group was immense by that time. We arrived and opened six bottles of champagne, and, after toasts and compliments of all kinds, they asked us to sing "La Lid Argentina."[29] As we began the first verse, all of our hats went to the floor, and everyone followed our example, and no one said anything except those who knew the song and helped us along. Everyone sang the chorus. At the sound of the last verse of "War! War! And death! . . ." the corks of another six bottles were popped, and there was a general toast for the Argentine Republic. My God, how beautiful!!!

It was about two in the morning when Cupertino and I returned to our tent. When we arrived we saw the light in the tent of the ladies I call my protected ones (because they really are in every way), and we went over there. My God what a horrible spectacle we saw upon our arrival! In the middle of the tent there was a corpse in a shroud. Two candles, one at its head and the other at its feet, gave off a weak light because of the four fingers of snuff that each candle had. The eldest daughter was keeping vigil next to the body, while the other three girls and their mother were sleeping nearby, done in by their sorrow and the vigil. From time to time a prolonged sigh or smothered sob followed upon the shudder of one of the girls, and then everything was suddenly profoundly silent. It is easy to imagine the horrendous impression this scene made upon us, especially if you consider that this came right after the semibacchanal party that we had only left a minute before. After a few moments of silence, the daughter doing the vigil answered a question of mine.

"It is our brother who died tonight. We looked for you in vain during his final moments but were unable to find you."

Good God, another wound for me! Who knows how I may have been able to help or what consolation I might have been able to give them? I have deprived them of it without knowing, just to go out serenading, while right near my tent at that very moment death was in the process of snaring someone else. We sat down for awhile, but what an insolent child that Cupertino is! As soon as he had sat down, he noticed that he was on the skirt of the prettiest girl of all, whom he watched sleeping with a strange voluptuousness without remembering what he had before him. Later, as he was making a sign to me, he placed his hand on the pure mouth of the sleeping girl. The girl keeping vigil did not notice, and this impudent boy continued doing it for a few moments, all the while making different signs to me. I looked at him harshly but in vain and pointed to the body next to him; he only laughed and continued to play around. I was mortified. Finally I arose and said to him imperiously,

"Let's go Cupertino."

At that moment the mother, the sleeping maiden, and all the others woke up. . . . We left after having done as much as we could to console them. The unhappy lady has now lost three of her children. Imagine the memories she is going to have of this pilgrimage in search of California gold.

WEDNESDAY, 11 JULY. *Chileans expelled from the gold fields*

Samuel wrote telling me that a great number of Chileans have just arrived in San Francisco after having been expelled by the Americans from the mines of Sacramento. I have been told that the injustices committed these days against the Chileans or anyone else speaking Spanish are horrible. Today I witnessed an atrocious injustice that beseeches heaven for revenge on the person who so cruelly abuses his power and strength. A Mexican had made a deal with an American to take twenty loads of freight for him. Today he was unable to pick up the freight because he lost three mules on the way and only arrived here at ten. As soon as he arrived the American had the train embargoed, charging him one thousand pesos for damages. The Mexican appealed, and the American said that if the judge ruled any other way he would shoot the Mexican. The judge, instead of ruling fairly on the Mexican's appeal, ruled that the Mexican had to keep the freight of the American and that its value had to be paid within twenty-four hours.

THURSDAY, 12 JULY. *Pedro Herrera*

The company of Don Pedro Herrera, which passed by my tent on its way to the mines several days ago, just returned. They are on their way back because the Americans threatened them and ran them out of the mines. They did not even have time enough to bring their equipment, supplies, and horses back with them. They made it here on foot and have had little to drink or eat since they left. These are all young sons of some of the most important families in Chile. Every day people like this come by my tent in more or less the same way. Those coming from San Francisco on their way to the mines do much of the same. I sure wish I had more comfortable things to offer these poor people.

TUESDAY, 17 JULY

The doctor has just come back from the mines and brings with him about fifty pounds of gold dust, which is what the men have taken out in six weeks. It looks like so far things are going pretty well for us, better than for many others. Maybe our mine is never going to yield any more than it does right now. I will have to settle for whatever we get.

THURSDAY, 19 JULY. *Cholera morbus*

More calamities are on the way. According to the steamship that arrived three days ago, cholera has made its appearance in the United States and in Panama. Six passengers aboard the ship also died, and everywhere people are scared to death of the disease.

FRIDAY, 20 JULY

Accompanied by the young Sanjuaninos, Coronel, my men, and Mr. Brentan, who showed up a few days ago, I left Stockton at eleven this morning on my way to the placer. It is terribly hot. Even in the deserts of Africa I do not think that the sun burns more. Right now I am writing this in my notebook in the shade of a beautiful pine tree, whose circumference is more than what three men holding hands could surround. This is the only way to be able to bear such heat.

SATURDAY, 21 JULY. *On our way to the mines*

We are about halfway there and are at a very beautiful site. We are at the shore of one of the forks of the Calaveras River, whose banks are covered on both sides of the river with oaks and pines and all kinds of vines whose shade is delicious. I have never seen anything like it. I took a bunch of grapes and could see that they are exactly the same as in Chile or in Buenos Aires. The only differences are in the leaves. The ones here are rounder and less undulated than ours. I am surprised to see how unripe the grapes still are, despite the fact that summer is so advanced. It also strikes me that we still see roses along the way as though we were in spring. Later we ran into four Frenchmen while we were waiting for the heat of the day to pass. They were carrying their equipment and making their way back on foot. They were as hot as we were.

SUNDAY, 22 JULY. *At the placer on the Calaveras River*

What a strange name that heads up my diary today. First of all, in California there are no pleasures, and, besides, the name itself is absurd, *Placer de las Calaveras.* Since when do skulls have life and pleasures in their dream of death, in their residence of misery, and amidst the deception of life that ultimately is nothing![30] But this is California, the land of odd events, things never heard of before, land of changes, land made up of strange things, magical land, a land capable of producing another Don Quixote to conquer all of its gold. This is a land where you can even speak of the pleasures of skulls!

We reached here at eight o'clock last night. I cannot portray or describe the impression this place made upon me, a place where I am going to live for two years of my life without any society other than that of the workers, with no other distraction other than constant work, with no change of scenery and no movement, not even for a day. It will be a life of sacrifice and pain and with no other consolation or hope of improving it than being able to finish out more than seven hundred or so days of work. Rochefort was in the Bastille for more time than that, for thirteen years, and yet when he emerged from his confinement he said that it had been like a dream.

Well, I am now here. Three of the men are sick. So far they have only taken out 1,200 pesos' worth of gold. It would be worse if we had found nothing at all. The time will come when we will not find anything, just like all of the rest of Eve's children who are around here. It is all a matter of pure luck, like with all mines. Before you know it, the lode has dried up and there is not a bit of gold left. I am going to do some panning myself, because I need some ounces of gold that I alone have mined. They will be a souvenir . . . and can be made into a wedding ring . . . or some other crazy thing like that.[31]

This afternoon I tried my hand for the first time, and the place where I washed the first shovelfuls of soil rendered up almost one-fourth of an ounce. Today is Sunday, and I should not have worked, but God knows that this gold will be destined for something other than just making me rich. It is to be spent on too sacred an object for God not to forgive my having forgotten one of his commandments. Well, now I have more than enough for that wedding ring. But I still need more.

MONDAY, 23 JULY. *Sickness*

Today four of my men are ill, and one of them has fever. We probably lose three or four ounces of gold for every day one of the men does not work. The gold for my rings is growing; today I got a bit more than yesterday. There is no power on earth that will make me work at this once I have secured the small amount I need for my museum of souvenirs and curiosities. There is no job that is more difficult than panning for gold. You have to work bent over in water up to your knees, and after a quarter of an hour your body feels all beaten up. Today the eleven laborers working here have taken out a total of 220 pesos.

WEDNESDAY, 25 JULY. *Mokelumne Hill*

They have discovered a very rich claim about five leagues from here.[32] It seems as though it was Mexicans who discovered it, but about 200 Americans made up an armed force and, as is custom among them, shamefully threw out all the Chileans, Peruvians, Mexicans, and anybody else who speaks Spanish. They especially have it in for the Chileans, though I do not know exactly why. Every day there are people coming by who have been thrown out of their claims. There is no other tyranny or arbitrariness as great as that carried out by this nation of free and republican people. There were groups of men who were told to leave within fifteen minutes or else their lives would be at risk. They have gotten rid of anyone who was in their way.

Despite all this, today I sent two miners there with supplies for an entire week. They will work under the orders of Mr. Alfredo, who is English but who passes for American. We shall see what happens. If they are allowed to work I shall send another two, and then another three, and so on, until the doctor comes back, and then he will be the American who goes there with my men.

THURSDAY, 26 JULY. *A burial*

Today while I was at the workplace with my men, I was called from the tent in a great hurry. It was the servant of an American who set up a half-mile from here. He asked me for three men to bury an American who just fell dead in his storehouse. He said that I should not hesitate to send them because they would be paid for however long it took. Besides, I was told that if I did not send them I should watch out. . . . To hell with the forced loan and the threat!

"Tell your boss," I said, "that the men are all busy and that when they are finished I will send them for free."

The servant went over to the tent of the Riosecos with the same demand, and there they gave him the three men. This dead man was French, and it was the French consul who had made such a demand. The consul was there by chance, as he was on his way to Stanislaus. And also, by chance, they found in his pockets the three pounds of gold that the dead man had in his.[33]

The laborers I sent to Mokelumne should have been back by now, but they have yet to return. Who knows when they may arrive?

FRIDAY, 27 JULY. *I lost my wife!*

Today a fatality happened to me that is one of the worst I could ever have imagined here. I lost my only consolation, my distraction, my love. I lost my guitar. This is a tragedy for me, an event that will mark my entire diary, a loss that I will lament as the greatest loss of all if I lose, as I think I shall, all hope of remedying it. First, the back of the guitar came unglued because of all of the heat, and I mistakenly gave it to the first person who offered to fix it. He put it in water to straighten it, and by today it was totally destroyed, broken into 9,999 pieces. I am like a widower or, better, like a lover who has just lost the illusions of his loved one. My God! At first I could only think of where I might find another guitar and how I could get it here if it came from San Francisco. Well, I have just written to Samuel and feel a little bit better now.

SUNDAY, 29 JULY. *Things to enjoy in California*

I do not know quite what to do without my guitar. I had never imagined that I would miss it as much as I do. Comparing it to the loss of a lover would not be an exaggeration. Actually, the loss of my guitar is even greater. A lover compensates the happiness she gives with long periods of sorrow and pain. But my guitar never ever causes me pain or suffering. Whenever I have it in my hands and a book in front of me, I can find something new, something to enjoy.

In order to forget about the guitar for awhile, I went out today with one of our men to do a little looking around. A walk is always lovely, and there is something poetic and mysterious about exploring unknown areas, especially those where there is no trace of anyone having been there before. We reached a place along the river, and we stopped at a type of pool it made. While the worker was examining the bank of the river, I reclined in the shadow of two large rocks that made a perfectly designed niche for me. The first thing anyone in California does when he is someplace new is to scrape the earth around a bit and see if anything appears that might look like gold. This is exactly what I did. I took out my knife and made a small hole, and in a second I saw two or three bits of gold. I told the laborer to wash a pan of that earth, and the first time he tried he got an eighth of an ounce! "It looks good," he said. The men will probably make two or three ounces of gold a day. It is too bad there is so little room to work right here, because the rest of the ground is covered with great rocks that are simply impossible to move.

MONDAY, 30 JULY. *Mokelumne*

It is midday, and the men I sent to Mokelumne have finally returned. Nobody kept them from getting there or bothered them in their work. They were only able to work for two days, mainly because they were staking out a claim to work. Even so, they have brought six ounces of gold back with them. Their workplace has been set up, and they have come back for supplies and more men for this coming week. It looks like that river is a bit richer than this one, despite the fact that there are few places left for them to work there.

They tell me that on the way back they met with some two hundred Mexicans who were on their way there. They probably let them enter because the place is very rich, and anyway they might find another canyon that has ten-pound nuggets like that one did at first.

By now our river is pretty poor, and you only get things from it with double the amount of work. Today the ten men were able to get a total of thirteen ounces of gold. Tomorrow I am going to send four more men to Mokelumne so that the work there can be a bit more productive for those left behind.

THURSDAY, 9 AUGUST 1849. *Recalling the day of my departure*

The ninth seldom comes around without my feeling strong emotions when recalling that we left Chile on the 9th of March. Only God and I know what was going on inside me at that moment. So five months ago today I left Concepción, and I have not yet even put in a fourth of the time I must spend traveling the world. The work of my men here is getting worse by the day. The truth is that right now I have only five men with me. The rest have gone off to other placers. The Herreras, who have come from Stockton, were with Samuel, though they neglected to tell him that they were coming up here. This is a great loss for all of us. Course savages! They were born that way and are bound to die that way, and, like the beasts they are, they do not realize the value of communication in this world. That is probably why they did not tell Samuel. I will get my chance to show them how much they have inconvenienced our enterprise by returning them the favor. With this type of people, making them suffer the same inconvenience is not a matter of revenge but rather one of education, because it is the only way to make them understand the damage they have done.

FRIDAY, 10 AUGUST. *The reptiles of California*

Last night the two men I had sent to the gulch discovered by the laborers of Don Maximo Peiro returned. All of it was false. They have been looking for gold ever since they left and have not found anything richer than this. The fact is that right now discoveries of gold are few and far between, just like the water in the rivers. I cannot wait for the doctor to come so that I can take off with half the men to try my hand at Lady Luck, who so far has been remiss with all the others.

There are probably few countries in the world with more snakes and other poisonous animals than California. A few days ago we killed an immense rattlesnake right next to the tent, and the day before yesterday we killed another one we found in the kitchen, which was nearly a yard and a half long.[34] Yesterday on my way back from the wash, as I came into the sunlight near some large rocks about six paces from the tent, my arm brushed up against the head of an immense snake that, at my jump of surprise, retreated into a crevasse in the rock. I threw hot water on it, and it came out furiously showing a long tongue covered with froth. We killed it right away, but it was not easy. It was nearly two yards long. This is another of these epidemics they have around here, where the Yankees, the Indians, yellow fever, or something else is always threatening your life. Fortunately, up till now I have come through all of these plagues pretty much unscathed. I escaped the Yankees in Stockton, and it will be pretty hard for them to take me by surprise the next time around.

SATURDAY, 11 AUGUST. *A ten-year-old rattlesnake*

I just killed an immense rattlesnake. I was writing when Candelaria came in shouting and saying that a giant snake had just about bitten her. I loaded the shotgun and went to see. There it was, completely curled up and asleep under a tree. I shot it and was able to kill it without damaging the rattle, which I really wanted to keep. There must be lots of California gentlemen who keep these rattles as carefully as they would keep a pretty gold nugget. The one I killed was ten or eleven years old. Today I wrote to Samuel, but I feel badly because I was not able to write Chile. It has been a long time since I last wrote there, maybe two months or more, and who knows how many more will go by before I am able to write again. If I am able to go to San Francisco in October, maybe I will be able to write from there.

TUESDAY, 14 AUGUST. *Back to Mokelumne*

This morning I sent Orellana back to Mokelumne again. That placer is the only hope in this area. Around here everything is pretty much finished, though the truth is that I only have four men, who barely scrape out about $10 each every day. I sure wish I had in Chile or in my Argentina some land like this here that yields $10 a day with hardly any work at all. Then I would be able to put one hundred workers to work and see what they got. As the saying goes, God gives cake to those with no teeth. . . . While waiting for the doctor I have not wanted to send these last four men over there, because with gold in the strongbox there is always a danger if you are completely alone. Either the Americans or the Indians are the ones who try to steal from big companies. A few nights ago they stole 2,500 pesos from Mr. Scollen, and he is an American.[35] His camp is not far from ours, and my company is three times the size of his, and so I should be careful. Today I again loaded my set of pistols and put aside extra rounds of ammunition and told my men to load their rifles. There is about $5,000 in the chest, which is the product of a month of work by my men, and we should at least make it difficult for them to steal.

WEDNESDAY, 15 AUGUST. *The day of the Assumption in other times . . .*

Today is a very important holiday that is filled with memories for me. Even with today being the anniversary of the Assumption of the Blessed Virgin to heaven and a day when the Church has prohibited all work, you can hear the sound of tools, shovels, and picks echoing off the cliffs. You can hear the blows of the men who work ardently because with every blow they may see the glimmer of gold. "Why do they work?" any normal person might ask. They work, I would answer, because this is California. Besides, I prefer them to work, even though it is against one of the five precepts of the

Church, because if they have time off they will irremediably go gambling and get drunk among the Indians and the Americans who meet there just so they can cause trouble. If you are sober you can avoid the trouble, but not if you are drunk. Last Sunday, about two in the morning, an American and an Indian with his quiver filled with arrows came by to demand that one of the laborers give them five hundred pesos, a pistol, and a rifle they had won in a card game. The best thing to do was to get quietly out of the way of those drunks, lest something nasty come to happen.

SATURDAY, 18 AUGUST. *Nothing new, more uncertainty*

The heat seems to be diminishing, and the water is getting colder by the day. It looks as though the season is about to change, and so maybe summer is ending. What a summer it has been for me this year. Twelve months of heat, and twelve months in which I have not felt the cold of winter. It is rather strange and perhaps rather frightening, because it must be a bit like eternity, where man does not experience the mysterious variability of the seasons. It is strange to have been eating maize and watermelon in January in Chile and then to have had the same fruits, just as delicious here as there, during the month of July in California.

SUNDAY, 19 AUGUST. *The gold of Orellana*

Orellana just arrived now from Mokelumne; he always seems to arrive between eleven and noon and is always complaining how hot he was on his way here. What that really means is that he is not one of those who enjoys rising early in the morning in California, which, by the way, is when it is at its most beautiful. He has brought fifty ounces of gold with him, the product of six days of prospecting for nine men. As we had expected, thousands of men converged on his claim and finished it up far before he "would have liked," to use his own expression. This means that they have no sites lined up for this coming week.

It is ten o'clock at night, and you can hear the happy snoring of some of the men who have been sleeping under the stars for the past hour. Farther off you can hear the sounds of a lively conversation of some fellow, seasoned with the idiotic and inelegant flavor of tobacco and a bottle of liquor. These must be some of the four or six other persons who are celebrating Sunday in their own way. I can also hear the far-off and vague sound of coyotes, which communicate their thoughts through their howls, which mix in with the bark of our dogs, Pluto and Tisi. There are a lot of living beings that are still on the watch at this time of night. I am watching out for my men and for the coyotes. As you can see, the society accompanying me on my watch is not very dignified. . . . But am I not in California?

TUESDAY, 21 AUGUST. *I got my way*

By now there is not much drinking water left around here, but at least it is good water. I have only four laborers in my charge plus, of course, all the gold. Mining is slow, and my men seldom get more than a half an ounce each. They work to keep themselves busy, not for much else.

The Californian who had that beautiful gold nugget the other day, which I really wanted but which he refused to sell to me for anything in this world, has just left my tent. He came to give me the same piece he had not wanted to sell to me before. Yet free things always have their price. . . . He needed many things and took a fancy to my Scottish dagger, which I naturally gave him for nothing. Before he ever gave me the gold nugget, it already had a place in my life, and so in one way or another it was destined to come into my hands. That is what ended up happening, and now it will be mine forever.

WEDNESDAY, 22 AUGUST. *Two hangings*

In the past few days in Stockton they have hanged two Americans and another one in Mokelumne at about the same time. The day before yesterday they hanged another one as well. Now in San Francisco and in Stockton, and in the placers themselves, a bit of order has been established. In Stockton an extremely strict jury has been set up, and it leaves no crime unpunished, no matter how small it might be; and punishments are rigorous. The strength behind this jury is the merchants themselves of Stockton. They catch the criminals, throw them in jail, and are also the executioners and the gravediggers. The jury votes on who the executioner will be because nobody wants to do it, not even if they are paid for the job. One of the most horrible decisions once fell to one of the most honorable men of Stockton, Mr. Sparrow, a business partner of Samuel, and the poor man had to run madly all over the place trying to find someone to replace him for a tidy sum. Finding the man cost him $200, but he would have given him a thousand or would have preferred to die before doing it himself. This is the news from Stockton. Samuel also says that he is very hopeful about the success of his business.

THURSDAY, 23 AUGUST

Daily two or three American ships filled with passengers arrive in port, and those arriving by land are much more numerous. More than 40,000 Americans have arrived overland. In every route out here you can find groups of between twenty and one hundred men, who are perfectly equipped with their packs on their backs, with their guns, their silk umbrellas or parasols. All together they look like an African caravan or some sort of procession on a rainy day. Chilean migrants also continue to arrive daily in California. The poor souls.

FRIDAY, 24 AUGUST

It is ten o'clock at night, and the two men I sent to San Antonio just arrived.[36] They say there is gold but that they have not brought any with them because they spent all four days looking for new sites to prospect. In fact, I think these rogues have spent their time mostly having a good time for themselves. They came telling of deaths of Mexicans and Chileans who did not even have people to give them a decent burial. They also said that just two hours from here they left a Sonoran and a Chilean dead under the light of the moon with nobody to bury them. They are shaken, and rightfully so, because who knows how many people had all their hopes placed on those two men who will never return.

    With the newcomers, my men have stories for the entire night. There is never a lack of entertainment when newcomers are around. In the meantime I must try to get some sleep so as to forget all the sadness in my heart. More than one good man has become a drunkard just to be happy for at least a few hours, the hours in which liquor has dulled one's spirits enough so as to take from him all recollections of the past and the future. That is how Martin forgot his own story of unrequited love, broken promises, and of the beautiful image of the loved one who had been the cause of his misfortune when he was twenty years old. . . . It always has to be a woman!

SATURDAY, 25 AUGUST. *Tales of the laborers*

    I got to bed about half past eleven last night, and as I was drifting off to sleep I overheard a conversation of the men. One of the travelers said that the day they had arrived in San Antonio a group of about twenty Indians had robbed all of the horses from the camp of the Chileans, including their own mounts. They and another ten men immediately got their guns and set off in pursuit, filling the camp with shouts of joy as though it was some sort of hunt, a manhunt that is. I was told that both the men and the Indians shot guns and arrows at each other at a distance at which it was impossible to hit anyone. Yet with each volley, the Indians let a horse or two go, and the first animals released were those of my men (certainly because they were the skinniest of all). They finally gave up all of the horses at the bottom of the hill, and so the hunt was continued on horseback. As they were about to get close enough to catch them, the Indians lit fire to the grass and disappeared amid the thick black clouds of smoke.

I do not know if the story ended there or if it was then that I finally fell asleep. Whatever, that is about as much as I know. I give thanks to the Lord that nobody was caught. For those poor people out here, there is not even a pretense of due process with these sorts of things. As soon as they were caught they would have been hanged for sure, just as though they were animals. They have hanged a lot of people already around these placers.

SUNDAY, 26 AUGUST

I was playing dominos with Tomás when Orellana arrived. He always has something doleful to tell. An Irishman who had been denounced as a thief was given a choice of three punishments by the jury: hanging, 500 lashes, or the mark of a thief and the mutilation of his ears. The prisoner chose the lashes, but by the time he had received fifty, his body was nearly destroyed, and he asked to be granted a final wish, and this was to be hanged. But whether it was for ill-conceived compassion or double cruelty, instead of giving him what he wanted they condemned him to the mark and mutilation. The executioner must not have been a very good surgeon, and he made the poor devil suffer a lot. It took him two or three blows to sever the first ear, bathing himself and the prisoner in the man's blood. He was no less barbarous with the second ear, despite the horrible cries of his patient. Bathed in his own blood from his head to his feet, the poor man received the indelible mark that would show him as a thief for the rest of his life. I am sure that nowhere is there justice as honest and severe as it is in California; you might even say it was the new Areopagus of Athens.[37]

Today Orellana brought with him four and one-half pounds of gold, which is the product of five or six days' work for nine men. He also brought some rocks completely covered with gold. He tells me that it is quite possible that the claim they are working right now might lead to a very rich lode in

44

the hill. I sure hope he is right. That way I will not have to desire anything else here in California.

MONDAY, 27 AUGUST. *A beautiful swim*

For the last six or eight days we have gone swimming every day in the Calaveras River. I have already mentioned what a picturesque and lovely river it is. The place where we swim is about ten or twelve blocks from here, which is nothing when you think we are on our way to swim. Any village would give millions of pesos to be able to have a river like this running next to it or to have for its gardens and alamedas the great pine trees or the variety of flowers that line the riverbank. Out here there are loads of extraordinary landscapes with wonderful vegetation. Imagine what it would be like if this river ran along the outskirts of a village. Yet those of us here in California cannot really enjoy all this beauty because we do not have our loved ones to share it with. You never enjoy things more than halfway unless the fair sex is there to complete the picture.

WEDNESDAY, 29 AUGUST. *The doctor is in Monterey*

I have just found out by means of a letter from Bauz that Dr. MacKay has gone to Monterey. I do not know why he went or how long he will be there. Just when my situation is most delicate is when he decides to prolong his trip. There are a thousand things to be settled, and these are on my mind all the time. His presence, or mine, in Mokelumne was necessary before but has become indispensable since last week, due to all the troubles the laborers are having. Many of these problems can be settled only by the boss. For example, the men should have damned up the river this week so as to be able to work in the middle of it, where they feel there is much gold to be panned. But I have ordered them not to do it yet because none of us are there to secure from the alcalde the rights to whatever we pan from the dried up part of the river.[38]

How much nicer it would be for the laborers who have been left completely alone for so long to rob all the gold and to do whatever they please. And what the heck am I doing here all alone, when I am hardly able to care adequately for the gold of the company? If those with sticky fingers only knew that my strongbox has a few pounds more than an arroba of gold, who knows what they would do. I do understand that Dr. MacKay made the trip because one of his boats arrived damaged in Monterey and he went to see to the repairs.

THURSDAY, 30 AUGUST

In my moment of sadness, which has afflicted me all day, I composed a waltz that I have dedicated to Mother. It is called "Memories of You, California." It may not be very pretty, but it sure is sad.

SATURDAY, 1 SEPTEMBER 1849. *St. Gilles*

Today is my day! Today is the feast day of St. Gilles the Abbot, and even though I am not a saint or an abbot, it is still my day.[39] Who knows, I may even decide one day to be an abbot and then even a saint. . . . Nobody was born a saint, and in this California it is pretty easy to become a martyr saint.

Today Camaño and Alfredo came back from Mokelumne. Camaño has decided to return to Chile because he is ill and fears that his bones may end up resting here in California. I think that, since he was saved once in San Francisco when his boat was lost, he will never die in this place.

Many people around here have come down with a mysterious illness. In miners it starts with a swelling of the feet. After that the legs swell until the skin opens up all over, and they become one big sore that seems to be immune to any treatment. That is the way they stay until death takes them, and there is never a clue to what disease they actually have. The legs of others end up becoming paralyzed to such a degree that they are unable to walk at all. This illness must be caused by the long hours of work in water up to their waists.

CALAVERAS, SUNDAY, 2 SEPTEMBER. *A day for hunting*

This morning we went out with Mr. Alfredo, shotguns in hand, to see if we could hunt a doe and three fawns that graze about a league from here. We had no luck because we never found the doe. We walked more than two leagues until we came upon some Indian huts made of stones and mortar. When we returned we were not as tired as we had feared. On our way back we found a grave. Who knows whether it was for an Indian, an American, a Chilean, or whomever? It had not been there more than two months.

Upon my return, Orellana was there waiting for us with four sick laborers. One has fever, another a terrible case of dysentery, another is covered with rashes, and the last one walked in with semiparalyzed legs. It has been a ruinous week for the company. Orellana has not brought with him even 600 pesos for an entire week's work. Besides, he says that he has little hope at all for any of the sites, which are fast running out of ore. Our business does not look promising, especially now that Mokelumne, the only placer that had a little gold, is also drying up, just like the one in Stanislaus. Nothing new has been found for some time.

MONDAY, 3 SEPTEMBER. *My hospital*

Today the tent was like a real hospital. Everyone is wailing and asking for help at the same time. The doctor has not come. What am I to do if I am not a doctor? It is true that we have a fully stocked medicine chest, but since I have never taken any medicine in my life I have no idea at all about it and would not know which one to use. I might even give them poison by mistake! Maybe I should let them go on complaining with no mercy and die without ever even giving them a simple painkiller or some other remedy. My situation is not a good one, but I prefer to give them hot water and rice for the dysentery and cold baths for the fevers rather than running the risk of giving them poison instead of medicine.

I have not heard anything from the doctor except that he is in Monterey. Good Lord! Another fifteen or twenty days will go by before he shows up. The company desperately needs a boss in Mokelumne. Who is to guarantee me that the men are not doing whatever they please up there? At times I almost get desperate here all alone without being able to somehow divide myself in two to take care of both sites. Who knows that we might be losing thousands of pesos because of his delay. In the future the facts and the consequences will speak more loudly than I.

TUESDAY, 4 SEPTEMBER. *My colleagues who are really not*

Orellana has left for Mokelumne. I am alone with the sick miners. A mighty good garrison to protect a strongbox with 8,000 pesos in gold dust! Some of the Americans in the "The Forty" have gone out along the isolated roads and fields to attack those who are returning with gold to Stockton or San Francisco. They say that there have already been five or six victims who have lost their lives, despite having given all their money in exchange for their lives. Bandits and murderers! It is almost impossible to hide from the men all the hatred I have built up for Americans. I wish I could find a worthy way to avenge all those they have repressed. Then they would see what it is like to abuse the power that the struggle between peoples and nations has placed in their hands. In Mokelumne they take away the richest claims of the Chileans and Mexicans just by showing up in much greater numbers with rifles in hand. Miserable people! They should come and try to take my claim sometime, attempting to scare me with noise the way you do with birds. Then we would be able to see whether or not my bullets will rip them apart as well!

WEDNESDAY, 5 SEPTEMBER

Mr. Milnes's colleague, who left here with the doctor, returned this afternoon. The doctor is in San Francisco and has said that in another fifteen days he will be here. He has bought 6,000 square blocks of land in the name of our company in Sonoma, not far from Benicia. I do not know what type of land it is. In a few months it may have tripled in value or maybe not. It cost 16,000 pesos. When we get there we will know whether it was a bargain or not.

THURSDAY, 6 SEPTEMBER. *An anniversary!*

Today is a big anniversary for me. This day marks the very first entry in my diary, because it was the day we left Catamarca [Argentina] for Chile as émigrés. It was this day that we bid farewell to our country amid the tears of our family and friends and we started a pilgrimage, as long as it was painful and filled with danger, without even knowing how many of us were to fall by the wayside two or three years later. Only a person who has been through it can understand how much suffering is caused for the person who one last time must turn his gaze, perhaps for the last time, in farewell to his country that he is forced to abandon. Only I really know what it is like to abandon your fatherland, because I also had to abandon Chile and my family to come here to beg in the deserts of California for hospitality and shelter from the least hospitable people in the world. In fact the people here are not really the sons of California but rather its conquerors. I will never be able to forget our departure and our family and friends, who, sensitive to our plight as expatriates, went along to bid us farewell. I did well to mention them all in my diary. I will always be grateful for that last show of sincere friendship. I saw them all cry, and since tears have something holy and sublime to them, they only fall when their masters, our hearts, feel true sorrow.

SATURDAY, 8 SEPTEMBER

The Californian who once gave me that beautiful nugget of gold has just left my tent. He came to ask me for a shotgun to kill a bear that has now come up to his tent three nights in a row. He says the bear is fat and big and he is afraid he will get into some mischief. I loaned him the loaded shotgun and asked him to tell me tomorrow morning if he was able to get him. We will see if my Californian is able to do it.

SUNDAY, 9 SEPTEMBER. *Hunting a ferocious bear!*

At five in the morning I was in my tent when a man sent by the Californian came to return the shotgun to me and tell me that the bear was dead and to go and see it. Since the morning was rather cool, I went quickly over there, almost as though it was exercise. I went with Camaño, who is leaving today for Chile and does not want to go without meeting the bear.

We are back now, and it really was an animal worth seeing. It was about 6 ft. long and about 2 ft. wide. The paws were not unlike those of a man, at least they leave that type of track, except that one paw of the bear is worth a half-dozen footprints of men. I have never seen anything quite so monstrous as the width of that animal's paws. That is why they can tear apart a horse with one swat. The head and neck can be compared to those of a calf or a bull about three years old. The eyes and the ears are too small in proportion to the rest of the body. Its mouth and snout are like those of a pig. The bear was black, and its hair was about two or three fingers thick. That darn Californian had more heart than I gave him credit for. He promised to skin the bear as carefully as possible and give the pelt to me.

MONDAY, 10 SEPTEMBER. *The ill, once again*

The epidemic of illness continues to afflict my company. There has been no improvement of those afflicted, and they seem to worsen to such a degree that death may well become likely, since the remedies we apply are of no use at all. As regards the others who were sick, one of them got better, and I sent him to convalesce in Mokelumne. Regarding our work, it looks like our claims have taken ill in the same way as the sick miners because they get worse every day. Orellana brought only 500 pesos' worth of gold with him yesterday. In the last two weeks the take of gold has been cut in two. According to him, there is little possibility that our luck will change, and there is no place to attempt to stake new claims because the entire area is overrun with men. Thousands come every day.

My Californian tells me that three bears, twice the size of the other one he killed, have come up to within ten to twelve paces from his tent. The growls of other bears have been heard nearby. I am afraid that they will end up liking my tent better than the others because it is better supplied. It would be a fine idea if the bears also made us have to stand guard the entire night!

TUESDAY, 11 SEPTEMBER. *The Americans*

Today more than twenty Americans came to my tent. They bothered me all morning with repeated questions. I am not exactly terribly fluent in English, and it has both bored and tired me to have to study and to answer everything to their satisfaction. Most of them had been in Talcahuano and in Valparaíso on their way here and spoke very highly of those ports and their inhabitants. None of them speak a word of Spanish, and yet they say they were very well received in Valparaíso. I told them that the best placer is over at Murphy's, and that is where they are going.[40] All of them are traveling with their rifles on their shoulders and a couple of six-shot pistols on their belts. I finally got rid of them; may God speed their journey.

WEDNESDAY, 12 SEPTEMBER. *Signs of winter*

This morning at daybreak it was overcast, with the wind out of the southeast. Now it has changed to the northeast, and the air is so cold that I have had to put on my winter coat. It is as though snow was about to fall and as though winter had come in two or three months early. Anyway, I prefer cold weather to the terrible heat of this past month. Every afternoon at sundown a cold, thick ground fog comes in. You can barely see the tops of the pine trees that stick out above the fog. It is really quite beautiful because the fog is only about ten feet deep, and so no matter how thick it is you can still see the tops of the tallest pines and oak trees. It is very poetic to see how they stand over the fog and lift half their bodies above it like immense giants, when all the other trees are shrouded in the fog.

FRIDAY, 14 SEPTEMBER. *The ruin of the placer at Mokelumne*

Six workers of the Riosecos have just come back from Mokelumne, tired of working with no take at all. Everything has ended on a horrible note, just like that. The rest of their company is coming back tomorrow and will not return there. The company of the Herreras has already left for San Francisco en route to Chile, as have others. They say that the number of those leaving and arriving amount to about the same. There is only one placer that might produce something over the winter, and the Americans will not let any living person get near. The Indians, led by a man named Polo, continue to make short work of anyone daring to go near their camp. There are a lot of paralyzed miners over there at Mokelumne, and so far not a single one has gotten better. The prices at the market in Mokelumne have dropped drastically, especially for foodstuffs. In fact, in a little over a month all of the immense trade that was centered in Stanislaus and other placers has gone to Mokelumne. Great losses await these merchants in Mokelumne now because, since it was the only really good placer around, they had all set up shop there and now all of a sudden the gold has dried up. Sales are everywhere, and a good shirt now costs no more than one and one-half or two reales.

SATURDAY, 15 SEPTEMBER

The Californian erred with his prey last night. He was all ready with his shotgun up in an oak tree, but the bear heard him and, after much growling, fled. Today he brought me the pelt and told me that the other one is bigger still. They tell me that there are between six and eight bears and at night they come within one or two blocks of the tents.

SUNDAY, 16 SEPTEMBER. *Indians*

It has been cold all day today because there was no sunshine and a cold wind has been blowing all the time. I think that winter is coming early and that before October we will have to dress warmly.

Orellana told me that the Indians killed several Americans and some Chileans who dared to go near their encampment. Right afterward another person came, saying that some Indians had told him that Polo had just been killed by another Indian and that his whole band had dispersed. He also said that the man who had killed Polo had brought his head with him in order to get the 5,000-peso reward that had been offered for him.

CALAVERAS, 19 SEPTEMBER. *Dr. MacKay has arrived!*

It is ten in the morning, and the doctor finally arrived after being away for two months and four days. I am about as happy about it as the sick people are. Doctors are looked upon with this sort of faith whenever people are sick enough to be afraid of death. The doctor has looked at the sick and says that even though some are gravely ill, there is still no reason to fear the worst. Besides the paralysis, two of them have advanced cases of scurvy, but the doctor thinks they will soon get better.

Dr. MacKay bought almost 16,000 square blocks of land in our name, which are laid out in the city of Sonoma, near Benicia. We have been told that the land is very beautiful and rich for nearly anything. It cost him 16,000 pesos in cash, which is really not very much money in California. The doctor says that before he left they had already offered him twice the amount of money he had paid for the land. It might turn out to be a profitable investment later on. Time will tell.

THURSDAY, 20 SEPTEMBER. *Back together*

Today the rest of the company came back from Mokelumne, which has dried up completely. They come here, where we have little to do as well, so the situation for the winter is fairly clear. Today at lunch, Dr. MacKay said that Alfredo and I also have a touch of scurvy. I looked at myself in the mirror, something I had not done in quite awhile, and I looked quite sick. At first I cursed my luck, but in the end I have been saved from greater plights in California. Losing one or two teeth will not make me look too badly in front of girls, and that is enough for now in California.

SUNDAY, 23 SEPTEMBER. *A basket of grapes*

Today my friend the Californian brought me a basket of very good grapes from one of those vines that grow along the banks of the Calaveras River where we go swimming every afternoon. According to the doctor, these grapes are very good for scurvy, and according to me, they are good for just about everything. What pleasure is to be found in seeing these fruits that are wild here and must be very carefully grown back home! I sure wish that California did not have all of those dangers that always seem to lurk when gold is nearby. Then we would all be happy, more like rich landowners than like exiles or immigrants.

The sick miners are in pretty poor shape, about like before. They told me today that they felt no better. It wrenched my heart to see them so close to death in a strange country without at least the comfort of having their families there for a final farewell. These thoughts must surely torment them! They have begged me for the love of God to send them back to die in Chile, even if it costs them everything they have earned so far and they lose the income they might have earned on the company sick list. I promised to do what I could for them, and by God I will do it with all my heart. I now understand just how much they all must be suffering.

TUESDAY, 25 SEPTEMBER. *An idea for a small expedition . . .*

We were planning a small expedition about three leagues from here, where, according to Moyano, who is from San Juan, there are fourteen or fifteen Indians with a large amount of stolen mules, horses, and cows. The doctor and I had planned to go there with our men, all fully armed, because, more important than the stolen animals, the Indians have a rich glen where only they can work. But we decided to wait until the judge comes and gives us the full rights of conquest over the goods we take from the Indians.[41]

THURSDAY, 27 SEPTEMBER. *More sick miners!*

Three more laborers have fallen ill or were already sick but just today have stopped working. They have the same pains as the other ones who are already bedridden, and they want to stop working for a few days to see if they get better. They are so frightened that they say they want to go to Chile before winter, even if it means that they lose everything they have earned here up until now. Actually I do not know how these men have made it through four months of working in the water without being used to it and have not fallen ill earlier.

They say that in the Mud Canyon placer a man found a thirty-pound gold nugget, and he does not want to sell it for anything.[42] It has already been deposited in Stockton in the house of Mr. Weber, and some people who have seen it tell me that it is good enough to be in a museum. These sorts of things are not strange around here, especially before we got to the placers, when huge gold nuggets seemed to show up nearly every day.

FRIDAY, 28 SEPTEMBER. *A matter of conscience*

I do not know what to do with the agonizing men the doctor wanted me to send to Stockton. Now they are beginning to believe that it was only the type of promise a doctor makes to a patient so that he will take this or that medicine. But that is not the way it is, because I truly want to send them to Stockton. In the past two days, however, the devil has had it that no wagons have come by going that way. Meanwhile they are getting worse by the day.

Some Indians, probably the same ones who have all the stolen animals, just murdered two Americans who were friends of my neighbor the judge. Today he came by to ask me to give him some armed men so that he could go after the Indians. I gave him everything he asked for. I wish we could all go with them, because it would probably be more profitable than working the river and getting next to nothing. They are probably in or near their camp now because it is the time of year they gather acorns, their favorite food.

SUNDAY, 30 SEPTEMBER. *A wagonload of sick men*

I just dispatched a *wagonload* of sick miners to Stockton.[43] Yesterday I was able to get this American to wait until today to load up his wagon. The whole thing filled me with emotion, and I shed tears with the men. The poor devils wanted to walk to where the wagon was, but their weakness and pains made them faint before having gone even twenty-five paces. When they came to, they began to cry and wail that they were going to die without even the comfort enjoyed by Christians. It was impossible for me to console them, and I forced them toward the wagon. Every step was accompanied by laments and curses of the gold, whose price has become so steep. It is impossible to portray the way these men suffered physically and morally and how they regretted having abandoned their families to come in search of a fortune that every day seems further and further away. Those of us who came to California will have to wait a bit more, because in all fairness after having suffered so much we should be able to enjoy some success later on.

CALAVERAS, WEDNESDAY, 3 OCTOBER 1849. *A dead man instead of gold!*

Today two of the men came from work to give me some interesting information. According to them,

"Right where we were working just yesterday we found a dead man, half interred, with only his underpants and hat on, and with no shoes."

It was funny the way they talked about such a simple and natural event around here in California. But what they said was correct. Just three blocks from here, there he was, the poor devil, one among the many who came to California in search of his fortune. He died as he dueled with one of the many enemies hovering around gold, wherever it may be, probably from fever, or perhaps from malaria, paralysis, or maybe he was stabbed. These are the fellow travelers of gold, wherever it may be. Some pious Christian, or perhaps the same person who killed him, buried him there, and now a poor little wooden cross as a tombstone says that here lies one of the many people redeemed by the Son of God on Calvary who has met his fate in California. The men put up the cross, and they pray every day before going to work.

Today it was very cold, cold enough to keep the men from working in the morning. With these little signs of winter, the men have decided to go to Chile no matter what and no matter who gets lost on the way. Now, whether or not they stay, and just about everything else, depends on me. Yet I depend on something else; I am waiting for a letter. As soon as it arrives I shall know what to do. The doctor has said that he too is willing to leave, even though the rivers of California are flowing with gold.

FRIDAY, 5 OCTOBER. *Scurvy*

Five more men have fallen ill, and the rest of the company is only able to take out about two ounces of gold per day. They complain that they don't make enough for food, and yet I have them there every day, and they might be unlucky enough to die for nothing. In part I certainly agree with them, because if you fall here you cannot pick yourself up, especially if you fall because you are becoming paralyzed or are ill in some other way. Yesterday, one of the men came down with an illness that was as unknown to me as was California before I set foot in this land. He jumps, kicks, and claws at his body as though he was possessed and screams, begging to be killed so that he may be freed from the pain that torments him. Last night while the others were sleeping I was awakened by the sound of his contortions. He says that he feels a pain in his heart similar to that caused by a red-hot iron pressed into his flesh somewhere on his body, and when it happens he loses his breath to the point of feeling as though he is suffocating. Since Alfredo gave him opium last night, he sleeps now as though he was dead. Who knows what type of disease has possessed him.

Mr. Scollen, the American judge who seems to have become my intimate friend since I began talking with him in English, has invited me alone over to his tent to have a drink. I do not like this type of invitation because it takes me away from my tent and my job, but I might as well keep him happy. Off we go.

SATURDAY, 6 OCTOBER. *Another basket of grapes*

My friend the Californian has again sent us another basket of wild grapes. These ones are twice as good as the ones he sent before. The bunches are bigger, the grapes themselves are larger, and the taste is even better, quite similar to that of grapes that are farmed in Chile. Now is when the grapes are at their sweetest and best, and this is when the Indians spend all day drunk from a certain liquor or vinegar made from the grape.

Speaking of Indians, four of them were here today acting as guards for the new chief who has taken over for the murdered Polo. All of them came into the tent naked with their quivers filled with arrows. All of them except the chief, who was dressed like a European and, instead of a quiver with arrows, had a couple of pistols and a fine dagger. In the eyes and gestures of this chief you could see the pride of a descendent of Polo. They have been accused of murdering two Americans and have come here to reach an agreement with the judge. The chief speaks a little Spanish and says it was not them but rather the Indians of José Santos, etc., etc. The judge has acquitted them and sent them off, telling them to come to his tent every Sunday.

MONDAY, 8 OCTOBER

Something good has to come from all this loneliness. Now I have something to distract me in my daily affairs, because I will always be able to study. With English there is really not much more for me to study; I translate and speak it fairly well, and I have a universal history, or encyclopedia, in English, which is what I read most of the time. I also have a large book of music with some lovely works, together with a beautiful geography in French, and the *Diary of St. Helene,* the *French Parnasus,* and several other works in French, which help me to pass the time. Finally I have the *América Poética,* which will help me to become a poet when I have nothing else to do.

SUNDAY, 14 OCTOBER

Mr. Biggs and Baus and I just arrived after a hike of almost two leagues. The only thing we brought with us from this hike was dirt and tiredness. What a difference carrying a shotgun today on my shoulder where a beautiful woman used to lay her head. That is how all Sundays are spent in California. There are no elegant tail coats or snow-white gloves. The only thing we have are dirt and shirtsleeves.

MONDAY, 15 OCTOBER

Today the men got a little more gold than in past days. The reason is that there is lots of water now in a stream that used to be completely dry. The men had to stop working on certain parts of the stream for lack of water, and those are the spots they are working now. On our walk yesterday we ran into an old man. He was about eighty years old and hardly seemed like a man his age. He was working as though he was twenty years old. He told us that he was a member of the Confraternity of our Lady of Mt. Carmel and that the scapular he showed us had saved him many times from the bears around there.

TUESDAY, 16 OCTOBER. *Another letter from Samuel*

Today I received a letter from Samuel. It might be the happiest day I have had since coming to the mines. With the letter he enclosed the portraits of our family that I had left in my baggage in San Francisco. Being able to look at each portrait made it a happy day for me. It was as though I was able to embrace each of my brothers and sisters and my parents. I tingled with emotion to have the memories flow freely through the portrait to my heart and soul.

He sent me a beautiful guitar, which I consider to be a gift of the very highest importance. I alone realize how important its absence has been, and I alone can truly value the importance of this gift. Samuel also sent me a large amount of fresh bread, which is impossible to find here in the mines unless someone gives it to you as a gift.

WEDNESDAY, 17 OCTOBER

The company of Mr. Biggs had a terrible riot in which the armed laborers threatened their boss. Last night six of the worst of them fled, and early this morning Mr. Biggs came to ask my help in catching them. He also asked the alcalde, who is taking the place of Mr. Scollen, who left yesterday for Stockton. It is now noon, and we just came from the tent of the alcalde, where we left the six rebels for safekeeping. I can see that I did the right thing when I dealt out severe punishment to some troublemakers and revolutionaries of my own just four days after coming to the mines. Since then my men have always set a good example for the other companies around here.

THURSDAY, 18 OCTOBER

For the past three weeks the men have hardly been getting more than 500 pesos per week, whereas before they were able to take out 1,200 pesos. All of the placers around here are about the same or worse than this one, and yet daily more and more immigrants arrive everywhere. This one is really the only one they do not come to, mostly because it is in a different direction from the rest of them, and so nobody hires wagons in this direction. I am happy with this because otherwise we would have had to change placers two or three times already, and this would not be easy with a company that has more than 400 quintals of material and tools. By avoiding these little trips I have been able to save more than four thousand pesos on each of them. It would only have been a little more expensive than that to get all of the material here from Stockton. The half-ounce each man takes out every day is not all that bad, especially if you add the peace and quiet we enjoy around here. Many others would gladly pay for it with gold.

SUNDAY, 21 OCTOBER. *Indians nearby*

Early today we went hunting with Mr. Biggs and Jim more than a league from here. A little beyond where we used to go swimming we found the tent of the Canaca Indians. They were resting after setting up their encampment. None of them spoke any other language than Canaca, and so we had no choice but to go back from where we had come. As I was following after some quail, I got separated from Biggs and Jim, and after having looked for them and firing shots into the air, I sat down under a great grapevine to look at the letters I received yesterday. I was there for more than an hour reading and rereading the letters, thinking of Chile, of Concepción, and thinking about what my family and my friends would be doing just now. I got so carried away that before leaving I scratched the names of some of the girls—the Rivera sisters, Delfina—into a nearby tree trunk with my knife.

WEDNESDAY, 24 OCTOBER

Three days ago a big batch of letters arrived, including the first ones to reach me from Chile. I spent all day answering them and also writing other ingrates who have not bothered to answer my letters. Today it was extremely cold, and at dawn there was frost on much of the water. Despite my gloves, it was too cold to take pen in hand until very late in the day. Last night the men lit fires twice in order to ward off the cold. I heard them all night telling stories and adventures around the campfire, and near daybreak they sang praises all together. I liked that very much.

THURSDAY, 25 OCTOBER. *A man hanged in Stockton*

According to news from Samuel, today an execution of an American was to take place in Stockton. They must have hanged him, which is the way they execute people here in California. It is much worse to witness the execution by hanging than one carried out by a firing squad. Those who are to be hanged are taken to the gallows in a tilbury accompanied by a priest, who is seated next to the condemned man. Yet the priest is little more than some trader who was seen shortly before bartering aboard some boat or carrying on his shoulders the goods he has just brought to his warehouse. This is the way a Christian Catholic who sees these executions finds such a horrible contrast between the farce used to accompany a man out of this world here in California and the imposing, solemn, and, if you will, even sublime execution in a Catholic country. Once the gallows have been reached, the sentence is read aloud, and the prisoner is allowed to say anything he wants in his own defense. After this, with the priest still seated in the tilbury, the noose is placed around his neck. At the indication of the executioner, the driver moves the horses, and the tilbury moves off with only the priest aboard. The condemned man is left swinging from the gallows amid the twitching convulsions and grimaces of impending death.

FRIDAY, 26 OCTOBER

Last night the coyotes made so much noise that they kept us awake nearly the entire night. Actually, when a lot of them get together, like last night, the order they maintain in their continual wails is admirable. Still more noteworthy is the way they suddenly seem to imitate the cry of men. The first voice starts, and the others follow along, making the same intonations and variations of voice as he does. They spend hours howling that way, and their howl is so mournful that they can come within twenty paces of the tent without exciting the dogs in the least. The dogs curl up at the feet of the bed and will not move. As soon as the coyotes began to howl about midnight, the men said, "They are out to accompany their dead." The men end up making comments about the howls of the coyotes being like the wails of the relatives of the dead: the one howling most is the one who has lost least and inherited most. The way they talk amuses me, and I just listen in silence, laughing to myself about the laments for the dead.

SUNDAY, 28 OCTOBER

Mr. Bous and Mr. Biggs just arrived. They are leaving for Stockton with the Riosecos tomorrow. Today is a day for farewells, a day of requests, of recommendations, of protests, etc., etc. Every one of my men writes his letter, and those who do not know how to write dictate the letters to others.

They make packages and bundles with gold or anything else in thousands of types of wrapping. Others make requests by word of mouth, little additions, reforms, and all types of things. As for me I have just wrapped my packages, and I also asked Domingo Rioseco to make sure that they all get delivered safely. That is about the way all of us spent the entire day, and it leaves good though slightly sad memories.

TUESDAY, 30 OCTOBER. *An assembly*

Last night before going to bed I had a full-scale meeting with the men. All of them came all of a sudden to where I was and sat down around me.

"What's up?" I asked.

One of them who had been chosen as spokesman stood up and came at me with the following request:

"Sir, as your grace can see we are not getting very much gold these days."

"And, what about it?"

"The Riosecos are leaving, sir. They are afraid of the coming winter, and it is possible that we are so worn out that no matter how much we are made to work, we won't get enough gold even to pay for our meals. We would like to follow the Riosecos even though that might mean we would lose some money."

This was more or less what they had to say, all of them, one after another. I told them that I was as aware as they were of the problems the winter might bring with it. They protested that, if I knew this, why was it that I had opposed the dissolution of the company when the doctor had been here. I told them that it was true, but at that time the problems did not seem to be nearly as big as they did now, especially with all the sick people and those who had been so weakened by the hard work. But I told them that it was impossible for me to change things now until we had a meeting with the doctor. This is about how the session ended.

WEDNESDAY, 31 OCTOBER

Last night after the meeting of the assembly about a possible return to Chile, I was lying in bed and having tea with Moyano, listening to him tell of his adventures during the war on the other side of the Andes, when all of a sudden I heard a voice from the road begin singing a part of *I Puritani*. I mentioned it to Moyano, who said he did not recognize anything at all. I thought I had been mistaken, but an instant later I heard the voice again and jumped up from the bed, saying to Moyano, "It's Samuel!" I ran out of the tent, but the singer was still on the other side of the ridge across from us. Moyano said, "It's impossible, it cannot be Don Samuel because he prefers to surprise you and normally sneaks up on you. I am sure." I almost believed him and was about to go back into the tent when I heard a new contralto voice on the ridge, and then I did not doubt for a second. Within a couple of minutes I heard the noise of a horse behind the tent of the laborers and all of a sudden the shouts of Samuel. My God! How wonderful, just when I least expected it! Samuel got off the horse and embraced me, always singing and filled with joy. I was so overwhelmed with the joy of embracing Samuel that I was unaware of anything else. I entered with Samuel, and all of a sudden there was the doctor. "Damn," he said, "you were so beside yourself that you did not even see me dismount and enter the tent! I do forgive you, though, because I can imagine your joy right now."

FRIDAY, 2 NOVEMBER 1849

Samuel and I have decided upon our plans, and we are determined to go ahead with them. Last night we agreed with the doctor to dissolve the company in accordance with the document of dissolution to be drawn up. Above all it is evident and has been agreed upon that this termination has been carried out under the sole responsibility of the doctor and for the reasons that he alleges. Thank God I am able to get away unscathed from all that might happen in the future. Let us see what I can do now in my own interests.

SATURDAY, 3 NOVEMBER. *The document dissolving the company*

Last night Samuel and I, together with the doctor, drew up the document terminating the company, and by now it has been signed by every one of the members. According to Article 1, the doctor has sole responsibility for dissolving the company and will respond to the partners for any further details. All of the members are free from now on and no longer have any obligation to the promoters, and they have full options on each part of the gold due to them, according to the contract drawn up in Chile, as well as to any other earnings derived from investments in gold in the name of the company as a whole. The total amount of gold dust we have taken out ascends to more or less 18,000 pesos. I will remain in California, but the promoters will pay me 230 pesos for my passage to Chile, even though a ticket on a steamer would have been more than 800. Besides, they will give me 200 pesos for personal expenses and another 200 and something as a commission for all sales in Stockton during the time I was there alone. The 300 hundred or more hundredweight of supplies that remain, together with the tents, the tools, the machines, and the other belongings of the company, will be sold to the highest bidder, who will be in charge of moving them (I already know what to do about this! . . .). These are the terms of the termination agreement, which was authorized by the district judge and witnessed by the proper persons. I will finally get a chance to make the promoters pay for their silliness and to show them just what they have lost by applying the damned Chilean system of continually putting restrictions on partners who want to speculate in a country like California. And they will pull at one ear when they realize this, and I hope they cut it off before getting to the other ear. Amen.

SUNDAY, 4 NOVEMBER.
The dissolution of the company and the arrival of winter

Winter came with Samuel. It came in suddenly and with great intensity, so much so that it reminded me of the winters of the south of Chile. For the past five days it has been raining day and night, and we have not seen the sun for a single moment. The doctor is desperate to leave because he is afraid that the winter might prevent him from returning to San Francisco and embarking for Chile. As soon as it stops raining he will leave immediately, no matter who is left behind.

Today he went to sell all the material and equipment of the company at the tent of the judge. Now he and the other Americans who have been there for two days are drunker than Friar Gorenflot of Dumas. Things seem to be going my way. All of the equipment is now easily worth 4,000 pesos, but there is nobody offering the doctor anything at all. And even if the judge offers to buy it, I doubt that the doctor will accept because of uncertainties regarding the payment, especially since he wants to be paid in cash right away so that he can leave for Chile. This is my chance to get my fair share! Well, let's move slowly; the storm continues to rage, and the drunks continue to drink. . . . The doctor has already made two proposals for me to take everything, and twice I have said no. I told him that I know very well, even better than he does, what this equipment is worth but that it would be impossible for me to get anybody to buy even a pound of it from me when I want to sell. These and other pertinent reasons helped me convince him that I have no interest whatsoever in what is left. Better be careful now, because if I am able to catch this chance, I will have been given more than my due, much more!

MONDAY, 5 NOVEMBER. *$4,800 for $800*

Today in one of his lucid moments the judge seems to have caught on to just how good a sale is at hand, and stumbling over to the doctor he said he would send the balance due as soon as possible. The situation was very critical, and we were only saved by the following turn of events. The doctor mistrusted the judge, and his proposal caused him to offer me once again the supplies and all the equipment. I asked him, "Do you want 800 pesos for the entire lot?" I kept silent at his surprise and his protests. That was an hour ago. Now the deal has been made for the $800, and the contract has been signed. Good move!

FRIDAY, 9 NOVEMBER. *One hand short*

What I am now copying into my diary is taken from a draft I have in my notebook. More than eight days ago I lost the use of my hand, and thus my diary has heard nothing from me. The day Samuel left, which was the 8th, I opened the chest to get a little gold to pay Mr. Scollen some company bills. I left the lid open as usual, and I do not know how but that immense iron lid, which weighs more than 25 lbs., fell and hit my two fingers that were near the lock. It smashed them. It makes me tremble to think of that moment when I almost lost consciousness from the terrible pain. Despite the abundant blood, my nails grew black as coal almost immediately. As the pain grew worse by the second, I ran to the stream like a madman and put my hand in the water. The shock of contact between my burning fingers and the cold water was so great that I nearly fell over. The idea of the cold water was probably a very bad one because the fingers swelled tremendously, so much so that you could no longer see the joints. I do not think I have ever felt such excruciating pain before. This has kept me from writing in my diary, though I have been able to scribble some things down in my notebook by taking the pencil between the thumb and the index finger of the good hand. Thanks to these notes, now I am able to catch up on the diary.

SUNDAY, 11 NOVEMBER. *I leave for Stockton*

Last night it rained so much that today the stream is completely filled with water. The men had left some clothes on some high rocks across from their tents, and these rocks have disappeared under the water, as have all the clothes. There was no way last night that I thought I could leave today, but the weather this morning is a little better, and so I was able to depart for Stockton at seven o'clock sharp. I do not like the idea of making this trip all alone, and especially when I have four pounds of gold with me, and when I am missing the use of my right hand. But the doctor is in such a hurry that I have to go today by myself, when tomorrow I could have been accompanied by someone. I think that if there is any trouble I should be able to pull the trigger of my pistol even though my hand hurts a lot.

MONDAY, 12 NOVEMBER.
At the Indian camp on the banks of the Calaveras River

Yesterday at five o'clock in the afternoon I reached this camp. After traveling about three leagues I finally came upon the tent of the Quirogas on the banks of the Calaveras River. I met up with Abel, who hardly recognized me, which wasn't surprising since the last time we had met was twelve years ago in Catamarca. I need not say that his look was that of an uncomfortable pilgrim in California. I was delighted to see this old friend of mine, and so was he. I stayed in his tent for nearly three hours, until way past sunset. Even had I come by earlier in the day, I would have stopped anyway out of curiosity at the great encampment of wintering Indians down there. I stayed in Mr. Lemon's house, and he took me to visit the Indians.[44] The first thing we noticed upon reaching the encampment was the way they made bread with the fruit of the oak tree. We were watching three Indian women at work. First they made a rectangular hole in the ground, which was then filled with sand. On top of it they lit a big fire until the sand was very hot. Later they removed the fire, spread out the sand, and cooked the acorns until they lost their shape and became a kind of thick paste. This was then forced through a type of strainer made of grass and was then set aside to cool in little baskets until it hardened and became a uniform paste. Later they cooked it again until the bread was ready to be eaten.

All of these Indians seem naturally pretty civilized, because they do not flee the white men. They are still naked, both the men and the women, and only put on a bear skin to protect them from the cold, though they take it off to work. It is hard to imagine a more horrible race of men. Only in the women can you occasionally find some whiter skin and better-looking features. I only saw two who were completely white and fairly attractive, and Mr. Lemon said that these came from a tribe that had mixed with Englishmen. Lemon made an interpreter talk and told them that I wanted to buy a bow and arrows. Right away they brought six or eight of them, all of excellent quality, and each owner went to great extremes to show how his weapon was superior in quality. Finally an old man came up with a terribly disfigured face, which sent shivers through my soul. When he was young this old man had fought for an entire day with a bear and barely saved his own life as he battled and killed it. The memorable deed is stamped on his face in the form of his multiple scars. He only has one eye, his right one, there is no trace of nose in his entire face, and along his forehead you can see five deep lines left there by the nails of the bear as he was gouging out the eyes and the nose of the poor Indian. The story of this famous Indian impressed me, and I had no doubt which bow and arrows I was going to buy. I gave him eight pesos for them, though the other Indians wanted to sell me theirs for only six. So my bow is famous after all! It is half past six in the morning, and everyone is still asleep. I am leaving for Stockton.

STOCKTON, THURSDAY, 15 NOVEMBER. *How things progress in California!*

Like with everything else in California, it is amazing to see the difference in Stockton from when I was here only four months ago. Stockton is now a beautiful city with lovely houses and with as much trade and population as the best of cities. It is both city and port, with all kinds of ships entering and leaving all the time. The panorama of Stockton now is magnificent. It is divided in two by a lake that is filled with all kinds of ships of every different size.[45] Going into one of them is like going into any warehouse on land. I don't think that there can be a better place to do business or a city that is progressing as quickly as Stockton. In about three days the bridge that crosses the lake and joins Stockton with the peninsula will be finished.[46] This bridge comes out right at the corner of Samuel's house.

The only real problem around here is that the ground is all mud and almost impassable, making it very difficult to get around. But this isn't anything for these Americans, because all of this mud will disappear when spring comes around. They have already ordered flagstones to pave the entire town, and by next summer it should all be finished.

SUNDAY, 18 NOVEMBER. *A purchase*

Yesterday I bought a vacant lot on the corner of the peninsula across from Stockton for 2,300 pesos. I paid 1,300 in cash and signed a note for the rest, which comes due in thirty days. These lots were originally sold for 1,000 pesos, while others went for $300. Mr. Thibault has one next to mine, and he won't sell it even for 6,000 pesos. We bought the lot from Mr. Lepencot. I do not know why he sold it to us at that price. Today he came to give me the deed to the property, and later Samuel and I will go to have a look at, sketch, and mark out exactly the property.

TUESDAY, 20 NOVEMBER

It is two in the afternoon. We just reached the encampment of the Indians, where we came upon a great funeral ceremony. The captain of the encampment, who had taken ill the day I came through here a little while ago, died yesterday, and today is his burial. No matter what they say, we all have some pretty silly customs in these affairs. While at first glance the customs of the Indians seem pretty stupid, the fact is that they are not too far removed from our own. The Indians lit a great bonfire, which was for the captain and all of his possessions, without exception. May God be witness to the fact that I truly believed that those devils were burning ham! The man set out to take the place of the captain is the one stoking the fire. All of the Indian women have their heads covered with ashes, and four naked Indians are there crying and making a thousand grimaces and gestures. Yet their crying has no tears and seems more like a chant. All the Indians have a leaf rolled up like a cigarette stuck up their noses, which makes them look slightly monstrous. They say that once the body has been reduced to ashes they will bury it right away. May God help them, but I don't have the time to stay around to watch.

CALAVERAS, THURSDAY, 22 NOVEMBER. *Back home!*

Moyano tells me that, in the seven or eight days I have been away, the men have seldom been able to work because the rain has not let up for a single day. Even so, they have given me 150 pesos in gold dust. Today the weather is lovely, and we will have to spend it unpacking all the wet gear.

You know, a man doesn't really know just how good his home is, even if it is little more than a hovel, until he has been away for a few days. I would not change my little camp bed, where there is a good fire nearby, for the best fireplace in Stockton, nor would I turn over my poor but clean bed in return for the best in any luxury inn. Last night I slept the sleep of a rich canon of some important cathedral. It was a good sleep indeed!

FRIDAY, 23 NOVEMBER. *It is hard to work these days*

Yesterday the men took out a little more than four ounces of gold, and I am almost willing to admit that it is a lot, considering how difficult it is to get work done. Taking your warm body away from the fireside to plunge it into water that freezes partially every night must be very disagreeable. But that is how these unfortunate fellows have to work, and I will be happy with what little they give me.

Today again is lovely, and it is wonderful to walk about on a carpet of green. There isn't nearly as much mud here as in Stockton.

SUNDAY, 25 NOVEMBER. *A Sunday with no rest*

Even though today is supposed to be a day of rest, I spent the entire day attempting to fix my tent, which sometimes tends to leak. I also changed the poles and the crossbars, fastening them all very securely, in order to raise it another 3 ft. Now I am not afraid of the winter, even if it is fiercer than it has been up till now.

MONDAY, 26 NOVEMBER. *The train has arrived*

The train finally arrived today after four days en route. Fortunately no problems have arisen. Juan de Dios Sánchez and Mr. Alfredo have come to spend the winter up here.

It is ten o'clock at night, and I have finally had a chance to sit down for a moment. I don't know how the Sonorans found out about the arrival of the wagons, but they showed up right away. Evidently misery was beginning to afflict these men because they are eating the supplies they buy right here. The exorbitant prices don't seem to bother them in the least as long as they can buy what they need right away. The articles that have sold the most are the beans, peas, flour, biscuits, dark sugar, jerked beef, wheat, and tobacco. They are willing to pay the hundredweight of these articles at 75 pesos and six reales per pound. I think that later on this winter there is going to be a very severe shortage of foodstuffs.

TUESDAY, 27 NOVEMBER

Just like yesterday, today I was delighted with the sale of supplies. Some of those who bought yesterday have come back again today. It almost costs ten pesos per day for them to eat, but some of them bought eight pounds of goods yesterday and are back again today for more. As long as I have supplies in abundance I have nothing to fear from this epidemic. But if the train does not return again pretty soon, in fifteen days I will have run out of what just arrived. Thank goodness the train is ours; if not, we would have to pay thirty-five pesos per hundredweight, or 105 pesos per load, to get the goods here. It is not very affordable, but it is much less expensive when the train is ours.

FRIDAY, 30 NOVEMBER. *One month less in California*

Another beautiful day, like all the others this week. And in less time than you can blink an eye, the month of November has come and gone. That means one month less of suffering. Every day I spend here is like an entire month. There is so much suffering around here that one has to put up with his own problems without complaining to anyone. The month of December is upon us, and it will go by like November, and then January will come and go! My God the year '50 is upon us, and I still have no fortune! I am surprised at what is really not surprising. According to the prophecy of Mardoqueo, by 1850 we would all have carriages, meaning that our fortunes would have been made. Well, even though this year I can't yet see the entire carriage, at least I can see its wheels. Maybe everything will work out by '51 and his prophecy will have been correct. If our luck is still not adverse, we will be satisfied to have fulfilled our mission.

MONDAY, 10 DECEMBER. *The first step of a serious affair*

The men who have been working near Quiroga's camp came by here, saying that a band of Americans came by to evict them on the orders of a judge that only the Americans had chosen. My men, who were not armed, came back before things got out of hand. But the 100 or so Chileans who are there and who have their winter houses, their supplies, and their companies there have said that the only way they will leave is if they are dead. The Americans were enraged at this display of defiance and promised to come back tomorrow and finish off those who refuse to leave. It is clear that this is all a trick, because there is only one real judge, and he is the one who is here. He has said that if they keep this up he will go with us to set things straight in a hurry.[47]

TUESDAY, 11 DECEMBER. *The affair with the Americans is getting worse*

Bravo! Things are getting pretty hot! Abel Quiroga has just arrived, fleeing from his tent right where the revolution seems to have broken out. Things seem to be getting worse. This morning five Americans went to work in Chili Gulch, and all the rest came back to kick them out with blood and fire, just like they had promised yesterday.[48] But to the surprise and admiration of the Americans, the Chileans who were on the defensive took the initiative and kicked out the five Americans who had first arrived. Since yesterday the Chileans have barricaded themselves in and have had an inexplicable enthusiasm. Things, however, might get worse for them, because the Americans they kicked out immediately sounded the alarm and asked for help from all over. It looks like something ugly is going to take place there, and that is the reason for Abel's visit.

Just when we were getting used to nice days, this morning the weather took another turn for the worse, much to my disgust. Now it is pouring buckets of rain, as though it were the great flood getting under way.

WEDNESDAY, 12 DECEMBER. *The Chileans dig in*

Today it rained the entire day without any relief, and judging from the wind it is unlikely that the storm will let up soon. It has also hailed, and it is cold enough to make the bravest of men cower when he is not sheltered. Meanwhile, Abel, Alfredo, and I play dominos, play the guitar, and sing songs. All of these pastimes are enemies of boredom, which is everywhere these days.

Moyano and one of his workers just arrived, as wet as ducks because of the deluge during their two-league journey. The Chileans have kicked out everyone who was not with them. They are as entrenched and proud as the heroes of Saragossa.[49] I do not think the Americans will end up laughing at them so easily as they did at the people from Sonora. For the time being, at least, the Chileans are secure, because with this sort of weather nobody will leave shelter for any reason at all.

SATURDAY, 15 DECEMBER. *I am the witness to a duel!!!*

Last night Mr. Scollen, drunker than Friar Gorenflot, came to tell me that, if I sold my supplies cheaper than his, with the help of the alcalde he would see to it that I was kicked out of here, even though I might be his best friend. Just so as not to lose our good friendship, I told him that I would do as he wished. All of a sudden he invited me and Mr. Alfredo to come eat and drink with him all night just to keep warm. We told him we were delighted and left. Later, halfway through the meal, which wasn't bad at all, he challenged another American to a duel for some reason that I do not fully understand. The American took a vase and broke it. In response to this threat, Scollen took both his pistols and cocked them. He took me by the arm and said to the American, "This is my friend, and he will be the witness to our duel." While he was aiming at his chest, and I was trying to grab the barrels of his pistols, the American got up, saying that he would kill Scollen with the same weapons Scollen wanted to use to kill him. Then there was a struggle between my Scollen and the American, each one trying to take hold of the pistols, which were still cocked. Then two other Americans came in against Scollen, but at the same time Jim came, and together we were able to take the pistols from him. I attempted to make a sign to Alfredo so that he would follow me out of that place. I left by the kitchen, and good-bye to that! These are the types of things that can happen to you when you least expect it around here. Good Lord, the things you have to put up with around these people just to keep safe!

The defeat of the Chileans

It is nine o'clock at night, and six or eight Chileans have just come in, hungry and cold, asking for shelter for the night. These men are a part of the group that seemed so strong just the day before yesterday. This group of men, including two young men from Santiago whom I know, say they were ambushed and were not defeated in a fair fight. This morning two Chileans had gone out to hunt, since it was a nice day, and were taken by the Americans, tied to trees, and told that they would be hanged if the Chileans put up any resistance. Twenty-two Americans came over to the camp of the Chileans and had coffee with them in a friendly sort of way. While they were doing this, they went about taking the weapons of the Chileans without their noticing, and, when they were fully disarmed, they surrounded them all and tied up the owners of the companies. Some of those they were going to hang escaped, despite the shots fired at them. I heard that they shot three or four times at Terán, who is from Nacimiento, and at Suterna, Picarte, and others, but missed them all.[50] One of the Chileans, a fellow from Santiago, grabbed the fellow who acted as the alcalde and threatened to stab him with the dagger in his right hand. Just then some other persons intervened and took the knife away from him. Thank God for the poor ones who were tied up, because this turn of events saved their lives. They were all taken to the house of the judge, who extorted 150 ounces of gold from them.[51] This was paid by six or eight of them, one of whom was Santiago Herrera. While this was happening, other Americans were sacking the tents completely, leaving nothing untouched. Moyano escaped and is trying to find a mule. I have no idea where he is, though he sent word that he would come tomorrow. And all this happened only a league from here, yet nothing at all like this has ever happened to me in all the time I have been here. As I said before, may the good Lord continue to watch over me! Right now the Chileans are having dinner and warming themselves by the fire. It feels very good to be able to do a favor for your fellow man.

SUNDAY, 16 DECEMBER. *More on the events of yesterday!*

The events of yesterday continue to occupy my attention, and I cannot help admiring how the entire chain of events took place. This conflict has also affected that privileged son of misfortune, Henrique Green. More than a year ago he left his home to take refuge in the Galapagos Islands for three or four months and then came to California to fulfill his ambitions, only to be thrown out again at every turn. He has just arrived here, after having left behind his laborers, and now he is on his way to Stockton to present a complaint against the Americans with all the others who stayed here last night. They had lunch and have just set off with the intention of taking justice into their own hands if they cannot find it in Stockton. May God protect them, but the situation does not look very good just now.

I sent another 450 pesos in gold dust to Samuel by means of Henrique Green, which is about our earnings for eight days. It is always risky to do this. I do not suspect the honesty of Green, heaven forbid, but I do fear that somewhere along the way a mistake will be made with the gold. Gold always tends to get lost or misplaced in one way or another. Anyway, two pounds or a bit more of gold is not a fortune.

TUESDAY, 18 DECEMBER. *A day for the elderly and for the convalescent*

Thanks be to God that today is a beautiful day; it is mild, and the sun is radiant. It is the kind of day that is so lovely that it seems to pay us back for all the past inconveniences caused by the terrible storm. But what I fear is that my joy—and the good weather—will not last very long and the bad weather will return with a vengeance. This month is the equivalent of the month of July in Chile and in Argentina, where there are also days like today. On those days, elderly women normally come out on the arm of some lovely daughter or granddaughter, who is actively pursued by young men who curse the old woman, etc. The ill also drag themselves out of the doors of their rooms, waiting for the arrival of the doctor so that they can hide and showing an expression of happiness on their pale countenances. Workers in shops take their wares outside, and tailors sit around enjoying

THE DIARY OF RAMÓN GIL NAVARRO, 1849

the sun more than anyone else and saying sly things to passersby, etc., etc. But I am not old, nor am I sick, nor am I a tailor. I have been exiled, or something like that, and I did what the prisoners in the Bastille must have done on days like today: I took my chair out into the sunshine, I tuned my guitar, and attempted to enjoy playing music, being the pretty poor musician I am. That is how I spent most of the day.

WEDNESDAY, 19 DECEMBER

Well, yesterday I said that the weather was so good that it couldn't last long. Today is a horrible day, rainy, cold, dark, and generally wretched. The wind has been howling since eight o'clock this morning. I am desperate to know what happened to Abel and his men the other day. Neither Moyano nor Infante have come yet, and I cannot imagine the reasons for the delay. Let's hope that they have not run into the same sort of bad times as the others. Regarding the Chileans who went to Stockton to denounce the events of the other day, here is what Jim just told me. Instead of complaining about the bandits that robbed them, the Chileans ended up lodging a complaint against the judge of Mokelumne, saying that they had not been treated fairly by him. The judge of Mokelumne was taken prisoner to Stockton because of the complaint lodged against him, and yesterday he was to be tried before the jury. According to Jim, the judge is not the least bit guilty, because he did not know that this sort of vandalism was being committed in his district. He says that if he is acquitted, as is to be expected, he will exact a painful price from those who brought him in. I fear that the poor Chileans are going to lose a lot more because of the unfortunate way in which they lodged the complaint.

FRIDAY, 21 DECEMBER. *Memories of my family*

It is noon, and the rain has not stopped since last night. The level of the water in the stream is still rising, and today Mr. Scollen took serious measures to protect his house, which might be carried away at any moment. Last night the noise of the river was so strong and scary that it kept us from sleeping. The stream is now so close that there were times when it seemed to me that the noise was passing right over my head. Today I can touch the water from my tent with a broom.

This makes three days that the storm has lasted, much like three days of fasting from good weather and from sunshine, which is really twice as bad as fasting from food and drink. For me in California, every day is a day of fasting, because I never eat anything other than rice and beans, and as a variant I have beans and rice, except for some days when we might have some birds or squirrels.

I bet my mother has been fasting these three days and has thought of us. She is probably wondering whether or not her children were also fasting so far away so that God might help them. Poor mother, she does not know how many things we fast from all the time around here.

SATURDAY, 22 DECEMBER. *A glimpse of fortune*

It is almost unbelievable how expensive supplies and shipments are around here. The needs of the consumers are such that they are willing to pay any price, no matter how high it is. And to think that I am selling things more cheaply than the other two stores around this district. A quintal sack of flour costs one hundred pesos; dark sugar is $1 per pound and one hundred pesos a hundredweight; a pound of wheat costs ten reales, and two hundredweight sacks of wheat cost $200 each; a pound of grease is worth twelve reales; candles, a peso each; tobacco, six pesos per pound; liquor, $5 per bottle and eight reales a glass; figs and nuts, twelve reales per pound; jerked beef, one peso per pound; chilli sauce, ten reales per pound; salt, ten reales; castor oil, one-quarter ounce of gold for each dose; and so on. Getting things from Stockton to here now costs $125 a load (eighteen leagues away), $150 to Mokelumne Hill (twenty leagues), $300 to Mercedes (thirty leagues), and more or less $180 to Stanislaus (twenty-five leagues). And still there is nobody who is really miserable yet, except when it rains a lot and they cannot work. When that has happened I have often given alms in the form of a plate of food to more than one poor devil who only has a shirt and some underwear to cover his bones, despite all the gold around here!

SATURDAY, 24 DECEMBER. *Christmas eve in California*

It is almost midnight, and since it was Christmas Eve we gathered around a great bonfire to drink mate and wish each other a Merry Christmas.[52] Now everyone is asleep, except for Alfredo, Biggs, and myself. What a contrast we would make if someone were able to observe us and compare what he sees to what is happening in the rest of the world tonight. Here we are drinking tea next to the fire, covered with soot, with our brows furrowed from the heat. Elsewhere in the world people are on their way to midnight mass with their girlfriends and lovers. I have a vivid recollection of the scenes from this night last year: what I did, whom I saw, how I enjoyed the company of those who were with me. Well, everything changes, and maybe by this night next year I will be missing the solitude and the peace of tonight in California.

WEDNESDAY, 26 DECEMBER. *The return of the Chileans*

Today is another lovely day. Since everything in California depends on the weather, it should not be surprising that the very first thing I write in my diary is news about the weather. Yesterday, perhaps because the weather was good and it was Christmas, I sold a bottle of cooking oil for $16, one ounce of gold, and another bottle of castor oil for $30. My goodness. The first of the two cost me five reales, and the other one $1, but that is how things work here in California.

The Chileans who went to Stockton to lodge the complaint returned and brought with them an order to take in the bandits, dead or alive, and another one for all the district judges, instructing them to help the men with whatever they need (weapons, horses, etc.). Right now all of the Chileans are in my tent.

THURSDAY, 27 DECEMBER. *The prefect's order is made known to the Americans*

It is noon, and Judge Scollen just left with the three men who brought the order to arrest the bandits from Stockton. There was much argument with Scollen because he says the order is not written correctly, since American citizens can never be arrested by foreigners. Yet the order instructs all district judges to help the persons charged with executing the said order from the prefect. At last Scollen went out alone with the three men to see if they can make the arrests on the strength of this order, though the bandits say they are not subject to the authority of Stockton or that of anyone else in California. They say they are the people and that only the voice of the people can elect their representatives, etc. Nevertheless, against the opinion of Scollen, Maturano went ahead to gather the Chileans in order to arrest the bandits by force, in case they do not go peacefully. There seems to be no other way out. Scollen is not at all at ease because there are many Americans and, according to him, the Chileans are not the ideal group for capturing them. Despite the order from Stockton, he is frightened by the entire affair. We offered to go along in case he needed more men, but he refused and ended up going out only with those who brought the order with them. I am afraid that something tragic is going to happen, something that will be splattered with blood.[53]

FRIDAY, 28 DECEMBER. *The Chileans get respect; they go out to arrest the Americans. The Chileans fight obstinately with the Yankees. Blood flows; it will all work out!*

It is two in the morning. Maturano just came in, and I can hardly get over the pleasant surprise his story has given me, despite its bloody nature. He reached the camp of the Chileans and told them all the things that had happened with Scollen and that he would undoubtedly not help them at all. He told them that it was necessary for all of them to go and take the Americans by force without waiting for the judge to bring them in. So, at dusk, thirty or more Chileans went out; some were armed with shotguns, others with knives, and ten or twelve with clubs. According to his tale, just when the Chileans were reaching the camp of the Americans, they were in the process of kicking Scollen and those with the order of the prefect out of the camp. They were laughing at them, telling them that the only authority lay in force and that the prefect should show up with force if he ever really wanted to take them in. Unfortunately for those who died, Scollen and his party took the wrong path out and missed the Chileans, who were advancing in order and in total silence. The Americans knew from Scollen about the advancing party of Chileans and were waiting for them, weapons in hand. As soon as the Chileans saw the camp at midnight, with all that light and the owners standing around waiting, they took more precautions, knowing that the bandits were waiting for them. There were more than forty Americans there. The Chileans ordered their lines, prepared their knives, their clubs, and their shotguns, and at a sign started their attack. One of them spoke English and at a hundred yards or so from the camp made known to the Americans the order of the prefect. The Americans answered with three or four shots. They waited no longer, and all charged the camp together. That is how the battle started.

The first Chilean who took an American by the neck to stab him with his knife was felled with a bullet to the eye (poor Jara!). Seeing him fall, all the other brave Chileans became totally wild. Maturano took out his pistol, aimed at the head of the American who had killed Jara, but it did not fire. The American shot a second time, and the bullet hit Maturano's pistol. Instead of getting a bullet in his head, the American had knocked Maturano's gun four paces away. The American was about to fire a third time, but this time Maturano got there first and stabbed his dagger into his chest all the way up to the handle. Just in case he had missed, he did it another two times, sending the soul of the American to hell.

Coming to the aid of the one who by now was already dead, a second

American moved up behind Maturano and was about to stab him in the back when another lad grabbed his arm, which was already raised, dagger in hand, ready to act. Maturano turned around and stabbed his new enemy in the neck with his dagger. He fell dead immediately and did not even have time to curse his enemy.

Another rifle shot went through the ear of a brave Chilean, and a bullet grazed the forehead of another one. At this supreme moment, with the upper hand and determined to finish off the enemy, the Chileans charged again. This time the Americans gave up the fight. The ones who had not fled fell to their knees. Even then, every time the Chileans saw the body of their dead comrade they wanted to make mincemeat of the Americans. Masters of the battlefield, the Chileans took twenty prisoners, including, fortunately, the most criminal ones. Five of them were badly injured, with little chance of survival, plus the two dead ones lying there. Not quite sure of what to do and without the prefect's order in hand in case someone tried to take the prisoners from him, Maturano headed this way with his troops and his prisoners. He came to ask me what I thought should be done. He also asked me to cheer the people up, because by now the euphoria of the battle had worn off and his men were not so sure they had done what they should. He asked me to tell them that I had seen the prefect's order.

I talked to them and returned to my tent. I persuaded them that they had really not done anything at all to go against the order of the prefect, and most of them who already knew me in Concepción took heart. After taking some biscuits, figs, and nuts for the trip, they left for Stockton, hoping to make it there by today. Boy are those scoundrels humble now, with their hands tied behind their backs! The man in charge of the prisoners, Santiago Herrera, came up to embrace me as soon as he arrived. When one of the most criminal of the prisoners saw the deference shown to me by his chief guardian and owner, he spoke to me in English and asked me to speak in his favor that he was a Christian and that he loved and respected the Chileans. I told him not to worry.

The leader of the Americans has a bullet wound in his chest. They asked me whether or not to leave him here, but my opinion was to put him on a horse and to take him with them. The way the Chileans flaunt their victory over the American prisoners is quite remarkable. None of that awkwardness and respect they showed before. Among the most brave was one of my old men, Pérez, who hails from Nacimiento. I am going to bed because I got wet crossing the river! Farewell until dawn tomorrow!! Everything will be clearer then.

SATURDAY, 29 DECEMBER

It is five o'clock in the afternoon, and there is no further news of the events of last night. Mr. Scollen went to the bandits' camp this morning and ran into two of the leaders who had escaped and who wanted to kill him because, according to them, he had led the attack of the Chileans the night before. They demanded the prefect's order, and Scollen told them he did not have it and, even if he did, he would not hand it over to them. They have sworn to him that the next time he comes by they will kill him, just as they will kill any Chilean they run into from now on.

This afternoon a young American from that camp came to sell me some venison. I just talked with Scollen, and we both think he is unquestionably a spy. Scollen will be prepared, and I am going to warn Biggs and his men to do the same.

SUNDAY, 30 DECEMBER. *Bitter nights in California*

Due to the events of a couple of days ago, for the last two nights we have stood guard all night. There are twenty-six men in all, and we have more than thirty guns and knives. We stationed sentries on the highest hills and stood guard with the greatest discipline, though nothing happened. The sign that Scollen and I have agreed upon to come to each other's aid is a gunshot. The night before last at half past twelve we heard a shot, which was the signal that the bandits had come back. We went straight off to Scollen's place with our weapons loaded. But when the twenty-six of us had climbed the first hill from which you can see his place, nothing appeared to be out of place, so we advanced in silence and in order. Just then one of Scollen's men shouted out that it was nothing and that the stupid sentry had gotten drunk and taken a shot at a mule. We returned to camp, furious and uneasy because these unpleasant surprises continue to occur.

It is noon, and all of us have just decided that Scollen and I should take two men with us and go to Stockton to find out the results of this affair and to get another order to capture the ones who are left, or at least one enabling us to defend ourselves in any way possible from those bandits. Today a Chilean came by who had just come from the American camp, where they were burying their dead. When they found out that he was a Chilean they wanted to kill him because they thought that he had been a member of the group that had attacked them. He got out of it because he spoke to them in English and was able to persuade them that he had just learned about those events from the Americans themselves. He also heard that ten Americans had set out to follow those who were taking the prisoners, but he knows of nothing more. Scollen and I will leave for Stockton at three o'clock in the morning.

MONDAY, 31 DECEMBER. *May God save me and always protect me*

We left Calaveras at midnight, and now it is five o'clock in the morning. Scollen, Jim, and I are in the Indian encampment at Lemon's place, about thirty miles from Calaveras. We reached here at dawn after giving thanks to the Lord for having arrived safe and sound. We took a detour so as not to go near the tent of the captain of the American rebels, and we came out at a tent whose lights could be seen from far away. We were very careful because we saw that we were surrounded by Americans but had no choice but to spur the horses on, with Jim taking the lead. When we were within twenty-five paces they told us to halt, and in an instant we were surrounded by fourteen or sixteen Americans with their pistols cocked. Another even larger group of men stayed by the fire, watching on. I had my hands on my pistols, awaiting the signal from Jim, when the captain asked him who he was. Jim answered,

"And who are you?"

"Where are you going?" replied the captain.

"It is none of your business," Jim replied, and spurring on his mule he passed by him, and the rest of us followed without really knowing what to do. And there we were with Scollen . . . and my God I had five pounds of gold in my pockets!!!

Well, now for the unfortunate end to this part of the story. The Chileans who had taken the prisoners, whose numbers had declined to only twelve because others had deserted, ended up being captured by fifty Americans from all over only ten miles from Stockton. This happened yesterday, and just when we were passing by that tent, the Americans had just arrived with their twelve Chilean prisoners. And those were the same men I had seen seated next to the fire!!

STOCKTON, 1 JANUARY 1850. *Arrival in Stockton and New Year's Day*

Yesterday at four o'clock in the afternoon we arrived here. All along the way everyone was talking of the troubles between the Chileans and the Americans. All of the Americans say the Chileans should all be hanged. When I arrived they asked me how many Chileans had been hanged, because everyone in Stockton is sure that the twelve have died. According to an American in Double Spring, three miles away, the jury met at Collier's place to judge them.[54] Some of the Americans who had been prisoners arrived here after being freed and were warmly received. The judge here is being blamed for the deaths that have taken place up to now and those that will surely follow for having allowed Chileans to arrest Americans. So far he has not said anything and may even fear for his own safety. The world of Stockton is red-hot, and last night there were multiple problems, due both to the fact that it was New Year's Eve and the Americans were all drunk, and to the affair of the Chileans and to the death threats against all of them.

Around two o'clock in the morning a group of six or eight men came by to give Sparrow a serenade. They sang wonderfully, with nearly divine voices, especially a base whose voice Sánchez and I greatly admired. We still have that beautiful music ringing in our ears. That is what happened last night, and the American singers only left just a little while ago.

WEDNESDAY, 2 JANUARY. *No news of the prisoners*

The steamship came in today but still no news from Samuel, who went to San Francisco several days ago. Since he does not know I am here, there was no letter awaiting me. Maybe he will come tomorrow.

There is no news of the unfortunate prisoners whom I left back in Calaveras. The most recent news around here is the news I brought with me, because rumor has it that they have probably all been hanged by now. People think that nobody will be saved, but up till now the most recent factual account is mine. The man who delivered the order for the arrest of the Americans barely got away to Chile, but the one who was with him along with three other decent young men are among those who were captured. People say there is little hope for them to save their necks. Maturano, the hero of the fight, is among the prisoners.

Once again, Stockton has changed so much that it is practically unknown to me. I have seen magnificent houses and luxurious hotels where before there had been nothing but rotten mud and filth.

THURSDAY, 3 JANUARY. *One who escaped and who hardly opens his mouth*

A Chilean lad just arrived from that fatal camp, but he is so frightened that he can hardly answer questions. The Americans took his horse, and he was able to escape by saying that he was Mexican. He knows nothing and has not seen any ill come to the Chileans. Thanks be to God! At least the fatal news has been delayed! Who knows but that perhaps God has determined beforehand how everything will happen. He never abandons the unfortunate innocent who implore him for his help. And who is more innocent than those poor devils? How have they done wrong in attempting to carry out the orders of the judge of Stockton? Anyway, I hope that the Lord will give them yet another reason to know his infinite mercy by saving them this time. Just imagine how many more hands will be raised unto Heaven in thanks if these poor devils are able to escape death this time around.

FRIDAY, 4 JANUARY. *The death of Rosas*

The steamship just arrived, and it brings Samuel with it! He was terribly fearful that his arrival would bring him the news of my death. The entire affair of the Chileans was so terrible according to the news in San Francisco that he feared even his brother might have gone to eternity. My God! Just imagine what I have escaped from, and so far it has not even cost me any money! My lot is nothing in comparison to that of those other unfortunate men, who have not only lost their possessions but have also been arrested, received blows, and may even have met their deaths.

Samuel says that in San Francisco there is horrible excitement among the Americans, some of whom are in favor of the Chileans and others who are against. This atmosphere has been further enflamed and exaggerated by an article published in a newspaper in San Francisco in which they say that many of the Americans were killed by Chileans who acted most dishonorably. Since I know the entire story practically firsthand, it is clear that the journalist does not. There is still no news of the Chilean prisoners.

Samuel has also brought from San Francisco a bit of news that is so important and of such great interest for Argentines like us that we did not dare to believe it, despite the apparent veracity of the account. THEY HAVE ASSASSINATED ROSAS.[55] My God, if it is true that he has died or has otherwise been done away with, what happiness we would all share!! All the Americans are happy at this news, almost as if it referred to the death of dictators like Nero or Dionysius, whose tyranny affected millions of men.

That itself proves that the death of Rosas is no small affair. They say he was assassinated on the 18th of October by a man who was disguised as Arana so he could get close to him.

SATURDAY, 5 JANUARY. *The mud of Stockton*

For the past three days the weather has been bad, with rain and wind off and on and lots of cold. The humidity and the mud in Stockton make life pretty impossible around here. In order to go for lunch at the inn, it is necessary to walk two or three blocks through a giant mud puddle up to your knees in mud. Besides, the poor pedestrian has to cross the river [slough] on planks and beams along the edge of the bridge, with his muddy feet slipping out from under him all the way. So far three or four men have fallen and drowned right away. What a difficult life around here, with dangers threatening you everywhere you go! It is funny how easy it seems to get gold around here and yet how many victims gold is able to claim for itself.

SUNDAY, 6 JANUARY. *Women for sale!!*

An American has come by to tell us about the opening of an immense hotel across from our house that cost 100,000 pesos to build and was constructed in only two months. Since it is opening at the beginning of next month, the owner came to tell us that on that day there will be twenty beautiful young ladies from every nation, each with her own room and additional comforts, and since the owners are friends of ours we will have preference in choosing the one or ones we like. How easily and naturally they sell the dishonor and infamy of women just as if they were a commodity, according to quality and price! And this among God-fearing people and with women from all over the world! My goodness, what a society! What a contrast to listen to the sounds of men singing at the mass of the Protestants coming from the place next door to ours. The priest is the owner of the warehouse, the deacons are his employees, and the altar is the counter where they sell their wares. This counter-altar is also used as a dining table and a place to be when they are getting drunk. Right now the priest is preaching, dressed just like he is when he is selling goods over the counter, and yet he gets so excited that he ends up sobbing in the middle of the sermon. He preaches against drunkenness, business fraud, and lack of respect for religion. He even names the sinners.

MONDAY, 7 JANUARY. *The fire in San Francisco*

Recently there have been big fires in San Francisco and in Stockton almost at the same time. In San Francisco an entire square block of houses was burned to the ground, including the beautiful Dorado Hotel, which was built in ten days, ready to use, costing 100,000 pesos. Yet this magnificent hotel is now even more lovely than before. It was rebuilt in just a few days, and the same thing as before is happening. Samuel was there when the workmen who were going to rebuild it were taking the measurements for the new building; at the same time they had to remove smoldering beams of the old one so as not to get burned. This is really California! The estimated losses for San Francisco are between one and two million pesos. Lots of buildings burned in Stockton as well, but nothing compared to San Francisco.

Today Samuel has come down with a bad cold due to all the time he has gone around with wet feet in wet shoes. He has been sick since yesterday, with no improvement so far. What the heck! What I find surprising around here is that people don't get sick much more often. Colds are really not very frequent at all.

Today the bridge of Stockton, joining the peninsula with the other side, should be finished. It is very lovely and seems to be as firm and consistent as all things built by Americans, despite their apparent simplicity.

TUESDAY, 8 JANUARY. *The results for the Chileans*

Samuel and I just returned from eating at the inn, where he had insisted on going despite his cold. After the inn, we went to Sosa's house to see the Chileans who had just arrived from Calaveras. My God, it is still difficult for me to believe what I have just heard and witnessed. The main leaders have been freed, Maturano is safe and sound, Herrera and Picarte had their heads shaved and were whipped, and some of the other men had their ears cut off. Holy Lord, what a sight to see a man with no hair or ears! Actually, seeing a man mutilated enrages you against those barbarians even more than seeing him hanged. Maturano was saved because he became friends, for whatever act of generosity toward a prisoner, with one of the most important Americans. Herrera and Picarte, whom I just spoke with, were saved because of a woman who entered the room where the jury was meeting deliberately to influence her husband in their favor. On the night of the 30th, Herrera and the other prisoners recognized us when we came so close to them, and he tells us that afterward there was an argument about having let us go through. Herrera says that there are still another six or eight to be tried tomorrow or the day after, and he doesn't know how they will escape. We will get the news when they return . . . if they return. One of those still a prisoner is the young and courageous Terán, who has been accused of having killed one of the Americans. I do not know how things are going to go for that poor man; I fear the worst.

WEDNESDAY, 9 JANUARY. *A beautiful gentleman*

Today while we were eating at the inn, some Frenchmen from the placers entered and asked to have lunch near us. Among them there was one who was extraordinarily beautiful for a man and whose voice would have gone better with a flirtatious young woman than with a young man used to working in the mines. The whole while we addressed him as "Sir," even though his beautiful eyes made a much more uncomfortable impression on me than that normally caused by young men, no matter how good-looking they are. All of a sudden he toasted with his glass, saying, *"A votre santé, Madame."*[56] At that we all opened our eyes wide, and, much to our regret, we were obliged to say something polite to the beautiful young man. At that point, she (for he must have been a beautiful young woman, at the very least) said to us, *"Voilà quelque fois, il faut se endeguiser en garçon pour necesité comme moi, et tromper les hommes malgré ma bonne foi, parce que ce sont les circonstances de California. Il y en a deux mois que je porte les avites que vous voyez, mais demain matin je en aurai l'honneur de me presenter a vous otres tel que je suis Madame Gregoire."*[57]

We are waiting to see the graces she promised to show, dressed in her own clothes, graces that we could only guess at for a person covered by a beautiful tail coat and trousers. Indeed, only the French women are really convincing when disguised!

FRIDAY, 11 JANUARY. *Californians like us are really uncivilized!!*

Today we saw Madame Gregoire once again, but this time wearing her real clothes. Obviously there is no need to say that she was twice as beautiful as when we saw her dressed as a gentleman. Now that there is something else to be seen in the inn, every day we end up spending six pesos only for food there! Sometimes I wonder what would happen if all of a sudden I was transported by some magical force to the imaginary theater I have sometimes thought of, one located at the center of some stuffy society. I wonder how I would fare and how well I would do with the young ladies in the midst of all the often almost ridiculous etiquette after having left California, where freedom reigns supreme in every way. It is a freedom that can be seen in everything from the carelessness in dress to the horrible danger for your life when the same freedom is used by the bandits!! Would they dare to criticize the lack of good manners, etc., in one, who, after two years of living among sailors, wanted to enter a polite society once again? I will see about this some day, I am sure, and it will be interesting to see what happens. Right now, however, it seems to me that the role of the popinjays, with all their good taste and perfume, is pretty ridiculous, as are the young girls who only admire men if they are elegant and despise them if they are not.

SATURDAY, 12 JANUARY. *The Chileans once again*

I just saw Santiago Herrera. He came to give me the news of those still held by the Americans. Some of the men were freed, but they were forced to witness the execution of the three condemned to be hanged. Two of those hanged were Chileans, and another was Mexican. Among the Chileans, young man Terán was hanged like the others, but he died bravely. He never complained or begged for anything. The only thing he said before dying was "I only regret not being able to kill two or three more of these bandits before dying." The other man they hanged was a Mexican whom I saw wounded on the night of the famous battle.

SUNDAY, 13 JANUARY. *The mass of the Protestants*

I just came back from a mass I attended out of curiosity. After entering the church it was impossible for me to leave, and I had to endure two half-hour sermons. My curiosity cost me dearly! The church is improvised in a type of inn where we eat at times when it rains. The owner of the place and one of the employees were the priests. The mass was celebrated at the same table where the people in the inn eat their meals, and the priests had no other vestments than the dirty clothes they wear every day. All of the faithful hear mass as they read in their Bibles (everyone noticed that I did not have any book). Before mass, they sang a part of a beautiful hymn very well. They also have genuflections, actions, and other gestures that are so strange it is hard to believe them unless you are there. I think the grimaces they make is a way of calling on the Holy Spirit, because just afterward one of the priests started his sermon. His sermon was wholly dedicated to criticizing how the citizens of a free nation like America would sell their votes to the government. In passing, he also mentioned drunkenness, took a few stabs at people's lack of religious spirit, and finished his sermon. The priest of the mass began his sermon with such intensity and solemnity, pausing at every word, that it lasted so long it made the first one seem light and short. After finishing, we all knelt with our eyes shut and our hands together. A moment later the priest and his deacon said good-bye with a "Good afternoon, my friends."

MONDAY, 14 JANUARY. *Sacramento*

According to *The Californian,* there was a fire in the city of Sacramento on the same day the fires took place in Stockton and in San Francisco. The most unfortunate part is that after the fire there was also an immense flood that engulfed the entire town, sweeping away entire houses and warehouses, hardly leaving brick upon brick. Some people think the town should be deserted entirely, and that would mean an additional great loss. This will have important repercussions here in Stockton because the price of everything will go up.

WEDNESDAY, 16 JANUARY

Since coming to Stockton I have had no news from my house and my business in Calaveras. I am pretty bored with being away, and even though life there might be uncertain, I would like to return as quickly as possible. After all that has happened, I am well aware that all of the hostility of the Americans is really only toward the Chileans, and among the Americans I have always passed for French. When I return there, I have every intention of speaking only French, if at all possible, until I leave the mines.

THURSDAY, 17 JANUARY. *Lies going around*

The steamship *Mint* should have come in last night, but it did not arrive then, nor all day today either. It is four o'clock in the afternoon; the rain has stopped, but it is diabolically cold. You can see smoke coming from more than 400 chimneys all at once, spiraling its way above Stockton, forming one sole dense and heavy cloud hanging above the city. Now Stockton looks like any other town in Europe. Being a town divided by a lake more than a league long and filled with ships all the time, it is as though it was an enchanted town, with ships tied directly to the warehouses on land. It is as though the bay was like the town square. The wagon traffic on the streets of town has made them almost impassable because of the mud. That is the way Stockton is now, as opposed to four months ago, when it was hardly more than a name.

Since the bridge has now been finished, day and night you can hear the continual noise of wagons and people with nothing else to do, going back and forth on the bridge and making it creak just for the pleasure of it. The bridge has the only pavement fit for use in all of Stockton, and even I want to dance a polka every time I cross it. That is, of course, if I can remember how to dance the polka. I have probably forgotten how, and by the next time I get a chance to dance I will have surely forgotten completely, though these are never very hard for me to learn. English took me more than six or eight months, and it is very difficult.

SATURDAY, 19 JANUARY. *Still no news from Samuel*

The effort it takes to get from here to the wharves, where the steamer docks are, is made worse when it is all for naught and your hopes are frustrated. It is only about a long block and a half from here to the dock, but today it took me a half-hour to get aboard the steamer, and I did not even get sidetracked along the way. There is no place where you do not sink up to the leggings on your boots in mud, and to raise one foot you first have to get it out of the mud, where it seems to be nailed. Except for the waist up, everywhere else on a person's body is covered with mud and water. There are times when I am willing to stay in my room for twenty-four hours without having more than tea and biscuits just so I do not have to go out to the inn to eat. Sufferings and discomfort are everywhere in California!

SUNDAY, 20 JANUARY. *Protestants and Calvinists*

It is now noon, and the mass and sermons that began four hours ago are still not finished. Just a little while ago I could hear the beautiful hymn sung at mass, and it reminded me of the hymns sung at our own church. It has been more than a year now since I last saw a priest of our religion or since I went to mass or took part in any of the acts of our Catholic Church.

From here you can hear clearly and distinctly the voice of the priest who is preaching right now. His voice is pleading, filled with tenderness and fatherly requests, and then it becomes threatening, as if it was one threatening revenge. By the way, I just found out from Don Jerman, who is here, that these preachers now are fanatical Calvinists. He is a Protestant, and he scorns and mocks the beliefs that led them away from the Protestant

Church. Mr. Lippincot is also mocking the sermon and mimicking the ridiculous postures of the fanatical preacher!! And yet each of these men believes truly and faithfully that his religion is the only true and holy one that exists.

MONDAY, 25 JANUARY. *Mesmerism*

Last night they came from the house they call a church to invite us to come and see mesmerism. We arrived there, and I was surprised to see that it was the priest himself who was the mesmerist. He put his hands on the head of the man he wanted to mesmerize and thrice moved his hands to the man's feet. The man being mesmerized involuntarily shivered all over, closed his eyes, and had tears streaming down his cheeks, all of which were signs that left little doubt but that he was completely mesmerized. A number of items were hidden in our presence, and at an order the mesmerized man woke up and found them right away. He then told Sparrow, whom he did not know, a number of business secrets that no one else knew! This was really more than admirable!

FRIDAY, 25 JANUARY. *The king of the thrushes*

Today for the first time I saw the king of the thrushes. What a beautiful and fanciful bird! When it stops raining, immense flocks of jet-black thrushes come down to the mud, and then all of a sudden in their midst appears one whose body is black like the others but whose head and neck above the breast are the most brilliant yellow imaginable. It is so beautiful and its appearance is so surprising that it truly looks like a king among his vassals. In every flock there is always one that appears when the rest are together. For Chateaubriand this would be just another act of animal instinct. Well, to each his own. It is a shame that he is no longer here to see such beauty.

SATURDAY, 26 JANUARY. *The Chileans once again*

Tonight an American who was part of the Calaveras bandits came here and told us the details of the conflict with the Chileans, laughing and enjoying telling about the cruelties and barbaric acts that his buddies had committed just as though they were funny and nothing more. He said that the last Chileans were made to sit where the Americans were when they were killed and that his buddies had shot their rifles at them. It was like taking shooting practice with the poor Chileans as targets. What atrociously inhuman barbarians! God will take care of the revenge for those poor devils; it always happens.

THURSDAY, 31 JANUARY

Today I have new motives to meditate on my luck after coming from Calaveras with Scollen. Sánchez told me that two hours after we departed, the Americans showed up looking for Scollen. Later they returned two or three times with an order from the judge to take him in as the sole guilty party for everything that happened that night. What fools! That very night they had him and the rest of us in their hands, and they let us by without saying anything. Thanks be to God!

FRIDAY, 1 FEBRUARY 1850. *The hotel in Stockton and my place*

I have just come from visiting the hotel that I wanted to see before returning to Calaveras. It would be impossible to find a more beautiful or finely appointed hotel in San Francisco or any place else in the world. It took Isidro and me more than two hours to visit the entire place, and during that visit we had loads of things to admire. The hotel is two stories high, both of which are lavishly adorned. The lower floor is for the storage rooms, offices, and other common rooms of the hotel, such as the confectionery shop, the liquor store, the washing room, the dining room, etc. Its walls are covered with extremely fine wallpaper in different colors. You find this attention to detail in the large rooms, the corridors, and in smaller rooms. All of the woodwork (doors, windows, beams) is painted in white, and the counters are varnished with designs of branches and other figures like that. The second floor is just as luxurious. It has twenty-five small rooms for another twenty-five prostitutes who are due in from San Francisco any day now. All of these rooms are luxuriously furnished and appointed, and their clean beds have mattresses and pillows filled with feathers. There are two beautiful dance halls, a salon for men, and another one for women. There is also a long string of rooms to rent and others set aside for lodging. In other rooms you can find all kinds of gambling tables and even a billiard table. Then you come to the balconies, which on one side look out onto the lake and on the other over the flatlands of Stockton. This is maybe the best part of this new and fancy hotel. On the one side you can see all the ships on the lake and those coming in from a distance, and on the other you can see those departing for or coming in from the mines. And right next to this building is my own lot. Could its location have been better?

Hardly! It must be worth at least 15,000 or 16,000 pesos now. They just offered me 3,000 pesos in cash for one-fifth of it.

SUNDAY, 3 FEBRUARY. *My arrival in Calaveras*

It is eight o'clock at night, and I just got home. After all the immense mud puddles I had to cross this morning on foot, I was extremely tired by the time I reached the camp of the "American bandits." They treated me with great friendliness. They asked me where I was from, and I said that I was Argentinean!! They said the proof of that was that I spoke English well. I satisfied their curiosity about recent news from Stockton and San Francisco. I went on to Abel's house, where I ate and only finished about the time of the Angelus. They told me the river was low, and, since it was so cold, I tried not to get wet. I hoped to be able to get across the river on my mule. But as soon as I was in the river itself, the animal got completely disoriented and started to swim, getting water up to my waist. By the time I got to the other side I was completely wet, and my books and papers were dripping with water. And that was not all, because I had to cross the same river another three times, and the same thing happened to me each time. God knows how! Later I had to pull the mule and myself through the terrible mire along the road. At one point I heard a gunshot and felt the bullet splash down in the water in front of me. The night was so dark that the only thing I could make out was a light at the base of a nearby hill. I reached for my pistols, but they weren't there because I had given them to my laborer together with the shotgun, because he had to come here on foot. Anybody who wanted could have easily killed me because I had no guns at all with me! But they have not killed me because here I am writing, and I still cannot explain that gunshot. I reached the river near our camp and got wet once again, but now I am back home, and none of that matters any more.

MONDAY, 4 FEBRUARY. *An unfortunate event*

Upon my return I heard the sad news of the death of the laborers of my French friends. What a shame! They were lovely people and good friends of mine. They were part of a group of twenty-five men that went to attack the Indians. After four days of marching they all got lost, and every man took the route home that he thought was shortest. The Indians found the young man Bertrand and his friend. They attempted to defend themselves, but they were far outnumbered by the Indians, who overcame their bravery. We know all this from a Mexican who watched what was happening at a distance and saw how the Indians were shooting their arrows at the two young Frenchmen who had been tied up. The poor devils! Around here it is so easy to die without even the comfort of having your family and friends nearby! Another group of men went out after the Indians and found the bloodied arrows and pieces of clothing but no bodies. They have probably eaten them by now!

THURSDAY, 7 FEBRUARY. *An Argentinean recollection*

Today I bought a head of cattle. Even though I am Argentinean and am used to buying cattle cheaply, today I did not hesitate to pay eighty pesos for an animal that wasn't very large. Even so, I think I shall be able to make up its cost with half the animal. After all, it is not so bad to roast the head of a steer once a year like you do in your home country. Thanks be to the Lord I was able to dine with Juan de Dios, who is what we call a "fat cowboy," and to eat the beef the way it is roasted by Argentinean gauchos. It is nice to be able to remember the customs of your own country from time to time.

A man named Tautimes from Sonora just died. I protected him ever since I arrived here in Calaveras, and he always responded to me with appreciation, respecting me almost as a father. He died of scurvy, like a lot of other men around here. Yet it is surprising how many of those dying are actually from Sonora. I think I know the causes: (a) the amount of liquor they drink all the time; (b) the way they go around without the proper clothing, sometimes with little more than a simple shirt and pants; and (c) the weakness and lack of cleanliness in most of them, who often spend months without even washing their faces. Once they take ill, they are so fainthearted that they refuse to get out of bed for anything at all. I have been able to observe all of this very well in the time I have been here. Poor Tautimes was one of the fellows who went on the expedition in search of the Indians, during days of great rains and without eating or sleeping.

FRIDAY, 8 FEBRUARY. *The ill*

Almost all of those who have scurvy have been told to eat meat in order to get better. My God! Had I not bought a steer, all of them probably would have continued to die because they only eat beans and jerky. This is how far the weakness of spirit of the men goes: they can see that these dried meals are killing them, but they continue to eat them, with no attempt at all to buy fresh meat in order to get better. I am selling fresh meat for only six reales per pound. Moyano told me that there is a man from Sonora who is dying of starvation because he was told not to eat beans if he wanted to get over the scurvy, yet the poor devil does not have the money to buy fresh meat. I sent him some meat just now, telling them to tell him to ask for whatever he may need until he gets well.

Moyano also told them to eat salads with watercress and coriander. It is easy to find all of this growing wild around here. The smell of coriander is everywhere, and you can see great quantities of fresh watercress growing nearby.

SATURDAY, 9 FEBRUARY. *The young Frenchmen*

My Californian friend from Angels Camp just came, and he brings very good news with him.[58] The young Frenchmen believed to be dead have turned up in Stanislaus. Even though they are covered with arrow wounds, it does not look as though their lives are in danger. Thank God! I am about as happy at this news as I would have been had they been more than just friends of mine.

Another two young Frenchmen just came in from Angels Camp, and they are completely famished. They also went in search of some Indians and ended up getting lost for three days. One of them met up with a bear. Unfortunately, he missed his shot and had to climb up a pine tree, which the bear was rattling but could not climb himself. The bear, however, was patient enough to wait there at the foot of the tree for the entire day and the entire night. The lad was able to outlast his hunger better than the bear could, and it finally went away, leaving the battlefield to its enemy. So far no expedition against the Indians has had any success at all. They have either defended their positions well, or bears, hunger, or cold have helped them to wage war on the miners.

MONDAY, 11 FEBRUARY

Last night the Indians came up almost to our tents. They robbed many things from Biggs's camp. From us they got almost all the clothes my men had set out to dry along the rocks. None of us heard them at all. If not, there would have been more than a small problem. These Indians are beginning to get too daring for their own good.

WEDNESDAY, 13 FEBRUARY. *The ninety-three-pound gold nugget*

Mr. Biggs just came back after having visited seven placers in Stanislaus. He is so thin that it is difficult to recognize him. He has been ill for a month now. He says the placer in Stanislaus is in horrible shape and the men spend long days without finding any gold at all. But for a few days now he has been carrying around a gold nugget that weighs twenty-four pounds. It was found by a miserable Sonoran who ended up losing it. I also know of an American at Murphy's who found a nugget weighing ninety-three pounds, with only three or four pounds of rock in it. I believe that the immense amounts of gold hidden in the bowls of California have not yet been found. Our children will have a better California than we do.

The Americans have kicked thirty Frenchmen out of Stanislaus with no resistance at all. I believe these Yankees are looking for another licking like the one they got from the Chileans. People around here believe that everyone will rise up against the Yankees this year, especially if the breakdown in the relations between the United States and England because of some violence is really true.

THURSDAY, 14 FEBRUARY. *Spring is here*

Today is a most beautiful day, and spring has at last shown its face. The precise way seasons change around here is noteworthy. Since it stopped raining twenty days ago, there has not been the slightest change in weather. Sometimes the lightest of clouds cover the heavens, which for the most part are clear and clean like no other place I have been in my life. There has not been any wind for this entire period, with only a hint of the slightest of breezes moving the leaves of the trees and refreshing the day when the sun heats things up just a bit at midday.

The green fields can be seen beginning at the very edges of our tents. Nature is so vigorous here that you can almost see the vegetation growing by the hour. The entire camp is covered with grass interlaced with a thousand types of aromatic plants and flowers that I have never seen elsewhere except perhaps in gardens and orchards. Here that wonderfully fragrant coriander is as abundant as the grass. Radishes and the most tender watercress make the most delicious salads that I have ever tasted. There has never been a more fertile land or a more propitious climate.

FRIDAY, 15 FEBRUARY. *Shattered hopes!!*

My friend the Californian came from Angels Camp today with Alfonso, who was the buddy of the two young Frenchmen. Acting on news from two friends, he went to meet them at Stanislaus but had to return, sadder than ever before, because not only had they not been found, but there is almost no doubt that the Indians ended up eating them. He came over yesterday with a Mexican who was with the poor boys. I had to act as an interpreter of the sad tale. The Mexican says they met up with thirty Indians, who charged them as soon as they came into sight. Seeing that they were vastly outnumbered, they attempted to flee, but later they were almost entirely surrounded, with no way out except by way of the river. The young men jumped into the river, but when they had swum to the other side they were once again surrounded by Indians. That was when they decided to fight, but their pistols and shotguns would not fire because the powder was wet. They were disarmed, and Bertrand's arm was pierced by an arrow, and his friend Felix had another arrow in his chest. The Mexican says that he then jumped into the river and went underwater like a duck and was saved by the darkness of the night. But more than a half-mile away he could still hear the clamor of the Indians. Poor Alfonso! He could not keep from weeping when I repeated the story of the poor young men to him. He says that what he regrets most is not having been with them at that moment.

SATURDAY, 16 FEBRUARY. *Quiroga and Argentina*

Today is the anniversary of an event marking the history of all Hispanic American republics but one that nobody is sure whether it was really positive or negative. It is the anniversary of the assassination in Barranca Yaco of the famous leader Don Juan Facundo Quiroga.[59] His destruction of the town of La Rioja in Argentina, his own country, is well known, as is the damage he did to many other Argentinean provinces. I am a member of the family that was among his first supporters and helped him come to fame. Yet I am also a member of the family he persecuted and attempted to ruin. He is the reason why my family is dispersed nearly everywhere, and yet I am more his passionate backer than his enemy. Despite the fact that Quiroga made many victims and shed more blood than anyone, he is much less guilty than the dictator Rosas in the eyes of most. He was the only one who wanted a republic and could have built one and was also the only one who could place an effective limit on the ambition of Rosas. He was the only one who could make the tyrant tremble. For that very reason, it is as clear as day that it must have been Rosas who ordered his assassination. Had this not happened, who knows where the Argentine Republic would be today.

SUNDAY, 17 FEBRUARY. *My birthday*

Today is a magnificent day, and it looks like even the weather wants to take part in my happiness. Today I am one year older. On a day like today I was born in the Jerusalem of Argentina, in the city of La Rioja. My poor mother probably recalls all the pains I caused her on the day of my birth! And how she would feel knowing that twenty-three years later her son would be thinking of her from the bowls of California!!! Last year I was poor, and turning twenty-two overwhelmed me. Today I am not yet rich, but I have twenty probabilities of becoming rich later on, if God only continues to protect me. But just now my situation is much different from that of a year ago. Now I am happy, if that is possible when you are far away from your family. Today my men ate rich, fresh empanadas, fresh watercress salad, and sweet potatoes, all of which are delicacies around here.[60] Today was a day for parties and for visits of many friends. Thank the Lord!

MONDAY, 18 FEBRUARY. *Calaveras is filling up*

Today an entire company of sixty or more Americans arrived. They come from Mokelumne, where there is no longer any gold to be found. This company is a small fraction of the 16,000 Americans who have come overland to California in the past few months. They say that all of North American is going to empty out into California and that it has become a symbol of the land of prosperity for all those who pray that prosperity will be theirs someday.

THURSDAY, 21 FEBRUARY. *American slaves among the freest people of them all*

For the past three days now there have been indications of a major change in the weather. Last night we had a real blizzard. All of the hills are covered with white mantles of snow that in places are 4 ft. deep. It is ten o'clock in the morning, and it is pouring rain. By now the twenty Americans who were working near my tent have left, and there are only three or four pairs of black slaves left who are freezing for their masters. My God! What an impression it makes on me to see slaves in California, slaves chained by Americans, who, more than any other nation in the world, stand for freedom!! These poor Negroes can hardly hold their picks they are so cold, and yet they do not move from the place where their masters told them to stay. Slipping out from under the masters' vigilance, they came over here to heat up a bit. These poor people are very nice and friendly. It is such a shame to see human beings, who in every way are just like us, have to drag chains around with them and have owners, as though they were animals!

One of the slaves begged me to play the guitar for them, since from where he had been working he was able to hear me sing "Lucy Long," which is a song about Negroes. I played it again with great relish as well as some other songs. You could see the happiness and pleasure it gave him. Finally I gave him a little liquor. As he left he thanked me very profusely for having given him "fire, liquor, and music," all for free.

FRIDAY, 22 FEBRUARY. *My California nights*

It is ten o'clock at night, and it is very cold out. The night is clear, and the heavens are filled with stars, but inside large logs are burning and giving off an exquisite smell. Around the fire there are nine of my laborers (I took on another two yesterday), Juan de Dios Sánchez, Mr. Alfredo, Moyano, and the cook. Right now one of the men is telling a story that has been going on for an hour. Everybody is listening to him with great interest, and his tale is only interrupted by occasional laughs that his comical style brings out. This was going on before I sat down to write in my diary, and it makes me happy to see the peace and tranquillity reigning in my house for all of these persons who depend on me. But the happiness turns to sadness when I think of how abandoned my own family must feel and how here in California I am alone without even one member to share this moment with me. What am I to do? Just put up with my solitude in silence and pretend to be listening to the stories of the men.

SATURDAY, 23 FEBRUARY

Last night three of the Negro slaves who were here before returned to beg me to play "Susana" and "Miss Lucy Long" again for them on my guitar. The poor devils were filled with pleasure to hear their songs so far from their own country. They joined in the singing and dancing as though they were among their own people. They thanked me repeatedly for all this, telling me that I was very good for them and that all the Negroes love me very much. Poor devils! They lick the hands of those who are good to them!!

SUNDAY, 24 FEBRUARY

Today is a beautiful spring day, a nice day to show off a beautiful sea-green tail coat, a velvet vest, a turquoise-blue tie, and violet pants. But where could I show all these things off? Where could I wear these fine clothes? Where could I do this and attract the attention of some beautiful damsel? Just as an imprisoned man dreams of fresh air and desires freedom, that is the way I have been dreaming these past days of my family, my friends, and my beautiful belles. Well, maybe one of these days all of these things I am dreaming will come to pass.

I believe that the most attractive placer around these hills is to be found in Calaveras, judging from the fact that every day there are twenty-five or thirty new miners coming in here. My king's camp (as my tent is known around here) is always filled with Americans, and my place is a meeting place for all of them. This is especially so for those who love music and are impassioned followers of the Argentine Republic. Last night some Americans told me that the only South Americans of the white race they had met were from Argentina and that all the rest were Negroes, or copper-skinned and beardless. This is what all of them, or at least the majority of them, seem to believe.

MONDAY, 25 FEBRUARY. *A new discovery*

Today we bought a young bull to celebrate the final days of February, which also seem to be the last days of winter. Prices everywhere are going down these days. The steer we bought the other day cost us eleven ounces in gold, and this one, only four. While buying the bull today I had a chance to see how good the Americans are with a rifle. Since we were not able to get the steer tied up, mostly because it was a pretty wild one, an American asked me if I would like to help him with his rifle. The moment he shot, the bull fell instantaneously, wounded as if lightning had struck him directly in the forehead. The American had shot from a distance of at least 150 paces from here.

THURSDAY, 28 FEBRUARY. *Month's end*

Well, we will see how March will behave with me. The month coming to an end, despite having only twenty-eight days and having many of them wasted because of the snow, has not been bad at all. Nothing bad has happened to me, nor to my health, nor to my business. My men have taken out 1,200 pesos in extremely rich twenty-four-carat gold dust. During this month a new and very rich placer was discovered. People say that some miners have taken out between three ounces and one pound of gold per day in big nuggets. This placer is on the same river as we are, about two and one-half leagues from here, near San Antonio. Next week I am going to send some of my men there.

MONDAY, 4 MARCH 1850

Today I sent six of my men to the new placer in San Antonio, some three leagues from here. We shall see if what the Americans told me yesterday and last night about getting a pound out per day and several ounces per pan or *batea* is an exaggeration or not.[61] I am sure that my men are the very best at this business, and they will get a lot of gold if the story is true. If not, it will just be another lie coming from that placer, like the ones before it.

TUESDAY, 5 MARCH. *Cargo has arrived, and lots has been sold*

I just received 668 lbs. of different articles I had ordered. The cost of the load has gone down from $150 per wagon to $60, or even as low as $15. The price of supplies has also gone down by nearly 100 percent; what used to cost eight reales per pound now costs four, such as oats, beans, jerky, salt, green peas, and wheat. Isidro told me that Samuel sold another 30 x 70 ft. lot for $4,000 in cash. This week's take, amounting to $8,500, has not been a bad addition to Samuel's treasure chest. Let's hope that the spring will continue like this. If so, I believe that, by the end of November, Samuel and I will be able to bid farewell to California, taking with us some 50,000 pesos.

FRIDAY, 8 MARCH. *Who knows what we have lost*

It is nine o'clock at night, and the three laborers I sent to the placer of San Antonio just returned. They say the Americans attempted to kick everyone out of there, just like they did the past time. My men found extremely rich sites. On the first day they took out 3.5 ounces each without ever even coming near the really rich part of the site. All of the gold is in nuggets and perhaps of the highest quality I have seen so far. Today my men went to work again, and twenty Americans, envious of all that wealth, came to take the claim from them. My men wanted to resist, but Juan de Dios convinced them not to. And here they are, with little more than what they got out yesterday, totaling some 200 pesos.

SATURDAY, 9 MARCH. *The day of my departure from Chile*

Today has been another nice day, but the atmosphere is heavy, and I think it will rain tonight. Big black clouds seem to announce the arrival of an important storm. The tops of the pine trees bend over with a wind from out of the southwest, which is an unfailing sign of heavy rains to come. I just came back from my vegetable garden of watercress with a good handful for today and tomorrow. If it rains, I will have more soon. This is the only good thing that the storm will bring me, because otherwise it will make me lose at least $100. This is how I tell the progress of the storm step by step. In other circumstances with a good roof over my head, I would even enjoy listening to the thunder from my bed. But here you tend to notice which way each leaf bends, toward the south or the north, and see in the smallest of clouds that pass whether it has other clouds to join it and form a big storm.

A year ago today I left my family and all the comforts of my home. Last year on the 9th of March the *Carmen* weighed anchor on the sands of Talcahuano, taking me away as I waved my handkerchief as a last farewell to Mardoqueo and saw the ship move away without ever knowing whether or not I would ever see my brother again. Thank the Lord that I am still alive!

MONDAY, 11 MARCH

In Stockton the price of land continues to increase because of all the immigration. More than 200 people come in every day, and this amounts to an increase of 72,000 men in only one year. How about those improvised cities of California! They have made an estimate of the total amount of gold taken out through the treasury of San Francisco last year, and it amounts to fifty million dollars in gold from the placers in California, not counting that which was taken out overland to Mexico and Sonora. San Francisco Bay is beginning to be too small for all the ships anchored there, even though it is the largest harbor in the world. I wonder what we will see for this year?

It is nine o'clock at night. A terrible storm, perhaps the worst one of this winter, started just about an hour or so ago. It had stopped raining for a moment, and I was with four Frenchmen whom I gave shelter to because of the rain. All of a sudden we heard a tremendous clap of thunder announcing the approaching storm. When we least expected it, a furious gust of wind left us in the dark and put out the fire with the same ashes it covered us with. Another gust of wind took down half the poles of the tent. If there is yet another one like that, we will end up being alone between the earth and the clouds.

THURSDAY, 14 MARCH.
The cruelest day of the winter. What a lot of suffering around here!

Today has been the worst day so far of this winter. Last night it didn't stop raining once, and today there were terrible winds all day, and so much hail fell that the ground was completely white with hailstones. When the wind finally died down, the hail became thick snowflakes. From dawn until about four o'clock in the afternoon, we did not have even the slightest respite from wind, snow, and hail. The river has swollen tremendously, and its waves are splashing against the rocks where my tent is tied. There is not a man, not an animal, not even a bird to be seen anywhere. It is as though everything was hiding so as not to be exposed to the storm. These days are horrible. Here we are, trapped between two hills, with only some canvas for a roof, at the mercy of the wind at every moment, with no more space than that within the tent, with no other company than sad thoughts, with no other beings or faces than those of the men, who are the only things reminding us that we are still men!

My God, being an immigrant in California the way I just portrayed it is really something! By contrast, just think of the life of the laborer in Chile as opposed to that of a rich man in California. Any reasonable person would prefer the life of the rustic there to that of the rich man here.

FRIDAY, 15 MARCH. *Looking over this past year*

It was about a year ago now that our company was first formed in Chile, and it is a good time to take stock of just what I have achieved in this period. Once the negotiations started, right away there were differences of opinion. Instead of the two of us who actually came, originally there were supposed to be four or six directors. There were debates and even some hard feelings. Families, even wives, took part in the decisions, and what began as a straightforward commercial venture of men ended up becoming the subject of drawing room conversations, and we spoke of little else. When all the stir finally died down, the directors were appointed. There were thirty young men who left Concepción, all of whom had the same objectives, similar ambitions, each of whom trusted the best arrangements of his company, and each one with his own plan and imagined castles for later on. My goodness, there were a lot of disappointments and a lot of bitterness once we reached the much idealized San Francisco. Learning in California has been difficult for everyone. Some of the men went back home almost right away, others made it to the mines, and by now all of them are back home in Chile eight months after leaving. Anyway, after a thousand sacrifices, I came to Stockton alone, which is where I sold supplies and I got the money together to get the entire company to the mines. It all cost me almost 7,000 pesos. With Dr. MacKay in San Francisco all of the time, for four months I had to handle the laborers all by myself. Doing my best and gathering strength from my own weaknesses, sending the laborers everywhere on foot, and often foregoing my own comfort and food, by the end of four months of work our company had 19,000 pesos in gold dust. Afterward, the company was dissolved, after having purchased a large amount of land in Benicia and twenty-one lots in San Jose, all of which are now a part of the company's capital. I bought the rest of the materials and tools belonging to the company, which were worth $4,800 but which I was able to get for $800 in cash. Well, after all this I was able to survive the terrible and bloody events of the 28th of November relatively unscathed.[62] During the winter, my eight men have taken out $4,000 in gold, and I have sold more or less $3,000 in goods at very good prices. In Stockton I bought a lot for 2,300 pesos, which at present is worth between 12,000 and 14,000 pesos, though two months ago they offered me $8,000 for it. As for this business, that is about it.

For six years now I have been studying one thing or another nearly every day of my life. This year I have studied English every day as well as universal history, and, thanks be to God, I can master the first and maybe even the second. This is my final assessment of this past year.

TUESDAY, 25 MARCH. *A vision*

Just when we least expected it, the rains returned accompanied by heavy winds. Two poor Americans arrived just now; both were soaking wet and terribly hungry. I just gave them some food, and right now they are warming up by the fire. Mr. Weaver also just arrived, and the ex-secretary of the British ministry came in with malaria to ask for shelter and something to eat. I gave him a couple of doses of quinine that I had, and he is delighted to be here and is now getting warmed up near the fire. Things of this world! Here is a man who has been admitted into the finest councils of the most powerful governments of the world, and now he is trapped in this miserable situation.

Today was a day of apparitions for me! The famous Maturano, who led the poor Chileans in the events of the end of last November [*sic*], just entered my tent out of an intense downpour. I do not know what sort of stroke of destiny let the captain off the hook while sending four poor devils to the gallows and having the others whipped to shreds. High judgments of the Omnipotent! Who knows what God has in store for him?

SATURDAY, 30 MARCH

Mr. Ward Smith, who was one of the richest merchants around with a fortune that some said amounted to nearly $400,000, went bankrupt the other day and blew his brains out. Samuel says that more bankruptcies are going to happen.

SUNDAY, 31 MARCH. *Easter Sunday*

As San Francisco progresses, corruption also makes great strides. There have been two dances held there where the boys and girls were in their birthday suits, without any clothes at all. There is another place where four beautiful girls play living statues, completely naked. One of them is Venus, another Diana, another Ceres, and the last one Minerva, all of them assuming positions that are altogether obscene. At that place you have to pay a peso to get in the door. My goodness! It is amazing what gold and wealth will lead people to do!

I will also celebrate my own Easter Sunday, just like everyone else. I had a sizzling roast cooked over the fire, and right now Mr. Casimiro is dressing a delicious salad of fresh and tender watercress. It would be difficult to have a more tasty meal. It is a good time to evoke memories of other years and other lands.

MONDAY, 1 APRIL 1850. *A fatal coincidence*

I received a package from Samuel containing letters from Chile for several of the men. Among them there was one for poor Terán. In others, friends and relatives send him very best wishes. I suppose I should go and ask the Americans who shot him where his grave is so that I can do many of the things I was asked. My Lord, what a fatal coincidence! The letters were dated 11 January, which is the day the poor man was executed by the Americans! Who knows but that his family was writing him with good wishes for his happiness and success just when the Americans were putting fourteen bullets into his body. Poor Terán! Maturano says that he was courageous until the very end. They were unable to get anything out of him as they took him to be shot, not a whimper, not a tear, not even a sign of pain. And even with fourteen bullets in his body, he still breathed hatred and defiance against his murderers. Only a shot through his head was able to do him in.

It is eleven o'clock at night. The moon has not come out yet, and the night is so dark that you cannot see anything even a yard away from your face. I was seated on my bench playing the guitar when, without any warning at all, two of the most horrible-looking men you can imagine suddenly showed up armed with rifles. I instinctively stopped dead in front of them and grabbed my guitar as though it was a stick. But they greeted me in good

English, and I invited them to sit down. Their hair, which looked more like a horse's mane than human hair, fell down over their shoulders, much as the hair of Indians often does; their hats were hanging down along their backs, their clothes were all torn and tattered, their faces were blackened with gunpowder, their eyes shown like lighted charcoal, and they smelled terribly of alcohol. They asked me for some liquor to drink, but I told them that I did not sell alcohol. Later one of them said to me in the most pure and elegant Spanish I have ever heard:

"Couldn't you send one of your men to bring a couple of bottles from the other store?"

"Of course," I answered.

He delivered his request to Muñoz, who, upon my signal, left and did what he always does: he hid behind the tent for awhile and then came back saying that they did not want to give him any because they did not understand him.

"I am going to bring them here, by God!" said one of the visitors, and he left.

The one who stayed behind was the one who spoke Spanish. He said to me:

"You should know Sir that, even though I am a Cherokee Indian, or a Yankee if you prefer, I have been in Buenos Aires, where they thought I was a pirate or a smuggler. They forced me to join the army of General Oribe for the provinces. I have been to Catamarca, Tucumán, San Juan, and Mendoza. I got tired of all that death and went to Chile. I went to San Carlos and was about to get married with a beautiful girl when the damned priest asked me if I knew about the articles of faith. I stopped him by saying that I did not profess the same articles of faith that he did, but rather I believed in Jesus Christ, in his passion, death, and resurrection for us, etc. My religion was that of a Methodist Protestant, which I had inherited from my parents. The result of all this was that they kicked me out of the church because I was not a Catholic and they took my fiancée away from me. I came back to the United States and became a volunteer, which in fact is like being a type of highwayman. And here you have me. For three years now I have been roaming these mountains with the Indians, and from time to time I come down to the tents to spend one or two pounds of gold for my own needs."

This was about where he was in his story when he noticed that his buddy was taking a long time, and so he said he had better go to see what the devil the guy was doing. He left about fifteen minutes ago. I am still amazed by our encounter, and what he told me seems like a dream. But Muñoz told me that it is all true and that he knows the fiancée and that he was in San Carlos about when this noisy altercation had taken place.

WEDNESDAY, 3 APRIL. *Girls should not be too curious!*

It is nine o'clock, and five Indians, two of whom are completely naked, just came in. Their leader, who spoke a little Spanish, made me understand that they had not eaten anything for two days and that they didn't have any money to buy things from people who did not understand and that nobody wanted to give them anything for free. He finally ended up telling me:

"Give me a little beef jerky and enough biscuits for five. Me no pay anything, no gold, nothing. But another time me pay everything."

His petition was too fair for me not to agree to it. I gave them the jerky, biscuits, and salt, enough for them all for the entire day. I told them to come back whenever they were hungry. Their leader spent almost an hour dictating to me the most common words of his language, and right now I have a good Indian vocabulary with almost all of the totally necessary expressions. According to what the Indian says to me, they too have a God "up there in heaven" and "a hell down below, very bad, lots of fire." Who could possibly ignore the existence of God, the sole creator of the world and of everything in it? The Indians have left now, but it is amazing how they can spend the winter naked as they are. Speaking of naked Indians, the last time I was in Stockton aboard the *Bella Angelita,* a young lady asked me what naked Indian women with necklaces were like.

"I am really curious to see them, Navarro," she said.

"Miss," I said to her, "if you really want to know what they are like, take off all of your clothes and look at yourself in a mirror dressed only in your birthday suit. . . . Indian girls are just the same, almost all of their shapes are entirely the same.

She blushed and covered her face involuntarily. It had just dawned on her how tasteless her question had been.

It is four o'clock in the afternoon. Four Frenchmen just came into my tent. One of them, who knew me pretty well in Stockton, introduced me to his colleagues and pointed to one of them, saying to me:

"Voici Madame Gremière que vous voyez deguisé en garçon."[63]

The gentleman's face turned bright red, though by now he must have been used to these sorts of introductions. I have never seen eyes as lovely as hers, nor a more frank and sweet expression on anyone's face. Just imagine how beautiful she would be adorned with her own clothes and using her natural charm! As he was weighing his gold, Bartolo said:

"But sir, tell me, have you ever seen such a good French lad?"

"And she is a male miss!" I replied.

I believe in God the Father, and nobody says it is a sin to be disguised!

THURSDAY, 4 APRIL. *My wheat field in Calaveras!*

On my way back with watercress I went by the wheat field I had planted and was delighted to see that some spikes of grain had appeared. Things really grow fast around here, and the wheat is already beginning to have grain. I intend to take good care of this field and of the bean field as well so as to see what this land is good for. It will be wonderful to show my friends and acquaintances in Argentina and Chile the wheat produced by the soil of California, right in the gold country. They will be delighted and impressed to see the robust grains and long spikes of wheat produced by the land that has also produced so much gold at the same time. Who has ever seen the mineral and the vegetable worlds so close together? Only in California, itself exceptional in just about everything in the world.

SUNDAY, 7 APRIL. *Murders in Camp Sonora. A visit from the Indians*

Americans always seem to kill people like you kill dogs. Here is what I read in the *Stockton Times* from Saturday, 30 March.

> On Sunday night last 24th March, at Sonora a man named Miles O'Connor drew a pistol to shoot some person who he considered had insulted him. He fired twice, but twice missed his aim, and killed two parties who were merely passersby. One of these unfortunate persons died on the spot, and the other on the following morning. The man who drew the pistol immediately took to flight, but authorities forthwith took measures for the apprehension of the offender.

It is four o'clock in the afternoon, and an Indian chief just came in with a group of twenty Indians, among whom there are ten or twelve women. They came to set up their camp about three blocks from mine, according to the chief, so that they can buy supplies at my tent. Since they are on the move, each them has his bed with him, his clothes, and any and all of his possessions. These, in fact, hardly amount to more than one or two beautiful baskets to make their acorn bread, and their bows and arrows. Only the wife and family of the chieftain are dressed, and the others are the way they entered this world. In order to show her position in the group, the wife of the chief has a bone as long and thick as a cigar piercing the soft part of her nose and coming down to her lip. The bone is so clean that it shines like ivory, but I think it is probably from some dog. All of these Indian women are extremely ugly, except two or three of the younger ones, whose youth makes them more attractive. Still, all Indians seem to be snub-nosed.

MONDAY, 8 APRIL

Today the Indians came back, and since it was Monday the chief was wearing a general's epaulets laced with gold. No matter that the coat is covering bare skin or that his feet look now like those of a peacock. The poor Indian doesn't have a shirt or shoes, but he sure has his epaulets, which cost him a lot. What a lucky guy who was able to sell them at such a good price.

FRIDAY, 12 APRIL

There is an unpleasant piece of news going around. García and his Spanish colleagues who live a league from here left four days ago in search of new canyons for prospecting. Since they left, there has been no word from them at all, and they only took supplies for one day when they set out. Six men looked for them all day with no luck. Today some Americans came in with the following information. About three leagues from here near the hills of Mokelumne they found a dead man who had been shot full of arrows by the Indians. They suspect that he was Spanish because all of the papers they found in his pockets were in Castilian. They were not able to find out anything more because they left as fast as possible, lest the same fate befall them.

It is true that these Indians are getting to be real thieves and murderers. The last time they ate my poor French friends, Bertrand and Felix, and now they commit another equally atrocious cruelty. It no longer bothers me when the Americans kill them like animals, because they end up harming everyone.

SATURDAY, 13 APRIL. *The way I spend my free time*

I get up before the sun comes up, and even though the snow is coming down hard I wash my face and arms. After getting dressed I take my *Geography* in hand and study the history of some country, its economy, its customs, etc. Later on I study expressions in English so as to increase my understanding of that language. I end up consulting its rules of grammar, the exceptions to the rules, etc. All of this takes one half-hour every day. Later I spend an hour studying or going over some piece of music on the guitar. In truth this is the study that is easiest for me and one that fills me with great pleasure. When I have done this, I take a volume of the encyclopedia in English; I carefully read the history of each nation, comparing its old and new borders. In fact, I end up building imaginary castles as though one day I were going to be the president or an important statesman of some nation. Then I read different French poets, I study the character of their poetry, and attempt to learn their verses and the most high-sounding words. By reading elegant French I am able to correct some of the mistakes I make. This is how I spend my time when I am not at work, and this is how life up here is bearable for me.

STOCKTON, 18 APRIL 1850. *Aboard the steamboat* Sutter

A couple of days ago Samuel wrote, telling me that he could not get away from San Francisco for the time being and that I should come and pay him a visit if I was not too busy in Calaveras. Since there are a number of business matters I want to consult with him about, I headed out right away. Stockton is entirely transformed, with another five or six magnificent hotels besides the Stockton House. But my goal right now is San Francisco. It is now nine o'clock in the morning, and I have already been aboard the *Sutter* for a half an hour. The whistle is blowing, and it is about to leave. I am writing from my seat on the deck, and Cupertino is walking fore and aft along the ship. The captain has just given the sign, and the steamboat is heading out slowly. The dense smoke that is coming out of the loophole makes it almost impossible to write. I think I prefer to sink a bit; that is, I prefer to go below.

It is now noon, and we have reached New York.[64] The captain is loading passengers and the mailbags, and I am writing in my room. There is nothing quite so lovely as a trip down a river aboard a steamboat. Sitting up there on deck and leaning over the railing is a way to spend hours on end looking at the beautiful countryside going by. For most of the way, you can almost cut flowers as you pass by, leaning overboard just enough to catch the roses as the ship glides past. Three leagues from Stockton we ran into some considerable danger. Someone forgot about the ship's boiler, and it took on more steam than it should have. When the captain realized what was happening, it was beginning to shake all over. He had to open four different valves to let the steam out. Everyone thought there was going to be an explosion, and we all ran to the back of the ship.

It is six o'clock in the afternoon, and we just left Benicia. We were there for twenty minutes to take on passengers and mail. When we were leaving New York we saw the steamboat *Mint,* which saluted us as it passed. We passed the immense steamboat *Senator,* which is going up to Sacramento with more than 300 passengers. It is like a giant sea colossus and is more than a block long. New York now has about 200 good houses. In its bay there are between sixteen and twenty boats at anchor. The terrain there is very rough, but it could be easily improved. The harbor is not well protected. In Benicia there are fewer houses, but there is more trade and movement than in New York. Its harbor is better and has better shelter. There are almost thirty ships anchored there.

It was nine o'clock at night when we arrived in San Francisco. It took us more than an hour and fifteen minutes to get across the bay and past the other ships on our way to the wharf. There are over 500 ships anchored there. And there is nothing quite so majestic as gazing at the gold capital of the world from the sea to see how it rises there above and beyond the myriad of ships, with all its millions of lights shining in all directions in such a way that they seem to make up different mathematical figures. Our steamboat approaches this city slithering its way like a fish among all those anchored ships.

Samuel just came aboard the ship with Blanco. He suspected that I would be on board. I wanted to surprise him. Damn, I would have been able to find the Lafayette Hotel on my own. We embraced and are heading home.

SUNDAY, 21 APRIL

Last night Samuel, Quevedo, Cupertino, and I went to the American Theater to see the *tableaux vivants.* It was a strange experience for a person like myself, normally so delicate and modest, to have decided to go to one of the most obscene spectacles you can see in the world. But my curiosity and desire to know everything about this place and this period made it impossible for me not to go. My motto is to learn all that I can about the customs of people and to see everything worth seeing in the entire world. That way I end up seeing just about everything. After seeing something once out of curiosity, just for the fun of it, I would consider it a sin for me to do it again. After making this caveat, I will say what I think of these "living representations" *[tableaux vivants]* and of the impression the show made upon me.

The "living representations" are made up of very beautiful women who are completely naked. When there is a man in one of the "paintings," he is normally covered from his thighs to his waist, all of which is rather unnecessary because everyone is really only looking at the women. Of the six representations, there were two of them that caught the attention of the public because of their beauty. They portrayed scenes of ancient history and of mythological characters.

What was a little strange was that I did not see or meet anyone who was impressed by the obscenity of the figures, but rather all seemed intent on admiring the beauty of the bodies of these naked women together with the ability of the artist to shape the statues. It seems pretty clear that a woman who is willing to be shown completely naked must be pretty convinced that she is beautiful. When all these figures are going around on a circular stage and are being carefully scrutinized by the audience, there is no way to fake a slender waist, a high and firm breast, and shapely arms. Up there it is impossible to fake anything; it is there precisely that one is able to appreciate the works of nature. In the middle of one of the *tableaux,* I cannot imagine what the loveliest woman in it must have seen, but all of a sudden she lowered her gaze and ended up laughing and undoing the entire scene, without the nearly naked man in it having done or said anything.

MONDAY, 22 APRIL

Last night in the beautiful Union Hall we saw four magnificent representations, that each had a beautiful girl of no more than eighteen years of age who was completely naked. They were all about average height for a woman. I have never seen anything quite so beautiful anywhere in any painting. But I can truthfully say that the last one I saw was really the best. In the Empire Hall there were eighteen representations decorating the main room. All of them showed beautiful women in different postures and positions, some dressed and others naked. The last of the scenes was the best of all. I must admit that each of these places was decorated with the most lavish of luxury and wealth that any man could imagine.

We heard a real violinist play in the United States Hotel. Before, I had no idea what an instrument like this played by a true artist would sound like. I will never be able to describe the kind of emotion that this violin produced in me, especially after a year of life in the wild. And all of this took place with the beauty of the women in living representations nearby. Oh, it is impossible for me to describe what it was like to hear a true artist for the first time. I was overjoyed, I suffered, I laughed, and I cried, and all of that in only a half an hour. My God, I only wish I could have had some lovely belles with me holding my arm during this experience!

Last night after hearing the violin, we went to visit Madame Lacombe. She greeted me with great affection, and I was delighted to see her. As we were leaving she told me to look at the painting she had on the wall. I could see that it was a painting with all of her disciples, and she could see that as I gazed at the painting I could not help but stare at Ursulita. She said, "It is a shame that Dorotea is not there to make the painting even more beautiful for you!!!"

San Francisco, Wednesday, 24 April

Like almost every day in San Francisco, today there is a terrible wind, almost making it impossible to walk in the street. The charm of this beautiful city for me is dulled by the wind, which only stops blowing at night and is then followed by horrible cold. Yet a stroll at night is wonderful. There is hardly enough time to go from one hotel to the next, picking out the music you like best or looking at the different things that most embellish each one of them. As soon as you are in the street, there are plenty of things to enjoy, beginning with the magnificent street lamps of different colors that adorn the entries of each hotel. The multitudes of people you can see at each hall or saloon are innumerable, as are the languages spoken all around you. I was once with two friends and was speaking to one in Spanish and the other in French when up came an English friend, and all of a sudden I was speaking with them in three different languages!!! San Francisco grows daily, and now it almost reaches Happy Valley, nearly one league from the main plaza.

Ever since I arrived here I have been going to the post office daily to see if there are any letters. So far, though, there has not been any luck. Every day three or four ships from Chile arrive, but there are never any letters. I do not understand all this lack of news and communication. It may be that my long absence has already begun to have an effect on my family and friends, or at least in some of those who should be writing us! Oh, patience; after all, that is why we are here.

Thursday, 25 April

After lunch today we took a walk and headed over toward the Telegraph.[65] This beautiful and useful edifice was only finished a couple of days ago. It is situated on the highest of the hills that grace the town, and ships entering the harbor can be seen from twelve miles away. The tower at the center of the building is very pretty and is very modern in taste, at least according to competent architects. Actually, I know about as much about architecture as I do about medicine.

When we came to Dupont Street, Samuel stopped all of a sudden in front of a pretty dilapidated house.

"Do you know who lives here?" he asked.

"Nice question; it is the first time I have ever seen it."

"Well, this is where Miss Regina Taboureux lives."

I only had a moment to peek inside, because Samuel started out again at the hunter's pace he usually uses when he strolls around town. But a bit farther away, I turned around and saw a girl leaning in the doorway. Oh my, did that bring back strong memories for me! How many times did I take walks with Juan and Mardoqueo, only to turn around to see if that beloved beauty was in the doorway!![66] Poor Juan, I wonder what has become of him. And poor me, forgotten by everyone while I cannot help but think about them all the time.

In a few days the largest steamship in the world, and also the most luxurious, is due in the bay. It is here to do the Pacific route. There are already another two companies, or lines, and this one will bring the total to four, which should begin to compete for business and bring the prices for freight and passengers down.

FRIDAY, 26 APRIL

Today we went to visit a great jewelry store that just opened on Sacramento Street. The owner is French, and his place is set up entirely in the Parisian style, with all the luxury and show of their nation. Nothing is missing that the most refined taste might want in pearls, stones, and jewels of all types and shapes. In the storefront windows there are different samples of their ware with wonderful little gold nuggets from the placers, some of which have been mounted and others that are just there on display in the window. The most amazing one had the shape of a little tree, and it almost looked more artificial than natural. The jeweler is asking 500 pesos for this piece. You can tell that he is an artist and that he knows how to assess the rarities and particularities of his merchandise. I probably have some nuggets in my own collection that are better than this one but that I have not valued nearly as highly.

SATURDAY, 27 APRIL

After lunch today, Samuel and I went for our usual walk to see what was new. As we passed Montgomery Street we saw a sign announcing a great concert by Herz for tonight. Anyone who knows that Herz is the most important pianist and composer in the world will be able to imagine what an aficionado like myself felt when he saw the billboard. In this country, where the passion for greed rules men's hearts like a despot, nobody is willing to miss the quarter of an hour taken from his precious time just to look at the announcement of the program of Herz. An event like this one does not come very often in life, and I made sure to get a program. We went to the French Theater and bought our tickets. Since I have the program in hand, there is no need to repeat the program of the concert here.

This concert also has something else that makes it very interesting for me. Our friend Madame Lacombe is to play during the second part of the program and will be accompanied by Herz. The piece she will play was composed by Herz, and the person who had the score was in Stanislaus. The day I left Stockton I received letters from Samuel, asking me to ask Isidro to go to Stanislaus with a letter from Herz to Ivanel, asking for the score. This was done diligently and cost $120, but the score arrived yesterday. Right now Madame is studying the score for tonight. What an honor for her to play in the company of Herz.

Yesterday we asked the jeweler to mount a couple of pieces of gold to give to Madame Lacombe at her party. I also bought myself a gold key for my watch.

SUNDAY, 28 APRIL

My Lord! My ears still seem to be ringing with heartfelt notes of Herz. It all seems like I have just awakened from a magical dream that only comes occasionally in life. It is as though I have just seen the seventh heaven and enjoyed for once all that our faith promises the just. It is impossible to describe what happens to a person in his heart and his ears in moments like those, just when the final curtain comes done. My God, these moments of intense pleasure beyond imagination are just the little drops you send those souls who are here in this vale of tears, struggling with all vices for your love!!

When Herz first came out on the stage, I swear I thought the theater would fall down because of all the applause. Three times he sat down to play, but three times he was obliged to stand to acknowledge all the applause. It was the first time I had heard Herz, and for the first time in my life I was convinced that, when men have reached this point of perfection in an art, they seem close to supernatural beings. A thousand ideas come into your head and, without wanting, you end up remembering the stories of witches and magic your wet nurse used to tell you. I had no idea at all what music was all about, and it is impossible to tell what it is really like to hear an artist like Herz. He played his "Storm at Sea," a work of his own, and as I listened I could imagine the swaying of the ship, the furious blows of the waves against its sides, and hear the thunder in the distance, so loud that it rang in your head. I have never seen or heard an imitation closer to the real thing. The creaking of the wind in the cables, the strong shaking of the sails unfurled in the howling wind or suddenly brought in; all of this was so clear that it was as though I was seeing and feeling it at sea.

Later Madame Lacombe came out, led by the hand of Herz, and once again the entire theater, especially the owner, trembled with excitement. I might have thought that, playing next to Herz, Madame Lacombe would not have looked very good. But strangely enough, just the opposite happened, because the influence of the artist turned her into an artist worthy of him. Madame Lacombe played so divinely that it was impossible not to adore her. After the curtain came down, the applause was so loud and so ardent that they finally had to come out again to play a number of encores. Herz's concert is now over, but I am still dreaming about it.

MONDAY, 29 APRIL

Samuel and I are staying in the Lafayette Hotel, next to the house of the Sorucos. These people have rented out the top floor of their house to a matron or an abbess of some sort of nuns, whose proximity I curse and whose presence I would like to denounce here before the eyes of God. In fact, they form a company not of nuns but of women of the world, a veritable French brothel, where their honor can be purchased for six ounces. There are some twelve or fourteen women available to the public, and all of them are very young and pretty. Every day we can see them on their balconies, as they make signs to us to come up and visit them. They are as lavish as a queen, and some are as beautiful as mermaids. . . . But all the illusion you might feel vanishes when you hear them speak of their trade the way the merchant speaks of his merchandise.

"Give me six ounces."

"It is too expensive."

"But I can give you so many hours."

"That doesn't matter."

"Then give me five."

"I'll give you four for the entire night. Let's get done with this."

"All right, my love."

San Francisco, Tuesday, 30 April

I saw Lacourt today for the first time since I left Chile. The poor guy is wandering about not really knowing what to do about his lumber business, which doesn't even give him enough profit to pay for shipments. I also visited Saturnino Correas, who is not doing well with his houses and his lumber business either. All of these old acquaintances of mine are certainly in a different position now than they were back in Chile. The wheels of fortune certainly change all the time, just like the whims of a flirt!

Last night I had another encounter that surprised me a little, at least at first. I was walking around with Samuel near the United States Hotel on our way to a violin concert when all of a sudden we happened upon Joaquín Jara, who was surrounded by men from different nations. He was dealing cards with, needless to say, a pretty sizable amount of other people's money at hand. A little farther on we found his employee Seledonio dealing at another table with a similar amount of money. This poor young lad, who started out in Concepción in acceptable company, had somehow gone astray. He was greatly surprised to see us, though he continued shuffling his deck as calm as could be.

Yesterday while we were out walking we saw two houses spring up seemingly overnight about two blocks from the bay. They hadn't even been started the day before. Today we saw something that was still more surprising. We went for a walk along the wharves near Happy Valley and discovered a regular railway. My Lord! All of the rest of us Americans have an awful lot to learn from the ingenuity of these men here in California! Big projects like this one are finished almost before they have been announced. Now the freight can be loaded on and off the ships in just a moment, without all those wagons moving up and down the docks.

Wednesday, 1 May 1850

Herz, who the other day had given his last concert before leaving the United States, just announced that he will play in the show of a famous magician who performed at his concert a few days ago. He will play twice, once with Madame Lacombe and again by himself in a kind of musical tour around the world. He will play "Yankee Doodle," a jarabe from Mexico, the "Carnival from Venice," the "Marsellaise," "God Save the Queen," the *sambacueca* from Chile, the Russian national polka, etc., etc.[67] All of these will be in one piece, a kind of medley with variations from each one. The concert promises to be as magnificent as the other one.

Today we went out to see the auction at a Chinese house. I was delighted and impressed to see such wealth, such luxury, and such beauty placed at the service of the comforts of life. The things done in silk were especially lovely, and I do not expect to see anything quite so nice again. On sale there was one especially lovely middle-sized room that was entirely upholstered in silk, with an elegant bed made of silk, from the draperies to the mattress covers, as well as a beautiful dressing room with all of its utilities and a lavish bureau. This last room is made entirely of mahogany, and it takes seven or eight men just to move it from one place to another. On sale there were also carvings of the Chinese imperial family, each made from a single piece of wood, all dressed in the most fanciful way imaginable. Nowadays in San Francisco you can see as many Chinese as Americans. There are also many Jews who have their own shops. The Chinese have some elegant inns, and the owners speak English very well. Here in San Francisco I have seen people from just about every place in the world.

Thursday, 2 May

The concert last night was just as good as the first one. Herz played all of the promised music divinely. The "Marsellaise" with variations and the "Carnival in Venice" were the most-applauded pieces. With that, Herz bid us all farewell. Who knows if I will run into him ever again. Last night I was seated in the first row, with the program laid out in front of me across the railing. Two Frenchwomen entered, and one of them sat down on my right. Just then Cupertino, who was next to me, gave me a sharp jab. The French girl was young and very attractive, though I never spoke to her before the intermission. She asked me if I was French, but I cut off the conversation with what was in fact a very pleasant "no." Later on, my foot brushed up against hers, and she moved away the first time. It happened again, but this time she did not withdraw her foot for the rest of the concert. Just then I stretched my leg a bit, and this made it a bit higher and closer to her. I said, *"Pardon Mademoiselle, je crois que je vous incommode." "Pas de tout, Monsieur."*[68] Things were going just right. My hand touched who knows where under my cape, and her leg was linked to mine. Samuel was laughing and pretty envious of me.

Friday, 3 May. *A portrait of a brothel and its women*

Tomorrow we must leave for Stockton. Sparrow came yesterday afternoon and left today at four o'clock on the steamship *Mint*. As soon as he arrived he asked us what the public girls who lived next door to the house of the Sorucos were like. We told him everything, and he said:

"I am going to sleep there tonight. You must accompany me as far as the door."

I invited Adolfo Rondizoni to come along with me, and all three of us set out. When we got to the door the mother abbess came out and told us very pleasantly to come in. As soon as she opened the door I could see the entire scene. Five or six of these girls were gracefully lounging around on easy chairs and couches stuffed with horsehair. Sparrow said to me:

"Come in for a moment and see the customs of these girls."

I have already said that this sort of thing is contrary to my customs and the way I am, but I want to see everything at least once in my life so I can know what they are like and make use of my experiences for my own betterment. So with my heart in my hand, I went in together with the others. I have never seen a receiving room more luxuriously appointed. Every one of the girls in her dress and her demeanor was like a duchess or a queen.

I sat down near a round marble table where there were books with beautiful illustrations. I opened one and read "The Two Dianas" by Dumas. I started to look at the illustrations while one of the girls gracefully sat on Sparrow's lap and another one on Rondizoni's. A young girl dressed in white, who must have been about eighteen years old, with a face, hair, and breasts that were more lovely than any others I had seen in life, came up to me and asked to sit on my lap.

"Do you want to sleep here, sir?"

Just as her dress was about to touch my legs, I moved my chair back suddenly. This reception confused and disturbed her and the rest of them. Since they were all looking at me, awaiting some sort of an explanation for my move, I was obliged to tell her in my finest English:

"Miss, I only came here to show the house to this gentleman, and I intend to leave right away."

"Even though you speak English," she said, "you can tell that you are French and that you do not like American women."

"Miss, you can sit here and speak with me if you would like, but I would prefer that it was not on my lap. Since I did not come here for the same purpose as my friend, I would be stealing from you the caresses that I have no intention of paying."

Who knows if there is some honor left in these women. She was greatly afflicted and went to sit down on the couch across from me. I continued to pretend that I was reading, even while I was listening to the dealings going on between the other girl and Sparrow. Just then the one who had sat on Rondizoni's lap said to me:

"What is he saying, sir, I don't understand him."

But Adolfo did not want me to be his interpreter and preferred to make himself understood with sign language.

I thought that my lovely young girl might have forgotten our dispute by now, but after the champagne had been served she took two glasses and came up to me.

"Sir, I am not inviting you to have anything with me, but please have some champagne like the others."

I took my glass and gave her many thanks. After that she started going up the stairs toward the bedrooms. I continued to be busy with "The Two Dianas" when I felt a beautiful hand take me by the chin. I turned, and it was her.

"You are a good-looking young man but stubborn and not very amiable."

"Thank you," I said.

Then she jumped like a little goat and went to give Adolfo a kiss, as if she wanted to make me jealous. My goodness, what women! Adolfo and I finally left Sparrow there and took our leave.

SATURDAY, 4 MAY

Our steamship to Stockton had engine problems, and we had to return to San Francisco until it was repaired. That night something terrible happened. We went to bed at eleven. After that everything got very confused, and I will write what I was able to jot down as it was happening.

It is four in the morning. Dawn has not yet come, and I am writing in the light of the flames that are consuming San Francisco! We were deep in sleep when we were startled awake by alarming and horrible cries of "Fire, fire, fire." I took my cloak and went out to the balcony. From there everything seemed to be lit up. I have never seen anything quite so frightful in my life before. It would be hard for anyone to portray the horrible sensation caused by the noise of immense hotels collapsing amidst the shouts of the crowds. The United States was torched and is now little more than ashes, just like the El Dorado, which followed it. Right now to the left I can see the Empire Hotel burning as well as the beautiful Park House, a hotel without rival anywhere, perhaps not even in Europe, which was finished yesterday and was supposed to open for business today. Right now all of it is an inferno. My God, what a horrible sight!! The flames coming out of the fourth floor are so great that they are almost kissing the roof of the

Miners Exchange, which stands on the other block. There is a black and dense smoke coming up from the flames, and all of this is accompanied by thousands of roofs and thousands of beams that break and crash down with a deafening noise made even more terrifying by the crackling of the flames. It is all part of a scene so terrible that it is hard to imagine. On the fourth floor of the Park House you can see the American flag raised high by the winds of the flames, all surrounded with long ribbons of cloth. It is as though the flag had Satan's soul and this kept it intact amid the flames that devoured everything in their path.

It is five in the morning, and Cupertino, Samuel, and I were able to save our gold, baggage, papers, and other belongings. We took refuge in the Catholic church. Providence is indeed protecting us. Had we not returned yesterday, by now we would probably have lost more than 6,000 pesos. Right now our Lafayette Hotel is burning like Troy did, and in an hour there will be no way to know where it once stood. What a terrible spectacle to see the entire place gone up in flames! Oh my, it is impossible to really describe the things happening here. So far two square blocks have gone up in flames, and the fire appears to be getting bigger. It is strange to see the burning sparks from the Park House come over toward us, ten blocks away. One of these sparks jumped over all the houses on Washington Street and ended up setting fire to the American brothel on all sides before touching anything else. You can see all the half-naked prostitutes running out into the streets, calling for help. What a frightful and strange scene jumping out at me from amidst all of the flames! Yet still more amazing is that all of the carriages and wood that were in the middle of the plaza have just gone up in flames, ignited only by the heat of the fire. Nobody can come within two blocks of the fire without getting roasted. And yet here we are safe and sound. I am going to take more notes on these events so that they can be consigned to my diary tonight or tomorrow.

SAN FRANCISCO, MONDAY, 6 MAY

Despite the fact that today is Sunday, all of the property owners are out trying to remove the debris of their burned-down houses and get started building new ones. The best thing that can be said of American ingenuity is summed up in the San Carlos Hotel, which was begun again yesterday and today has all of its card tables back working, as well as many lavish paintings, with the only difference being that the roof is made of canvas for now and will remain that way until a new one can be built. A total of eight square blocks with about 400 houses burned down, and the total amount of property destroyed comes to about five million pesos. *Caramba,* that is a lot of property! The fire has still not been completely put out, and at night remnants of the fire can be seen. Three men, a father and his two sons, were burned in the United States. My Lord, this is what has made the biggest impression on everyone. What a martyrdom these poor devils must have suffered!! Right now, according to the *Pacific,* two men have been arrested and are suspected of being the arsonists. I wonder what the conscience of a person who has set fire to a city like this one must be. It was an act that caused great misfortunes, losses, and deaths. Whoever it is, he must be a North American.

Samuel and I could not find the place where our room was in the Lafayette until we came upon a bronze cot that had been devoured by the flames and the iron strongbox that was still intact where it had been left. I cannot help but give thanks to Providence for having made us come back for the fire and save our most important belongings from the Lafayette Hotel. Today construction on a new hotel started. It will be twice as grand and should be finished by next Saturday.

STOCKTON, FRIDAY, 10 MAY

It is two o'clock in the afternoon, and we just returned from taking a walk around Stockton with our friend Quevedo, who was very impressed by all the progress that can be seen around here. By now the peninsula has become twice as attractive as the other side of town. New houses spring up practically every day. The best hotels are on this side of town, and the best house in town, which belongs to Mr. Weber, is close to my own lot. We just came from visiting Weber's house, and we were greatly impressed by its beauty and by how much it evidently cost. It is situated on the peninsula just near the lake, and with its gardens and belvederes it looks like an enchanted palace. Samuel's house was started yesterday and should be concluded in about twenty days. It has an even better location than Weber's and will be no less beautiful. It will be a shame to have to sell it again in November.

STANISLAUS, SATURDAY, 18 MAY

After some days in Calaveras, we decided to come to the Stanislaus placer. We left at nine o'clock in the morning, and, after having crossed immense mountains, we reached the river at two o'clock in the afternoon and crossed it without any problem at all. Quevedo was hungry, and so we asked for some food in the inn. They served us boiled meat and fish with onions.

Since it was pretty bad, we did not stay very long. We reached Cupertino's house at four in the afternoon. The town of Sonora appears to have really taken on airs of grandeur. It has some beautiful houses, nice streets, and luxury hotels and a population of between sixteen and twenty thousand souls. Today all of Stanislaus is in a veritable uproar because of the $20 tax that foreigners are charged every month. Yesterday the collector came here, and, seeing that everyone was willing to greet him with guns and knives instead of with $20, he went to the new Bolivia camp. To his own misfortune, the first person he sought to charge was a Chilean who had just arrived. He told him he did not have the $20 yet and that he couldn't leave his job because he only had barely enough to eat with. The collector took out his six-shooter, but before he could do anything the Chilean had sunk his dagger up to the handle in the chest of the collector, who fell with hardly a gasp. There were another six stabs, but they didn't matter much because the collector had died from the first one. There wasn't an American who came to his aid, even though there were more of them than there were Chileans. Some of the poor Chilean's countrymen gave him some money and a horse, which he mounted, and he left the placer for Stockton as easy as can be.

SUNDAY, 19 MAY

All night last night the movement and the revolution in the works have been gathering steam. The events of yesterday seem to have frightened all the Americans, and nobody whispers even a word. For now the foreigners seem to dominate. Early this morning the crowds were pushing up to see a scandalous lampoon aimed at the sheriff of Stanislaus. It is obscene and insulting and is designed to scandalize the Americans. There were three more along the street, and people were shouting, "Let's get the sheriff."

It is noon now. There are 2,000 foreigners who have gathered in the other camp and are marching on Stanislaus. They are headed by Chileans and Mexicans. Another 4,000 Frenchmen should come any time from Mormon Bar. They all have decided that, if the demands of these 2,000 are not met, the glove will have been cast down and the challenge made, and the results will decide who is the master and who is the slave. While General Caseus is deciding, the meeting about the demands heats up, and everyone gets their weapons and buys the gunpowder they need, no matter what the price. Quevedo was taken as the interpreter by Elordi, the main foreign leader, a man much esteemed by the general. As usual, it is the Argentineans: one is the leader of a good cause and the other the interpreter in a matter of life and death.[69]

MONDAY, 20 MAY

When night had fallen and everything seemed pretty quiet, a temporary agreement for twenty days having been reached, all of a sudden 100 Americans arrived, showing their banners and cheering. A number of misdeeds were committed last night, and it looks like things are going to get worse. Even though the events have ended up filling the roads out of town with bandits, we decided to get out of this fire with Quevedo no matter what. It looks like God has deigned that I am supposed to be present at all of these California revolts. I hope nothing bad happens to us.

As a precautionary measure we secured a safe-conduct pass from General Besançon, who advised us not to move until the problems had passed.[70] But we had already made up our minds. He gave us the pass along with a letter of recommendation, normally given to any American or to any other person who has rendered services to Americans.

TUESDAY, 21 MAY

Yesterday after getting the passport from General Besançon we got ready to leave as quickly as possible, because the situation was getting more dangerous by the minute. Last night armed Americans from all over arrived. The French set up their general camp near Columbia and sent out messengers in different directions in order to get the call to all the French, Chileans, and other foreigners. By the time we were ready to leave, large groups of men were cutting off the streets. Across from the sheriff's house there was a garrison, but they would not allow any armed foreigner to go past. We had nothing to fear because they had seen us speak with the general on very friendly terms. That way we left with no fear. In front of us there was a Frenchman who had a truncheon, or at least a stick that served as a truncheon. Following orders, the Americans stopped him and asked for his weapons. He said he only had a club. They tried to take it away from him, but he jumped back and escaped. He had not gone more than three paces when an American took out his gun and shot him to death. It was just at that minute, with the curious crowd beginning to gather around, that we left hastily, just in time to see that last convulsions of the dying man.

Thank the Lord that we were able to get away safely from all the misfortune that the death of a Frenchman in these circumstances may well have brought to that region. We reached the river around nine or ten in the morning. There we had lunch with a group of eight or ten Frenchmen who were on their way to join up with their compatriots. They brandished their pistols in front of the Americans as if to say that nasty things would happen if they were made to pay the $20. For the time being the Frenchmen have nothing to fear and the Americans keep their mouths shut, saying nary a word.

We reached Calaveras at four o'clock in the afternoon, and after all the turmoil in Stanislaus it was a great relief to see that my mansion there was so peaceful.

WEDNESDAY, 22 MAY

It is two o'clock in the afternoon. Two hand-delivered messages have come in, just two hours apart, to call all Frenchmen and other foreigners around here to come to their aid. The last one just left my tent on his way to the camp farther up the valley. He says that the alarm continues to increase and that there will probably be a battle tomorrow if the Americans attempt to impose their projected $20 fine. After reading the message, the Frenchmen around here left, after having bought some guns, gunpowder, and lead munitions from me. This looks like it is going to be a pretty nasty affair.

SATURDAY, 25 MAY

It is seven o'clock in the morning of our memorable 25th of May. Before dawn I got up and gave the first warning shout, and everyone jumped out of bed. Yesterday I had each of the men clean his rifle and gave him enough gunpowder for today's salutes to the May sun.[71] Before the sun had even come up, there were fifteen men lined up to salute its very first appearance. In fact, our little formation made a pretty sad contrast to the calm and the silence of the men and the nature itself of our encampment in Calaveras. It did not look like anyone was really ready. Only the birds seemed to be cheered along with us at the impending appearance of the sun amidst a beautiful dawn. I could not help but be moved at the sight of a fistful of men ready to celebrate these sacred memories amid the hills of California, where everything is crushed beneath the empire of ambition. What a great pleasure to see that around here there are still Argentineans who, amid all this misery, might just be willing to sing the arrival of the day in which freedom placed all of them on an equal footing with all other men. Oh no, I do not think that the thousand and one shots fired today in Buenos Aires meant more to our nation than the simple way in which we too showed that we were her children. Despite the long years of emigration and of work and suffering in California, our love of the mother country is still pure, healthy, ardent, and filled with hope.

At the first sight of the sun we fired our rounds and continued firing amid all the cheers and chants for more than an hour. We shot some 200 rounds, until the entire encampment was covered everywhere with smoking wads.

CALAVERAS, MONDAY, 27 MAY

Yesterday Abel came to visit us, and we spent a beautiful day together. At two in the afternoon Jesus, the chief of the Indians around here, came with three or four other Indians. Quevedo was able to satisfy his old desire to meet this famous Indian. The day before yesterday Jesus' wife was also here with four other Indian women, and they were all teased to no end by Emilio, until finally Manuela went away, telling me "that man was much bad." Abel left after lunch and promised to return next Sunday.

Speaking of Sundays, after fifteen months of not having heard mass or a priest, I went to San Francisco with the natural desire of going to mass. I went to the Catholic church the first Sunday I was there and was able to see that what Samuel had said happened to him happened to me as well. I was scandalized to see the people in the church behave with so little respect for what they were witnessing. I saw women coming into the church with caps, and even some with great bonnets covered with flowers and other trimmings, just as though they were going to the theater. All of these women were among the few Catholics around here. Most of them are Irish. When the Sanctus of the mass came, nobody knelt down, and when the priest raised the Sacred Host, none of these women even bothered to take off their hats. No matter how acceptable these customs may be around here, they are of little benefit for our religion. They take away much of the holy and august nature of the ceremony, even in the eyes of those who are most indifferent in matters of tolerance. That is what my first mass in such a long time was like, and the same impression was repeated on other Sundays as well.

WEDNESDAY, 29 MAY

The Stanislaus affair, which caused so much alarm, has ended up being settled in the most friendly manner, at least for the moment. The thousands of foreigners who had gathered in the Columbia camp have now gone home, as the authorities accepted their proposal to reconsider their decision regarding the disputed law. Considering the present state of the mines, $20 is really a pretty hefty sum. Everyone thinks that the damn tax has really ended up making everything surrounding the business of mining more difficult. The merchants, for one, will certainly be ruined if the law is not repealed. Commerce survives thanks to the miners, and many of the miners are foreigners. They will certainly leave before paying such an expensive tax, and once the foreigners leave the mines all of the commerce around here will dry up. Since three-fourths of the inhabitants of California are foreigners and they are the ones who take out most gold and spend it everywhere . . . the logic is pretty clear.

FRIDAY, 31 MAY

I received letters from Samuel from San Francisco in which he tells me that in a matter of eight days we will be the owners of the most beautiful ship in the entire San Francisco Bay. It is a lovely frigate that is only seven months old. It will be ready to sail any day now, and so we hope to send it off toward the end of next month. Samuel has already seen the consul in order to exchange its Chilean flag for an American one and to call it the *Elisea Navarro* instead of its present name. Poor Elisea, I am finally able to place your name on the first ship I own.[72] It will be a source of great joy to see that name of yours on any and all paperwork pertaining to the ship.

STOCKTON, THURSDAY, 6 JUNE 1850

We have returned to Stockton once again. Last night we went around to the different hotels in town. Every day the number of hotels increases, and they are better and better, more luxurious, and more comfortable. After visiting five or six, we ended up at the Branch Hotel, where a good Mexican musician plays the piano. This is the best hotel in town. Though its paintings may not be as nice as those of the Dickson, they are live paintings. In other words, they are made up of exquisite public women. There must be six or eight of them.

Last night I was near the man who was playing the piano. We were talking about music, about Rivera and Calsadilla, when I noticed the noise made by the soft rustling of a silk dress.[73] I turned around and saw the most beautiful and elegantly dressed woman I have ever seen. My sudden impression was so strong and she was so fascinating that I couldn't help staring into her eyes. This darn apparition was standing on the top step of the staircase, and she had both hands on the frame of the doorway where I was. The effect was that the wind was blowing her dress onto my legs, and the smell of her perfume was overpowering for me. From this position her slender waist was entirely free from the obscene looks of the visitors and the gamblers. After allowing me this vision of her eighteen years of beauty, she came down the stairs between the pianist and myself, where there was just barely enough space for her to get by. This action might have perhaps been considered an honor for anyone else, but for me it was too bold. It is a funny thing, but all the fascination that this woman caused in me at first went who knows where because of the poisonous contact between her legs and mine. It was only then that I remembered that she was a prostitute and that anyone with six ounces could be the lord of her honor. It was then that my self-respect returned to me, and I said in a pretty audible voice and in my best English, "I thought that beautiful women were never audacious." And without waiting to hear her reply, if indeed there was one, I disappeared into the crowd of people going around to see the different *tableaux vivants* in the hotel.

FRIDAY, 7 JUNE

It is half past five in the afternoon. We just came in from a tour of the new stores and houses of Stockton. None of them are as beautiful, as well built, as tasteful, or as elegant as the house owned by Samuel and Sparrow. The windows from the top floor look out onto the lake, and from the front of it you can see the entire peninsula and the lake. The facade is painted imitation marble, and inside it is decorated in mahogany. The balcony goes all the way across the front of the house and is held up by columns like the "S" of a violin. Since I am not an architect I cannot really explain how beautiful the building is. It is finished, and the only thing left to do is for Samuel to move in. The peninsula is almost completely built up by now, and the best buildings are close to my own lot, right next to where the wharf is going to be built. We shall see how much they give me for it.

CALAVERAS, TUESDAY, 11 JUNE

Sparrow has just invited me to a dance, or something like it, in the house of an American who spent many years in Mexico. Last night he promised to take us there so that we could dance with the man's daughters.[74]

CALAVERAS, FRIDAY, 14 JUNE

There is something strange about the climate around here. A couple of weeks ago it was as hot as in the hottest days of summer, and now, much later in the season, the days are as cool as they have been all spring. At night it is necessary to get under lots of blankets if you want to sleep without being cold, and during the day, with only my red shirt on, I am really cold. It is surprising that these big and sudden changes in the weather do not harm one's health. I remember that last year I could not stand the heat, and it was necessary for me to always have a bottle of lemonade next to me. Is it possible that I have gotten used to it and that now I am almost a Californian? Now that I have been here well over a year, it doesn't seem to bother me any more. Who knows what new place I will have to get used to next? It is as though a person's life is always one of wandering, especially for one who is young and has an ardent soul and an ambitious heart, as I do. When I was in Catamarca the only thing I really wanted to do was to leave there for someplace new. I went to Chile, and there my aspirations multiplied. I wanted to be rich, wise, and happy; I wanted to wander the world over. In Catamarca I would have been happy with what I had in Chile, and once there I wanted to have wider limits to my aspirations. Then I came here to California, and during my first year the same thing happened to me, and my ambition doubled once again. I have achieved what I wanted, but can I consider that all of my aspirations and ambitions have been met? Not at all! After being in Chile I wanted to travel to California and no more, and once here I wanted to know all of the Pacific, and I made myself a promise to fulfill that desire. Now my final goal is to travel in Europe, and God knows that if something doesn't stop me I will also do that. And afterward? The day will come when I shall aspire to something really impossible, and then the impossible will be the end of me, or just maybe I will once again end up with what I really seek in life.

CALAVERAS, SATURDAY, 15 JUNE

Today is as cool as the previous days. The amount of water in the creek is increasing, instead of the opposite that happened this time last year. The fields that were so lovely have dried up, though this year there are multitudes of flowers, as beautiful as those of springtime. My wheat field is ready to be harvested. Amid all the rocks there are areas where the wheat is very high. The grain is almost as large as it is in Chile. I believe that with a little work these fields will yield more than a 100 times of what they cost. In a few days I will put a little of the wheat aside and keep it as a souvenir of where I spent so much time, in the guts of California, where I set up my home before anyone else. It must be very nice to be able to see afterward things that remind you of the smallest details of the place that became famous in a person's own life history for a thousand and one reasons. I can imagine myself looking at this wheat of mine in those other worlds and telling my relatives and my friends of the events of California.

CALAVERAS, MONDAY, 17 JUNE

It is noon, and the weather is still surprisingly good. Right now the cool breeze of these past days is blowing again. As always, silence reigns in Calaveras. Scollen has already left. The great company of Negro slaves has been replaced by another one just like it of Chinese laborers. All day long I see the stupid faces of these men who are so civilized and refined in the arts and so brutish in their customs and habits. Like I said, everything is in silence. Everything, that is, except my California tent, which is the only one around that seems like a real establishment, a factory of hundreds of working arms. From a block away you can hear the harsh and dry sound made by mills and the soft and rhythmic sound of the roasting machine used to make the cereal meal.

Like with all great machines, every man works to the noise of a tool and enjoys whiling away his time by singing to the beat it makes. That is what the men do when they pack the cereal meal, as they sing to the beat of the music of the machine that makes it. Right now I can hear all of them singing. I love that, much like the owner of a factory loves to see his men singing while at work.

Today the factory, or actually the men who make it work, has been most active. Right now they are tying up the last sack. That makes a total of seven hundredweights of cereal meal for today without any special effort. The mill is one of the best ones I have ever seen and is possibly without equal in California these days. I am pretty sure that if we continue to do seven quintals per day, by Saturday we will have pretty much finished with the business of the wheat.

SONORA, WEDNESDAY, 19 JUNE

It is about time I stopped saying Stanislaus, stealing the real name of the town of Sonora granted by Congress only four months ago now.[75] In fact, it is quite a town, much better and with twice the trade than of many towns in Chile or the Province of Buenos Aires.

I went to Stanislaus to sell my load of cereal but will have to return to Calaveras empty-handed. All of the encampments of Stanislaus have nearly been ruined by that darned tax law. Yesterday I met more than 300 men who were going to Calaveras because there they do not have to pay the tax. That means that there is no business at all for the merchants in Stanislaus. Nobody is buying or selling anything. The ones who have the most merchandise are the ones who feel the greatest pressure. I am returning without having sold the entire lot of cereal, because there is nobody who wants to put up the $1,500 needed for supplies in those circumstances. Well, maybe I will sell it at Mokelumne Hill.

CALAVERAS, THURSDAY, 20 JUNE

Yesterday upon my return from Stanislaus, a letter arrived from Samuel confirming the rumors I had heard there about another fire in San Francisco that was even bigger than the one I saw. Samuel speaks of it in his letter, and he also includes a supplement of the *Stockton Journal,* where details are given of this new and horrible misfortune for San Francisco. The fire happened on Friday the 14th. It started at seven o'clock in the morning in the bakery on Sacramento Street. It happened in the oven of an owner, who had been warned three times that morning by a neighbor across the street before it actually started to burn. (Now that I think about it, Samuel and I met my French woman friend from the theater there in the shop. I think her father is the owner.) The fire spread from seven to half past ten, when it was stopped at Post Street. In the other direction it burned all the way to the wharf and was only stopped by the water. It looks like that lovely Clay Street, which was spared in the earlier fire, was also burned and with it our friend Lacombe's store as well. It was the only loss of any of our really good friends. All of the hotels that had survived the earlier blaze went up in flames, and this time ten square blocks were burned, as opposed to the eight blocks of the earlier fire. For now the estimated damages amount to five million. Despite being a larger fire, the merchant houses were able to salvage some of their belongings.

I do not know what the inhabitants of San Francisco think of these events. I do not know what sort of spirits they have for rebuilding yet again a city that seems to have been damned by God. Anyone who has not seen fires like those of San Francisco has no idea of what hell must be like, especially if we embody its torments in these fires.

Samuel also said that he is ready for any eventuality regarding the house in Stockton, and from now on he has written it off as both a profit and a loss for him. It would be a shame if what every one says is the best house in Stockton were to burn down.

FRIDAY, 21 JUNE

It is not very hot today. In fact, there is a breeze that sometimes cools you more than you really need. Two hundred men from Stanislaus have just come to this placer. Right now it is two o'clock in the afternoon, and the string of ants seems to have no end. The miners of California have simplified to the extreme the gear they absolutely need. It consists of a small iron rod on their shoulders, with the wooden bowl [pan] for the gold and a blanket for bedding hanging from its end. In this way they are ready to move in any direction, and they can walk great distances if necessary.

My little cereal factory is working wonderfully. I think that by tomorrow all of the work will be done, because there are only four or five quintals of wheat left to process.

Here is a quote from the *Stockton Journal:* "A Chillian was murdered by a French companion on Saturday last about ten miles from Stockton on Knights Ferry Road. The two were seen coming along the road together, engaged in conversation, when the Frenchman stopped suddenly, looked around as if to see if he was observed, and the next moment leveled a gun that he was carrying in his hand at the Chillian and shot him down. Some Chillians rode up directly after and took the murderer prisoner but afterward surrendered him into the hands of some Americans, from whom it is said he made his escape. The Chillian died almost instantly and was buried near the scene of the outrage."

SATURDAY, 22 JUNE

Right now Orellana is sewing up the last sack of cereal meal. The factory has done its job. We have made forty-four sacks of 100 lbs. each. Today I sold four and still have another forty for further orders. Silence has returned to my tent, as the noisy roasting machine no longer beckons to passersby, and the mills now sleep in peace.

MONDAY, 24 JUNE

A letter from Samuel was just delivered to me. He must have left for San Francisco aboard the steamship after having settled the accounts on the house. The final balance amounts to 50,000 pesos in clear profit after taxes and all other expenses. It is not a bad profit for the full year that has gone by since the business was set up.

TUESDAY, 25 JUNE

The men finished their contract with me and are leaving today for Stockton. They will embark for Chile aboard my ship next week. My company is the only one that has been able to fulfill its contract in every way. My men have been faithful to me to the very last moment, and every one of them will take more than 2,000 pesos in gold with him, which amounts to half of the gold we have mined. It is fortune enough for men who have never earned more than a real a day before.

STOCKTON, SUNDAY, 30 JUNE

Yesterday I came down to Stockton in order to board the steamship *Tehama* bound for San Francisco. The steamer moves out across the lake of Stockton and goes past beautiful buildings on both sides, while I am seated on the deck and am able to write all this in the notebook for my diary. What a beautiful sight is made by a steamship leaving Stockton, with its tall chimney sending out clouds of smoke trailing behind us, its imposing vent, and its immense motors on each side, like the arms of a robust swimmer who travels great distances with each movement. Besides this, it is all lavishly adorned, and this is its maiden voyage. Many halls would give anything to be as well-appointed as this ship.

While the steamship was blowing its whistle for departure, I was leaning on the railing and watching some people fishing, when one of the fishermen said to his companion, "Don't you see, there is a dead man." As soon as he said that, men and boys began to gather around at the news, until finally the authorities showed up.[76] The president of the commission made a diver go in and threw some ropes down. In a couple of minutes the body was on the wharf. It was probably an American who fell in when he was drunk, at least that is what his body, with no bruises or injuries, seemed to suggest.

The bell calling us all to lunch has just rung, and I am really hungry.

SAN FRANCISCO, I JULY 1850

At five in the afternoon yesterday our steamship anchored in New York. We had hoped to arrive by two, but there was not enough fuel, and the going was very slow. The moment the ship arrived, we went ashore with Mix, a young American friend of mine. He invited me to go to a hotel to have a drink, and we would be able to see some lovely lasses. That we did, though it was necessary to go through a veritable cloud of fierce mosquitoes. We did not stay long, because no matter how pretty the girls were, the damned insects were too much to bear. We returned to the steamer, which had loaded up with coal and was ready to go.

Last night at eight we arrived in Benicia. It took us three hours instead of one to get there. We figured that we wouldn't arrive for quite a while, and so we went to our rooms to sleep. It is now six o'clock in the morning, and we cannot dock because of the fog and because we have run out of fuel. They have just thrown two sofas and several chairs into the boiler. Let's see if that will get us to the dock, which is still a few blocks away.

TUESDAY, 2 JULY

When I disembarked from the steamship in San Francisco I was greatly surprised by the horrible damage caused by the latest fire. It was difficult to get to the Lafayette Hotel because I had to go through ruins that were not there when I last left San Francisco. Yet the damage from the earlier blaze cannot be seen anywhere. Five magnificent hotels have already been finished, and they are 100,000 times better than they were before the fire. Their luxury is enough to catch the attention of the most refined European. It is really amazing to see so much magnificence in the work the hotel has put into its oil paintings and its lovely portraits, and all of this is destined to feed a voracious fire at the least expected moment. Every day San Francisco seems to be the most interesting port in the world. According to today's statistics, there are 528 ships anchored in the bay. It must be as they say, because you cannot see the water in this immense bay because of the veritable forest of masts of all the ships.

WEDNESDAY, 3 JULY

I have just come from the *Elisea*. I am now a man who has a beautiful ship with the name of my sister Elisea. Samuel bought the ship just before I arrived and was lucky enough to only pay 4,200 pesos in cash for her, when previous proposals had all been for more than 6,000. The ship has all the qualities we could want. It is entirely new, can carry 300 tons of cargo, and has two cabins as well as ten rooms for passengers. It used to be called *Elvira* but has been rebaptized and registered under the name of *Elisea*.

It finally looks like my dreams are beginning to come true, at least in part. In fifteen or twenty days the *Elisea* will leave for Chile. Getting the ship equipped is costing a lot because here everyone and everything, from the captain and the sailors to the water itself, must be weighed in gold. We are working on it to get things together as best we can. We shall see how many passengers the *Elisea* will take to Chile. Up till now none of the ships leaving San Francisco have taken more than twenty passengers, and these have gone at pretty low prices.

THURSDAY, 4 JULY

Today is the famous 4th of July, the anniversary of North American independence, and also the anniversary of the crimes perpetrated by the Americans in California last year. What a disgrace for a good North American not to be able to celebrate the anniversary of his nation without having to be ashamed at the same time to belong to the same nation as the bandits of San Francisco, who are the most criminal and barbarian in the world!

We went to the planting of the flagpole in the main plaza, and it was really pretty curious. All the Americans threw coins into the foundations of the pole until the entire ground was covered. The pole is some 250 ft. tall and is the most beautiful and straight pine tree I have ever seen in my life. An American had made a small mine of gunpowder right where the celebration was going to take place, and when the 300 men began to dig the pit for the pine tree, the mine blew up and set fire to the clothing of some of them. Everyone sure must have thought that was a great idea!

SATURDAY, 6 JULY

Today two lovely new wharves were finished. They are both three or four blocks long. In San Francisco there are now six wharves, and these are still not enough to facilitate the maritime traffic in the port. They have built some very nice houses in the sea, more than four blocks from land and with streets as long as the wharves themselves. We just might have a Venice in San Francisco if the population continues to stretch out into the bay.

San Francisco weather is certainly strange. We are in the middle of the summertime, and while the heat is almost unbearable in Stockton, here you need a cloak to get around. At dawn a dense fog makes it impossible to see more than thirty paces away. This fog is humid and thick. At noon a strong wind comes up and holds up traffic in the bay. The fog leaves and the wind, which is worse, comes and takes over. A five o'clock in the afternoon the wind stops, and an intense cold takes over. You have to be made of iron to weather a climate like this!

TUESDAY, 9 JULY

Today the steamship *Isthmus* came in with 300 passengers. Samuel and I went aboard, and we just returned. This steamship is new here and is as large as the other ones and as comfortable as the largest of hotels. We saw some young women on deck who were very dizzy and pale. Today six young girls were sold at a type of auction. They had come in aboard the *Eliza* from Mazatlán, but when they got here they had no way to pay for their fare. Three of them were pretty, and their value naturally was twice that of the other ones. Good Lord, around here it is little more than a shortened version of the markets for women in the Orient.

WEDNESDAY, 10 JULY

In another fifteen days we should have six lovely artesian wells in San Francisco. They are being dug simultaneously around the town, and there are immense storage tanks for each one. The well in the plaza is about three inches wide and two feet deep, though it is hard to know just how far they will have to go before finding water. Once it is finished, the water will spurt thirty feet into the air before flowing into the great storage tank, which is eight or nine yards from the well and is already finished. Then we will have a lot of water, and the fires here will not do so much damage.

THURSDAY, 11 JULY

We still hope the *Elisea,* which is taking us longer to equip than we had expected, will set sail on the 20th of the month. It looks like we are going to have a lot of passengers. Normally, ships do not carry more than twelve or so at this time of year, but already twenty tickets have been requested. It also looks like we will have some first-class passengers, and that will help make us a tidy profit because each of them will pay $200 for their fare. Right now there is only one for sure, but another four or five have seen Adolfo about it. We had thought of stopping in Callao [Peru] or in Central America someplace to pick up local products, but since we are carrying so many passengers, their fares will make up for two normal trips. Should we stop, we would only prolong the trip, and this is what interests us least. Our goal is to get it to Chile as soon as possible.

SAN FRANCISCO, SUNDAY, 14 JULY. *A dozen ties*

Samuel said that he had to go to his English lesson and so would not be able to go for a walk with me. I went out alone without any particular destination. I went to the Empire Hotel, and as always I looked carefully at the different paintings there, almost as though I had never seen them before or as if I were a famous painter who was able to look critically at all the aspects of the painting. All of the paintings here are beautiful, and it is easy to spend a half an hour gazing at them every day. In the entrance to the Empire Hotel there is the loveliest painting I have ever seen. It portrays the wife of Putiphar, who is grabbing the cape of a half-burned Joseph, himself struggling to get away from her.[77] It is difficult to imagine a more beautiful and seductive woman, and the effect is made even stronger by the expression of passion written all over her face and in her large and languid black eyes, rather than by her white arms that are attempting to hold the chaste Joseph. The horror and desperation in the young countenance of Joseph, on the other hand, is as natural as can be. After looking closely at this painting, all the rest seem to pale by contrast. There is also a beautiful naked woman in a very large painting whose body could yield many lessons for a discerning artist. This painting has nothing at all obscene about it and is a source of pure admiration for art. The talent of the artist makes you forget the immodesty of the scene portrayed. The woman's smile and position are so natural that at first glance you really think that you are looking at something alive and animated.

After this painting there is a portrait of the famous Lola Montes, who, after revolutionizing Europe, came to be the princess of "N" instead of being the queen of Bavaria. She is a beautiful woman, and there is no misunderstanding why she caused such great passion. The sad part of all of this is that after this painting, placed among some others about not very moral subjects, there is one of the Virgin Mary contemplating her beautiful baby Jesus in the manger. The pure and modest beauty of the Virgin and her child makes a stark contrast to the obscene nature of the other paintings. Twice we have attempted to purchase this painting, but they did not want to sell it to us.

I then went to see the paintings of the other four hotels, and at the last of them, the Parker House, I ran into Rufino. Later we returned because we were ready for some sleep. Walking along Montgomery Street I saw that there was an auction going on with a pretty big crowd. We entered for a moment just in time to see that they were offering three reales for a dozen summer ties. I offered six, and here I am with a dozen ties for six reales!!

WEDNESDAY, 17 JULY

Last night they murdered a woman near the Napoleon Hotel, where we are staying. The murderer is a Mexican who tried to get away after his deed but was arrested and is now in the jail. People say that this woman had been dancing happily with her murderer just before this all happened. Who knows what happened between them later to cause her death.

Two nights ago there were some horrible stabbings in a tavern in a fight involving some Frenchmen, Americans, and Chileans. A Frenchman was treacherously murdered by an American after the first dispute. They say that because of this murder yesterday some eight or ten Frenchmen got together and went to demand justice at the house of the sheriff, swearing on the honor of France that, if justice was not enforced, they would take cruel revenge on their own. I think the sheriff took things seriously because yesterday he jailed two of the participants in the murder.

There is no place quite like San Francisco to make events like these seem to disappear amid all the daily commercial bustle. There are deaths by stabbings, robberies, and rapes almost every night. Yet it is hard to find more than three or four lines about the events in the *Alta California,* because it all seems so insignificant when placed beside all of the events that happen here every twenty-four hours.[78]

Like nearly every day, today the thick wet fog moved in around ten in the morning and stayed here until noon. Then a horrible wind started blowing and lasted until half past five. We went out to eat in the hotel at four and could hardly make our way because it was blowing so hard. Afterward, however, the wind died down, and things have become much nicer.

THURSDAY, 18 JULY

News of proposals and cost estimates from two different companies regarding the construction of a railroad from San Francisco to Boston have reached us here from North America. Both of them promise to lay 3,000 miles of tracks in five years and say the trip from San Francisco to Boston will take six days. The calculations and estimates seem to be done so well that the project may be feasible and might be accepted almost unaltered by Congress.

This news has caused great excitement in San Francisco, because all of the merchants are thinking that with the railroad they will be able to get answers to their requests in only fifteen days. Just imagine all the movement there would be in California with a railroad link to the east! Just imagine how many passengers from both continents would travel only for pleasure! If this ends up becoming a reality at the same time that the Isthmus of Panama is opened up, it would be two of the most celebrated events of the nineteenth century.

Today the sailors of the *Elisea* have stored the water for their trip. Here the water costs nearly $300, whereas anyplace else in the world it would be free. This is how expensive things are in San Francisco! It is true that we have put aboard almost twice what we will need for the trip, just in case something happens. Ships coming in from Chile often arrive with people who have died of hunger or thirst. There should be no problem, because the *Elisea* will take with her 6,000 gallons of water and provisions for three months in case the trip turns out to be a long one. We have doubled all of the supplies that the captain requested. At least that way our conscience is clear.

MONDAY, 22 JULY

At nine o'clock this morning I came off the *Elisea* after having bid everyone farewell. The tears came down my cheeks when I heard the anchor weigh, urged on by the sad song of the sailors. As the sails were being raised, my men in tears bid me adieux. Poor boys! I love them as though they were my own sons. As the boat started moving I was tempted to let myself be carried away, but the boatman shouted, "Sir, the ship is leaving now." Finally I gave my last instructions to the captain about the passengers and got off the boat.

I just returned from Telegraph Hill, where I went to see the *Elisea* off. It was as light as the wind. My poor sister Elisea! I entrust you with the lives and the interests that the ship bearing your name carries with it. Make sure that my hopes are not dashed and that everything turns out all right. Farewell and safe journey.

TUESDAY, 23 JULY

Yesterday at ten the *Elisea* set sail for Valparaíso and Talcahuano carrying fifty passengers with it. Adolfo Rondizoni is the chief mate, and the captain is the German Detjen. The crew includes the captain, a maître d'hôtel, and a cook, who earn $750 per month until they reach Valparaíso. Alarmed by the morbid news of ships reaching Chile with people dying of hunger or thirst, we doubled all the provisions needed for a two-month journey. The supplies cost us more than 2,000 pesos, not counting the cost of getting the ship ready for the trip. There is a doctor aboard for the security of the passengers. We have not skimped on anything to guarantee a pleasant and safe journey for the passengers. It is the first ship to set sail for Chile equipped as it should.

We have sent Mardoqueo 1,000 pesos in gold nuggets and another 650 in a letter of credit drawn against Mr. Blanco in Valparaíso. To take advantage of the good size and comfort of the ship, I had wanted to get a load of trifles together to send to my family. In the end I hardly had time to write and much less time to go around getting the load together. I am only sending Mardoqueo a beautiful shotgun and a rifle with all the necessary implements, all of which cost me $100, which was not at all expensive. I am also sending four paintings to please the eyes.

STOCKTON, SATURDAY, 27 JULY

I am back in Stockton once again, and yesterday the *Tehama* returned to San Francisco. It carried with it a letter of mine to Samuel sending him 800 pesos in gold dust to be delivered against my account at the Sorucos and to reclaim my IOU for that same amount.

Stockton is improving by the day. Some of the houses are as beautiful as those in San Francisco, and the streets have been so built up that there are few vacant lots left. Yesterday we visited all the hotels in town, whose levels of luxury and comfort are not much different from those of San Francisco. So many of them have been built recently that probably some will end up closing for lack of business, much as happened in San Francisco. In the old part of town you have the Branch Hotel, where there are six beautiful women. Sometimes they dance or walk around amid the elegantly dressed crowds. The best part of this hotel is its music, mostly selections from operas. A bit farther east is the beautiful Union Hotel, where the music is based on two violins, a flute, and a guitar played by Lucero. Across the street on the same corner is the El Dorado, which is now the most popular of them all. A bit farther south along the same street you have the Mexico Hotel, the Dickson, the Weaver Club, and other second-level hotels in buildings that are still pretty imposing.

On the peninsula we now have the best and most sumptuous buildings, some of which are without equal in size, taste, or lavishness, even in San Francisco. Among them, the four-story public office building, the Corinthian Theater, the New York Hotel, and the Stockton House Hotel are worth mentioning. The commercial establishments are also luxurious and well built.

In another few days the beautiful wharf destined for the steamboats on this side of the peninsula will be finished. The artesian well across from the theater will also be finished pretty soon. The fire hydrant and the fire department have been completely fixed up. On the other side of town there is another good-looking hydrant with three hoses. This is what Stockton looks like today, just fifteen months after it was founded.

CALAVERAS, TUESDAY, 30 JULY

I have returned once again to Calaveras. We arrived at two o'clock in the afternoon. I met Coll, who looks fat and well. He was talking with Gutierrez and another fellow who were in the house. This house of mine, which just a few days ago had so many people in it, is now a bit lonely. It is as though everyone left Calaveras when I did. I miss the bustle of my men and even the silly conversations I had to listen to. It is clear that there is no situation in life that a man cannot get used to or that he will somehow not miss in the end.

THURSDAY, 1 AUGUST 1850

It is eleven o'clock at night. It is time to assess the events of the day and to distract myself from the matters that are weighing upon my heart. I sure owe a lot to this diary of mine in these moments of bitter sadness, because only it can distract me from thinking of my family, my friends, and my days of hope. It saves me from the suffering of having the happy past memory be compared with the reality of the present. So, let's see. . . . Let's think of more indifferent matters.

Today I saddled my mule before the sun rose and left with Coll for the San Andreas Camp. There was nothing much there. I could not find Ramón, who had left for Mokelumne Hill on Tuesday. I was in several tents to sell some mules, and everything I saw made me sad. I entered a mess hall made of straw, where there was a woman with pretty coarse looks. I sat down, and later other men came in who had to sit next to me because there were no other free chairs. After a little while I looked across from me, and a cloud of sorrow came over me. There was a mirror over there, and I could see myself in my mining uniform, much like a Spanish bandit, with two men at my side who just as well might have been the good thief and the bad thief. My God, I do not think I have ever seen figures that reveal vice and corruption better, especially if you add to all this the figure of the woman, the house, the filth, and the stench of drunkenness. All of a sudden the memory of my family, of my previous encounters in the best of salons, and of my present position flashed into my mind. The clash of present realities and past memories was unavoidable. I got up, humbled with a heart oppressed by sadness, and left without finishing the business that had brought me there.

FRIDAY, 2 AUGUST

Just like last year, today I am in the mines, only this time I am getting ready to leave them forever. This day is one to bid a solemn farewell to this place that for two years has been witness to all the emotions of my soul and all of the secrets of my heart. This farewell is written on a piece of paper that also has flowers in memory of the moment and the place.

CALAVERAS, SATURDAY, 3 AUGUST

It is five o'clock in the morning, and I am about to leave for Stockton, bidding farewell to the mines. Good-bye a hundred times over to my house between two hills, where I have known so many moments of peaceful happiness. Farewell a hundred times over to a place that I came to before anyone else had set foot here, to a place where I made most of my fortune. In the long run, everything is heartfelt in life, especially when it is a matter of saying good-bye. Even the captive will shed a tear of sadness when he leaves the cell he has been confined to for so long.

STOCKTON, SUNDAY, 4 AUGUST

Yesterday at noon I reached the house of Mr. Lemon and Mr. Davis feeling pretty terrible with a strong headache, due perhaps to the oppressive sun en route. The sun had never seemed so hot to me before. Since I had not eaten I decided to have lunch, just in case that was the cause of my weakness. I sat at the table and ordered but could not eat anything. Finally I had two glasses of lemonade and returned to my mule once again.

As I passed the river, the water looked so clear that I felt like washing my face to see if my heaviness and this sort of fever would go away. Not a good choice! I washed my face and my head and lay down under a tree to get out of the sun for awhile. I took a book in English called *The Queens of France* out of my saddlebags and started to read. The pains and the fever grew, and finally I thought that I was really getting sick and might be forced to stay along the route in the hands of some Americans. This thought gave me renewed strength, and I mounted my mule quickly, almost as if I was well. I traveled another two leagues until I could not stand the fever that seemed to be burning me up. I stopped at a tent, had a large glass of lemonade, and left again.

"How far is Stockton?" I asked an American.

"Fifteen miles," he answered. It might as well have been one hundred miles for me. I set out at a gallop to get there before becoming completely incapacitated by my illness. But it was clear that as each mile passed I was losing strength, and my sight was clouding up enough to make it hard to see the road. I suffered that way for about twelve miles, while the sun seemed to be burning much as iron does as it is being made into steel. I could tell that my vision was growing distorted and that I was unable to know just what was the best thing to do. All of a sudden I felt a horrible pain in my entire body and a complete collapse of my entire being. I attempted to dismount the mule, though it was more like falling off the animal. I was able to drag myself over beneath a nearby tree. I do not know what I did for the hour and one-half I was there, whether or not I slept or was unconscious, who knows. I finally was able to get up a little bit and saw the mule grazing about a block away. I got there as best I could and mounted again. But Lord, what suffering! Every step felt like my entire human machine was being thrashed and was about to completely break from the next blow. I dismounted another three times to rest. I was finally able to drag myself half-dead up to the house of the Quirogas, where Samuel, who had just arrived from San Francisco, came out to greet me. I was so weak that I could hardly tell him what was happening to me. Today I feel a little better, but I am far from being well. I have a high fever and little desire to eat. There is no part of my body that is not racked by aches and pains. It looks like my farewell from the mines was a bad omen.

STOCKTON, MONDAY, 12 AUGUST

The signs of improvement in my condition yesterday and the day before were only passing because today I feel worse than ever. I was almost out of my mind when I got up at four o'clock in the morning and went out to the balcony to see if breathing some fresh air would make me feel better. It hardly did. Then Samuel got up, and I told him how I felt. He said, "I will make you take an emetic, even if I have to tie you down." Rojo went to get the emetic. As far as I can tell, there is no way to get out of it this time, so we shall see just what happens.

TUESDAY, 13 AUGUST

Today I feel much better, thank God. This time my improvement might be real. Rojo came in again, and, like the good friend he is, he prepared the emetic and helped me get through the entire day. The emetic has had an entirely unexpected effect on me. I have gotten rid of more bile than all of the water I have drunk these past fifteen days. The last emetic was so yellow, almost red, that I was frightened, thinking that it might be blood. I asked Samuel to look at it, but the doctor said not to worry, that it was only bile. Samuel was delighted to see that the emetic had at last had the desired effect.

After that, I fell asleep for a couple of hours, and when I woke up it was as though I had never been ill. This was the first real illness I have had in my entire life and the first medicine I have ever taken. I feel as though I have lost the virginity of my nature after having given it the poison of the chemist!

WEDNESDAY, 14 AUGUST

Today Samuel made me take a purge, just in case, even though I told him I felt so well that I did not need anything at all. He insisted, saying that it was necessary the day after having taken an emetic. He was only able to give me senna, since I refused to take castor oil.

MONDAY, 19 AUGUST

Last night I was in the Italian Theater, and the show was great! Madame Rossi was divine in her hood; she really looked like a fifteen- or sixteen-year-old Andalusian girl. The polkas were lovely and very well danced. I am no longer surprised that Lola Montes was able to derange the king of Bavaria. Last night the applause for Madame Rossi was so thunderous that the house almost came down. The stamping of the Americans was so strong that one of the columns holding up the floor broke, and everyone feared that the theater was about to collapse. Well, I wonder what kind of heart a woman who dances so well really has. I wonder if she really knows how to love or if it is only a flirtatious nature that sustains her much-celebrated art.

It is half past four in the afternoon, and Madame Rossi just come to my room to invite me to have some macaronis with her at her table. She told me that Samuel was there with her, and if I do not go along he will have to dine alone with her. I thanked her but said that it was still not time

Ramón Gil Navarro, circa 1853. Daguerreotype in color made in Valparaiso. Courtesy of María del Carmen Ferreyra.

The Navarro family. The photograph was probably taken in Valparaiso circa 1856. Seated, *left to right*: Doña Constanza Ocampo, Navarro's first cousin and wife of Don Ventura Ocampo; Don Samuel Navarro, Ramón's brother; Doña Parmenia Navarro, Ramón's sister. Standing, *left to right*: Don Ventura Ocampo; Don William Perkins, husband of Doña Parmenia Navarro. The original photograph is the property of the family of Dr. Fernando Allende Navarro in Chile. Courtesy of María del Carmen Ferreyra.

(top right) The diary of Ramón Gil Navarro. Ramón Gil Navarro papers, 24 March 1845–8 June 1883 (BANC MSS 81/159c, vol. 1). The Bancroft Library, University of California, Berkeley. Courtesy of the Bancroft Library.

(bottom right) Pages from the diary of Ramón Gil Navarro, currently held by the Bancroft Library at the University of California, Berkeley. Courtesy of María del Carmen Ferreyra.

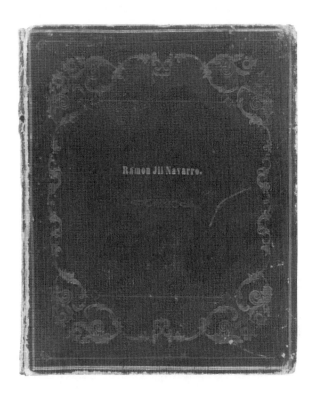

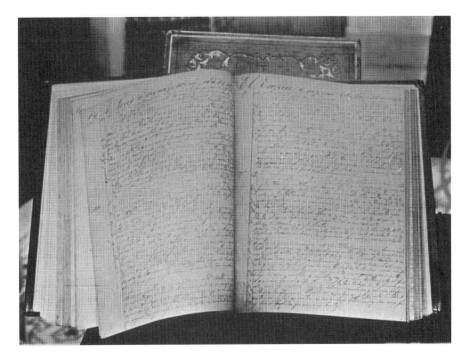

Memento) Stockton 8bre 27 1851. Lunes

Esta el dia hermosísimo. El sol no quema sino lo muy bastante
para quitar el frío. Nada anuncia que estamos en invierno, ni
oriento en Murcia, ni nubes que empañen la luz del sol tan her-
moso... Tampoco hai nubes en mi alma que le empañen
con la luz dela dicha... Si, en vez de nubes que marcan tem-
pestades en mi alma, hai reflejos de divina felicidad conter-
plando natura El... Pero Dios mio! que horrible es la accion
de las injusticias en este mundo! cuando yo estoy llenos
cuanto puedo desear para ser feliz, hai dos seres infeli-
ces que cuentan en el calaboso las horas que les restan de exis-
tencia a mas la tormentosa idea de morir ignominiosa-
mente la hora mañana a las 3 dela tarde con Amilcs de tes-
tigos del suplicio de su infame y deshonra...!!!

(top left) An external view of the notebook in which Navarro would jot down his daily experiences in California. Courtesy of María del Carmen Ferreyra.

Pages from Navarro's California notebook. Courtesy of María del Carmen Ferreyra.

San Francisco Bay full of ships, circa 1850–51. Zelda McKay pictorial collection (1905.16242.106). The Bancroft Library, University of California, Berkeley. Courtesy of the Bancroft Library.

Photograph of Ramón Gil Navarro taken in California circa 1851. This photograph is mentioned in four different letters written to family members in June 1851. Courtesy of María del Carmen Ferreyra.

Gold washing in Mariposa County, California. Etching, circa 1850. Robert B. Honeyman Jr. Collection of early Californian and western American pictorial material (BANC PIC 1963.002.0268—A). The Bancroft Library, University of California, Berkeley. Courtesy of the Bancroft Library.

Byrnes Ferry on the Stanislaus River in Calaveras County. Oil painting, circa 1860. Robert B. Honeyman Jr. Collection of early Californian and western American pictorial material (BANC PIC 1963.002.1366—FR). The Bancroft Library, University of California, Berkeley. Courtesy of the Bancroft Library.

WELLINGTONIA   GIGANTEA.

Giant sequoia not far from the original camp of Ramón Gil Navarro in Calaveras County, near the headwaters of the Stanislaus and San Antoine Rivers. Color lithograph, circa 1850. Robert B. Honeyman Jr. Collection of early Californian and western American pictorial material (BANC PIC 1963.002.0374—D). The Bancroft Library, University of California, Berkeley. Courtesy of the Bancroft Library.

for me to eat. I was able to observe the effect my not having accepted her invitation had had on her. If what I suspect is true, she won't be able to stand my refusal.

TUESDAY, 20 AUGUST

Today it is not as hot as it has been these past days. All day long there has been a breeze that has been fresh and agreeable. Work in the mines has picked up, now that it is not quite so hot. Big operations have been set up on the channels of the Stanislaus and Mokelumne Rivers. Nevertheless, the Calaveras placer is still the dominant one, having the highest yields.

STOCKTON, WEDNESDAY, 21 AUGUST

The steamboat *El Dorado* has brought with it the news of the sudden death of the president of the United States, General Taylor. All of the newspapers in San Francisco have large columns on their front pages adorned in black. Even the *Stockton Times* today has come out with a special edition about his death. None of this seems to have had much of an effect on the Americans in Stockton, yet I think that this death will soon bring new elections, and there may be widespread disturbances in different states.

Last night at half past eleven I was still reading in my bed when I heard the voice of Samuel and of this Rossi woman in the stairway. A moment later she entered into my room. The first thing she said to me was:

"I never thought you were so ungrateful. After my promise to you last night, I believed you could keep your word to go to the play. But now I know that I am not worthy of your friendship even though it would be the greatest hope for me."

Really she promised last night to get a pass for me and at the same time to make me a sign with her hand that only I could understand, indicating that the ball was for me. But I wanted to know if she remarked my absence from the play. Now I am certain of her sentiments for me![79]

THURSDAY, 22 AUGUST

An invitation to all the citizens of Stockton has just been published, exhorting them to contribute to help rescue from misery some 20,000 immigrants who are coming overland from North America and who are in danger of starving to death unless somebody sends help in time. Does the *Stockton Times* really think that foreign merchants living in Stockton have forgotten all of the outrages heaped upon them by the sons of North America?

FRIDAY, 23 AUGUST

Fifteen days ago a very interesting club was opened for the citizens of Stockton. Weaver is the owner of the place, the same German I took into my house in the mines for fifteen or twenty days when he was ill. Today I received an invitation from him to come to the club as one of his best friends. There is a billiards room for gentlemen aficionados and another room for chess, dominoes, cards, and all kinds of other games. There is a library with a reading room where you can find all the newspapers in California and the United States. There is another room for pistol-shooting practice, fencing, etc. Finally, there is a room where refreshments, ice cream, and all kinds of sweets and liqueurs are served. I did not turn down the invitation of my friend, though I only plan to use the library and the newspapers. The rest does not matter much to me.

SUNDAY, 25 AUGUST

It is half past eleven at night, a most beautiful night indeed. The full moon is shining over the lake and all the ships anchored on it, casting a thousand shadows of masts upon the terse clarity of the water. Some boats filled with people can be seen moving from one side of the lake to the other fishing for trout, which at this time of night come up close to the wharf. The theater on the peninsula is completely lit up, as are all of the hotels. What a wonderful sight to see a city divided by a beautiful lake filled with ships in anchor. There is nothing missing in this town except for perhaps a few more lovely damsels to grace its streets.

STOCKTON, 26 AUGUST

Last night we spent two hours enjoying the fresh air on the balcony together with the Quirogas, Sanchez, Rojo, and Rossi and his wife. Since I had my guitar with me and it was such a lovely night, I ended up inviting Juan de Dios to go out and give a serenade with me. The only person asking whom we were going to serenade was Mme. Rossi. I said we would sing to just about anyone. We went out but really could not decide whom to awaken with our songs, whom to bother. The only one we could find who was worthy of our songs was our buddy Rufino.

We began to sing at his house, playing with both guitars, and before we had finished the second verse we were surrounded by a multitude of people, Yanks more than anyone else. They thanked us and invited us to have a drink with them, but we refused because it was already pretty late.

That is about how Stockton nights are spent.

Today Mme. Rossi invited me for supper, and when I refused she asked whether or not I feared dishonor by dining with her. I said, "If that was the reason, my brother would not dine with you either."

Since we were alone at last, *she told me everything, she avowed everything.*[80] Well, *my love's confession is received. . . . Oh, I am happy now and cannot refuse her invitation to dine. Oh, she is very pretty indeed.*[81]

TUESDAY, 27 AUGUST

The two fire-fighting brigades came out with their men to do exercises. We have spent a very amusing afternoon watching the dexterity of the firemen and laughing at all the people who got wet. One group of them was on the wharf and started the fire pump, aiming their hoses at the men who were on another corner more than 40 yards away. At that distance the strength of the pump carries the water very high. It looks like we are safe from fires.

The post office just opened today. I have never seen one so lavish and well appointed. I find it hard to compare it to any other, because not even the post office in San Francisco is as good as this one. I feel this urge all the time to go to my mailbox so as to be able to observe the elegance, the tidiness, the order, and the goodwill of the people who work there. I wonder when the day will come when we will have places like this one in South America.

STOCKTON, SUNDAY, 1 SEPTEMBER 1850

Today is the day of St. Gilles, but it is no different from any other, except perhaps for the fact that it is even hotter. It is now ten o'clock in the morning. At nine we went to eat at the hotel, and from there Samuel, Abel, and I went to the Protestant church so as not to lose the habit of going to church, no matter what faith it was. We have just returned. In church we only saw women and young girls in their bonnets, with their Bibles in hand but looking elsewhere. The gentlemen were sitting around comfortably reading the newspaper while the priest was saying mass. The minister was the last one to arrive and came in on the arm of his wife, who left him at the foot of the altar, from whence he went up and began mass by reading from the Scriptures.

MONDAY, 2 SEPTEMBER

Today at four in the afternoon, Madame Rossi embarked with her husband for San Francisco. For a number of reasons, over the past three days I have not been able to look at her or speak with her. She asked me why, and I told her that it really wasn't anything at all. According to my brother, she thought I was angry with her and that was why I had not spoken to her. Anyway, as she was getting aboard the boat she asked my forgiveness several times over and was very moved as she held onto my arm, which was holding her up. I pretended not to understand her. She went into the ladies' room and closed the door. She was carrying her child with her and with tears in her eyes said to the little one, "Ask the gentleman for forgiveness for your mother." I could no longer keep from kissing her, and then suddenly she was gone and all was forgotten.[82]

WEDNESDAY, 4 SEPTEMBER

I got up very early today so as to enjoy the coolness of dawn and went out to take a walk. Instinctively I headed east because that is where the best shops are. I walked for about two miles without really thinking how far it was. As I was being distracted by people milking cows at the different dairies, all of a sudden I came upon a cemetery that I had never seen before. I was startled, and without really noticing, a feeling of sadness came over me because all along I had been on my way to visit the dead.

There were a multitude of crosses, but only the tombs of the Mexicans have them. All the rest are in their graves, which are very well appointed, considering that they have been improvised. All of the tombs of the Americans have nice epitaphs written in large and beautiful letters. The funny thing is that there was only one grave of someone over fifty years of age; all the rest were for people between twenty-five and thirty, in the prime of their lives. Instead of coming back saddened, down deep I was content with that sweet conformity a Christian feels whenever he ponders death.

THURSDAY, 5 SEPTEMBER. *The horse race*

Stockton seems like a great city, especially if you judge by the noise its inhabitants make when they come out in the evening to enjoy the cool air. This afternoon the streets were filled with beautiful carriages with well-dressed men accompanied by lovely ladies.

Today Samuel, Sparrow, and I went out for a horse ride. We went to the same place where a month ago (3 August) a horse of Sparrow raced. I was not there at that famous race because that was they day I was close to death from my illness, though nearly everyone else in Stockton was. The race was supposed to be for 15,000 pesos each, though Sparrow and Navarro only bet 3,000. Two jockeys ran the mile race. From the very start, Sparrow's horse raced ahead amid the hurrahs and shouts given to the participants. Going over that race kept us there until nightfall.

SATURDAY, 7 SEPTEMBER

Samuel went to San Francisco and has written saying that our mailbox is filled with cobwebs rather than letters. According to him, two of the strongest banks in San Francisco, the Nagle and the King and Wm., have gone under. Samuel says that so far people have withdrawn some 200,000 pesos from the bank. Actually, the bank was looking like the palace of Louis XVI during the French Revolution!!

SUNDAY, 9 SEPTEMBER

In Stockton all business activity appears to have come to a halt. The only thing moving are the rents people get on their property. Sparrow and Navarro's, one of the most beautiful, lavish, and well-situated houses in all of Stockton, is filled with tenants, and Sparrow has had to give up his room to yet another tenant. His house has the best views of any in town. One side faces the lake, and the other one looks out onto the southern part of the town. The main facade looks out over the lake, and you can see the movement of ships as far as a mile away. From his balcony you can see the ships move about the lake and can even hear the shouts of the ships' captains. The entire house is lavishly wallpapered, and the floors of the rooms are covered with red carpets, which go very well together with the velvet and green wallpaper on the walls. The house is very lively because of all of its tenants and because of the theater orchestra staying in one of the rooms on the second floor just across from ours.

SATURDAY, 15 SEPTEMBER

There is news from San Francisco. They are placing wooden planks on the sidewalks of the city so that this winter there will be no mud at all. All of the hotels are once again at the peak of their importance, and the police have allowed musicians in all of them. So San Francisco is again looking like the San Francisco of old. As time goes by, people are beginning to forget the fires, that is, until the next time fire comes when they least expect it.

A petition has also been subscribed by all the merchants here to get the sidewalks and streets ready for winter, much as San Francisco is doing. The amount of activity shown by Stockton is really admirable, and its growth by leaps and bounds in every way is most striking. Despite the fact that business is very slow, there is a new and lavish house going up just about every day, almost as though there was as much gold now as there was last year about this time.

Monday, 16 September

This past week an American woman, Miss Sheldon, died, and her death has caused about as much bustle as the death of President Taylor of the United States. The female sex around here sure has lots of value. Every day men die, and nothing is done for them, and the newspapers say nothing of their deaths. The dead young lady, on the other hand, is carried in a casket placed on a wagon drawn by black horses led by elegant young men and followed by just about everyone in town.

Stockton, 17 September

Dawn today was lovely, but now it looks as though it is going to be quite hot. It is half past eight in the morning. The carts with the day's supplies are going back and forth, ringing their immense bells to remind the sleepy merchants that there is still time to deliver them their bread, their milk, the vegetables, etc., etc. The bells of the hotels, especially those of the Chinese Hotel, the loudest of all, are also ringing to call their residents. On both sides of the lake there are multitudes of people unloading cargo from ships and receiving steamboats as they come up to the docks. I can see loads of movement in the streets and the lake of Stockton, despite the fact that it is still a little early.

It is eleven at night, and I have just returned from the Ainzas' home. They are two Mexican friends I have here in Stockton. I stayed longer than I had intended and only left after having tea. It was a lovely night with the moon lighting things up as though it was daytime. There is a cool breeze blowing that softens the heat left from the day. There is a great silence reigning in Stockton. You can only hear the applause of those coming from the theater.

I have just gone by the theater on the peninsula, and they are showing more *tableaux vivants*. Once again the exhibition of naked women!

WEDNESDAY, 18 SEPTEMBER

The steamboats *Sagamore* and *Dorado* have just come in with the fatal news of the fourth fire in San Francisco. Samuel did not write about it, but I have the *Herald* and the *Stockton Extra,* which give details about the fire. This is now the fourth time that San Francisco has been ravaged by fire, and the only explanation is that the town has been damned by God. The fire began at eight o'clock in the morning on Jackson Street in a house called the Philadelphia House, between Kearney and Dupont. The fire progressed rapidly before the fire pumps could arrive, though at least they prevented the fire from consuming other city blocks nearby. An entire square block was razed, and the losses amount to at least $500,000. Mr. Rossi, who was there, is on the list of those who lost property. It is the fourth time his house has been burned.

It is now half past eleven at night. At sunset I again went to the Ainzas' house. Hoping to give me a big surprise, they brought out *El Democrata,* a newspaper from Mexico, in order to show me a poem by a fellow countryman of mine against Rosas that was "the best we have seen so far." At the very outset I realized that it was the great poem by Marmol against Rosas on the 25th of May. We discussed all of this until about eight, when they invited me to go to the theater with them. I excused myself, saying that I had already seen the *tableaux vivants* in San Francisco, though their insistence was such that I could not refuse.

The company is made up of seven women chosen from among the most beautiful in order to represent, totally naked, a thousand scenes from mythology. There is nothing more artistic than the marvelous perfection represented by these women in the statues, the goddesses, and everything else we could see last night. It is indeed surprising to observe that all the nudity does not bring to one's sight or thoughts any sign of obscenity, but rather the beauty of divine art carried to its pinnacle of perfection. Venus entering her bath accompanied by the Graces was a wonderful scene! I cannot imagine what the Venus of mythology could have had on the young Venus entering the bath completely naked in the theater tonight! I kept the program because it might be interesting to look at it later on.

We left the theater, and since the night was so lovely we took a stroll. We went by Dr. Craig's place, and they urged us to enter. Mariquita was the first one to speak to me about the tyranny of my windows, which had been shut for three days, and about my absence. . . .[83] I never thought that these few minutes of conversation would make me so happy. I feel satisfied about everything now.[84]

THURSDAY, 19 SEPTEMBER

I still cannot get out of my mind what I saw last night at the theater. More than the *tableaux vivants* themselves, I cannot help but be surprised by the insolence of the American character in all public acts, even on the most formal occasions. Last night the theater was full, but each person spoke and said his own particular obscenities a propos of the scenes as though he were immersed in a conversation with three or four friends. After this, there was also whistling, foot stomping, shouts, barking, and braying in their own way in order to show their enthusiasm and applause for the artists. Few nations are as brutal and insolent as the Americans are.

Two women from the Branch Hotel who were dressed up last night as men were also at the show, and they shouted a thousand obscenities and applauded the artists on stage just like the rest. As we were leaving the theater, I was walking down the staircase with Ainza when I saw one of those women fall down the stairs and take three or four men with her. They rolled down like a ball until they hit their heads in the street, amid all the hurrahs and applause from the others, as though they had done it just to be funny. I was also pushed by one of those tumbling down the stairs but was able to grab onto the banister. Another one took Ainza's poor uncle with him, and he nearly killed himself from the bad fall.

WEDNESDAY, 25 SEPTEMBER

We have had to come back up to the mines. On our way to Jesus Maria today we came upon a horrible spectacle. Moyano and I were immersed in a good conversation when we ran across the bodies of men who had been murdered moments before. The blood was still flowing, and their bodies were twitching in their final agony. My Lord, what a horrible scene! The murderers must have been pretty close by. What were we to do? I only had my knife, and Moyano had no weapons at all. I do not want to die that way, even though I would sure sell my life and the gold I was carrying at a very high price.[85]

CALAVERAS, NEAR THE CHILEAN PLACER, THURSDAY, 26 SEPTEMBER

It must have been two o'clock in the afternoon when I reached this placer, after spending five or six hours in search of Rodriguez, whom I came to meet here.[86] Yesterday, after finding the bodies of those poor devils, Moyano found someone to accompany us to Jesus Maria, and I wandered around until I found the placer where Rodriguez was working. He is in good health.

I can hardly believe how close I was yesterday once again to the knives of the murderers. Every time I think of what we had before us for a few minutes, my entire body trembles. One of the bodies appeared to be a Chinese man, and he had a wide wound on his forehead that must have been caused by the blow of a stick or some club, judging from the damage to the head. He was still moving his leg, and his body was entirely covered with the blood he had lost in his convulsions. The other one was completely dead; his brains had been blown out by a bullet. He appeared to have rolled over a couple of times and was lying there dead, with his face in the dirt. It was about the most horrible murder I have seen since coming to California.

CALAVERAS, FRIDAY, 27 SEPTEMBER

It is eight o'clock in the morning, and I just arrived from Francisco Estuardo's, where I was invited to have some chocolate. There are two small inns, and each of them has live music that is played all day and all night. That is where some Mexicans love to dance the jarabe.

It is half past five in the afternoon, and the sun just set. There is a great multitude of people gathered in the little plaza like when crowds are demanding an execution. At noon I was invited by the judge to be a member of the jury to judge a Mexican who robbed $1,600 yesterday. I refused under the pretext that I was balancing the books of our operation. Well, the jury was formed, and the prisoner was tried. Now it is half past five, and the five Americans just came out of the judge's house to take the prisoner to the gallows. He took off his serape and his breeches, etc., and he is walking amid the members of the jury with a roll of rope under his arm that is going to be used to hang him. The fatal noose has already been placed around his neck. More than 200 men are following the jury out to a nearby forest in order to witness the execution as I am writing this account in my notebook for my diary. It is nearly dark now, and I cannot see anything else.

It is eight o'clock at night, and I have just come up to the little square, which is vibrating with people dancing and drinking in different taverns.

There is a large number of people at the hotel who are dancing to the music as they let out ferocious shouts. Who could believe it?! I am a scrupulous young man, and I have only gone to see this so that I could write about it. But there the only thing I could think about was my past life. I wonder if anyone is thinking about me right now?

SATURDAY, 28 SEPTEMBER

It is six o'clock in the morning, and I have saddled my mule in order to leave for Stockton, against the advice of Rodriguez and other friends who told me not to go alone. Yesterday a friend arrived from Mokelumne Hill and said he came across a murdered Chilean along the way and that it took them a lot of work to bury him. That means that all the roads are crawling with bandits. What am I to do? I have no choice but to leave now, and there is nothing I can do about it. May God help me! The price for my life will be high, and I swear upon my mother that many bandits will die first if they really want to murder me.

It is half past two in the afternoon, and I just reached Stockton safe and sound, thanks be to God. Just before I arrived they brought in on a cart the body of a man who had been attacked some ten miles from here. The man is now in his home and is still breathing. The doctors are trying to restore life to him. I was carrying four or five pounds of gold with me.

SUNDAY, 29 SEPTEMBER

Last night I was near the window of my love. I heard her speaking and I was near her without her knowledge. Perhaps she did not know that I had arrived. I made my first visit to her, and she will pay me very well with her kindness.[87]

STOCKTON, MONDAY, 30 SEPTEMBER

The day before yesterday I arrived from the mines after a trip of eight days. While I was there, there was almost one death or murder per day. The animosity toward foreigners in the mines is no longer as bad as it was before, but many Americans have turned into bandits, and they will murder travelers for no reason at all.

The mines are about as always; some men get loads of gold, and others don't get hardly anything at all. This makes some people complain about the mines, while others seem to be very happy. Nevertheless, the shortages of gold are more noticeable now than they were before. The daily wage for workers is about three pesos, which is too high for the placers.

SATURDAY, 5 OCTOBER 1850

I suppose that by now I have forgotten all those little things demanded of the young by social etiquette. It has been two years since I last had any dealings with young ladies or was able to dance or to be anywhere where etiquette was demanded. Here it is important to remember that I am young, and just two years ago I was about the best-dressed and most presumptuous lad of all. Now I no longer know what it is that society calls social address. Next Wednesday I would have had to remember all of this because Miss Dickinson is getting married. She is one of the richest young women in California and the only one in Stockton. Thank God I will not be here then. Otherwise I would have been hard put to avoid the dance at the wedding party. We shall see what there is to do in San Francisco on Wednesday.

SUNDAY, 6 OCTOBER

It is half past eight in the morning. More than twenty bells, some French, some Chinese, some American, are ringing at once, making a confusing and ill-defined noise. Anyone who does not know why they are ringing might think that it was a number of churches calling the faithful to worship. In fact it is just the opposite. Each one of these bells is beckoning its members, whether it is to workers at a company or merchants at the inn or the gamblers at the hotel or lovers of good coffee. The bell of the Chinese inn is the loudest of all. What a shame that none of these bells is calling the Catholics to worship at church!

It is half past ten at night, and I just returned from Dr. Craig's house. I was there to ask if he needed something from San Francisco. She asked me to think of her, and she promised to think of me. My Lord, what a strange and surprising thing for me, and yet I feel pretty happy.[88]

SAN FRANCISCO, TUESDAY, 8 OCTOBER

I arrived in San Francisco, which was almost totally unrecognizable. All of its streets have been covered with planks of wood, almost as though they were the dance floor of an exclusive salon. Hills as high as 15 ft. that used to disrupt traffic on many streets have entirely disappeared as though by magic, and now streets are almost completely level, and inclines are gradual. The hill at Clark Point was cut in half to make way for a new street. Jackson Street was raised twelve feet, just like all of its houses, and now is at the same level as other streets in the city. All of the streets have been covered with planks, and this winter there will be no mud in San Francisco. These public works will cost 1.2 million pesos and will be paid by the government and by the citizens in equal parts. Here I have seen done what they told me about China when I was a child, that the entire country was paved in porcelain. According to this tale, San Francisco does not have a better floor than China!

WEDNESDAY, 9 OCTOBER

Yesterday the steamship *Carolina* came in with fourteen passengers who had died on the trip from Panama to San Francisco. All of the passengers had died from cholera, which is now wreaking havoc in Mexico and Panama. Yet they have not made the ship undergo quarantine here, even though it has aboard the scourge that God uses to avenge the sins of humanity. It is as though God had hidden from the knowledge of doctors the cures for this disease, as though he wanted to use it for his just revenge.

There are now five beautiful piers in San Francisco, and the middle one is five blocks long. Ships can tie up to these docks now with great ease even when they are very large. These wharves grow longer every day, and they work on them all the time. These works must cost as much as putting planks down all over town. The surprising thing is just how fast the steam engines are able to raise immense posts that are the foundation of the docks. Each time the machine hammers a post, with the force of twenty or thirty hundredweight, the post goes into the floor of the bay another fifteen feet. This is repeated over and over again, almost as quickly as I can tell about it.

THURSDAY, 10 OCTOBER

The newspapers today say that cholera is now in the city. Three people who died from the disease were buried yesterday, and today there was another death. With the large population living in San Francisco, this promises to be horrible. They also say that there has been a case of cholera in Stockton in the house of Sparrow and Navarro. Poor Samuel wrote me yesterday and did not say anything about this. Yet Deitton, who just came in, told me that he witnessed the case of cholera in the house and that the victim was a friend of his who was taking a stroll in the morning and at two was on his deathbed. Only five hours, my Lord! May God's will be done. I just wrote people in Chile and have not mentioned a word about the danger to our lives over here. Our friend Camilo Soruco died of cholera in Panama, and he did not last even six hours. May God have mercy on the persons who need us in this world.

SAN FRANCISCO, SATURDAY, 12 OCTOBER

Yesterday there was still no news from Samuel. I was desperately anxious. Around noon I went to Emilio's house. There I met my buddy Rufino, who said as soon as he saw me, "The other day you got a letter for me from the steamboat and did not deliver it until much later, and this time I have played the same game with you and have held the letter that arrived for you on the *Sagamore* until just now." "Damn," I said to him "you should not play that way with the peace and tranquillity of a man in these circumstances."

The letter was from Samuel. In it he told me about the death of the person who fell ill the day before yesterday in his house and who all the newspapers said had cholera. Samuel said that he only lasted six hours. Even though everyone says he had cholera, he prayed to God that it wasn't true. He described the horrible scene of spending the entire night separated by only a wall from a man dying of cholera.

MONDAY, 14 OCTOBER

Today another letter arrived from Samuel, and he is well. He says the cholera there is not as bad as they had thought.

TUESDAY, 22 OCTOBER

In San Francisco on the 9th, I was introduced to the niece of Rosas, Emilia Mansilla de Tucksbury.[89] I have never seen a young lady so entirely polite and cultured. During my visit, at times we had to speak in English or French as was required by different people who came in. She speaks both languages well and is both pretty and elegant. She learned from a friend of hers that I wanted to be introduced to her, and without any special ceremony she went to Miss Caddis's house where I was and said to me:

"I have heard that you wanted to be introduced to me. The fact that you are a fellow countryman and the desire I already had to meet you have made me disregard all possible etiquette."

What a nice woman! And I know why she wanted to meet me: in Buenos Aires she was the intimate and inseparable friend of my cousins. This famous young lady made both Manuelita and the sister of Rosas very jealous because of the fact that it was clear that she was preferred by the young men from Buenos Aires, the emissaries and nobles from Europe, and all the men at Rosas's court. She is truly worthy of being loved, because she is even impartial with respect to the crimes of her uncle, the dictator Rosas.

THURSDAY, 24 OCTOBER

The steamboats just came in. The number of deaths from cholera is going down. In Sacramento, however, as many as fifty persons per day are dying from the disease. The newspapers are saying that as much as ten percent of the population of Mexico has died from cholera. Rumors have it that yesterday and today there were deaths from cholera here as well, though I have not seen any.

FRIDAY, 25 OCTOBER

Seven or eight days ago, a Jesuit father came by here with the idea of setting up a Catholic church.[90] I knew that he was coming with big problems, mostly because he only knew French when around here it was going to be a church for English and Spanish speakers. I went to seek him out and explained to him that the purpose of my visit was to translate for him whatever he wanted or needed in order to help him out. I also volunteered to see Mr. Weber so that he might give some land for the church. He was so grateful that he embraced me in tears and called me a brother in Jesus Christ. Right away he asked me from what region of France I came from, but I told him that I was not French but Argentinean. "You speak French so well that I might indeed have been mistaken," he said. By Sunday we will have heard mass, the very first one in Stockton! What a wonderful thing! We will at last be able to die Catholics if and when that cholera finally comes to get us.

SATURDAY, 26 OCTOBER

A few days ago in San Francisco a little adventure happened to me that I do not want to forget. On the ninth, after spending some time at Mrs. Eugenia Caddis's house, I retired early to my room at half past nine. I read *La guerre des femmes* until about ten, when I blew out the candle thinking that I was ready to go to sleep. I was wrong, because it was hard to get to sleep. From there I could hear the shouts of the drunkards, the noises of the carriages outside, etc. At last everything seemed silent, when all of a sudden I heard steps on the staircase and whispering like that of thieves or lovers. I thought it might be my friend who still had not come in. It should be remembered that my room was only separated from his by a very thin wall. I was attentive, listening carefully. Then I heard them coming to the door of my room on tiptoe. I was grabbing for my knife when a very familiar voice said "Navarro." I kept quiet to see just where things would end up, and then I listened to what they said.

"He still hasn't come in, or he is already asleep."

I heard no more. Soon they opened the door to the other room, and I could hear them close it after the steps of a couple of persons. I could hear a female voice chuckling, and I recognized the cute and flirtatious laugh of a young woman. I went up to the wall and put my ear up to it in order to hear the little lies and promises that lovers exchange. What a world! My poor friend does not know that I have really got him now, that I know his secret as well as he does, and that I have heard what he said. Yet it is also true that only I will know it. I finally got cold and went back to bed, where I was awakened all the time by damned laughs of that little girl, poor thing. Well, it looks like those who think they are equal to me are in fact less than I am. I can see that after what came out last night. He finally has something to be ashamed about.

SUNDAY, 27 OCTOBER

Today at half past ten we had our mass. The priest gave a lovely sermon in French. What a wise and easygoing man this priest is. The more I get to know him, the more I recognize his merit and ability. He comes by our house almost every day. Thanks be to God that we finally have mass on Sundays here.

MONDAY, 28 OCTOBER

The Jesuit priest asked me today to accompany him to some houses as an interpreter, because he wanted to tell Stockton Catholics about the new church. Our visit was successful, and right away we were able to collect $100 in alms. As we were going by Ricorder's house, a woman came out begging me to tell the father to go and absolve her mother, who was dying of cholera. Father left but still has not returned. Who knows what happened.

STOCKTON, TUESDAY, 29 OCTOBER

Just like yesterday, once again today I accompanied the Catholic priest on his visit to a number of homes in Stockton. He approaches all Christians, no matter what their state or profession. This morning we left the Robinson warehouse and were going down the street when we passed a house.[91] The priest stopped and said to me in French, "Why don't we enter here?"

"My father," I told him, "this is not a good house."

"Are there bad people here?"

"No, but it is a house of women. . . ."

"So much the better. In all countries it is the women who are most charitable and religious, or at least they pretend to be so."

In order to put him straight, I said, "But no, my father, this is a brothel, where all kinds of lost women gather and sell their honor in order to survive."

"That is even better. I am delighted to know that. If the shepherd only cares for the sheep that remain in his flock and abandons to the wolves the ones who have gone astray, he would not be a good shepherd. *Allons mon cher, entrons.*"

"Father, I have never entered one of those houses in my life, I confess to you upon my honor. Even the air you breathe in there should be avoided."

"We are going to do a good deed, and the person who is working for the good has nothing to fear." We entered, and he greeted everyone with the greatest pleasantness possible, speaking to them through me. I shall always remember this scene. The women gave the priest $50 in all.

WEDNESDAY, 30 OCTOBER

My Lord, what a terrible tragedy!!! A few days ago the eight steamboats operating out of Stockton started to compete and lower their fares, at least $2 from the normal $18 and $25. Others went further still. The *Sagamore* placed an add in the newspaper, saying that it would pay $1 plus food to any man who embarked to go to San Francisco. Yesterday it left here with more than 200 passengers on board bound for San Francisco. This morning I was on the dock watching the *San Joaquin* arrive when even before it had tied up someone aboard shouted "The *Sagamore* blew up yesterday as it was leaving, and more than 100 men aboard have drowned." My God, the news is true, and all of the passengers told stories of the fatal accident. It is still hard to believe this tragedy took place. How many times have I taken this steamboat to and from San Francisco? The last time was just a few days ago. I feel like I escaped again, just as though you have not been destined to die for one reason or another. But in compensation, the second captain, our intimate friend Charles, did indeed die. It is a horrible thought.[92]

THURSDAY, 31 OCTOBER

We are still in a state of shock at the news we got yesterday. Hearing how the bodies of those on board were dismembered sends shivers through all of us. A number of people were torn into three or four pieces, and arms and legs have been found a block away. The ones who did not die in the explosion ended up drowning. It is really horrible to hear about the disasters of this explosion, because it is the first time it has happened in California. Our poor young friend Charles. He was so full of projects and expectations, already rich, and with something that made him love life so much in this world, and now in eternity.

SATURDAY, 2 NOVEMBER 1850

May God be thanked a thousand times over!! We have before us the *Stockton Journal*, which gives details of the explosion on the *Sagamore*, and it says that our friend Charles escaped in the most supernatural and incredible way and is alive and well in San Francisco. And to think that I had him dead and buried days ago! It is truly incredible. I have kept the newspaper so that people can read again later on all the details it gives of the miraculous salvation of our friend. This is really much more than surprising.

SONORA, SATURDAY, 9 NOVEMBER

Several days ago I had to set out for the mines again and make the tour of several placers. Last night I arrived here in Sonora, a city whose houses hardly pale in comparison to those of Stockton. This town is very pretty, with its trees in the middle of the streets and with the gold works right in the patios of the houses themselves. It would be hard to find a more fanciful sort of layout. The court of justice has already been set up here and occupies a nice building. There are three or four beautiful hotels, and occupancy is high in all of them. They also have music, but it is not as good as in Stockton. The best hotel belongs to our friend and compatriot Elordi.

SUNDAY, 10 NOVEMBER

Sundays are beautiful and pretty curious as well in Sonora. All of the miners from the nearby areas come into town to spend the day and get supplies and other necessary items for the coming week. Today seems like a real fair here in Sonora. Gamblers are the ones who do most business. By the way, I ran into Cupertino, who has taken to gambling in order to survive. It hurts me greatly to see how he derives satisfaction from doing what his own conscience dictates against. If I had to earn my living this way, I think I would contemplate suicide. Yet it is also true that nobody knows how much Cupertino has had to suffer and all the sacrifices he has made before finally being forced to go to the gambling table. Those of us who are far from desperation and misery can afford to have more scruples than those strictly required of a man of honor. But, my Lord, to die of starvation! And that is what would have happened to Cupertino had he not gotten into gambling.

SONORA, MONDAY, 11 NOVEMBER

Last night Cupertino introduced me to Madame Amelia Mezzara, the loveliest lady in Sonora. She is really very pretty, and she sings quite well. Accompanied on the piano, she sang one of the loveliest arias I have ever heard, and she also made exaggerated compliments when she heard me play. She said to Cupertino, *"Je vais parler comme si votre cousin Navarro en eusset pas ici, et je dis qui il me parait parfaitement bien et que sur tout est il un joli garzon sur ma parole."*[93] Poor Cupertino naturally did not understand anything at all, but I thanked her for her honesty and generosity. It is true that the poor guy does not understand or speak French, but love knows all languages, and Cupertino is happy where a lover can be happy.

TUESDAY, 12 NOVEMBER

It is six o'clock in the morning, and I will be leaving pretty soon for Calaveras. Last night I was invited to have dinner at the house of Madame Amelia Mezzara. We were having a very pleasant time until everything was disturbed by an American who is supposed to be both the most valiant and the most mischievous person around. He called at the door and wanted to come in and have a drink, but the madame said that she would not let him in. He became furious and insulting and said such shameless things that I was about to go out. He told Mrs. Mezzara that she was a . . . I wanted to go outside, but her husband prevented me. The insults came again, and this time I finally went out with Cupertino despite everything. Cupertino had his pistol, and I got mine from the room, because this Villefort fellow had his gun in his hands and was saying that he would kill the first person to come out and then would do the same with the lady. We finally went out . . . and Villefort shook our hands, saying that he had nothing against us. We had a very difficult time convincing him not to shoot his six bullets at the door. Finally, he invited us to have dinner even though it was two o'clock in the morning, but we had to accept so as not to upset him again. We went to a hotel, where the owner served us a dinner, and the revelry did not end until dawn.

TUESDAY, 19 NOVEMBER

Well, well, I was completely mistaken yesterday in thinking that the few clouds would not bring water with them. Last night at about two o'clock in the morning I could hear it sprinkling outside. Now it is noon, and it continues to rain, though not very much. The first rains of the winter of 1850 have finally arrived. What a difference from last year!

You can see the people of Stockton with their trousers stuck into their boots in order to avoid the splashing mud. You can also see those darn boots with six soles that seem (and are) so inelegant in the summer but are so good to keep the moisture and the mud out during the winter. Am I destined to wear these boots instead of the elegant patent leather galoshes of Chile? I do not think so. We shall see how much need there is.

Now that I think of it, today is the anniversary of the great earthquake that ruined Valparaíso in 1822. Up here our winter has come in on the best possible footing.

WEDNESDAY, 20 NOVEMBER. *The* Elisea

Today we have received letters from Chile. Actually I say "we," but in fact it is Samuel who received the letters. These letters bring with them the news that the *Elisea* reached Chile safely and happily on the 20th of September. The trip from San Francisco to Valparaíso took only fifty-seven days, a time hardly equaled by any other ship. The passengers made it there perfectly well, and during the entire trip there was not a single mishap. It is hard to imagine all the enthusiasm and happiness the arrival of the *Elisea* has caused among all of us. The fact is that she has made us shed the type of tears of joy that can only be expected on the happiest of occasions. Thank God, for I am content and happy at this moment. I may not be rich yet, but I am much happier than many rich people just because I am the owner of the *Elisea*.

SUNDAY, 24 NOVEMBER

After lunch Rojo and I went out, and, like good Catholics, we headed for church. When we arrived we discovered that the door was shut. Father Arnau is ill, and there will be no mass today. One of our main Sunday attractions has just vanished! What were we going to do on a Sunday? After all, praying at home alone is not quite the same as praying in church, where you can set such a good example for all of the young ladies? I guess we really have no choice in the matter.

MONDAY, 25 NOVEMBER

The steamboats have not yet arrived, even though it is after twelve. Maybe they too wanted to respect the day of rest and have put off their departure from San Francisco until this morning. No, I don't think so. Americans are much more merchants than religious persons, and they wouldn't waste ten cents on a religious event.[94]

Up until today there has been no rain for over a month to announce the coming of winter. Since then the days have been beautiful, but as cold as the loves of old women and as sad as the recollections of exiles.

WEDNESDAY, 27 NOVEMBER

The *Union* just arrived at the dock with the Mobile Guard of Paris, made up of 250 men, all dressed in uniforms with rifles of the light infantry.[95] They carry with them their cornets, their bags on their back, their lieutenants, their captains. It is as though they were actually on duty. The Americans could not help but admire all of this, because it really is an impressive corps and could do great damage if they really set to it.

THURSDAY, 28 NOVEMBER

It is noon, and you can hear the bugle of the French battalion as it marches off to the mines as though it was going to battle. They are all going in columns, eight deep, with their guns on their shoulders and their packs on their backs, moving with precision to the orders of their officer. It is as though I was seeing a battalion of Napoleon's guard. The Americans are going to have a bad time of it with these old soldiers from Algeria.

FRIDAY, 29 NOVEMBER

It is ten o'clock at night, and I just returned from taking a walk with Rojo. The human condition is really something! He leaves his house in search of something to distract him from the monotony of his life and the sadness of his thoughts, and anyone he runs into ends up being affected by the same sadness that affects him. We went to the El Dorado Hotel, and as soon as the musician saw that I was there, he said he was going to play selections from *Norma*. And it is true, he played *Norma* wonderfully. Yet every note was like the blow of a hammer to my heart, and every change in tone or beat sunk me into double sadness. I guess there is no other solution. The only way to really enjoy the visit to a garden or anything else is if you have a beautiful young woman on your arm with whom to share the beauty of life and of the flowers. Whenever you want to enjoy music freely, with no anxiety and no suffering, you must have a beautiful someone with whom to share a request, a reproach, a farewell, a word of love, or each heartfelt note of the sad aria. This is what I was missing as I was listening to *Norma,* and this is why I returned home sad and pensive when it was over. My Lord, who will I be sacrificing my life to, my youth, my aspirations! Who will be the one who repays me with an "I love you" for all my sufferings in California!!! Oh, I do fear that I may never even find that angel created by my fantasy because of the lack of real persons to think of.

SATURDAY, 30 NOVEMBER

Everything continues to be pretty quiet here in Stockton, with that type of tranquillity that characterizes cities that have grown accustomed to the daily bustle of life and accept alterations with a certain calm. The steamboats blow their whistles upon leaving, and I can see the *Dorado,* the *Corning,* the *Union,* the *Fashion,* and the *San Joaquin* from my balcony; each is spewing smoke from its engine rooms and announcing its impending departure for the traveler, who can hear it in the inns, hotels, cafes, and restaurants, mixed in along with all the other sounds of city life here. This is what Stockton is like on the 30th of November of 1850.

STOCKTON, SUNDAY, 1 DECEMBER 1850

Since Father Arnau is still ill today we have not had mass, much to my regret. As my exile in California has grown longer, I have become more religious and a better Catholic. After getting elegantly dressed this morning, as though I was on my way to some important ceremony, I went out with Rojo to take a walk after lunch. We crossed the bridge and stopped for a few minutes at a large watchmaker's shop, whose owner was intent on telling me that last night they had broken one of his shop windows in order to steal his wares but that he had alerted the neighboring shop owners with his shouts and had frightened the thief away. Later we went up El Dorado Street, which is always filled with people as though it was the county fair. We went into the hotel, and, as soon as he saw me, the musician played me the cavatina from *Ernani,* which was perfectly played. Later we went to the Placer Hotel, and the musicians were playing an American march that we didn't like at all. We also visited the lovely velvet-covered scene of the exaltation of Pius IX but did not stop for the following scene made up of twelve naked women taking a bath. That is when we left the Placer.

We went up Central Street toward the Stockton hospital, past two brothels and one dance house, with its sign "for tonight" placed on the door, and then up Mr. Dickinson's street. We were going to go in to play the piano a bit, but Dickinson and his girls had gone to church. In this way we wandered around that street until we reached the river without hardly even noticing what we were doing. There we walked along its banks for awhile and turned back.

Before getting back to Central Street we ran into three women, all elegantly dressed in silk. Since we thought we recognized them we decided to follow along. As they were entering their house we caught up to them and could see that it was Mrs. Peck, her sister, and the widow. We came back from our stroll a half an hour ago, and Mix, Rojo, and Samuel are now playing chess while I am writing. I do not know what will be of me for the rest of today.

It is now midnight. Stockton is asleep in some parts, and in others it is wide awake. The great lanterns of the Placer Hotel give off still more brilliant lights through their colored shades. The numerous lights of the Dorado are so bright that it looks like they just changed them. In the middle of the lake you can see another brightly lit population, made up of the sailing ships and six or eight steamboats not due to depart until Monday. You can see the lights through the numerous shutters drawn on each ship, making a lovely string of lit-up spots in the distance, kind of as though it was an immense palace on the day of the fete. This is what the night of December 1st is like in Stockton.

TUESDAY, 3 DECEMBER

Mr. Weber, a true millionaire, just married Miss Murphy, also a millionaire.[96] The poor little thing! They made her marry all those millions, and I can assure you that her heart is as virgin of emotions and lacking in love as that of a four- or five-year-old child. There is no doubt about it, the paleness of her face and the languor of her glances shout out that what she really wants is the love of a young man her age who would love her with all his soul without ever considering her millions. Oh well, that is how society seems to work.

WEDNESDAY, 4 DECEMBER

Yesterday Samuel was asked by Mr. Mix to be his best man at his wedding with Miss María Craig. Yesterday and today both the groom and his best man have been very busy with the preparations destined to bring about as soon as possible this happy day for the groom. "Blessed and praised be the night of the married man" are the words and verses of who knows what poet. Important news: the kind, style, and quality of the wedding and the dance we are going to have, the dresses to be cut, the bodies to be straightened out, dances and steps to be noted, new styles to be used, etc. All of this goes with the wedding. Thank goodness that my diary, ever hungry for things to observe, is going to have matters to deal with other than the monotony and sadness of my life. The wedding will take place on the twelfth, and we will see all the decorations, the wigs, the corsets, the Yankee dress coats, the English feet, the solo part in quadrilles, the waltzes, the polkas, etc., etc. My poor diary is going to go out of its mind with pleasure.

It is five o'clock in the afternoon, and Samuel just left with Mix for San Francisco. They have gone to get the groom his clothes for the big event, as well as other ridiculous things that I will probably end up mentioning later on. They almost missed the departure of the *Union* because we were all so involved in a chess game. When we reached the dock it had already pulled away. He was finally able to board.

THURSDAY, 12 DECEMBER

It is half past four in the afternoon, and Samuel and I just arrived at the Petit Hotel, where we had gone for lunch. I was surprised by the beauty and size of a gold nugget we saw there that was found by one of the French soldiers visiting here. It weighs twenty pounds and is of the purest gold I have seen. I could hardly believe it, but now, since I had it in my hand, like St. Thomas, I can no longer doubt. Last year some nuggets were found weighing as much as thirty-four pounds, but the gold was not as pure as this one. When I asked the soldier if he would sell it to me he replied that he was going to take it to San Francisco and show it to all his friends and then he was going to invite all of them, together with a certain Madame N. N., to drink to the health of Napoleon and then to that of the Republic.[97] I told him I thought it was an excellent way of using it.

An hour ago we received a letter from the groom, announcing that the ceremony would be tomorrow. But over at the Dickinson's house they said that a second announcement had come, saying that the ceremony would take place tonight. We left thinking that we too should have been told of the change, which is what ended up happening because I have the new announcement before me right now. There is no question but that the groom is in a hurry. We have all dressed in a hurry, and Samuel and Rojo have already left to pay a visit to the bride. I do not want to forget anything, nothing at all, that might pertain to this marriage, and I want to remember the clothes I am wearing tonight. My trousers are sky-blue, the suede vest is embroidered in white, the tie is turquoise blue, the tail coat is black, my watch and its chain (the presumptuous best man wore a new watch), a black hat, white gloves, etc. Well, it is time to be off. We shall see what happens and will speak of it tomorrow morning. The night is beautiful but cold.

Friday, 13 December

Today I shall steal a few minutes from the invitation I have to spend the day at the house of the newlyweds in order to take a moment, a few minutes, to jot down some notes that might be of interest to me later on as fragments of this drama in which I have been destined to play a leading role. Before all else, my diary should know what it has not known before, and that is that the woman who was betrothed last night to Mr. Mix is in love with me with all the fire and passion of a first love, with the madness of a fifteen-year-old, and with the poetry of the purest of loves.[98] Even though I have never said anything to her, I swear by the Lord that I was hoping to make her my fiancée.[99] Yet I never said once to her that I ever really loved her in so many words, despite all the things my actions may have stated with total clarity. I am aware that she does not love the man she is marrying and is giving in to pressure coming from someone. It is a mystery to me, but I shall find out in the coming days. We shall see. She is extremely distraught at having her will forced, perhaps by her father or by her unworthy groom. (A man who takes a women, still a child, who has told him a hundred times she does not love him is always unworthy.) I protest before God and all mankind in the name of her happiness against the violence of last night, against her enforced consent, and may whoever is responsible receive his just punishment for the crime perpetrated yesterday.

164

By the time I had arrived at the wedding party, the first quadrille had already been danced. Mariquita paled when she saw me in front of her with my hat in my hands, *ceremoniously* offering her my congratulations.[100] After having done that, I went with Agustin to one end of the hall. Yet wherever I went, there were her eyes, searching for mine. They were eyes filled with tears and filled with the most tender and sorrowful expression that a sacrificial victim can have. Since I was not dancing (I did not dance at all nor did I even move my feet the entire evening) and was trying to get away, several times she came near and said "And you, Mr. Navarro, aren't you even going to dance a waltz with me?" "No miss, many thanks." This invitation was repeated several times, but I was more stubborn than anyone else and was even less willing to give in, and so I stood there next to the door of the second hall with my arms crossed. Nobody could have seen envy in my face because, my Lord, I am too proud to envy anyone. Besides, what reason for envy could there be in a man like myself, who is the first one she loves, before God and the world, no matter how much he may take possession of her body? And wouldn't I have been a hundred times before the groom in this position if I had not wanted to react to her entreaties and agony in silence? No, in my face it was not envy that could be seen but rather an expression of protest against this violation, the expression of foreboding for this immense error apparently celebrated happily by all, but which for three of us present is so terribly unfortunate. I was the only one there who did not take part in anything. Like an automaton, I watched the dances, the men, the girls, all of them, without showing for a single moment any pleasure or any sadness or any willingness to take part in the party.

Later on everyone went out to dance quadrilles, and since Mrs. Clements, her bridesmaid, was sitting alone on the sofa, I sat down next to her. By chance or by design, Mariquita came with her dance partner right in front of me. With her arms dangling down along her body and her hands intertwined, her head resting on her right shoulder, pale, and with an expression of the greatest agony, she looked to me more like the statue of sorrow than the bride and queen of the entire party. As long as I live I shall never forget these moments in which she looked at me from that position as though she was begging for forgiveness and for compassion. That sadness revealed all of the terrible mystery of this marriage within me. Madame Clements noticed the afflicted and doleful attitudes present in Mariquita's sorrowful looks at me. Turning to me, she started the following dialogue in French with me.

"What does this mean, Mr. Navarro? What is the matter with Mariquita? Why is she so sad, so pale, ashen when she looks at you?"

"I am sorry, Madame. Perhaps all of this that you think and notice does not exist at all, and so perhaps you are wrong."

"No, Mr. Navarro. She is suffering, I am quite certain of that."[101]

Later, before the quadrilles had finished, seeing once again the semblance of Mariquita, who was evidently doing little to hide what she felt from the people gathered there, Madame Clements once again said to me in French, "Mr. Navarro, there you have Mariquita, a young girl of sixteen years of age who is bidding farewell to the world and whose face and demeanor are proclaiming this to anyone who will listen." What a tremendous prophecy, my God. I shall remember it forever, and I shall weep for her as Jeremiah did at his own prophecy of the ruin of the Holy City.

An hour later all of the guests had gone into the banquet room, where the dinner was splendid and lasted a long time. Only I was not there, only I, who was the closest friend of the household. Oh no, I could not authorize with any single act of mine this iniquitous farce, where the happiness of one of the creatures most deserving of happiness is bandied about. Three or four times the groom himself and Mariquita came to complain of my stubbornness in not wanting to accept anything, but it was all in vain. I entered and left with the same ceremoniousness in my words and actions. That is how the wedding night passed. That is how the night passed, which will eventually decide if it was one of happy or unhappy memory. That is the way the drama in which fate gave me a role to play ended. There are bad omens in this entire affair, among whose mysteries some crime has been perpetrated. May heaven not have this crime punished later on. If it does, it will fall upon the head of he who committed the crime, and the regrets and repentance will come later on. We shall see what time says and what becomes of this marriage held on the 12th of December of 1851.

STOCKTON, TUESDAY, 17 DECEMBER

While we were eating this afternoon at the Petit Hotel, we heard a great ruckus coming from the front door. There we saw about fifty men gathering around an American wagon bigger than a house that had stopped at the hotel to get its last supplies on its way to the mines. As I said, there was lots of noise and a crowd of people all around the wagon. Despite our curiosity, we stayed at our table until the maître d' came in and told us that all the commotion was about the *nuns* from the Branch Hotel, who were going to the mines. Through the windows of the hotel I could see that divine and incomparable face of Judith, who has caused so much admiration in everyone because of her beauty. What a shame it is, how much it pains me, to see a woman as beautiful as she is, perhaps the most beautiful woman I have ever seen in my life, turned into little more than a whore who sells her honor to the highest bidder, to both the rich and the poor at the same time. He who sets the course of things in this world must know the reason why he made a whore of such surprising beauty. How many disconsolate men might she have left behind her had this woman of angelic beauty also had the honor of her sex, the modesty of a young lady, and the respectful continence of a married woman? My Lord, I can only imagine how many men would have gone crazy over her and how many crimes and abuses would have been committed because of her! Now, however, everyone is her owner. And envy and jealously, which have caused so much harm in the world, can have no place in her. Now she is not the forbidden fruit to excite the greatest greed among men. Rather, everyone sees her, and if he wants her, he possesses her, and if not, he pays her no heed. I might have been the first to go crazy over her had her soul been like her body, but the poor thing right now only inspires in me a pity bordering on contempt.

FRIDAY, 20 DECEMBER

Last night about ten o'clock there was a great noise of the strangest and most beautiful instruments you can imagine. The Chinese bells, which seem able to awaken the dead, were ringing like crazy, as were bugles and a thousand and one bells from the wagons of suppliers, the sounds of hammers, and a thousand other instruments I do not know. Played all at the same time, these instruments made a noise that is impossible to compare with any other. If you add to that the shouts of 100 or more men, you can get some idea of what this noise was really like. I heard all this, but I had no idea what it was all about, until Samuel told me that it was a serenade given by all the Stocktonian rogues for the marriage of a young man with an old woman seventy or more years old. This is a custom in the United States, and when the disproportionate couple tries to free itself from ridicule, it has to give 200 or 300 pesos, depending on how much money they have, to the members of this society, who then turn it over to the orphans' home. The police have nothing to do with this entire ritual.

MONDAY, 23 DECEMBER

Today at noon we went to show the painting of Stockton to our friends Morales and Mix. Mr. Cresi told us that unfortunately it had already been boxed for shipping. We were disappointed that they could not see it, because it is really a magnificent painting. It is eighteen feet high and twenty-two feet long. It is as lovely as a painting can be and shows a charming panoramic view of Stockton divided by the river, with its sailing vessels and steamships, etc. In it you can see each and every house with its name and exact color.

WEDNESDAY, 25 DECEMBER

It is lovely this morning. At half past eight the sun is beckoning with its warmth, perhaps to those who froze last night. The temperature went well below freezing, and the frost was as thick as any I have ever seen. The water in the lake was frozen this morning, and all of Stockton, including the surrounding fields, looks as though it were covered with white sheets. This is how I can imagine it must have been only an hour ago. I can hardly write, and I may have to give up because of the cold.

Despite the fact that this is the greatest holiday in the United States, last night there was not as much bustle and movement as there was last year or like there is normally in other civic and ecclesiastical holidays in North America. Aside from some gunshots fired into the air and a few canon shots from Weber's house, there was little else to remind us that this was the eve of the birth of the redeemer of the world.

After lunch we went to the Catholic church, thinking for sure there would be a mass, but we only found the following notice on the closed door of the church: "There will be a Catholic service at eleven o'clock on the peninsula in front of Centre Street."[102] We attempted to locate the new church on the peninsula but could not, even though we looked everywhere. I finally tired of the search and went home. Samuel just arrived and said he was able to go to mass because he found the church and the priest, who had been paid by Weber and who had said three masses today.

SUNDAY, 29 DECEMBER

It is half past ten at night, and Samuel and I have just come from Dr. Craig's house. He invited us over, and, after my customary refusal, Samuel said to me, "Ramón, you should go. You haven't been over since he got married, and your absence might make people start to wonder." Still, I said I would not go, and so he left with Rojo. For a half an hour I sat there alone in my room thinking, with my head on the desk. Finally I got up and decided to go over there for a visit. I took my cape, fixed my watch, put on my gloves, and went out.

The poor *negra* was very surprised to see me come in, and it was hard for her to conceal her feelings.[103] I sat next to her, and she could hardly catch her breath she was so moved. They had been playing cards, and since everyone arose when I entered, the game came to a momentary halt. Soon, however, Samuel took his cards and continued playing. As soon as he had dealt, however, the Morales women came in. Thus the circle got larger, and so conversations could become a bit more private.

"I thought you were never going to come again and that you had probably forgotten all about me."

"That is the way the world is," I said, "and I would have preferred not to come. In fact, I should not have come, but society tells us to lie, and so I pretend to be here."

"So you would prefer not to have come?"

A long conversation followed upon this question. Later everyone danced. Finally she asked me why I had not gone to the Christmas dance.

"Was it because I was there, Mr. Navarro?"

"No, Mariquita."

"Yes it was. You avoid me whenever you can."

"Perhaps."

"Would you be kind enough to dance something. I would very much like to see you dance."

"You know I do not dance."

"Of course you do. It is just so you won't have to dance with me."

"No miss, that isn't it."

"Come on, please, make an effort."

"I cannot, and I do not want to."

Later on I asked her, "Are you going to dance?"

She answered, "And you?"

"No, I am not. I already told you so."

"Well, then I am not going to either."

Samuel told me later that the entire gathering went from being a happy occasion to being one of sadness the moment she saw me.

STOCKTON, WEDNESDAY, 1 JANUARY 1851

Last night there was a dance, and we rented our piano to Mrs. Sharp, who was the hostess. I bought a ticket for Samuel but had no desire for anything in the world to go to the dance. But when I came here, Samuel and Mix told me that they would not go either if I did not come along. I bet that right now all of them regret having urged me to go, because it was a dull party. The only young girl was Mrs. Sharp's daughter, who was not worth a darn, and a niece of Weber, who had little to be said in her favor. Mariquita was there, but when we saw there weren't any real ladies at the party, at a secret signal we all left at half past ten, even though Mrs. Sharp was urging us to stay for the dinner. At the party I said hello to Mariquita but saw no more of her until Samuel suddenly called me and said,

"Do me a favor. Sit here and keep hold of this chair next to Mariquita for me until I return."

"Oh you must be very miserable just now," she said, "because you have no choice but to sit next to me."

"Why?"

"Because I have been observing you all evening, fleeing from me and finding pretexts so as not to come near me."

The poor girl. I had thought that she was more ungrateful than she actually is.

After the dance around midnight there was tremendous commotion and movement all around Stockton. All of the bells were ringing, hunting cornets were playing, as were violins. Just about everything was being played, and all together there was a tremendous racket. The gunshots, rockets, and other fireworks all made the noise twice as loud. There were a few fights and robberies of some importance. Most of the merchants around here have formed a group to demand the creation of a corps of night watchmen to guard the streets of the city at night. We shall see what comes of this.

THURSDAY, 2 JANUARY

They have begun work on the Placer Theater, and the word has it that it is going to be twice as good as the Corinthian. This is what Stockton society is most interested in, especially after the bad times for business during these past three months. Now, instead of wagons carrying freight there are elegant carriages of all types, and instead of workers there are elegant couples strolling around town.

FRIDAY, 3 JANUARY

The only news from San Francisco is about the double poisoning of two artists there. According to the papers, the woman felt that the tenderness and affection she showered her lover with were not reciprocated, and so she took poison, just like that. Her lover, they say, loved his woman more than she thought, and, unable to bear the thought of surviving her, he took poison as well. Neither of the two survived, and all of the newspapers say the affair is strange enough in San Francisco to be worthy of the best capitals in Europe.

SUNDAY, 12 JANUARY

It is half past nine in the morning, and I just came back from a visit to the bathhouse with Soruco. There I had a little adventure that I have been enjoying for awhile now. They gave me a card with the number of my bath room, and that is where I went. Later, after a handsome bath lasting a half an hour, I started to get dressed when I heard the door in the room next door open. At the same time I heard the voice of a woman whose accent I recognized as Mexican. I could tell that she was starting to take her clothes off because I could hear the rustle of her silk dress, etc. Just then I turned my gaze in that direction and realized how I could satisfy my curiosity. . . . The wall that separated the rooms was only about 7 ft. high. This was going to be my chance! As soon as I heard her get into the bath, I put a chair next to the wall and peeked over it. . . . My Lord, what beauty! A few drops of the water she shook from her wet hair fell upon my face, and they were as hot as fire. I was watching her bathe for five or six minutes without her noticing anything at all. Goodness gracious, what beauty! Perhaps it is because naked bodies have something of extra beauty in them. Just so that my vision would not be harmful for me, I called Soruco in English, who was in the adjoining room, and told him everything. The poor devil was discovered as soon as he showed his head, and at the sight of him the beautiful woman let out a terrifying cry. Fortunately, we were already dressed and able to escape into the large room before anybody noticed.

MONDAY, 13 JANUARY

Yesterday we took one of the nicest walks you can take in San Francisco. Most of the town's residents were heading over to Telegraph Hill, and Soruco and I took the same route. The entire hill seemed to be covered with a green mantle, and there the richest satin shoes were showing off with the greatest gallantry. The view of San Francisco from Telegraph Hill is one of the best you can get. There is nothing more magnificent. In the distance you can see the bay with its 600 ships at anchor, and you can distinguish the smallest masts and spars of each of them. We stayed up there until four o'clock, when we came down to eat.

At night we were able to see the best work shown yet at the French Theater. It is called *La Luisette,* or the *Singer of the Streets of Paris.* The vaudeville songs brought tears to the eyes of more than one spectator. Afterwards, at eleven o'clock, we went to the masked ball, and there that famous girl from Chillán who used to live on the corner opposite my tent came out to talk with me.[104] What a surprise!

For the past two or three days I have been crazy to buy a guitar from an artist that is being sold at the music store. It is the best you can find, and they are asking $150 for it, the same as its factory cost. My Lord! We shall see. . . .

STOCKTON, THURSDAY, 16 JANUARY

Today may be one of the happiest days I have had in a long time. Today I am to pay her a visit, and as the time approaches I am trembling like a prisoner awaiting his final moments. Well, I must remember that I am an Argentinean and should be a bit braver. In fact, women make me tremble more than men do. Well, let's go.

It is half past two in the afternoon. My Lord, when I said that today might be one of the happiest days in my life, I was not mistaken. I have just returned from my visit and am hardly able to contain my heart, which wants to break out of my chest because it is too small for all that happiness!! Now I know all, everything a lover would want to know. Poor little thing! She loves me with all the sincerity of her soul, with all the purity of a first love and the purity of a virgin. Oh, anything I say about our conversation will hardly do it justice. Generally I am as incredulous and difficult to make happy as they come, but today I cannot ask for any more. "*I will never be able to refuse you anything,*" she said to me.[105] I will have to remember this every time I remember the happiness that was mine today. The poor little thing! She may have suffered even more than I have . . . and I was ready to blame her!! My Lord, how unfair I was! How happy one is when he is loved by such a beautiful and ardent creature with a love that is akin to love itself!!!

FRIDAY, 31 JANUARY

After returning from San Francisco, I found Madame Mezzara here in Stockton. She was the woman I met in Sonora in October in highly dangerous circumstances for me. If I am not mistaken, that bandit Villefort, may he rest in peace, wanted to put a bullet into me and almost received one of mine because of the insults heaped upon Madame Mezzara in my presence.

A few days ago there was a very much talked about concert in the Corinthian Theater given by Madame Mezzara and a few of us who participated as pure aficionados. Spectators have seldom left a concert happier and more grateful, especially because the concert was offered free of charge. Madame Mezzara was as beautiful and as charming as ever. The entire house seemed like it was going to come down, such was the applause. She is so young and so beautiful that her singing and musical ability cannot but drive you crazy. After the concert they threw many bouquets of flowers on the stage, and one of them is now mine. Her last song about the swallows drove people crazy and made many of the spectators cry. The three of us played on our guitars the allegro of a fandango, which turned out marvelously. The third act was made up of Negro songs sung by six young Americans disguised as American Negroes and imitating their voices perfectly.

TUESDAY, 4 FEBRUARY 1851

I am going from one contradiction to another and am always alarmed for one reason or another. Today, even though something positive happened, I am restless and more upset than ever. Yet my diary does not know many of the events leading up to today, and these will be necessary if my sad story is to be understood. So I will mention some of the events that have happened to me in the past month.

Without my really noticing, it looks as though my behavior since the day of her wedding has tended to put distance between the two of us. For anyone who has been loved as I have with the ardor, madness, and passion of a first love, there is no possible explanation for this behavior. The truth is that perhaps I should have warned her or let her know of my intentions before she was affected by them, but I always kept myself at a distance and was indifferent to things happening around me. My trip to San Francisco and my stay there, however, seemed to annul my previous indifference. But my Lord, how could I ever have dreamed that I would forget a love like this, just like that? Upon my return from San Francisco I went to her house for the first time in twenty days or even a month. I found that she had not forgotten anything and nothing had changed; the entire affair lives on in her memory as though it had been engraved there forever. Against my wishes, I saw her alone, and I trembled because of the conversation we had, especially considering what she is for me, the woman and honorable wife of another man. What mystery this entire affair seems to have! She is madly in love with me, and yet she gets married! How they must have influenced her pure and good heart, taking advantage of the inexperience of fifteen years! They have terrified her and forced her to surrender in the name of "happiness." May they all be damned, and may the future unhappiness of this angel fall upon their conscience.

SATURDAY, 8 FEBRUARY

Why else open my diary except perhaps to cry in it? How else should I react to this unique event in my life, one so profoundly intimate for me? Being inclined to secrecy and mystery, as befits my nature, I have hidden all of this from Samuel, though perhaps he really understands it all. And now there appears to be a third party who knows what my soul is going through and how it is being tormented every day. Why did Amelia have to become the mistress of her sacred secrets?[106] Why did she delve into the secret sensations of Mariquita's heart? She has cried on Amelia's breast, telling her troubles to her and the secret suffering behind each of her tears. She should have kept silent. The damned weakness of women always causes happiness at first and then is ultimately fatal! Why could she not have suffered in silence? . . . Well, at least no crime has been committed yet, and that comforts me. I am not guilty of the fact that another man has bought or acquired a body whose heart belongs to me so justly from its first beat of love. And she is not guilty if they have sacrificed her will and inclinations despite her unwillingness. . . . But my Lord, what will become of that poor little thing later in her life when I am unable to offer her any relief because I must remain distant from her?

SATURDAY, 22 FEBRUARY

The day before yesterday, Amelia, her husband, and I went out for a walk with Mariquita. The fields were beautiful, and the walk was good for all of us. My memory of the day is a special and happy one, and I will treasure it, especially in times of unhappiness like these. This must be the way one suffers when pain is inflicted by others even though he has done nothing wrong. How passionately I received that first token of this ill-begotten love from that innocent young creature. I only wish I could be her guardian angel and look after her as her best friend. I would be content with that eternal and beautiful token of hers, which is sufficient to bring back to me the happiness without remorse and the sadness without guilt that has afflicted us. Yet there is the intent of a crime against me that kills the generosity and chivalry of my heart and beckons it to revenge, a worm that has never before moved my heart and soul. A vile and ugly deed has been done against me, a truly criminal atrocity. It was only the intention, that is true, but the effects would have followed on the intention if the victim had not offered herself up for the sacrifice. When she objected to these intentions because of the love she felt for me, in a totally unworthy and cowardly way they let it be known to her that she should fear for my life. When she attempted to resist the threats, she was shown a pistol and a testament and was told:

"Miss, you will be the cause of my suicide and the crime that follows."

My God what a miserable villain through and through. There is no love or madness that can excuse such an action; it was worse than raping a pure virgin, worse than murdering her, worse than killing her after stealing her honor!! And amidst all of this she is so virtuous, so good. I have not heard any of these infamous things from her, not even a word, but my proof comes from elsewhere, and I have no doubts. So they were going to unjustly make an attempt at my life? How could they have forced her will and her heart vilely and unconscionably without caring for the unhappiness and distress that would be hers for the rest of her life? And what about the possible destruction of my own projects, my career, and my future? Well, there is no longer anything linking my heart with generosity and chivalry to those who have offended me so vilely!!

MONDAY, 24 FEBRUARY

Sunday was another sad day for me. But I do find some things that made the day at least bearable, if not happy. I must summon all of my iron will to awaken me from this sleep, so that I may find a more pleasant and less desperate situation than this one. Yes, I could do it, but what about her, the one who is dying of a broken heart? And for her, the only light on the dark horizon of her future is her poor Ramón! What will become of her when I am not here to encourage her in an existence that is dragging her down with no prospect and hope for the future!!!

SATURDAY, 1 MARCH 1851

The weather today is lovely. If it continues this way, Amelia, Mariquita, Samuel, Mix, Mezzara, and I will all go for a walk. I am the first to be invited, of course, but I may not go. Why go? I will be unhappy, and those who suffer for me will end up poisoning her walk. She says that she will have more poison in her heart if I do not go along than if I do.

This life of mine is made doubly unbearable by the suffering and the pain, with hardly any hours of pleasure at all. She suffers and cries more than I, it is not surprising, but she is the cause of the suffering we both share. Cannot anything be done about it? If God does not come to our aid, we are both going to be very unhappy. Today she told me that I, too, was responsible in part, because I never made any proposal that let on to how I felt.

"Bah!" I replied, "Love does not mean marriage. It may be a consequence, I admit that, but the word love has never in itself implied marriage. I have never thought that. Those who are gentlemen and those who love with purity and honor are already spouses before God, even though the mere rite of a priest only confirms a pact made by two hearts. I have never joined the word "matrimony" with love, and so I am not at fault."

Good gracious, what have I improved by saying this? Nothing at all!

"My God, my Ramón, take my life, take my honor if you want, but at least show me that you forgive me and that you do not abhor me. Smile at me, if only for once. I can only see anger in your eyes and can never hear words from you that are not filled with bitter and cruel sarcasm."

Tears were streaming down without my even noticing, but a moment later I responded, "Your life, my angel, would only make my life more miserable if you were to lose it. If your honor was without purity and honorability, I would not be able to love you. So it will not be I who asks you for your honor."

MONDAY, 3 MARCH

The walk planned for yesterday ended up taking place with everyone except myself. You can imagine what a sad excursion it was, with more tears than smiles. Samuel told me that while they were in a boat on the river at French Camp, Mariquita twice said she was going to throw herself into the water.[107] At one point she grabbed a handkerchief out of his hands that had my initials, saying "This handkerchief belongs to Ramón." Poor Samuel, who really did not know what was going on, was stunned. Quickly she became ashamed of having been briefly carried away by a momentary fit of madness.

STOCKTON, WEDNESDAY, 5 MARCH

I still cannot imagine just how unhappy I am. Still stunned by the sharpness of the blow inflicted upon me, it is difficult for me to think about or to look at my own unhappiness. In any case, I will begin telling my diary, *the only thing that faithfully keeps my secrets and my sorrows,* what I am going through.[108] Since this looks to be a day that will mark an important period in the poor history of my life, I should not keep anything about it to myself.

I left here at nine o'clock, as is my custom, and went to the warehouse of Agustín.[109] After an hour we took a walk and went by Mariquita's house. There she was with all her belongings, ready to go to San Francisco, and by her look I could tell that she had suffered a terrible shock. She told us that a prisoner would go to the gallows more willingly than she was going to San Francisco. I am so upset, it is hard for me to remember the things she said. She went inside and about a half an hour later came out with a letter "for Amelia." . . . It was to be her farewell before going to San Francisco. We got up to leave, though we had to stay for a moment because she was all alone. I ended up staying on, and Agustín left. Her first words were:

"Poor Ramón, we are no longer going to suffer as much. Now we have a friend to comfort us. My brother Agustín knows everything. I have poured my heart out to him, and he has shown great interest in us!!!"

I will never be able to explain the torture and surprise this revelation caused in me. A moment later I got up to leave, and my only words were the following: "We are lost forever now, and before God I blame you for it."

Outside, I ran into Amelia, Samuel, and Mezzara and the two brothers. I did not want to be with them, preferring to be here at home alone with my suffering!

Yes, I have just received a terrible blow, the first of its kind in my life. I have just received one of those decisive blows in the life of a man that either cures or kills his passion, one of those blows that will always influence the life of a virtuous young man and that opens up to him the path of vice, corruption, and wantonness for all passions at once for the first time. . . . From now on I am divorced from virtue and honor, and I will raise perfidy and revenge to the altar of my heart. What is the result of twenty-two years of purity and perfect virtue? What is my prize for the austere honesty in both my public and private lives? What is the prize for having never seduced a young maiden or taken a wife from her duties? What is my prize for having dispensed only honor to more than one virgin who has fallen into my arms and for having religiously respected her purity without having given even a clumsy kiss, without having picked even one petal from the flower of her virtue? Those who have known me since my childhood, people who are witness to my spotless conduct, if they saw me now in my present state, they would all urge me down the path toward depravity. Whenever I have been together with young people anywhere in the world, in any language, even though I may have seemed like a fanatic and a silly puritan, I have done nothing else than preach the virtue and purity of men with regard to women. Never has a priest spoken with greater conviction and fervor than I on this matter, and even if I have not convinced them that I was right, at least they have respected me and recognized that I was well above them on this point. . . . And all of this for what? Damn!! May those who have offended me and robbed my happiness fall beneath the weight and justice of my revenge!!

THURSDAY, 6 MARCH

It is three o'clock in the afternoon, and I have just come from Mariquita's house after having seen her for perhaps the last time. That vile, lying, and miserable Agustín, now the lord of the confidence that Mariquita, in all her honesty and good heart, placed in him, has gone up to her husband, exactly the way that Judas sold Christ. Fortunately there has been nothing criminal, and he has not been able to make any accusation, because there was nothing that was not worthy and pure between her and myself. Thank you, my God, for her, because she is still the pure and faithful spouse of her husband. Thank you for her alone. As for me, may your goodness protect me, and may destiny run its course.

Mix informed Samuel about what he had heard from her brother and asked to have a meeting with me today. I have just come from there, and even though somewhat greater harmony seems to have been achieved, thanks to his many protests of friendship, my heart still has something sticking in it. Mix started by telling me what he had heard from her brother and Mariquita herself. Since everything boils down to the fact that we love each other, I really had no defense at all. It would be terribly long to recount the entire meeting in detail, though I certainly was triumphant in every issue raised. At one especially heated moment, I arose and said:

"Well, if you are a gentleman, as it seems you are, and if you feel that I have offended you, let us not waste any further words. Take a pistol as I have, and let's start walking off the distance."

Samuel heard this as he was entering with Mariquita. Things calmed down because Mix said that he had never thought ill of me but that I loved María and she loved me at the same time. At that, Samuel and Mariquita left once again.

"Whether or not I love her only concerns God and myself. It is an affair of my heart, and if no actions have been taken, why are you complaining? And anyway, since I love her, who knows which of us has a greater claim to her love, you or me?"

"I, who am her husband."

"Yes, her husband, in a marriage made by the fear of a pistol and the clauses of a last will and testament."

"You have no right to meddle in affairs that are not of your concern."

"It just might be that they concern me or did concern me at one time far more justly than they do you."

"Nevertheless, if you are a gentleman, you know there is nothing more you can do about this affair."

"You are right," I replied, "and I will give you proof of it by not ever setting foot again in your house, no matter how you became lord of your wife after having purchased her. As far as I am concerned, I am the lord of my own heart, and from afar I will love her or will not love her, as I please."

"I never thought this scene would go so far as having you say that you would not come back to my house. I would never want that to happen."

In another moment of special intensity and indignation, at the suggestion of further suspicions about me, I arose from my chair and said:

"Look me in the face and we shall see which of the two is a greater criminal toward the other. (I was referring to his threat of an attempt on my life if his marriage proposal was refused.) I know what you were thinking and attempting to do against me, and the worst part is that you have confessed it to a woman friend of mine. Should your memory fail you, try recalling an excursion to French Camp. What happened there was truly criminal and contemptible! I have not spoken before of your threat and the type of offense you were planning against me because I am generous by nature, but what is your justification for demanding honesty of me, when you have outraged and offended me in what is most sacred and beloved for me? And just how mad could you have been to have dreamed about, or perhaps even attempted to bring about, my ruin? Well, then, which of the two of us is the one who has justice and equity on his side? Clearly it is the one who in his generosity has forgotten and forgiven all!"

It is hard to imagine the damage a carefully aimed blow can inflict, especially when it weighs upon the conscience of the person receiving it. He attempted to excuse his actions by saying that much of it was false and that they were words that had come out in excitement and desperation. Samuel came in at that moment with Mariquita and the Judas. I then said to Mariquita:

"Thank you, Miss, for the hours of agony I have suffered since last night. Thank you for the first real wound and disillusionment that I have suffered in this world; I owe it all to you. If our pure and honest secret had had anything criminal about it, right now I would be mourned by my brother and my family and you would be a widow. I have reaped the punishment because I forgot that, after all, you were only a woman like all the rest of them.

All of this was said in front of her husband and everyone else. Samuel made me shake hands with Mix and the rest in a sign of renewed friendship. Only time will tell what we end up being.

Friday, 7 March

Many hours have passed, and the minutes I have counted one by one as I was devoured by pain and sadness. It still seems like the horrible reality of my misfortune is but a dream. I saw Mariquita yesterday for the last time, after having stabbed her in the heart with my words of reproach as I took leave of her. . . . I left the house yesterday, despite all the good words, with my mind made up. I will never return there, and, if at all possible, I will never see her again as long as I have the misfortune to remain in this country, where I have received the first real disillusionment of my life as a young man. Will I be able to keep this promise? Will I be able to live without the friendship of one who was so beloved before? Will I be able to see her as simply a vision, a kind of apparition at one moment of my life? Will I be able to endure the fact that my brother can spend hours with her in the greatest of friendship and harmony and not be able to attach myself to her through him? Will I be able to get away and not succumb to my pain? Yes!!!! Yes, I will be able to do it! I never before realized what my heart was capable of once its pride and self-esteem have been offended. Holy passion, I venerate you, because even though you often are able to cause me harm, in the end you will either save me or throw me to my grave. But at least I will not suffer as much or have to count the hours of torment. Pride and self-respect, that is it. . . . My pride, which has been often so harmful to me, will save me this time.

At four o'clock yesterday María embarked for San Francisco with her husband and our Judas. Everything is over for us. Now there is nothing on this earth to link us together. May she continue on her path, as I travel down mine, through the labyrinth of this life. . . . No, I have nothing to be ashamed of. I have loved her with tenderness, with purity, with the passion of a first love. I have venerated my love without having ever stolen a kiss from the purity of her virginity nor her dignity as a spouse. She is pure and without stain, and I have no pangs of guilt. . . .

My God, who could ever portray the way my soul is suffering right now. Even though it may be profane, I will say *Non est dolor sicut dolor meus, et non est que consoletur me!!*[110] Oh pain, eat away, devour my soul, tear it apart, but you will not triumph, and even though the agonies of your martyrdom keep me from thinking, there will always be a ray of light of religion and another of hope in my soul.

SATURDAY, 8 MARCH

Today is both an anniversary and a coincidence of great sadness for me. On this day in 1849, I bid farewell to my family and to my mother. I felt like I would die from the heartbreak of tearing myself away from her arms to embark en route to this world where I have only had pains and afflictions, hard work and misery. The 8th of March was a day of mourning for me and for my family. . . . And here we are on the 8th of March, two years later, and again I am distraught by the weight of my suffering, with no remedy or hope. . . . On that day I lost my family and my home; on this day my heart is still bleeding from my recent suffering. . . . It is the 8th, and I have no loved one, no illusion, no friends, nothing at all. . . . Everything has been lost, save my honor.

At last everything has finished, and only the memories remain. Right now she is gone and maybe has not even thought again about the person she used to call "her Ramón." . . . And her husband, what do I owe him? What can I possibly owe him after he vilely got her consent, thanks to a gun and the clauses of a last will and testament? He was the villain who persecuted an angel whose purity was destined for me because of her love. In the eyes of God and of men, he stole property of mine. And what do I owe her brother? He was ungrateful to the friendship I had offered him, and he was villainous enough to tell María that I had seduced a young lady in Chile, just to cull the favor of his brother. . . . He also betrayed Mary and violated the secret she confided in him upon his word of honor. Damn, I shall pay back all the things I owe him, no doubt about it!

SUNDAY, 16 MARCH

Today I saw María for the first time since that fatal 5th of March.[111] She went to San Francisco and returned, but I only ran into her by chance. I was taking a stroll with Agustín and Pancho Ainza after lunch along Channel

Street, and suddenly we saw them only about twenty paces away coming toward us. María was there between her husband and Judas, and I was between Pancho and Agustín, so there was no way to avoid the encounter. Even had I wanted to cross the street so as to avoid them, there was no time. As we met, they all greeted us with great courtesy, except for me with my hands in my pockets all the time and refusing to acknowledge even their existence. . . .

STOCKTON, TUESDAY, 25 MARCH

It is two o'clock in the afternoon, and I have just come back from the hospital, where I was invited by Dr. Lasvignes to witness an amputation. My goodness, what a horrendous spectacle! When we got there we found the patient lying on his bed, wailing every time the pain became more acute. He explained to us that yesterday he had gone hunting and on the way back had stopped at the El Dorado. He leaned his loaded shotgun on the bench where he was sitting. It is hard to tell just what caused the accident, but the shotgun went off, and the shot went through his thigh bone. When we got there, the other doctors came in and decided to amputate his leg between his thigh and buttocks. Captain Adams, whose family is in the United States, asked if the amputation would be dangerous, and they replied that no, it would not. Nevertheless, he entrusted his family to the charity of all of us there. Dr. Radcliff took out his instruments and started to sharpen them in his presence. God, what a horrible thing! He was placed on a table surrounded by the four doctors and myself. He was given chloroform and soon lost consciousness. Dr. Radcliff stuck his tremendous knife into him as though he was an ox and after reaching the bone realized that he had erred the joint. The patient trembled and came to his senses despite the chloroform. He made us all weep with his cries of pain. He was given more chloroform, and the doctor continued to cut. The operation took eighteen minutes by my watch, instead of the three it was supposed to last. When his leg finally fell to the floor, Captain Adams's soul left his body as well. As far as I am concerned, the poor devil was murdered by his doctors.

SUNDAY, 30 MARCH

Almost a month has gone by since that fatal 5th of March, and I have only seen Mariquita a couple of times. I have news of her from Samuel, who visits there every night but no longer goes during the daytime. He tells me that she is devoured by a profound melancholy. It is true that she seems to have lost everyone at once. She lost me, she has lost Samuel, her father, her brother, her friend, her mentor, and she has lost Amelia, her only comfort. Samuel, who used to be practically one of the family like I was, does not go as frequently as before, and when he does he hardly abandons the cool politeness with which he treats everyone. If they invite him to lunch, he never accepts. Before, he used to eat there almost daily. Mariquita cries all the time, and when she is alone with him, she asks:

"How is Ramón?"

"He is well, thank you."

"Hasn't he anything to say to me?"

"No, Miss."

"Oh my Lord, what indifference! What a horrible change!"

She spends her nights and her days without seeing anyone else except her husband and that modern-day Judas.

And what about me? It looks like things are coming back together for me. I seem to have regained my will, my pride, and my self-respect, much like any other man. With my heart in pieces I witness day after day go by without seeing that poor victim, yet I am happy to see the coming of night and see that I have overcome yet another day, as things should be. I said that I would never return there, even if it tormented me, and, true to my promise, I have not returned.

MONDAY, 31 MARCH

It is three o'clock in the afternoon, and something terrible just happened. Amelia has just poisoned herself. I was writing at my desk when she came in for awhile, only to leave after two or three minutes. I continued to write when all of a sudden I heard the desperate screams of a woman and lots of steps and blows, like when some great and sudden tragedy has just occurred. I ran to the room and on the way came upon Pietro, who was weeping. I went past him and entered the room. There Amelia was lying on the floor, writhing with convulsions. But she did not take her eyes off me and exclaimed, "Here is another one who torments me innocently." Everyone stopped for a moment, but soon we all concentrated on the care Dr. Lasvignes was giving her. Nobody knows why this poor woman would do such a thing. Yet the doctor is hopeful, even though the dosage she took is more than enough.

It is now midnight, and I have just come back from my turn at Amelia's side. For the last two hours she has been resting amid her delirium in the arms of Samuel and Pietro, her husband. I have just spent my hour and am coming back to get some sleep. Still, I will probably think instead of sleeping. What strange things Amelia said to me just now as I held her. "You are killing me, Ramón. You are cruel because you do not love me!!" What does this mean, is she saying the same things to the others in her delirium? Samuel says that when she was with him she was always talking about me. What have I done for her to be this way with me? But why would she hold me so tightly in her arms if I was the one making her suffer?

TUESDAY, 1 APRIL 1851

Amelia is still horribly ill. After getting past the poison, the illness appears to have taken another route. The doctor speaks of inflammation and worries about her health if inflammation does indeed occur. What a horrible tragedy to die in California at twenty-two years of age, so young, so beautiful, so clever, and so virtuous! What a tragedy for her husband. Poor Pietro is inconsolable. His reaction is hardly an exaggeration, given the reality of things. Samuel, her husband, and I take turns at her side. She is suffering horribly, and the doctor's orders are that she should not be allowed to sleep for a single moment. How that poor creature suffers when the opium makes her sleepy and each of us does his best to keep her from sleeping! Poor thing.

It is half past one in the morning, according to my watch. I just came from my turn at her side, and her husband has taken over. I will try to get some rest or at least write in my diary a bit in my room. What an amazing thing! What does Amelia have with me? Why is it that she does such strange things when she is in my arms? Again the incoherent words, completely out of context but which have such sad meaning for me. "Let me rest my head on your chest, Ramón." "Oh, you abhor me and look down on me all the time." Later, "Put your hand on my chest, Ramón." "What suffering, I am being devoured." "Can't you feel the beats of my heart?" These words and others like them. She always seems to think that I despise her, and then all of a sudden in her convulsions and her delirium, she says words that surprise me and whose meaning is completely foreign to me. Why does she want to be with me more than she does with the others?

FRIDAY, 4 APRIL

Amelia is no better, despite all the efforts of the doctor. There is no imminent danger for now, but the illness has become more complex, and now it will be very difficult to cure.

The bishop came by to pay us a visit. He took advantage of the visit to see Amelia. Perhaps due to his wisdom or because of the world he belongs to, he felt that she was suffering morally as well. Without telling her that he wanted to hear her confession, he said he would like to be of comfort for her in all the pains she seems to be suffering. She agreed, and they were alone for a half an hour. Amelia had confession, and she seems to be more relieved right now. Afterward, the bishop bid us farewell and left with the two attendants traveling with him. He gave us a thousand thanks for all the help we had given Father N., his missionary up here. He told us he would keep in touch from Monterey. He speaks English, French, and Spanish very well.

Saturday, 5 April

The fatal 5th is here once again. My sufferings have changed from being active and tormenting to being passive, though they are much the same as before. It has been days now since I last heard from María. Samuel is now the only tie between us, and he has hardly gone by their house lately because of the illness of Amelia. Who would believe it? After so much friendship, such confidence, to have been reduced to oblivion. After so much love and so much suffering, we are now no more than strangers in each other's lives. . . .

Tuesday, 8 April

The illness of Amelia continues, though the doctor is now a bit more optimistic about her chance of recovery. I should have left for San Francisco several days ago, but her illness has kept me here. I shall depart this afternoon.

I know nothing of María and shall depart without seeing her. Perhaps it is better for her and for me. I am amazed to see that the memory of her does not upset me. Perhaps I am being a bit unfair. The fact is that, as time goes by, my intense emotions and feeling of aggravation appear to take a different road. I am saddened, but now the calm has returned to a certain extent, and the suffering is no longer feverishly intense. I hate those who offended me, but my desire for revenge has lost much of its strength. I always need to forgive. But no! There are people who do not deserve forgiveness. Poor María, who knows how much she must be suffering.

San Francisco, Wednesday, 9 April

It is four o'clock in the morning, and we just arrived at the wharf of San Francisco. Dawn has still not come, but from here this new Babylon is lovely to behold, with its thousand hotels all lit up and its magnificent houses strewn all over the hills and even on top of them, without any apparent order, as if on a whim, yet all strictly lined up along the streets and the plazas of the town.

The bay is no less beautiful with its web of masts looking like a cloud. The masts of the 600 ships anchored here certainly give that impression. Light can be seen in the windows of many of them, and from time to time you can hear the sad and rhythmic cry of sailors moving an anchor in order to change the location of the ship. In the roving hotels you can see dozens of men, half of them drunk and the rest singing. One of these hotels has just gone past our steamship and is going to go around the bay, picking up a sailor from each steamship, a criminal from each prison ship, and a deserter from each warship. This is what the Empress of the World looks like as she sleeps here upon my arrival at four o'clock in the morning.

SUNDAY, 13 APRIL

I have been in San Francisco for a few days now, and anyone who knows the city will not be surprised by the fact that I have yet to visit my diary. The truth is that there has not been a single unoccupied moment since I arrived. There are so many wonderful things to see and admire, much more extraordinary than can be seen any place else in the world. There ends up being little time left for practically anything else. Of course, I could give up eating, but that is necessary to stay alive, and so there is not much choice. Every night there is theater in different parts of the city, new and luxurious hotels to visit, great artists to admire, etc., etc. Tonight there will be an important show in the Theater of French Vaudeville, and I will then go out later to give Emilia the serenade I promised.

By the way, I have been seeing that enchanting girl daily, and she seems much like a princess, since she has received the compliments of more than one duke and the gallantry of more than one European envoy while at the side of her uncle Rosas. Since my arrival our friendship has grown and become one of great confidence and even intimacy. Thanks to our long conversations, she knows me well and I her. She never mentions her uncle Rosas, nor do I. The esteem and friendship I feel for her is always reciprocated by her completely. She has never had a better friend, at least that is what she said to me as we talked on our way from church to her home the other day. What a lot of virtues grace the soul of this creature, who is doubly beautiful in her body! She is not a woman like the rest and does not disguise her feeling or deceive others with her actions.

I deceived her last night by saying that I was returning to Stockton, and it was so convincing that I even bid her farewell at four o'clock. At midnight, Leguisamont, Cupertino, Lucero, and I went up the steps of her house to give her a serenade. We sang beautiful sad songs, "La palidez" and "La estrella," with three of us playing the guitar, and later I played a magnificent andante and allegro with Cupertino. As we were leaving, a window opened, and she said, "Thanks Navarro." This morning she could not find the words to thank me for the surprise and the serenade but told me that she had suffered a lot and that the next time we should sing and play something less sad.

On the way home we went to the balcony of Madame Caddis to give her a serenade as well. We had begun to tune our guitars and were getting ready to sing when a fellow came running by crying "Fire!" and pointing in the direction of the hotels and the plaza.[112] In a moment a thousand voices were crying "fire" everywhere, and the police and the firemen began to run down the streets. But the fire was nowhere to be seen, and in vain we tried to tell them that it had been a drunk who had sounded the alarm. There was no way to stop the panic; thieves were running everywhere, and there was a great commotion. And amid all this consternation, we hardly noticed the fact that we were standing there with our three guitars until Leguisamont said to us, "Pretty soon they are going to take all of this out on us because we are poor meddlers, singing to beautiful women with no money in our pockets." This joke was followed by another and then another. I will not forget last night easily with all of Leguisamont's madness and jokes. Since the alarm and panic continued unabated, Leguisamont ended up persuading us to hide our guitars and to get out of there fast. We finally hid the guitars underneath a house and went out to see what was happening. By then everything was beginning to quiet down, so we went back and got our guitars and finished our serenade, which was as well received as the first one. But it was really hard to keep from laughing as we sang thanks to the silliness of Leguisamont. It sure is going to be hard to forget last night!

MONDAY, 21 APRIL. *Letter to his father in Chile*[113]

After not having rained for almost the entire winter, it has more than made up for it this past month. This rain is really good for the mines, which are the source of all money around here. If you add to this the abolition of the tax on all of the foreign miners, it is beginning to look like business is going to get better in every way. You already know the way I send news about business here, but I'll say it to you once again. If when we return we have something with us, it means that things have gone well for us, and if we don't bring anything at all, it means that all was lost. I am tired of sitting on all the fortunes and good business deals done here in California, because at times it seems like it is easy come, easy go.

WEDNESDAY, 23 APRIL. *Letter to Rudecindo Rojo in California*

As the population, trade, and wealth of the capital of the world grows, in San Francisco you can see new convents all the time. Even if you were looking for the strangest of things, you would probably find it in San Francisco. One of these marvels is a new convent for Chinese women. . . . I am not quite sure which order they belong to, but the fact is that the community lives on Jackson Street, a couple of blocks above the Polk Hotel. For men like me, with religious principles and social ideas, these houses are out of bounds, yet they also awaken the curiosity of any young man eager for news from the world. Since I am unable to go there and see their convent, taking notes in my notebook about their lifestyles, their customs, and their cloistered condition . . . I am happy to spend a couple of days walking past the place just to get an idea of what a beautiful Chinese woman is like. Well, my friend, I was amazed to find so much beauty worth admiring after having seen so many horrible Chinese faces. I had imagined that I would run into women with dark or at least tan skin and small noses, kind of like you, with no eyebrows or eyelashes, etc. Instead, it was just the opposite. They were as white as Englishwomen, with pointed noses and dark hair like Andalusians. I saw two particularly beautiful ones. It was surprising to see them all dressed in the latest French styles. I had imagined they would all be dressed in silk, without any heed to fashion. They demand one ounce for a two-hour visit, at least according to the sign on the door. The other recluses have lowered their price to $8. Not surprising, considering all the women in San Francisco nowadays.

THURSDAY, 24 APRIL. *Letter to D. Juan Ocampo in Concepción, Chile*

Yesterday Ainza and I went out for a walk to enjoy the beauty of springtime on the banks of the San Joaquin River. As we were coming to the outskirts of Stockton, we caught sight of a group of Americans making the following spectacle. One of the Americans was dressed in an alb and a cincture, with a beautiful choir cloak of purple tissue embroidered with gold, and was dancing a polka amid the laughs of the others. We were irritated to see how they were desecrating vestments this way, and so we went up to the dancer and asked him where he had gotten them. He replied that he had bought them from one of the American volunteers in the war with Mexico. We asked him for the vestments in order to show them to the Catholic priest and promised to pay him for them. Right now I have them in my room, and I hope to see the priest this afternoon when he comes over. You sure see strange things in California. In fact, you come upon things that would be hard to believe if you had not seen them. A polka, an alb, and a cape all together on the streets of Stockton!

The underground mines for extracting lode deposits that have been discovered recently in Stanislaus and Carson Creek have Stockton and all of San Francisco really excited. They have people's imagination going as much as the first discovery of gold in California and are the subject of as many lies and exaggerations as that first one was. The fact is that the mines are reaching the real mother lode, and shares are going for exorbitant sums. In one at Carson Creek, four Americans found a gold nugget from a certain vein that is worth $200,000, and it only took them four hours of work to get it. This was in the newspaper today. They have already begun putting big machines in the mines in order to work these veins, which are flush with as much gold per square block of terrain as all of the placers where gold is washed. They have already discovered veins in almost all of the existing placers.

SONORA, THURSDAY, 1 MAY 1851

After returning to Stockton for a few days and seeing that Amelia was very slowly getting better, I went to Sonora on business. I arrived in Stanislaus on Monday. While they were attending to my horse and preparing my room in the hotel, I went for a walk to the ranch of the Indians. There are some 500 Indians, both men and women, who have their little ranches all together. Yet it is almost impossible to see the homes, even when very close, because all you can see is perhaps a tree or two or some bushes. Some of the Indians seem to live in cellars or, perhaps better, in dugouts rather than in houses. I was walking in the encampment amid their huts, when it seemed that the ground was sinking under my feet. At that moment an Indian woman with a child on her back came out along with her husband. By means of sign language they asked me not to sink the roof of their house. I then noticed that I was standing on the roof of a type of dugout dwelling or cellar.[114] There are many Indian women breastfeeding infants, and many of these children are very white. That can only mean that their race is gradually mixing with the Americans.

I arrived in Sonora at noon on Tuesday. As always whenever I have been away, I am invariably surprised at how much this town has progressed in its buildings. Its population has grown as well and may even be larger than that of Stockton. The lavishness of its hotels is great and is far from being much less than that of any other big city in California.

MONDAY, 5 MAY

Yesterday was a day of magnificent expectation for any foreigner in Sonora. On Sundays, all of the miners from the surrounding areas come into town, and Sonora becomes a truly charming and festive place. There were many different attractions. There was a bullfight, theater, and a fight between a bear and a bull. William Perkins and the rest of us preferred the theater, and there they treated us to a work of Robert Macarvé that made us laugh until we were silly.[115]

A letter from Samuel just arrived telling me about the fire in San Francisco that, both in terms of human lives and of commercial establishments, was the greatest and most fatal of any so far in the city. It took place between the third and fourth of this month! What a fatal coincidence, a truly fatal anniversary of the fire that desolated the city last year just now. This time the losses amount to twenty million. When the steamship bringing the news to Stockton was ready to return, San Francisco was no longer more than debris and ashes!

TUESDAY, 6 MAY

Another fatal coincidence! We just received a message from William sent by Samuel. Stockton no longer exists anymore either! The fire started last night in the magnificent Placer Hotel, and it was impossible to stop it until it had devoured much of the town. Those of us on the peninsula have been completely spared, but all of our friends elsewhere have been pretty much ruined. Poor Agustín! I was not there to help him save anything at all. It was the only time in which I might have been useful to him, and this time bad luck had me far away.

Here is the object of general surprise and of false or maybe certain conjectures: Why is it that San Francisco burned at the same time Stockton did? Could it not well have been arsonists? The stagecoaches left this afternoon for Stockton, and all of them were filled with passengers.

I think that I will go to Calaveras tomorrow to see Rodríguez and Morales.

SONORA, WEDNESDAY, 7 MAY

It is nine o'clock in the morning, and I have just left for Stockton. I had breakfast with William, and he accompanied me for three or four leagues. It is cloudy today, and the views are lovely with all the pine trees and other trees all fresh and gay in the absence of a hot sun, though the days of spring are beginning to wane. I am going to Calaveras and must still traverse that horrible Melones hill and the bad inclines of Stanislaus. I have never seen worse roads, not even in the mountains of Chile. But I am well mounted and have my pistols and knife with me, and these are awfully good company.

It is eleven o'clock in the morning, and I have reached the Stanislaus River. I am writing while the boatmen prepare the boat and put my horse aboard. The river is lovely and crystal-clear, so clear that you can see your face in its waters. This river crossing is done amidst beautiful pines and willows. I had seen oil paintings and daguerreotypes of this place before, and the countryside is truly worthy of the paintings. There is a two-story house that rises amid the tallest pines on the riverbank. The curtains of its windows are lavishly adorned with blue cords. At this moment, just as I am passing by, I can see the angel who adorns this enchanted house. Farewell, my beauty! You do not know that I have seen you and that I carry you with me in my notebook. No, you know that I have seen you, and you have also seen me and have said to me, "A traveler who has silver in his saddle, a rich knife and the best pistols in his holsters, who has a rich watch and chain hanging from his vest, and who makes notes in his notebook cannot be just any traveler." Yes, all of this was said just as that damned beauty was entering her room.

It is half past six in the afternoon, and I have just reached the house of my uncle Rodríguez and the one of Morales in Calaveras. It is starting to get dark, and I am as tired as can be from the long trip. I passed by Melones, and it is filled with miners. Soon I got to the placer of Angels Camp and ate there. As I was passing the last tents, a Frenchman called me by my name. It was Mr. Cros, who used to be the French consul in Chile. I got off my horse, had a bite to eat in his house, and continued my journey. Adelaida and my Mrs. Teresita are doing quite well. The first of them is as happy and as pretty as she can be at fifteen years of age. They made me eat while I was jotting down the last notes of the day in my notebook.

SATURDAY, 10 MAY. *Letter to William Perkins*

After having traveled yesterday and the day before along those horrible roads, the like of which I have never seen before, I reached here at four in the afternoon, as I had promised my dear William. Really, I am willing to go ten times to Sonora, but I would prefer not to cross the mountains of Stanislaus. They are so high that as you are going up them it is like reaching the clouds, just as the when you are going down it is like descending into hell. As I was going down the mountain, I saw the form of two women in a forest. "*Allons!*" I said to myself, "who knows but that this little adventure might well pay me for the ruggedness of the route." I went a bit farther and realized that they were Cahuilla Indians. It doesn't matter, I said to myself, as long as they are pretty. Anyway, my calculation misfired. There is no question but that it was a mother and her daughter, because the young one was hardly fifteen years of age. As soon as they saw me, who knows whether it was my figure, my pistols, or my knife that bothered them. In any case, before I had time to say anything, they flew up the hills as though they were deer who were used to bounding over the rocks and boulders.

TUESDAY, 13 MAY. *Letter to D. Rudecindo Rojo*

Here the only news worth mentioning is about business; it is good news, and it was brought by letters coming from Chile. One of the letters mentioned the following useful item. Mardoqueo sold my ship, the *Elisea,* for nine thousand pesos and bought the *Carmen* for $5,000. It was supposed to sail for Peru to load anchovies and sugar. My friend, as you can see, everything down there is working very much in our favor.

STOCKTON, WEDNESDAY, 14 MAY. *A dream!!*

It is noon, and I just came back from the countryside, where I went for a walk with Amelia. I can hardly write, and my entire body is trembling. I have been back from Stanislaus for five days now, and during that time, hour by hour, minute by minute, I have seen a dream born, grow, take shape, and become overwhelming. It is something that for me has no name, especially considering the short experience I have had in the affairs of the heart. I still don't understand what I am seeing and feeling. How am I to know what this is and explain it, if I do not even understand it?

I left the house this morning at nine o'clock and took Amelia out for a walk with me. Stockton was aglow in what was the loveliest day of spring. As we left the city behind, I was trembling but still had no idea of what was going to happen. We hardly noticed anything because we only heard what we were saying in our conversation. We passed by beautiful places filled with exquisite flowers, we picked some of them, and then continued our walk in no particular direction. All of a sudden we came upon a lovely forest about a mile out of town. There was nobody there but us, and we were thrust into a profound silence, with no noise other than the beating of our hearts. I found myself alone with her leaning on my arm, as lovely as charm itself. All of a sudden I could not speak and was trembling from head to foot, unable to explain my emotion, with not a word to say and not knowing where to go. My Lord! And she was trembling even more, and her beautiful chest rose and fell as though it was about to explode. Neither of us said anything; we had nothing to say. Finally, after a couple of minutes of terrible struggle, I said let's go on, and we continued the walk. We left the forest and entered another one, and then on to another one, until we finally reached a small thick wood made up of flowing rose bushes, with the ground covered by thick and smooth grass. The roses gave off a sweet and soft fragrance, as did the other flowers and bushes of the wood. It was like a room, a room that was closed in on all sides by the rose bushes. The ardent imagination of a poet could not paint a lovelier sight. It would be impossible to explain how I felt after entering this poetic and mysterious place. I was out of my senses. She trembled all over and held her face in my chest.

"My Lord, what is all of this?" I finally asked.

"And you, why are you trembling more than I am?"

Two or three minutes passed in which not a word was said, while we embraced each other very tightly against our hearts. I could feel the beats of her heart against my chest, and the contact with her firm and round breasts drove me crazy. My God, who could ever paint such a scene?

"Would you like to sit down here a moment and rest?"

"Yes."

I took my jacket off and placed it on the grass. She sat on it with me at her side. For a second our eyes met, and we trembled as if something frightened us. Without saying a word, I took her hand and held it tightly in my own. I felt her lips touch mine in a long and ardent kiss while her arms were holding me tightly to her body . . . and a moment later . . . My God, it was like a dream!!

THURSDAY, 29 MAY

It has been fifteen days now since I last opened my diary. That means that during this entire period I have been extremely excited, spending days of sheer happiness together with others of bitter suffering and bad memories. For three or four days now I have been alive without living. In other words,

I have been living the most forced existence any man could possibly live. I go from my room to the warehouse, from the warehouse to Ainza's house, and then again to my room, but no place do I find repose or tranquillity. I am truly unhappy, and in vain I seek for something to lessen my suffering, to comfort me; yet there is nothing like that to be found. Only today was I able to find something like what I am seeking. In accord with the general nature of most men, who are petty, egotistical, and miserable, when we suffer, what we would like most is for everyone to suffer, and we only find some comfort or at least resignation when our suffering is general and is shared by others. That is how I have figured that I could be a bit less unhappy, by comparing my bad luck and moral guilt of unknown origin with that of another whose problem is considerably worse!!

So it is half past three in the afternoon, and I just returned from the place of the gallows where a young Irishman, whose trial has been going on for some time now, was hanged. "Here you have," I told myself when I saw Mack with the noose around his neck, "here you have someone who is more miserable than I am, and he is going to die the most ignominious of deaths amidst the curiosity of more than 3,000 spectators." This is how miserable men like me are able to bear their own moral sufferings! But getting back to Mack, of the hundreds of men I have seen executed, I have never seen one more stoically indifferent and filled with tranquillity. He came to the platform of the prison perfectly well dressed with a cigar in his mouth. He reached the gallows and walked up the last fatal steps almost gaily, as happy as if he were going into the El Dorado Hotel. He had on a black frock, trousers, a vest and a black tie, a felt hat, and a rich and clean white shirt. He looked like he was getting ready for his wedding. He spoke for more than a half an hour, telling his story and his crimes. As the sheriff finally placed the fatal mask over his head, he took one last look and made a sign to the cart. "Farewell," he said and was left there hanging in the air after falling through the trap door. I had my watch in hand, and his agony lasted two minutes and twenty seconds. That is how Mack died at twenty-three years of age after, in his own words, having allowed himself to be dragged into a corrupt and criminal life.

SATURDAY, 31 MAY. *Letter to D. Saturnino Correas*

Samuel finally left for the mines today with Mr. Perkins. Don Casimiro Rodríguez, who had a store in the mines, has written us from Melones, telling of the wealth of the mines and offering us a chance to participate in a company along with three Spanish friends of ours. He has bought a partnership in the original mine. The day after his purchase, $25,000 in nearly pure gold was taken out of a mine right near ours. There are now twelve men working for us. Samuel has gone there to settle the ownership in a more formal way in accord with American laws. That is why Mr. Perkins, our best friend, has gone with him.

STOCKTON, SUNDAY, 1 JUNE 1851

Pretty soon it is going to be three months since that fatal 5th of March without my having been with or spoken alone with Mariquita. Last month Samuel, Perkins, and I went to pay Madame Clements a visit. There we ran into Mariquita and her husband. Even though I knew beforehand that I was going to see her there, still it was difficult for me to handle the emotion our encounter caused me. It was still more difficult for me to understand her own reaction. I shook Madame Clements's hand and that of her husband before taking my seat near a table, without ever greeting either Mariquita or her husband. A quarter of an hour went by without my even looking at them or saying anything to anyone, except to the boy of Mrs. Clements, who was on my lap. Finally Mariquita got up, and, with the pretext of freshening up, she went into a bedroom that only I could see since I was seated directly across from the door. As soon as she was in the doorway, she stopped without going all the way in and, turned around, started to stare at me openly with her arms crossed on her chest and with no attempt to hide it. My Lord, I myself have said that speaking with your gaze is nothing but a farce and the illusion of poets. How mistaken I was! But that I were able to translate all the feelings and sadness her eyes and her look expressed in those three or four minutes! Finally she raised both of her little hands to her lips and seemed to give her soul over to me with the kiss she sent. Two or three minutes later we got up to leave the same way we had entered, only this time I could not take my eyes off Mariquita on my way out.

SUNDAY, 1 JUNE. *Letter to his father in Chile*

Samuel left yesterday for Sonora. On his way, he is going to go by Melones, where Rodríguez is. There is nothing richer in California than that placer, and all its mines are lode mines rather than the typical placer mines where the gold is washed. The day I went by the mine, the four partners of another mine came out with $80,000 as the product of one day's work with 12 miners. You have to see all this wealth to believe it. When I first went by, it was only a small placer with a few tents, and today it is practically a city with more than 300 houses. According to my most recent information, the lots there are worth $300. They have already painted and lithographed entire blocks of the town. This is about how everything in California is improvised, from towns to fortunes. People make and lose millions, but that never discourages the spirit of its inhabitants. I do not know when, where, or how, but the day when we ourselves are owners of a stake in one of the mines cannot be far off.

MONDAY, 9 JUNE. *Letter to Rudecindo Rojo in Sonora*

You may already know from Perkins that we are now the owners of three mines, two of which have gold in sight. The one we have yet to begin working is a lode that may be as beautiful as the original one. . . . I sold a quarter of one of the other mines for some $300 in cash, just so I could have something to live from while waiting for the work at the mines to begin to pay off. So, my friend, I hope that when we leave California we will have made our fortune, no matter how illusive it has proven to be so far.

CALAVERAS, WEDNESDAY, 11 JUNE

It was nine o'clock in the morning when Agustín and I left Morales's house for Melones. Since I know how far it is and how bad the road is, I rather doubt we will make it today, especially since there are several visits to be made along the way. At ten we arrived at Dr. Craig's house. There was nobody there, so we went to find him at work. The poor old man came out to meet us with a shovel and a bucket in hand. He asked us right away about Mariquita. I had already asked Samuel to ask her to tell him that I was coming, but she never answered. The poor guy doesn't even know that Agustín no longer goes to his daughter's house and that, because of all the conflict with Mix, she is completely isolated, even from Agustín and Manuel, her own brothers. Nobody goes by the house except Samuel, and he does not do so as often as he did before. As Agustín and I walk around Stockton, whenever we go by his house we see all the doors shut, with the sole exception of the window of her room, where she always is up there watching us pass by. It was very sad to see Dr. Craig. He knows that I loved his daughter and that she was mad about me. In other words, he knows everything. He continues to hold me in the highest regard and cannot help but feel sorry for his daughter and for me.

At half past one in the afternoon we reached the second river of Calaveras, just where I spent almost two years of my life. This place is witness to so many bitter hours of sadness, to so many tears shed in loneliness and silence, to so many of my innocent pleasures. It is the place that was witness for two years to all the emotions of my soul. There is the place where my bed was covered with flowers, there is the place where my desk was, there are the four pillars that were used for a table, there is the pole of the tent where my guitar used to hang, and over there is the place where my wheat field was and where you can see wheat even now, just beginning to ripen. Oh, once again I can see the phase of my life just as it was. Now that I am here, the only thing missing is an altar to my own memories.

MELONES, THURSDAY, 12 JUNE

Yesterday at six o'clock in the afternoon, Agustín Ainza and I arrived here in Melones, after going by Calaveras, where we visited Milnes, the Englishman who lived with me when he was at the mines. Afterward we stopped for awhile at another placer, looking for some of my men who I had been told now had a mine of their own. We ate in Angels Camp, and after a three-hour ride we finally reached Melones in the late afternoon. This is an entirely improvised town, filled with people and merchants from all over. These days it looks like the meeting place for just about everyone and the object of the greed of all those seeking their fortune. Since the terrain is pretty rugged here, there is only one very long street, which runs along the only terrain that is more or less flat. Lots here are worth as much as 3,000 or 4,000 pesos, and there are loads of speculators. I just came from meeting with Rodríguez, who has bought some other land and part of another mine. I have just signed a contract with Vera to sell him one-quarter of a share for $300 in cash. I am also negotiating the sale of another quarter of the same share for $500, which means that by the time I return to Stockton I will have $800 in gold, a sum that should be enough to pay for my trip and all the discomfort of the road.

It is now about midnight, and a great tragedy just occurred, one from which, you might say, we have just been born again. An hour ago Agustín and I went for a walk around the hotels here in order to listen to the music being played. We were listening to the music at the Lavetour Hotel, along with about 500 other persons, when all of a sudden a fight broke out on account of two women, a Mexican and an American, and their husbands started shooting at each other. The news spread like wildfire, and before anyone had a chance to leave the hotel, all of a sudden there was a ferocious gunfight going on, with Mexicans on one side and Americans on the other. Ten or twelve bullets whizzed over our heads and killed or wounded another ten or twelve men nearby. The only noise to be heard was the noise of men killing, along with loads of swearing and blasphemy in every language. The Mexicans finally won, and the Americans either fled in terror or are hiding in the houses of peaceful Mexicans. Agustín and I got out whatever way we could, and we were able to get home and get our pistols and knives, ready to make any insult pay a high price. Three Mexicans were killed, and another four were wounded; an American died and another one, who is a captain, is still breathing but probably won't make it until tomorrow morning. One of the dead Mexicans has nine bullets in him! It is as though everyone decided to empty his pistol into the poor guy.[116]

Melones, Friday, 13 June

Damn! After the tragic events of last night we decided not to stay another moment in this place. But today when we asked for the horses in order to leave, we were told that the Americans from Murphy's had taken them in order to chase after the murderers of the captain. May the devil take the damned captain's body and soul, for all I care! Here we are trapped in this labyrinth, where a person's life always appears to be hanging by a thread.

Friday, 20 June. *Letter to D. Saturnino Correas*

Samuel is leaving for Melones tomorrow in order to straighten things out at the mines and, if possible, to settle our rights with the alcalde. This person, whom you seem to fear as a future partner, is as good a person as you can find. Anyway, he will be little more than a partner because Madero, Rubio, and ourselves are running the business.

Monday, 23 June. *Letter to D. Rudecindo Rojo*

Bored as always on Sunday nights, last night Agustín and I went out to steal some reseda from that garden through the gate. They saw us, though I think only she recognized us. Well, after this little adventure, half amorous, half thieving, like most of our nocturnal flings, we went by the Episcopal church, which was completely lit up and filled with people. The bishop was preaching to 200 faithful, with his hand on the button hole of his tail coat and the knot of his tie over his left shoulder. He was so caught up in what he was doing that he seemed to be unaware of anything else. I found nothing really special about his sermon, and so I cast a glance around at the female element in the church. They were all old, ugly, and some of them were even squint-eyed. I was pleased to see that the Episcopal church does not even have good-looking women. The beautiful women all seem to be reserved for the Holy Roman Catholic religion! As we were returning home, near the corner of El Dorado Street we heard a tremendous noise. When we got there we saw that a rat had upended the shelves of the apothecary's shop, and the floor was flooded with the contents of broken jars.

WEDNESDAY, 25 JUNE. *Letter to Samuel Navarro*

There were deaths and lots of disturbances during the latest fire in San Francisco. They caught the arsonists, and the mob wanted to hang them right in the middle of the fire. Other innocent people were detained in one way or the other. At the shout of "arsonists," the mob began throwing rocks and things at them. They only escaped miraculously. Another Frenchman was surprised with certain goods down by the large wharf, and the mob took him as a thief. Paying no heed to the fact that he said and swore to be an honest man who was just saving his belongings from the fire, they took him away, put a noose around his neck, and strung him up. Fate would have it that the pole on which they were hanging him took pity on the poor man and broke under the weight of his body. Just then some of the members of the vigilante committee came up and recognized him, saving him from the mob.

STOCKTON, SATURDAY, 28 JUNE

Today it is not too hot, though it is much warmer than these past few days. Samuel has written me from Sonora and still does not know when he will be back. I do not think it will be soon because he wants to make it to a dance that Perkins is going to give for him and for some other friends.

Speaking of Perkins, I just received a letter from him, sending me a copy of the *Sonora Herald,* where they published a beautiful speech of his given at the Masonic party that took place yesterday. The speech is magnificently written and does justice to President Perkins, the head of the Masonic society of Sonora.[117]

Stockton is recovering its old form. By now, almost the entire town has been rebuilt, and there are very few blocks remaining of those burned during the last fire. The houses are not as lavish as they were before. This is because they are going to be built with bricks. Everyone appears to be getting ready to manufacture bricks.

SUNDAY, 29 JUNE

As always, today I went to mass. On our way there we saw that people were already leaving the church. That is the only place where María can see me for a few moments, and it is not surprising for her to be very punctual when going to church, certainly much more so than I am. It is pretty terrible to profane the house of God by using it as a place to meet. But, my Lord, wasn't our love holy and pure? In fact, I feel much more moved, more excited, by the fact that it is in the house of the Lord where I can get my only comfort, the only pleasure to see the object of a love that was as pure as it was unfortunate.

I can hardly believe what I am seeing and feeling. It is seven o'clock at night. After supper Agustín and I went out, as is our custom, and after a long walk we returned near Mariquita's house. As we were going past, she came out and stopped in the gallery. There was no way to get away, and so we kept on walking, though I do not know whether or not she recognized all the strong emotion welling up in my chest. As we were going by her door, to my surprise she asked us if we wanted a bouquet of reseda. I stood there as though I was petrified, unable to utter a word or make any movement in reply. Agustín left my side and went through the gate of the garden. Mariquita gave him her hand and later took two bouquets of reseda. She gave one to Agustín and then went to cut another bouquet. My goodness, what a moment of anxiety it was for me! To think that she was going to say something to me, that she was going to give me a bouquet, that I was finally going to touch her hand. All of this went through my mind at that very moment while she was getting the bouquet for me. She finally finished, and coming over to where I was, she put her hand on the gate and gave me the bouquet without saying a word to me but saying a thousand things with her eyes. I was so transfixed that I do not even remember whether or not I thanked her. Finally, coming to my senses I said, "Let's go, Agustín" in a firm voice that had nothing to do with what was going on in my soul.

Now I have the branch of reseda before my eyes as I am writing, and I can still hardly believe it all. Yes, I can smell its exquisite fragrance, and as I squeeze it in my hands I feel like I am dreaming. Can it be that Mariquita continues to love me with all the passion of before? Could it possibly be that her crime was only an error for which she repents and weeps bitterly? Could it be that she might be worthy of my love?

TUESDAY, 1 JULY 1851. *Letter to D. Saturnino Correas*

The day before yesterday they caught a thief in Campo Seco, and the judge of Sonora took him away from the mob that had gathered to lynch him on the spot. An hour later there was a meeting of the respectable citizenry, including Mr. Perkins, and the thief was once again condemned to be hanged. This time they went up and took the prisoner from the hands of the sheriff and hanged him from the first tree they found along the street. The entire execution lasted only fifteen minutes.

FRIDAY, 4 JULY

What a strange day this has been. I just escaped a bad accident, and now I have just escaped another one.[118] It is seven o'clock in the afternoon, actually at night though there is still light. My life has just been spared, and once more I feel as though I have just been reborn. An hour ago, Agustín came with his carriage, and both of us set out for a tour around town. We had gone three or four blocks when, just as we were passing in front of the Phoenix Hotel, the horse went wild. After ruining the front board of the carriage with his kicks, he furiously took off, completely unbridled, down Market Street amid the cries of more than 200 persons. "They will get killed, stop them, stop them!" We couldn't do anything because we no longer even had hold of the reins. Finally, we could see our death come near as we approached the bridge or street that runs across from Mr. Duval's house. We reached that point, and before we could do anything the carriage broke into a thousand pieces. We fell, and even then the horse continued to attempt to kick us three or four more times, though fortunately he failed. At the end of it all, the remains of the carriage had flown over us, but we were not hurt in the slightest. This is indeed a miracle; this is what being born again is all about!

STOCKTON, SATURDAY, 5 JULY

I had just returned from my crazy tour around town with Agustín and was thinking about all those scary events of only one day, all of them so strange and potentially dangerous, all of which made it seem miraculous that I had come out of it all in one piece. While thinking of all of that, my door opened, and Alfred Mix came in. It is difficult or even impossible to say what a surprise seeing him caused in me, to see him coming to shake my hand as though we saw each other all of the time, especially after all that had happened between us. He sat down, and since every second weighs heavily on you when you have to enter into explanations, he looked me in the eyes and said:

"Ramón, I am here in my and in Mariquita's name to ask you to come tonight to a little get-together we are holding in our home." I had been warned already by Samuel that they were hoping to have a dance as a pretext for our reconciliation, and so I did not delay a bit in replying to him.

"If I can be useful for anything at all, I will be happy to be there. Please tell Mariquita that I accept." He breathed a sigh of relief, as though a great weight had been taken from him, and, since the time seemed to be dragging out (when there is pain, things always go slowly), he got up and said good-bye.

Imagine all of the things that went through my soul in that everlasting instant. To see Mariquita again, to speak with her, to hold her hand, and to dance at last with her! It all seemed like a dream yesterday. How am I to start, what can I say to her? Or, perhaps, what will she say to me, after all the pain she has caused me? Yet I have the feeling that I will not say anything to her and she won't say anything to me. Just by dancing together we will say as much as we ever could with our tongues, that is for sure. With these thoughts in my mind, I began to get dressed for the occasion, despite all the tears and silliness of Amelia. . . . She has found another thing to suffer about: having me see Mariquita again and go there with her husband and Samuel, leaving her behind.

I left the house about eight, beautifully dressed like some sort of a French dandy, because that is the way the master of the dance had to be. When I got there, the hall was already filled. I entered and stopped to get ahold of a thousand really unknown emotions in me. It took just a moment. I went straight to where Mariquita was, and in no time I extended my hand to her and said:

"How are you, Miss?"

"Very well, thank you, Mr. Navarro. I can see that you are a bit late this evening."

"I do not believe that I am being impolite. I did not think that anyone would notice whether or not I came earlier or later."

"Oh sir, how wrong you are."

Just then Samuel and Agustín came up with Alfredo and took me over to the refreshment room so I could have something.[119] The critical moment had passed, and I went back to my natural indifference and coolness. There were three or four dances, and I watched the people in the dance hall. After a few quadrilles, I saw Mariquita coming over to the room where I was along with another two young ladies.

"Mr. Navarro," she said, "why are you here if you have no intention of dancing in the parlor?"

"Miss, if you would be so gracious, it would be a great pleasure to dance a waltz with you."

"Delighted."

"Thank you very much."

She took a glass of champagne and gave it to me, inviting me to toast with her. A moment later they played a waltz that rang in my heart like the trumpet on the day of our final judgment. I did not hesitate a bit. I entered the parlor, took hold of Mariquita, and went out to dance. Will I ever be able to portray what happened inside me when I took her hand and later her waist and began to dance? I said not a word and, true to my words, did not open my mouth until after she did. All of a sudden the following words came to my lips, which contain the entire conversation and made everything hinge on her reply:

"Adhuc diligis me Mariquita."[120] Her reply was only for God and for me, and only God has a right to judge her at all.

After the waltz I came home and found Amelia in bed. Poor Amelia. She was so happy for my early return, having left the dance early just to see her and to comfort her. Later I returned to the dance and, after it was over, stayed on with Mariquita, Mix, and Samuel until three o'clock in the morning.

TUESDAY, 15 JULY

It is half past six in the evening, and I have just come back from Mariquita's house. I went there to take comfort from my complete loneliness. At four o'clock I was left completely on my own. Amelia finally left, accompanied by Samuel and Pietro. She is going to France and to her family, together with a lady and old Captain Labarun. So I am completely alone at home. I had been trembling as this day approached, but it has passed without being as painful or loathsome as I had feared. Poor Amelia. For the past fortnight her life has not seemed real, and her eyes have been wet with tears at all hours. The poor creature has been crying disconsolately all the time, as she thinks of having to take leave of us and of Stockton forever. My Lord, what a beautiful heart! When God was making a perfect being for this world, why didn't he give another head to go with this golden heart and another more adequate will to accompany that beautiful face? There are few creatures I have ever seen, however, who are able to possess as much grace and beauty as she does. She is beautiful like few are; knows English, French, and Spanish as though they were all her native language; sings exquisitely whatever there is to sing; and is the daughter who carries in her the blood of the most important man in France. She was educated by the wife of the king, admired and respected by princes, and is beloved the world over as the privileged goddaughter of the queen of France. Poor Amelia. She is so deserving of better luck in life. I have never seen such a surrender to love as hers. There never was a person more seductive, more delightful, more passionate, and more worthy of being loved.

As they were telling her to tend to packing, she responded, "They are so unfair with me, they want to take from me the only hours I have left with Ramón. They finally want to kill me off." It is true. They would have really hurt her had they not allowed her to spend these last hours, as she called them, with me. In the end, however, she cannot complain, because the farewells were done much as she had wanted. Few days has she been able to be as alone with me as this last one in Stockton, as she cried the tears of a separation that might never end, the pain of happiness lost. She wept with me as she said amid her sobs, "I know that now I am exchanging my happiness in life for my own death." She was so beautiful, weeping with such serenity, shedding oceans of tears from her heart and not from her eyes, as is the case with most women. I, too, seemed to weep the entire day. Poor Amelia, should we never meet again I will always carry your memory with me.

"Thank God, Ramón," she said as she continued to weep, "that, on such a sad day, I have finally been able to bid you adieux in the happiest possible way." We went over to Mariquita's house, and her suffering was very clear as once again the two of them met. Who knows what ideas were in her head when she saw Mariquita and me together, just when she was about to leave, perhaps forever.

A thousand times she asked me to return to our forest of roses during her absence. I shall do so as often as I can, and while there I shall always recall the walks we were able to take so many times. I could not bear to go aboard the ship with her. I accompanied her to the wharf, and from there I went to Agustín's house. I did not dare to return directly home, and so from there I went to Mariquita's house, where I spent much of the afternoon. All of this is very sad indeed.

THURSDAY, 24 JULY. *Letter to D. Andrés Herrera, San Juan, Argentina*

One of the newest and strangest things in California are the effects of the lynch law. Courts with this name have been established in towns all over California. The honorable inhabitants of this country are tired of having their rights trampled, their interests undermined, and their lives put in jeopardy by the bandits and thieves who either escape or are acquitted when arrested by the police. The citizens have formed a court made up of honest men and have established their own police force to safeguard the interests of each town. For now, the measure has been successful. The other day in San Francisco they captured a bandit called Penkins. Even though it was midnight, a bell was rung and a jury of citizens was convened. The man was tried in the plaza and was convicted and sentenced to be hanged. In vain the armed forces came up in the name of the law to take the prisoner with them. The sovereign people, however, defended their rights with their pistols, and the soldiers ended up fleeing. As they took him to the gallows, he confessed to all of his crimes. In any case, they had caught him in the act that very night. Something similar happened the other day. This time it was a bandit called Stuart. The trial was held in the middle of the plaza, and for over three and one-half hours the prisoner confessed to the most horrendous of crimes. According to the newspapers, after his confession he was sentenced to be hanged. At four in the afternoon the prisoner was taken out by six thousand men to the wharf on Sacramento Street. There a Protestant minister exhorted him to repent, a noose was placed around his neck, and, at the shout of the crowd, he was hanged from one of the pilings used to tie up the ships. Everything was silent as the prisoner was swinging there in the air, twitching with his last contortions. On the 18th of the month another two prisoners were hanged in San Jose in the same way. I wish we could establish a system like that in our own countries.

SACRAMENTO, SATURDAY, 26 JULY

It is half past three in the afternoon, and I am at Fort Sutter, the famous place where gold was discovered in California. There is so much to admire and praise here, in these half-crumbling walls that make up the fort and in Sutter's memorable mill, where the first piece of gold was discovered in '48, a discovery that gave name to all the wealth of California and that brought migrants here from the world over.

At four o'clock in the afternoon I reached Sacramento. As a city, it seems a hundred times better than San Francisco. It is on the banks of a river that carries its name and is located on a beautiful plain. There are immense trees along the banks of the river that give the city the air of the countryside, all of which contrasts admirably with the beautiful buildings of a great city. The hotels and the main streets, and all of the theaters, banks, and other official buildings, are beautiful and are made of brick. Commerce Street is ten or twelve blocks long and is as beautiful and abundant in lavishness and merchandise as anything imaginable. The El Dorado, the Magnolia, and the Queen's Hotel are among its best hotels, and their lavishness is twice that of hotels in San Francisco. There are other places to stay, including the Crescent City Hotel, the France, the Sutter, the South Carolina, etc. I am staying at the Sutter Hotel.

It is two o'clock in the morning. I left the American Theater at midnight and came back to bed. After sleeping for an hour and a half or maybe two, all of a sudden I heard from my room the cry of "Fire, fire!" I got dressed right away, and since, apart from my clothes and my bag, I did not have much except my cape and my pistol, I went out into the street, saying to the night watchman:

"Farewell, my good man, just in case the hotel burns down and we do not see each other again."

An entire block burned. The fire was finally stopped because they demolished several houses and a three-story hotel that was beginning to burn. Almost at once more than six thousand men came together. What a grandiose spectacle! Four companies of firemen were working, helped by the same men who had gathered at the scene of the fire. The fire finally was put out, and calm returned. As I entered the hotel I ran into some young women who were nearly naked or only half-dressed, who asked me, "Sir, is the fire over?" "Yes, it is." What pretty young girls to be so frightened . . . !

MARYSVILLE, SUNDAY, 27 JULY

It is seven o'clock in the morning, and I am at the Crescent City Hotel, where there are more than twenty stagecoaches getting ready to leave for different nearby towns. I have never in my life seen more lavish stagecoaches. I just got aboard a yellow coach, whose inside was upholstered in scarlet velvet, with reclining seats covered in blue velvet with golden and silver trim. There are twenty-five leagues between here and Marysville, and we should make it in four and one-half hours. My ticket there has cost me three pesos. Now, that is what I call progress!

It is ten o'clock in the morning, and we are in Nicolaus. The horses are being changed, and I am making use of my time to write in my notebook.

As we were crossing the American River, the horses lost their footing in the river. We had to close the windows of the coach so as not to get flooded with water. The first pair of horses broke off, and we were stuck in the middle of the river. The drivers had to jump into the water, retrieve the horses, and hitch them up again with great effort. It finally got done, and we were able to continue our journey.

It is noon, and we just arrived in Marysville. We walked around most of the town before coming to the United States Hotel. I am writing in my notebook while the servant of the hotel is saddling the horse that is to take me to Verano, or Camp Sonoreño. The town is beautiful to see because, much like Sacramento, it rises from the banks of the Marysville River, along which you can see the steamboats and cargo ships that supply the mines from San Francisco and Sacramento. There are loads of lavish hotels decorated with portraits and other costly paintings. But what I noticed most is the brothel, a lovely three-story, luxuriously decorated building, where you can see that curtains on all the doors and windows are made of Indian silk of different colors. As I was going by, I could see six vestal virgins who live there, all of whom were lovely, if indeed there can be beauty of the flesh where there is no soul.

It was two o'clock in the afternoon when I reached what they call the *Veranito*. It is about five or six miles from Marysville, and this is where the muleteers stop and where you find the best of the fruits sold in San Francisco, Sacramento, and Stockton. I met with Mr. Mariano Alvares, who received me as though I was the promised Messiah. To start with, he gave me two beautiful watermelon, better than any I have ever seen before. Afterward he invited me to a good lunch. The poor guy is worth his weight in gold. It was such a hot day that his watermelon sure came in mighty handy.

SACRAMENTO, TUESDAY, 29 JULY

Last night in Marysville I was able to listen to some of the best orchestras you can find in California. It is strange, because while there I was also able to see some of the most beautiful women, be they French, Mexican, or American. All of them were more or less employed in the hotels. The truth is that some of them were sitting honestly at the bars with their husbands, while others were with their fake daddies, playing lansquenets.[121] What corruption to see old men, fifty or sixty years of age, who for some monthly stipend will accept the name of a young lady, probably a prostitute, and will be with her in public only for show, blind and deaf to all that goes on around their "daughters." There is corruption and poison at all ages and states of life. I saw two or three men like that in Sacramento and in Marysville.

I can recall now that when I reached the town of Nicolaus on my way to Marysville, where the stagecoach stopped, I ran into poor old Captain Sutter, the man who discovered gold here in California. He does not have enough money to eat, and he was sitting there with his six-cent pipe in his mouth. What a world, where only fortune, both good and bad, holds sway! That man, who was the owner of Marysville and Sacramento, who was paid 12.5 million pesos for the land, that man now doesn't even have a small piece of land to call his own, and he gets his food from charity. My God, the fortunes of this world are but questions of vanity and little else.[122]

THURSDAY, 31 JULY. *Letter to Rudecindo Rojo*

Yesterday I came from Sacramento and Marysville. Did you know that both of these towns are really lovely? In many ways, Sacramento looks even nicer than San Francisco. The architecture of its buildings is often strange, but they are very beautiful and luxuriously appointed. It is difficult to imagine what the city of Sacramento is like without actually seeing it. Yes sir, if Don Quixote were to resuscitate, he would think that Sacramento was an enchanted town. The night I was there, there was a great fire. The way the wind was blowing the flames, I couldn't help being happy that I was able to see the town the day before it ceased to exist forever. All of a sudden, however, four companies of firefighters came up, and before I could figure out just what they were doing, they threw their hooks around a three-story hotel and pulled it down. With that, the fire had to stop, almost against its own will. As I was at the Sutter Hotel, I got my watch, my pistol, and my book and went out into the street without really noticing the way everyone else was hurrying to save their furniture and other property. And, you know what? Before the fire, I had been dreaming about Mrs. Stark, who had been simply divine at the Tehama Theater that night. Well, as I was going out of the hotel with all of my belongings and "with the hope of not having to pay my bill the next day," I ran into Mrs. Stark on the main staircase dressed in her nightgown. My lord, what beauty!

THURSDAY, 7 AUGUST. *Letter to Samuel Navarro*

Yesterday Mix received a double purge whose effects may well be difficult for him to overcome and may endanger his position and perhaps even his future. He had thought that his elected office was for one year and that he still had another three months in power. Yesterday the *San Joaquin* published an order coming from San Jose that stated that elections for recorder were to be held on the fourth of next month. Imagine the effect this will have on Mix, who was happily dreaming, with no thought at all to elections. Now there are already three strong candidates, with the most fearsome being Dr. Ward, because of all his popularity. Mix is probably going to lose his post.

THURSDAY, 7 AUGUST. *Letter to Rudecindo Rojo*

There is not much news in your letter, but one item is worth the world because it talks of the disappearance of one of the worst men who ever infested life in Sonora. Yes sir, all of the citizens of Sonora today must be delighted with the end met by that bandit Villefort, whose name and the clothes he wore were those of a gentleman. What a strange thing. One by one all of the evil men who have created such exceptional troubles in California are disappearing and are being replaced by good people. All of those gamblers in Sonora are little more than impudent criminals, yet they are tolerated because they have been able to drag into their excesses all of the good men who might otherwise have thrown them out like the filthy reptiles they are but who did not because of their contacts with them. In this way, Mike, who was just hanged here, was able to count on certain gentlemen as "friends" in Sonora. They were men who used to be well heeled and refined but who ended up gambling with him, drinking in his house, and having orgies together with him . . . of course, "all honestly." Well, Villefort finally died after all the evil he brought with him. He is leaving behind many friends and perhaps even admirers among the aristocracy of Sonora. As I say, it is really a strange thing but with all of these gamblers and people hanging out at the hotels with their pistols at their side and their cards in their pockets; all of them end up either at the gallows or murdered by someone like them, between one drink and the next.

TUESDAY, 12 AUGUST. *Letter to D. Valentín San Fuentes in San Francisco*

Yesterday our partner, Rodríguez, came here from the mines with the best of news. Recently they have reached metals that leave little doubt but that gold is but a few yards away. Of all of the mines being worked nowadays in Melones and in other places, few offer greater hopes for their speculators, and none have miners who are happier and more enthusiastic. The reason why Mr. Rodríguez has come here is to meet tomorrow or the day after with all of the partners, because by Saturday we will probably have gold in sight or at least the ore we need to grind for gold. Lots of things have to be shipped to the mine, and your presence is absolutely necessary if things are going to be done properly. My brother Samuel was at the mine, and while there his horse fell, and he broke his arm. He had to go to Sonora to get it mended, but he will be here for the meeting.

STOCKTON, WEDNESDAY, 13 AUGUST

It is eight o'clock in the morning, and I am taking the stagecoach to Mokelumne Hill to go to the mines of Calaveras. Yesterday at Mix's house I saw Scalante himself, who said he could not find the road to the Golden Star mine and that I should take the load he was carrying.[123] I did not want to wait and am leaving right now by stagecoach. It is sure different to travel now than it was in '49. Nowadays I enter the stagecoach as though I was on my way to a dance, with my book in hand. I sit back and read *Rose Foster* and only remember my journey when they call me to lunch or dinner.

It is noon, and I just arrived here in Calaveras. I was hoping to meet the muleteer on the bridge to show him the road to the mine, but there wasn't anyone there. I went to get a horse to set out in search of him, but there was none to be found, no matter what the price. I suppose that I will have to set out on foot for the mine. It is annoying after coming here in such a beautiful stagecoach. Darn these muleteers, it is always their fault.

THURSDAY, 14 AUGUST

Last night I was on my way to the ranch with a book under my arm, almost as though I was a preacher or a missionary with his breviary, when I heard the noise of a wagon coming up behind me. I waited, and indeed it was a wagon coming toward me. I told the Americans in it about my misadventures and was friendly with them. They were kind enough to bring me here in their wagon. They also told me how to find the muleteers. Today I did just that, and I was able to show them the route to the mine. Now I am waiting to return to Stockton. A stagecoach should come by between nine and ten to take me there.

STOCKTON, WEDNESDAY, 27 AUGUST

It is eight o'clock in the morning, and I am leaving for Sacramento on my second trip to that city. I took the best stagecoach going there, and I think it should be a pretty comfortable journey. I was at Mariquita's house last night, and she was well, though rather sad. If her husband loses the elections it will not bring anything good for the poor thing. Maybe she will have to leave Stockton if her husband is forced to move elsewhere. Actually, I don't think anything can take her away from here. She has so many acquaintances, so many friendships, that it would be very hard for her if she had to leave. Her husband and her father are rich enough to start up any business around here they want. There is no doubt that losing an office that pays more or less 20,000 pesos a year is bound to be felt.

It is noon, and we just reached the house of Miss Hallen, where we spent an hour having lunch and changing the horses of the stagecoach. It is a beautiful day, certainly not as hot as we had feared. The loveliest of all, however, is Miss Hallen, who speaks with us while she is setting the table, as well as the different plates of game they serve: venison, deer, rabbit, quail, etc.

We made it to Sacramento at four o'clock sharp after a very successful journey. The entire town, both beautiful and charming, has just washed its face. Its streets have been swept and watered down in a way that brings out their freshness and is thoroughly delightful. It is like an enchanted town, with the beauty and luxury of its buildings, the multitudes of people filling each street and sidewalk, and the warehouses and shops contributing to enliven the town with their wares. I have taken a room at the Crescent City Hotel, which is where the stagecoaches bound for all of the nearby towns depart from. It is the easiest way for me to get the coach to Marysville.

It is half past nine at night now. I ate at the great New Orleans Hotel and afterward went to the Tehama Theater, where I had been the last time I was here. When I got to where it was, I could not find it. Who knows, I wondered like a Sevillian for his *Giralda*, if they haven't carried it off someplace? Later on I met with a gentleman who cleared up the situation for me by telling me that eight days ago the theater burned down along with the other buildings on the block.

THURSDAY, 28 AUGUST

I have taken the eight o'clock stagecoach for Marysville in the most elegant three-passenger coach available. The say that the twenty-five league journey will take us four hours and twenty-five minutes. A beautiful woman from Mazatlán just got aboard and took her seat next to me. She has beautiful eyes, skin as white as paper, and is about sixteen or seventeen years old. I am the only Spanish speaker aboard and have been her interpreter for the rest of the passengers. What a shame. . . .

We reached Marysville at half past two in the afternoon. During the trip she kept me entertained with the stories of her life. She says she left her husband in Sacramento and has come here to visit a sister. She invited me to the Napoleon Hotel, where she is staying. She is so lovely that it is impossible for anyone to say no to her, and so I told her that I would drop by. In fact, I have not intention at all of dropping by. It may or may not be honorable, but the best thing with dice is not to play with them!!!

MARYSVILLE, FRIDAY, 29 AUGUST

Yesterday upon my arrival in Marysville, I got off at the United States Hotel, where I stayed for an hour to rest and wash up, and then headed out for Verano, or Camp Sonoreño, in the stagecoach that covers that route.

The people around here are like the people from Sonora in Mexico. Everything is like one big dance, and most of the people are Mexicans. I came yesterday and found Mariano Alvares in a fiesta like all the rest of them. They served me watermelon and all kinds of other tasty things to eat. I read until the sun went down. As soon as it got dark, the music coming from two little hotels began to gnaw away at my patience. I went to bed at nine o'clock and from there could not help but hear the music, the songs, and the sounds of the dancers. It must have been about midnight when the noise of a big fight involving a hundred men or more awakened me. I could hear their swearing right near my bed along with the voices of two or three women who appeared to be the cause of it all. There were gunshots, knifings, and curses. It lasted most of the rest of the night.

MONDAY, 1 SEPTEMBER 1851

I returned to Stockton yesterday and was met by very grim news. What a sad affair to start my diary with this month. The things I am going to recall in this diary of memoirs today will be very sad and very painful.

My poor father. After a laborious life of 50 years, after having served his nation in the highest posts with no attempt whatsoever to enrich himself, after having been the most just and honest man in his country, he was cast far from his nation and his home and made to earn a living for his family after much hardship and at the risk of his own life. After having lived an exemplary life of austerity, after having been called by all those who knew him "the virtuous and the irreproachable one," he was forced to come to Chile to die as an exile, far away from his children.

It is as though his illness and his death are but the work of his sorrow and melancholy. I have never seen my father ill, ever, and in Chile he always had excellent health. Isolated on the ranch in Cucha, only seeing his family in the winter, often alone among barbarians, dedicated to material work by day and to mental labors by night, he forged ahead without thinking of this vale of tears and of its moral consumption until it was too late. In his letters he has been foretelling the end of his days, but we have just imagined them to be mere observations made under the influence of his sorrow in the hope to get us to return. We were wrong.

He died fifteen days after coming to Concepción. At last I have the comfort of knowing that his death was exemplary, as was the history of his life. The day of his death (30th May) took place just when it looked like he was getting better. In the morning he said he was going to die that day and that he wanted to get up and walk to the temple in order to be prepared. Against everyone's exhortations and advice, he got up from his bed, went to church, went to confession, received the holy sacraments, prayed there for more than two hours, and returned home as peaceful and happy as if he was well again. Then he sat at his desk and wrote a long letter of farewell for me and another one for Samuel, arranged all of his things, and wrote his last codicils. Then he said, "Now I am going to bed to die." The entire family gathered in his room, and he bid farewell to them one by one with total tranquillity and was completely in his right mind until the moment of his death, which came an hour after taking to bed.

What an amazing end to the life of a just man. He took his leave of this life with total serenity, with no sorrow, with no remorse. It was almost as if the end came without pain or suffering, as his eyes closed with gentleness and no contortions to reveal his agony. Whenever I stray from the path of honor and integrity, as one who is less virtuous than his father, I will always remember his life and death as an example, as the guide to the way we are supposed to lead our lives. . . .

SUNDAY, 14 SEPTEMBER. *Letter to Samuel Navarro*

Last night was lovely, and you could see many boats with young boys and girls on the lake, beautiful carriages on the peninsula, and all kinds of couples along the docks. All of this ended up getting disturbed by the sudden noise of drums, bugles, and bells, etc. I thought the cause was probably some wedding of a twenty-year-old man with a seventy-year-old widow. You know what the tradition is in cases such as those. Lots of people began to gather and ask one another, "What's the matter?" By this time a crowd of some 200 people was following the music, and like many others, Agustín and I began to get alarmed, thinking it might be something like a revolution. The procession finally stopped at the docks, and the man who seemed to be the head of it and who was dressed like a big spender stopped on a cart and made signs for the musicians to stop playing. Everyone was silent, and not even a fly was moving. It looked to me as though they were about to apply the lynch law to some prisoner. "Gentlemen," he said with great composure and gravity, "today is Saturday, and therefore there is no doubt but that tomorrow is Sunday." And without another word, he headed off to the sound of the music, doing much the same at every street corner. What do you think about that?

SUNDAY, 14 SEPTEMBER. *Letter to Samuel Navarro in San Francisco*

A sad and horrible event has all of Stockton talking this morning. It was the suicide of that young man Castro, who was Urbina's colleague. Dr. Lasvignes just inspected the body at the order of the coroner and the justice of the peace, and the statement of the doctor reads as follows: "The man has committed suicide with a pistol, and the poor devil survived the shot by three-quarters of an hour." The events are as follows. Dr. Lasvignes ran into poor Castro at four o'clock yesterday afternoon and asked about his colleague Urbina. Castro did not answer and went right on past. The doctor says that he started to cry as he left his side. At half past four he looked very sad as he went up to his room. At five, a pistol shot was heard by the rest of the tenants and people living in the building, but since a pistol shot is so common around here, nobody paid much attention. By today they had noticed that the poor young man had entered into his room but, very much contrary to his own habits, had not yet come out either at night or during the day. So they put a ladder up to his window and went into the room. The poor devil was still kneeling next to his bed with his brains all over the place and his pistol a couple of feet away. It seems that before shooting himself, he had doubted as to whether to kill himself with a pistol or with a knife, and that is why there was also a knife next to him on the bed. There was no letter or anything at all that might have said why this guy had reached such a desperate situation. What is known around here is that Castro had requested and had received the hand of a young girl who is the daughter of a rich family from Contra Costa. He had spent between four and six thousand pesos in getting prepared for the wedding. It looks like all of his golden hopes became acute disappointment, either because the father was going to go back on his word or because Castro might have seen a certain "robustness" in the young girl, instead of her fine and delicate waist, and that this did not seem either right . . . or elegant . . . to him. The fact is that this disagreeable event made him return to Stockton, but by then he had changed entirely. The days that passed between that moment and yesterday, the last day of his life, were marked by a horrible sadness and a stoic indifference to everything. Evidently the whim of the little ranch girl to fatten her waist and lose her elegant flexibility seemed to be in such bad taste to Mr. Castro that, on the very eve of giving her his surname, he decided to take leave of this world. He said that there was no honor or fidelity in the so-called weak sex and that in reality it was very evil and horribly damaging for any poor devil who fell into one of their nets here in California. This affair is the subject of conversation around here. If instead of California we were in Chile during the winter, more than four old women would have burned their heels sitting around the brazier, telling the event with all its details as they were finishing off their mate.

FRIDAY, 19 SEPTEMBER. *Letter to Samuel Navarro in San Francisco*

Since yesterday the Ainza girls have been gracing the town of Stockton with their beauty. Two of them are very pretty. Especially Lola, the youngest, who is as slender and gracious as can be and has eyes as black and expressive as those of Lola Montes, the queen of Bavaria. None of the others are ugly, and all of them are very polite and gracious. They all sing and play instruments in a way that only Amelia and Madame Lacombe have done before.

I am sending you a little money, don't know quite how much. Before the steamship leaves at four I will put the number of hundreds or thousands I am sending you. Pretty soon we will begin to put all sorts of zeros in our register book, now that the mine is beginning to pay off. *By Jingo!* I really like this mining business . . . today you are poor, tomorrow you are rich, today in heaven, tomorrow in hell. But we will not be stupid, *my dear brother, if only we could* strike it rich in the mines, *by Jingo!* We would go to Europe with all of our thick thousands, we would buy some paintings in Versailles, we would buy printing presses and whatever else we fairly well pleased, and we would come back to the Argentine Republic to destroy Rosas and his family (*by Jingo*, everyone except for Emilia . . .) and not leave behind any trace of his race! We will visit the world, so we might as well count our thousands as though they were the hairs on our heads.[124]

SUNDAY, 21 SEPTEMBER. *Letter to Samuel Navarro in San Francisco*

The biggest news today in Stockton is the arrival in this world of His Royal Highness, the prince of Stockton, N. N. Weber. Last night Mr. Weber came in person to fetch the doctor, who at the time was busy figuring out how to make his bed without moving from his easy chair, all the while reading the *Court of London.* He left and only returned this morning, telling us of the happy arrival of the little Weber boy in this world. He is so pleased that he really doesn't know what to do with himself, and the proof of it is that he is expecting a handsome recompense for his services.

TUESDAY, 23 SEPTEMBER. *Letter to Rudecindo Rojo in Sonora*

I am hoping to go to Sonora to start up a store that will keep me busy for the four months I must still stay in California. You'll come with me then, won't you? Oh, do not be alarmed. It is not a service I want to do for you, but rather a favor I would like to request of you. You could come and live with me, and we could have a good room there, with our fireplace for the winter and our books in all sorts of languages (which you know well). We would also have our piano, our guitar, and all the new music available. We could live like real people and also make money all winter. What do you think? Will you come with me, buddy? I can just hear you saying that you cannot refuse me anything I ask, just as I cannot refuse anything for you. Let us not speak anymore about this until the time comes.

I just received letters from Chile postmarked only twenty-seven days ago. What do you think about that? When letters from the United States take at least a month, the twenty-seven days from Valparaíso is really amazing!

The news we received regarding business matters is as good as it can be. They are asking us to return to Chile as soon as possible because we are needed there. They say we will lose thousands in potential earnings if we do not attend personally to our business ventures. Besides, they say that here we are not doing anything really worth our while. The truth is that our present venture in the mines may look that way, but things may change dramatically very soon. The special rights for the two steamships we plan to set up along the Bío-Bío River in the south of Chile are just about done, according to Mardoqueo, who also tells us that we can count on his help. With two uncles in the court, he thinks it is pretty much done already. With this privilege in hand, by itself the concession would be worth fifty or sixty thousand pesos if we were to sell it, though we would never dream of doing something mad like that. We have already received the letters from the United States in answer to Perkins's proposal accepting the business company and offering their capital and the steamships as long as we get the proper rights. In the next steamship there will be blueprints and tonnage that the small steamboats need to have to sail there. Together with the other business we have in the south of Chile and the ships sailing out of Valparaíso, this new venture could turn out very well. For this reason we are being urged to go there as soon as possible. Samuel is leaving on October 1st, and as soon as he is gone I will put into practice the little business plan in Sonora I mentioned to you.

SUNDAY, 28 SEPTEMBER

Three or four days ago I received letters from Amelia sent from Panama. Poor Amelia; always suffering, always unhappy, but always the same in her feelings. She says she has suffered greatly during the voyage. The malicious captain showed himself to be a despicable man, and this has merely added to her suffering. She met a young Argentinean-American doctor aboard, who offered her his friendship and helped her as the doctor on board. She says she expects to suffer even more as they cross the Isthmus of Panama because there are dangers to be overcome and many leagues to be walked on foot. Poor Amelia! Conceived in misfortune, always unhappy wherever she is and however much she has been loved and cherished by everyone. She told me to remember the 14th of May and all of its events, and should she die, she will do so with my name on her lips as she recalls that day. Thank you, Amelia. Should I die, I shall pray for you and for myself to God and for the happiness of those who have loved me.

STANISLAUS RIVER, WEDNESDAY, 8 OCTOBER 1851

It is noon, and we are on the Stanislaus River. I took the stagecoach this morning at six o'clock on my way to Sonora. We are waiting in a magnificent hotel while the passengers are served a meal and the horses are changed. This hotel is lovely and is built on the very banks of the river, with views of the surrounding fields and of other nearby places. The main room is completely filled with paintings that seem to be obscene to me, though others may think of it as a quality.

The ranch of the Indians is two blocks from the hotel on the other bank of the river. I have just taken a walk around their miserable huts, just when the Indians were returning from fishing with immense salmon and whole strings of trout. This is how these poor people earn a living. Each one of them is now busy preparing the lunch, while the women are rocking the children on their knees. It is surprising to see that there are about eight or ten of these Indians who are as white as paper, though their hair is still a bit black. These must be the sons of Yankees. The race is now beginning to become mixed and will continue to do so until all of the Indians disappear.

It is half past six in the afternoon, and we just reached this little Babylon of Sonora. The town is lit up with its street lamps and the lights from hotels and other stores and shops. Around the town you can hear a type of indescribable and imprecise noise coming from the different types of music being played in the different hotels. In each one of them there is a beautiful girl at the bar and another one at the gambling table, attempting to attract people and crowds to the hotel. Without a girl there can be no hotel, without a beautiful one there can be no business, without a woman there can be no business or anything else.

STOCKTON, SUNDAY, 12 OCTOBER

I have been here in Sonora for four or five days now. Despite being with my best friends here amid all this bustle, with all the artists and music, I am as sad as a man in jail. What a night last night was! Samuel just wrote to me, and in his letter he said, "Mariquita is pregnant."[125] What sort of news is that to cheer sad people up!

Today is Sunday, and all this movement about town is really worth noticing the first time you see it. You can hear music in all of the hotels, and each one of them is crowded with people. It is not surprising because the entire mining population within three leagues of here comes into town on Sundays. There must be thousands of them. Every half-block or so you can see another immense crowd of people surrounding a man who stands out above the rest, who is shouting and making a thousand gestures while he is showing some sort of ware he wants to sell. Then two, three, or more groups of musicians come by almost together, each of which has a juggler or a clown along with them, inviting everyone to come to the theater, the bullfight, or the acrobatic show at night. Boy, what I would give to be in Stockton right now!!!

SONORA, MONDAY, 13 OCTOBER

It is nine o'clock in the morning, and I am leaving Sonora for Melones. Yesterday I learned from the miners who had come from the area surrounding Melones that our mine was beginning to be profitable. Everything in

California tends to be exaggerated, and this bit of news has been exaggerated here as well, to such an extent that, in Sonora, people began trying to ingratiate themselves with the owner of a mine capable of yielding twenty-five pounds of gold at first try!! What miserable people! Everyone lies cleverly, and they are all servile enough to kiss the feet of someone they think is rich. As far as I know from the news that Vera brought me, according to Rodríguez the mine is yielding a profit of $500 per load. And that is considered fabulous *wealth,* with all due emphasis on the word!

It is noon, and I just reached Melones. My uncle and partner Casimiro Rodríguez was not there, and a woman told me that he had headed out for the mines early in the morning and would soon be back. The house is entirely unoccupied, and I am here alone, except for the rats that run across the counter from time to time.

It is half past eleven at night, and the moon is as bright as I have ever seen it in California. I was able to take a walk and enjoy the beauty of the night and was even able to jot down a few lines of poetry that came to me after having read some of Lamartine. I came upon a greasy and beat-up book by Lamartine, his *Les Confidences.*[126] What great satisfaction it gave me to find this book here in the very guts of California, amid all this solitude and on a night like this. I asked my uncle about the owner of the book, and he told me that it belonged to a traveler who had forgotten it there, and since then it has gone from hand to hand around the miners of Melones until it ended up the way it is now. My goodness, it would have been hard to find a treasure greater than this one. I had never read this book and had actually looked for it many times. The story he tells before beginning the memoirs, about the way he used to keep a diary from the time he was very young and what it was worth and what it meant for him, filled me with amazement to see how a worm, an atom, a nothing like I am in comparison to him, instinctively did the same thing he had. For me, my diary is my life, my comfort, my second existence. For him it was the same thing. I couldn't help but copy down a few lines mentioning his diary. There they are at the beginning of my diary, and whenever I or anyone else wants to know what it means some day, he should read the words of Lamartine, and he will know.

MELONES, TUESDAY, 14 OCTOBER

It is nine o'clock in the morning, and I am on my way back to Sonora. Last night I read and wrote about Lamartine's *Confidences* until the candle went out. Today I awoke still under his spell, and my soul overflows with tranquillity and happiness.

It is eleven o'clock, and I have just come down the immense hill of Melones. I am now by the river, where I am waiting for lunch before continuing on my way. The house of Mr. Murray is on the same bank of the Stanislaus River. It is a lovely country house, with its balconies, its garden, its plants, etc.

It is half past two in the afternoon, and I just reached Sonora. As I went by the Lecoq Hotel, Miranda and his miss invited me to dine with them. Everyone is filled with adulation. Our mine is doing excellently, and it looks like we will soon sell half of it for 12,000 pesos. I have with me some samples taken from the works themselves, and I bet I will be able to do some good business in Stockton or in San Francisco.

SONORA, WEDNESDAY, 15 OCTOBER

It is four o'clock in the morning, and I am heading out for Stockton. Last night I didn't sleep at all. At half past eight I left Carmelita's house with Enyart. Later we returned and went with her and her husband to have some chocolate at an inn that is famous for its chocolate. After midnight we went out with Mademoiselle Virgine, who says to me in good Spanish, *"alma miya."*[127] Afterward Enyart and I came upon a little burro in the street. Since the moon was so beautiful, it occurred to us that it would be fun to play with the burro. Enyart got on the front, and I was on its haunch. Accompanied by several young men, including Cupertino, Galán, Samorain, Galup, and others, we entered the Lavetour Hotel riding the jackass amid frenzied applause. It was really a sight for all of the people there to see the treasurer of the town, a member of the congress, and his friend Navarro, *both pretty high-ranking gentlemen,* sitting atop an ass accompanied by twenty young men.[128]

STOCKTON, THURSDAY, 16 OCTOBER

After my return to Stockton, I took a bath and went right over to Mariquita's house, where I was able to visit her and the Ainza sisters at the same time. They were eating when I arrived, and when I refused their invitation, one of them said as she laughed:

"Men with 50,000 peso mines no longer eat with poor people."

"On the contrary, they are precisely the men who do eat with the poor, just so they can save their money. After all, all rich men are misers."

I saw no difference at all in Mariquita, and I think that all this business about being *enceinte* is all a lie. My God. *Serait il possible, sa finirait d'un seul coup avec . . . Mais c'est impossible!!!*[129]

FRIDAY, 31 OCTOBER. *Letter to Francisco "Pancho" Herrera in Calaveras*

I am very sorry, dear Pancho, not to be able to reply affirmatively to your request for me to find you a position here in Stockton or in San Francisco. Your honesty and ability would make you a better candidate than most, but if you do not know English, around here it is as though you were a deaf mute, and having a mute salesperson or clerk is never a good idea. Why don't you stay there a bit longer while I see if the strikes we have begun in the Golden Star mine or in the one in Melones continue. In Melones we just made our first strike a few days ago, and it paid $250 in gold taken from 6 arrobas of stone. If things continue that way, we will be getting thousands of pesos per week. That being the case, you would be better off staying out there than being here next to your cousin, whom you should also consider your brother. So I advise you to wait, and if the good luck in some of my mines continues, I will let you know when to come with me.

STOCKTON, FRIDAY, 28 NOVEMBER 1851

It is four in the afternoon, and I have just witnessed the execution of Roberts and Wilson. It was a beautiful day today, almost as if to lend a note of sarcasm to the death of the two victims. At noon the people began to arrive on horseback and in carriages from the surrounding areas. By two o'clock the gallows were surrounded by nearly 6,000 men and women, not counting the street alongside the prison that was just as full. The two criminals appeared just at two o'clock. Wilson showed up with a cigar in his mouth, exhaling clouds of smoke, apparently indifferent to the entire matter. As he took his seat on the wagon, he asked, "Which one is my coffin?" Then he sat on it, and the wagon took off. They were taken up to the gallows, and Wilson took the one on the right and Roberts the one on the left. Roberts had little to say, asked for forgiveness and to be prayed for. Wilson, on the other hand, spoke for more than a half an hour by the watch I had in my hand. You could hear his voice three blocks away, and I have never heard more blasphemies than those he uttered. He told the story of his life and his crimes amidst a profound silence. At times he laughed and was even able to make others laugh, telling about the different events of his life. "I know I am going to hell," he said, "but I don't care. I want to die bravely and not like an old lady. Farewell girls." As he said this, the trap door fell, and his agony began. It lasted twenty minutes. The other prisoner died right away.[130]

As far as we are concerned, there is very little to be said about business here. Samuel will tell you about the only business affairs we have. I do not like to talk of hopes, and so for now it is probably better to say nothing. Nevertheless, our position is the following: "I and Samuel . . . or Samuel and I, for a change." Speaking only about the work of the two mines, there is really not much to say, because those talkative miners have said more than enough already. One of our mines, the one in Melones, is now making a profit, and it could probably be sold for forty or fifty thousand pesos. As far as the other one is concerned, it just became ours a few days ago. It is called the Golden Star, and our partner San Fuentes (the brother of the former minister) says, "we are done with our troubles and all our hard work; we have just discovered gold at a yield of six to eight ounces per load, which means about $150 in pure gold for six arrobas of ore." I do my own calculations in the following way, 500 loads of metal will give us $75,000 net profit. The mine of Melones is valued at $50,000. Total sum: zero net profit divided by "hope." That is all I have to say to you about business, "hope."

Here in California I can get some of the best works in French and English only two months after their publication in Paris or London, but it is hard to get classical Spanish authors unless I send to Mexico City for them. . . . Here there are newspapers that are filled with the stories of a thousand and one nights, with news, and even advice on how to get rid of fleas or rats. Yet every day there are more of them, and they are doing much better. If the Spanish-speaking population here were not so indolent, even here in California, by now we would have started one already. In our recent discussions on the matter with the Ainzas, the Iñigos, the Riveras, all our Mexican capitalists, we proposed you as our correspondent in Chile. They already know you from your letters and would be delighted if you accepted. As far as I am concerned, Mardoqueo, I would like to get involved in something like this and learn about these things, without, of course, forgetting about my other occupations here. This is the best country there is to learn how to entangle things of all kinds with your pen. Here there are no restrictions whatsoever on newspapers, nor is there any press law here to limit a person's freedom of expression as represented by the pen. In California everyone answers in the way they are addressed. If it is in a newspaper, they answer in a newspaper. If they are socked, they hit back; if it is by a pistol, they use a pistol in return. Insults are seldom used except in exceptional situations. Explanations are seldom demanded; but when they are, they are given fully.

SATURDAY, 10 JANUARY. *Letter to Amelia in Le Havre, France*

The first thing I do in the morning after getting dressed (you know, I have become the dandy of Stockton since I received the load of clothes from Mr. Doile's tailor shop in Valparaíso), I sit at my desk and write in my diary until lunchtime. . . . I am also doing very well on the guitar. For three months now I have been practicing a lot and am in really good form. I have taken a great love for my instrument. I have also been writing a book of very nice poetry, or at least the Stocktonians say so. The book has been circulating and has received very undeserved applause. I will send you a copy when I have time to make one, though it may take awhile because it is quite long.

I am also translating the *Mysteries of the Inquisition* from English and have already done a volume. This type of work distracts and entertains me in my room. As you can see, my lifestyle has not changed very much. There have been two dances since the 4th of July in the Mixes' house and many more in Agustín's. I have gone to all of them but invariably have returned without so much as taking the waist of a girl to dance a waltz, polka, or anything else. You know what? There are three hearts around here who live and die in the warmth of my gaze, but I am no more responsible for any of that than you are, more than 100 leagues from me here in California. It is not surprising. I am really the only young man around who they say is worth the trouble, and thus I am the object of women's whims coming and going all the time.

SUNDAY, 18 JANUARY. *Letter to D. Agustín Herrera in San Juan, Argentina*

There have been two new strikes in our Golden Star mine in Calaveras and in the one in Melones. Since we have been working now for almost two years at this darned speculation, we have considered the possibility of selling off the mine in Melones, which is the more productive one, in order to underwrite the work of the others or to move someplace else, much as the swallows do when there is a better springtime and better flowers elsewhere. They have offered us 10,000 pesos for half, but we want twenty thousand for the entire mine. The representative of the English company has returned to San Francisco with our proposals, and that is where the business will be settled by our agent, who has also gone there. Samuel will be leaving for Chile on the first of next month.

STOCKTON, TUESDAY, 20 JANUARY

Every time I am happy as I have been for the past two days, every time my heart is filled with joy, the thought that something negative is just around the corner always comes to me. I have been wrong many times, probably most of the time. Yet since I have grown used to being happy, I can't help but think that fate has made me drunk with joy and satisfaction so that it could set a trap for me and make my fall all the harder. But I might be mistaken. Why should I mix these somber thoughts now along with the happiest moments of my life? Why commit blasphemy now in the midst of well-being and good fortune? And what about those moments when your soul is the prisoner of depression and misfortune, moments when it is understandable to use blasphemy to get the darkness out of your system, to alleviate the pain? No, I should not believe that I am happy now just because it is all a trick being played on me. I am happy because my soul is at peace and it enjoys a good fortune that is impossible to explain. Thank you, my Airam.[131]

It is always interesting to see how certain things always seem to get twisted in real life, how they can become incredible. If it were to happen in a novel, I would think it was pure invention. *Actually I can hardly believe it myself. Neleb, incredibly enough, is more in love with me than ever.[132] Yesterday evening she said it to me as plain as can be and told me just what was happening in her heart. By my God, this is horrible! Being so proud, you would think that she was asking for a little friendship, instead of this love she has never felt before but confesses now for the first time. I listened to her calmly, but when she said, "My Lord, how unhappy I am!" and began to cry, I could not restrain myself, and I too shed tears alongside her. She has said things that were enough to break your heart. . . . But, my Lord, what am I to do? I do not know how this will work out. It is a truly terrible thing. And the countess of Landsfeld would die of sorrow if she ever found out that another woman loved me.[133] The poor countess, still but a child, loves me more than all the others combined. It is impossible for one not to love her when she is so gay, the gayest of them all, when she is so young and so naive. She even said to me, "Sir, I love you so much that I would like you to demand from me some sign of my love, and you will have it." It is beginning to seem like all of this is a farce, but it is all as true as my name is Ramón. What am I to do? And what would happen if Airam knew that two other woman were crazy in love with her Ramón?[134]*

STOCKTON, MONDAY, 2 FEBRUARY 1852

The weather today was lovely, and it looks as though there will be no more winter. I received letters from Amelia and her mother that were mailed from France. Poor Amelia is ill. It is truly sad to read her letter. Who would believe that she would still have a strong and fervent memory of me when she is in the true capital of the world. It is the same sentiment she had for her Ramón, as she used to call me, when she was here. Later on I shall copy some parts of her letter in my diary. For now it is enough to jot down that she is in one of the best hospitals in Paris, along with four or five other women of high rank who are ill like she is. She expects to be there for four months.

THURSDAY, 5 FEBRUARY

It is half past eight in the morning, and I am off to the Golden Star mine to settle a disagreement that has arisen between some of the miners and the director, our partner San Fuentes. It is cloudy today, and I have left with only my winter frock coat for cover; no poncho, no cape, nothing else. But I am riding our trusty horse Kate, and I have my five-shot pistol at my side.

At half past two I reached the Calaveras ranch, still ten and one-half leagues from our mine. I was completely soaked. It rained for about ten or twelve miles of the journey, but I did not want to stop. At about half past six in the afternoon I reached Mr. Wakes's hotel in Calaveras. En route I ran into Benavides, a young Chilean who came along in a wagon. We made the rest of the trip slowly as we spoke of Chile and of the Argentine Republic.

GOLDEN STAR MINE, CALAVERAS, FRIDAY, 6 FEBRUARY

I left this morning around seven o'clock, after having slept tolerably well. I ate dinner around eight with Benavides, and we retired about ten o'clock after a stroll around the moonlit fields. It rained the entire way here. The journey was four leagues, and on the way I stopped at an inn to have some French cognac. As I was leaving, seeing that I was very wet, the owner of the place said to me, *"Sir, I will lend you an Indian rubber coat for the rain, and you can return it to me when you come back."*[135] Thanks to the coat I was able to stay dry until I got here at about six o'clock in the afternoon. The disorder and disagreements I found upon my arrival saddened me. We will see what can be done. I went into the mine on a pulley wheel. That underground dwelling is completely lit up and filled with twists and turns. It is certainly impressive.

GOLDEN STAR MINE, SATURDAY, 7 FEBRUARY

It is half past eight in the morning, and I am leaving soon for Stockton. We shall see if I make it there in good time or not. I am very happy because I was able to settle all the differences here that last night had made me fear that all might be lost. The company has been renovated and has begun to work on another lode that looks like it is rich with ore. We have already taken out 100 hundredweights of this metal, and who knows how much more there may be, perhaps even of pure gold. Get ready, world, we are on our way!

FRIDAY, 13 FEBRUARY

It is half past two in the afternoon, and I just returned to my room. Since Samuel and I are leaving for San Francisco, at nine I went to say good-bye to Mariquita, and I was there until just now. It is a sad day that I accompany my brother, who is leaving for Chile, a sad day that I must bid him farewell. At four o'clock in the afternoon Samuel, Alfredo, and I will board the *Kate Kearn,* bound for San Francisco. Saying farewell to so many beloved people and things has cost Samuel far more tears than he had ever expected.

SAN FRANCISCO, SATURDAY, 14 FEBRUARY

We are staying in the New Orleans Hotel but are having our meals at the sumptuous Loving House Restaurant. After disembarking, we went to a barber shop. At the sight of my beautiful hair, the barber decided to give me the latest fashion in hairstyles that has just made it here from Paris. I agreed, and, my goodness, what a beautiful hairstyle! Art can make beautiful things that are not but makes them doubly beautiful when they already are beautiful to begin with. It is too bad that my women can't see me coiffed like this!

SATURDAY, 14 FEBRUARY. *Letter to Mardoqueo Navarro in Valparaíso, Chile*

As you know, Samuel leaves for Chile this month. As for me, I hardly have the cash to put stamps on my letters, though everyone else seems to think that by the time I see you, I shall be a rich man. Do not think, dear Mardoqueo, that I will not return unless I am rich. No, I do expect to be rich, but in any case I will come to embrace you even if I have to work on board to pay for my fare. Since many of our business ventures have failed, the way I shall refer to them in the future will be "I have so many thousands in the register" or "I do not have enough for food today." This may be positivism carried to an extreme, but that is what I will do, unless our business dealings yield a profit that must be sent to you in Chile or in Argentina.

SAN FRANCISCO, WEDNESDAY, 18 FEBRUARY

It is twenty past seven in the morning, and the steamship *Panama* taking Samuel has just fired the cannon shot announcing its departure. He spent last night with us, and we all got up this morning at four to accompany him aboard. How sad it was to see the three of us alone at that early hour in the streets of the immense and populous city of San Francisco. We did not run into anyone as we crossed the streets and the docks in silence, as though we were being taken to the gallows. When we reached the steamship, we went to the cabin destined for Samuel, he requested a candle, and began to write his own codicil, while the rest of us walked about on deck. It is not really possible to describe our farewell. Samuel gave me the sealed document, but we did not take our leave because I told him that I was going to get some books for him. Just in case I did not make it, he bid me farewell, and I said to him, "God, Fatherland, and Liberty." By now the shot has sounded and he is on his way, leaving us behind. This afternoon I am leaving for Contra Costa, and Alfredo is going to Stockton.

CONTRA COSTA, THURSDAY, 19 FEBRUARY

It is eleven o'clock in the morning, and I just arrived in Contra Costa, across the bay from San Francisco. I embarked at ten on the steamship *Cangarro,* and it took us an hour to get here. This country is beautiful, and its topography is the same as Coronel, on the other side of the Bío-Bío River in southern Chile.[136] I was so delighted by the similarities in its trees, grass, pastures, and quality of the soil that my imagination took hold and had me believing that I was about to meet with General Ribera at his ranch in Coronel, the stage in another time of scenes of love, happiness, and sorrow for me. How far those days now seem for me! Yet the fact of the matter is that I am now in Contra Costa.

I met with Leguisamont, who around here is known as Mr. Doctor and enjoys the reputation of being a good doctor and a good Argentinean, a good friend for these good people. I was only with him for a few hours but laughed so much at his stories and his wit that I am exhausted already. At five o'clock in the afternoon, Leguisamont and I came to Mr. Valdes's house near the harbor, where it will be easy to get to the boat bound for San Francisco tomorrow morning.

SATURDAY, 13 MARCH 1852. *Letter to Samuel Navarro in Valparaíso*

The weather was waiting for you to leave before starting its deluge here in California. It has rained for ten days without interruption, with no break, without seeing the sun a single day. At the same time there have been windstorms that were so strong that they blew the roofs off many houses, almost as though they were made of feathers. On Saturday the 6th, the first crest of the floodwaters filled all the sloughs. It was on Sunday the 7th when we got our first hint of the strength of the flood that was going to devastate the town during the coming days. On Sunday night at eight, the bridge behind Mix's house was washed out. At nine, the butcher's near the Page Street bridge, a brick building, and the market where the bear had been were all washed away (including the bear). At ten, the bridge there was also washed out. By that time the water had reached the Ainza house as high up as the gallery and was running down the streets as though they were rivers. It is interesting to note that all of the bridges and houses carried off by the slough were stopped by the great bridge near our house, thus backing water up through the entire town. At midnight, Enyart and I came back from the Ainzas, and we crossed the old bridge with water up to our knees. We went up to our balcony and were able to see the most grandiose spectacle imaginable. Stockton seemed to be resting on a lagoon, and the noise of the sloughs in the silence of the night made the scene even more solemn. It had stopped raining, the sky had cleared, and the moon was shining as though it was noon.

All of Stockton was on the alert, half of it on that side and the other half on this side of the slough. "There she goes" you could hear people say to one another at every creak coming from the bridge across from our house. The poor bridge struggled in vain, and at exactly one o'clock, under the pressure of the increasing current and with the two bridges and the three wooden houses pushing against it, the bridge finally gave way with a horrible noise and floated majestically in one piece down the raging river, with all the houses and other bridges behind it. At that point a cry of horror went up from 2,000 people, because the floating bridges and things behind it were going to take out the last bridge left in town. Imagine all the anxiety and the fearful looks as we watched the bridge flow down with all the rest behind it until it hit the next one, on its way to washing it out as well. When they arrived, there was a tremendous crack, and the houses and bridges broke into a thousand pieces against the old bridge, which, as it always had, continued to stand there unmoved. All of a sudden you could hear a great "Hurrah" go up. Even though the water rose another 4 ft. and flowed over the railings of the bridge, it remained firmly in its place. Two other houses with lights still on inside them flowed past us but also broke up as they hit the bridge.

On Monday and Tuesday the water continued to rise, and on the 8th and 9th we had to use boats to get to the other side of the slough. Yet yesterday, without even waiting for the waters to subside, they began rebuilding the bridge across from our house, and by the time the sun had gone down they had also begun on the one near Mariquita's house. Do you think they sunk the posts in with a machine? No sir. I cannot explain to you how they constructed the bridge, but it is bigger and much more secure than the other one. Besides, it was completed in only twelve hours! *Suficiat pro Stockton.* The newspapers will tell you about the floods in Sacramento and in Marysville, which have also been destroyed.

SONORA, THURSDAY, 1 APRIL 1852

Yesterday I left the Stanislaus River and made it here at noon, having covered the thirty-five miles in three and one-half hours. It is four o'clock in the afternoon, and the storm that began yesterday after my arrival continues unabated. It is pouring rain, and last night it even hailed a bit. Sonora is, as always, like an enchanted city. The music from its many hotels and its commerce mix together on practically the same streets and give the town a curious appearance. All of the movement around here is truly noteworthy. Alex and my other friends are all doing pretty well. Rojo is a servant at the Lecoq Hotel, and yesterday he came out to serve me when I arrived, without either of us expecting to meet in such a situation. Cupertino is now the treasurer of the Spanish Dramatic Society that has been improvised here. William will come from Sacramento in a few days.

FRIDAY, 2 APRIL

The storm is still raging unabated. The weather is horrible, as sad as All Souls' Day and as uncomfortable as any day during Lent in Catamarca. It must be because I am kind of depressed and everything seems sad and horrible to me. There is no doubt that the weather contributes to this feeling in a world in which a young man comes into society pure, clean, and filled with attractiveness, only to wallow in its mud, where everything is misery and corruption, knavish, ruinous, and underhanded, and where even the most honest gambler squanders his fortune and his time in hotels and gambling houses. What a difference and what a comedown from the way I used to live in Calaveras.

Cupertino and I have composed and arranged a couple of tunes for two guitars that really sound divine. Alex and Dryfous, who are playing *Damon and Pitnias* on Sunday, asked us to perform at the theater in the company of the artist M. Planel.[137] But I turned them down because the tickets are not free.

SATURDAY, 3 APRIL

It is midnight, and I just came back from the theater with Alex. In the work, he played Pitnias and Dryfous played Damon. The tragedy was lovely. We were all moved to tears during most of the scenes. The day and night were lovely, much as they often are in Melones, that is if any night can be lovely when I am away from Stockton. How difficult it is to be away so many days! As a poet-uncle of mine often says, "Past glories are like a noose for good thinking." Today I composed a waltz I called "Rapture" that is really beautiful. Maybe it is because I composed it under the influence of the memory of my Airam! She must be really unhappy, but our fate is inexorable, and it can do whatever it wants with us, no matter how strong our will is.

SONORA, MONDAY, 5 APRIL

It is nine o'clock at night, and I just returned to my room. Alex, Dryfous, and I went to the circus. After everyone had arrived, the entire tent came down amid a thunderous noise, causing some injuries to those who happened to fall beneath others. Fortunately, we were in the middle of the circus and had not taken our seats yet. They set up the tent again, but again it fell down. On the third try it was no better. We finally came back without getting our six-peso ticket refunded. Perkins has just come in bearing excellent news. He brought with him letters from Samuel and a long letter from my Airam, which is enough to fill anyone with happiness.

THURSDAY, 8 APRIL

I just remembered that today is Holy Thursday. Who would believe that only eight years ago my Holy Thursdays were spent at school and for many years I celebrated it with great joy and veneration. Now I am in California, in the town of Sonora, with a position and prospects for the future that are very different from the ones I had in those days. Around here nobody seems to even notice that today is Holy Thursday, nor is there even a hint in the town that suggests that today is the day before the death of Jesus Christ, the most important man ever to have lived in the history of this world. The town is filled with movement, but all of it is commercial movement. The stagecoaches from Stockton, Columbia, Jamestown, etc., have just arrived and have passed just under the window of the room where I am writing. It is a lovely day, perhaps the loveliest of this entire spring. Thousands of birds are singing in the great oaks standing across from the Lecoq Hotel, and their song mixes with the music from the hotels in a beautiful and very special concert. I wonder what the people, my friends, and acquaintances of my country are doing right now as I am here thinking of them, right when my thoughts transport me to those far-off places? I wonder how many of all of those people are thinking of me?

FRIDAY, 9 APRIL

Another lovely day here in Sonora. Around here it is always possible to see and hear the same hustle and bustle around town. It is Good Friday, and fate has it that I should be here in Sonora. After lunch, Jorge and I went for a walk along the side of the hill where there is a great canal. On our way back we entered the town from the side where the Spanish district is located. All of a sudden we caught sight of a group of boys who appeared to be busy tying a man to a tree trunk. When we got there we discovered that the boys had made a large effigy of Judas. They had dressed it perfectly, and they were stuffing it all over with firecrackers and gunpowder, in the pockets of its dress coat, vest, and trousers, while others were tying it to a post, getting ready to set fire to it on Holy Saturday. I was delighted with this encounter because at last I was able to run into people in Sonora who at least remember the great events of this day magnified by the sacrifice of our Savior.

SONORA, SUNDAY, 11 APRIL

It is midnight, and I just returned from the theater with William. It was a hard day yesterday and another one today, all the time thinking and thinking about people in Stockton. Yesterday I learned that my Airam would soon be leaving Stockton. We finally decided to go to the theater and see some French vaudeville called *The Colonel.* It was pretty nice, and at least it distracted me from my own dark thoughts. Four members of the troupe, especially two young girls, danced an Aragonese jota wonderfully.[138] Then a German lady sang "La Italiana" as well as I have ever heard it sung in all of my life. Thank God I am returning to Stockton tomorrow morning at four o'clock. But the four hours between now and when the stagecoach leaves are going to seem like an eternity to me. Today I received letters from Samuel sent from Panama, one from Mardoqueo in Chile, and another one sent by Rojo's wife from San Juan in Argentina.

STOCKTON, WEDNESDAY, 14 APRIL

I reached Stockton yesterday afternoon. I have never in my life seen plains like the ones we traversed this time on our way from Sonora. No poet's pen could ever portray the beauty of those natural gardens, nor could the brush of a painter copy this prodigy of nature. Every time the stagecoach stopped, I gathered innumerable types of flowers, each one as lovely as can be. It is a shame we did not reach Stockton faster because the sun soon wilted them all. As soon as the stagecoach arrived, I met Agustín and Juan Crisostomo, who came to meet me. Yesterday I visited the house of Mariquita and was received like a long-lost brother. It was so good to be there.

THURSDAY, 15 APRIL. *Letter to Samuel Navarro in Chile*

I have just come back from Sonora, where I had begun my letter. The reason for my sudden return is the following. Before leaving for Sonora we had made a proposal to the government to translate the laws, public documents, and the Senate record, etc., and accompanied it with a certificate from the authorities stating that we were able to render these services suitably, etc. Well, three days ago the proposal was taken under consideration, and they sent us an official letter, including part of the Senate record and a law to be translated. They said that if the translation was good, the committee set up to examine it would accept our proposal outright. Unfortunately I was in Sonora, and when the letter arrived telling me to return, I was only able to leave the next day. So by the time I got here, it was too late to even examine the translation that had been made and sent off the day before. This annoys me a great deal, because even after it was done by the doctor and checked by Agustín, etc., you know very well that they are no judges in the matter, and I have found a number of defects in the drafts that make them look pretty silly. They could not wait for me any longer because the committee only gave us forty hours to do the translation. Yet Dr. Craig, "my supposed colleague," says that there is no doubt but that the offer will be accepted, because everything has been done just how the Yankee wants them to be. What does please me is that my name is not on the translation, thanks to the fact that I was absent. This will lend weight to their consideration that I am the one who would have done it best. If we get this job it won't be all that bad, because it will mean $10 more or less of income per day, and the work for me is only a game. I wish I could let you know the final decision, but it will still take another three or four days.

I just now received the last letter from Panama, which was sent on the 23rd of last month. Thank goodness you at last seem to be on your way. All of the girls have told me that they are writing you, and I am going to pick up their letters right now. All of them are saying that each one has written the best letter. A remarkable thing! I was told that the very first thing Lolita did when she opened her letter was to run and measure it against the others. You can imagine the surprise of Lola when she started to read your letter and found these words at the beginning: "I am sure that you are going to measure this letter against the others in order to test my friendship." . . . All of them brought their letters to me and had me read them as soon as I entered the house. It is too bad that they couldn't write more, but they were not allowed much time to write the letters.

MONDAY, 26 APRIL

Last night I danced for the first time in a year. They say I did so beautifully and that it looked as though I was used to dancing every day. What surprised everyone most was that I was able to dance the schottische without ever having done so before. It was nice of them to be so complimentary. I am happy now, and I owe it to my Airam. What an angel of virtue you are! You deserve all happiness, but your life is filled with the unfairness caused by destiny.

STOCKTON, SUNDAY, 2 MAY 1852

Today has brought me many happy memories. After mass, all of us young friends accompanied the Ainza sisters to their house. I can never forget the angels who represent our nation. We had just received details of the last events leading up to the fall of Rosas. It was easy for those with me to see my joy. Since they know the enthusiasm the colors of my country's flag elicit in me, they all went out together and a half an hour later came in dressed exactly alike. It was impossible to tell them apart. Mariquita and Lola were dressed in pure white, with long, wide sky-blue ribbons around their waists. Sitting together holding hands, they looked like two angels fallen from heaven. I was ecstatic seeing these two ideal girls in all their beauty and elegance, and these angels were representing my nation and my happiness. It overjoyed me to see them together, almost as if they were mine, as if it was something that belonged to me.

FRIDAY, 7 MAY

Alfredo arrived this morning on the steamship, and he will be leaving for the north with Mariquita next week on the 12th, five days from now. Poor Mariquita, what horrible agony and torment she is suffering because of having to leave Stockton! She is leaving with her husband, but she is leaving behind in Stockton her sisters, her friends, the memory of her past happiness. In other words, she is leaving the theater, where she has been happy and a queen for two years, in order to go to the jungles. She is leaving a brilliant society and refined friends in exchange for crude miners and repulsive Indians. She is leaving behind her beautiful house and its comforts for ranches with only canvas for a roof, with no shelter, no cleanliness, no beauty. Oh Lord, if that was the only thing, it would all be glorious! She only has five days left here in Stockton.

It is half past ten at night, and I have just returned from the Ainza house. Mariquita was there, and we were all practically in mourning at the news of her departure. It looked more like a mortuary than anything else. This is all increasingly appearing to be a general disrupture of happiness and well-being. Everything now is affected by it. She has been suffering all night, and the vitality of her spirit appears to have fled from her countenance. All of her freshness and gaiety appear to have wilted all of a sudden. I can only imagine what it will be a day from now, or in a month or two, or in a year from now. May God have pity on this angel, who can only hope for joy in heaven and on earth from Him.

SUNDAY, 9 MAY

Today I composed a song entitled "Disillusion." I composed the music this morning in twenty minutes and the lyrics, among the best I have ever done, in another twenty minutes. You can see more than one meaning in all of it. Poor Airam. It is dedicated to her, and it is about her.

234

FRIDAY, 14 MAY. *Letter to Madame Foulon in Le Havre, France*

Mme. Foulon, you cannot imagine how the mines are able to drive people crazy. There is madness in them, and people end up being enchanted much like Don Quixote. You dream of gold as though you were a poet, and you end up neglecting everything. You forget your friends, your pleasures, and even your love. You turn the mine into your lover, and you give it your soul, your thoughts, and your existence, as if it were a young girl who had driven you crazy. You always have pen in hand, making millions and millions of calculations on pieces of paper, much like Robert Makaire does, dreaming up banks the way he does, along with the bankers, the nobles, and the kings, without ever thinking of anything else. Oh, my Lord, Mother Foulon, I too have begun to dream, but I am dreaming of my fatherland, my home, the property of my parents, and a secure $2,000 income, much more than of the millions that might come from the mines.

WEDNESDAY, 19 MAY

It is noon, and I just returned to my room from Mariquita's house. My Lord, how many cruel trials are You to send this soul because of all of the mysteries and sad recollections! It has been eight days now since she left Stockton, and today all of her house's furniture and utensils were sold at auction. The most insignificant things for the buyers were for me filled with both joyful and sad memories. The bidding started with Eduard's bed and ended with her couch. My diary is witness to the fact that I have never made any mention of my present indigent situation. No, that I have never done, but today I have greatly regretted in my heart not to be able to buy those items that belong to me by right of friendship. When I saw the tea set go . . . those little cups that on many memorable nights have been entwined with events of my life. I was always seated to her right whenever tea was served. Only I know all of the great and special memories they hold for me. I was finally fortunate enough to see how the entire silver tea and coffee sets went to my friend Mr. Masterson. The dining room and table were next, silent witnesses to all the loveliness reflected in the mirrors, and to all the treasures, beauties, and mysteries that objects hold for those of us who have used them. Those mirrors have witnessed so many beautiful party dresses, dance dresses, negligees, all secrets of the mysterious charms of her beauty. When the bureau and her boudoir went . . . Later it was the couch, upholstered on that famous 8th of December by Samuel, my poor brother and her never-to-be-forgotten best man. The last to be sold was the horsehair couch, the center of her memories, her favorite piece of furniture, her bed by day! Lord, I will get ill if I continue to think about it all.

STOCKTON, TUESDAY, 25 MAY

Three years ago today I arrived in Stockton. My life has undertaken many different twists since that 24th of May, 1849, when I reached here for the first time. I was poor then but was heading up an expedition that seemed to promise fortune. At that time there were no more than two or three tents in this town that today has so many and such high-quality buildings. I set up my tent right where the wealthy brick warehouses of Page & Webster now stand. You can still see on the corner the trunk of the immense oak tree that I had my men cut. That trunk, or three-quarters of it, served as a night table near my bed. In it I had nails where I could hang my watch, my tweezers, my scissors, etc. That is where I set my candle so that I could read at night before going to bed. That invincible, silent, and insignificant object to everyone else was witness to my long bouts with insomnia and sleepless nights I had at the time, for fifteen or twenty days at the very least. That is where dawn took me by surprise as I dwelled upon my uncertain future, on how seemingly dim the horizon of my own life was. Yet some months later that same tree trunk had to hold the weight of thousands of pesos in gold, the initial foundations of my fortune. Now the place where my initial tent stood is worth thousands and thousands, and that trunk now has other owners, other fortunes, and other secrets to keep.

The 25th of May of 1850 found me as a man who had already made a good part of his fortune. At least I was rich by my own standards and expectations. After a year of work in the mines, after suffering up there with my men all of the rigors of summer and the snows of winter, after having saved my life from a thousand dangers, I was back in Stockton, I had invested two or three thousand pesos in real estate and had invested another similar sum in my house in Calaveras. I was even going to San Francisco to buy a ship to send to Chile. I bought the ship, I changed its name, I called it the *Elisea,* and I put my men aboard along with fifty passengers and the rest of my capital in gold. I put Captain Detjen in charge of it with Rondizoni as first mate, sent it to Chile, and stayed behind to see what fate and fortune would bring me. Later I was delighted to have been able to send all of this to my family. Everything else was easy for me. My idea at the time was to leave on the same ship, but my brother Samuel was staying here, and there was no good reason to leave him alone. I returned to Stockton, and it must have been later that the theater of the many joys and sorrows of my life, the theater of the famous events for the poor history of my life, took place.

After returning here I met Mariquita, the only young girl in Stockton. The windows of her house were the ones that heard the first serenade I gave in Stockton along with Sánchez. That serenade, which later was to be so important in her memories and in mine, marks a very important period of my life, as well as an important one in hers. The 25th of May of 1851 came after the horrible fire of the 4th. Mariquita had married in December of 1850. On March 5th, those days of tribulation for my soul began, those days that stand apart because of their bitterness and adversity, those days that brought with them my absence from her house for four or five long months, despite my friendship and that of my brother with her family. During that period I paid more attention to my pride than to my heart. After those events and that long absence, the 25th came round again. Amelia had lived at the time for a few months in our house with her husband. It was for her that a group of Argentineans sang a serenade on the 25th of May. My memories of Amelia are noted elsewhere. I got this idea in my head to give another serenade that night. I got my guitar, and in the company of the Argentineans who had sung with me in the house, I went out and gave the celebrated serenade last year at this time. It was right near Mariquita's house and her bedroom, only separated from her by the thin wall of the house. Later she was to tell me that after four months of my being absent from her house, the notes of my guitar in that serenade fell upon her heart like drops of molten lead . . . but they filled her soul as though she were in ecstasy. There was a beautiful moon, and it was two o'clock in the morning. Afterward we sang another serenade to Agustín in his house, and on our way home we sang the Argentinean national anthem at the bridge. That is how the 25th of May of 1851 ended, amidst such joy and as a prelude to the happy days that were going to come afterward and that now are gone forever.

And where am I this 25th of May? My diary can say where, as can the letters I wrote today. My Lord, what a difference between a year ago and today! I can say along with Varela, "What a May it was, what great happiness, not even memories of it are granted by the Tyrant who stole them all." How true it is! In my destiny there has been a tyrant who stole much happiness from me, together with many years of good fortune.[139] It is a cruel and wicked tyrant who is now being paid for his evil ways with the contempt of those who once followed him. He is a tyrant who has on his conscience and even on his grave the weight of a dark crime, which horrifies those who even hear him recount it. It is a crime known to the entire world, which will be paid for today and even more tomorrow. His victims are noble by birth and noble in their hearts. More than hatred, they feel sorry for him. He will forever be sorrowful in payment for what he and his crimes made miserable, and this will serve as a warning for all those who come later with ideas like his and sins like his against God and society. May his life be an example to later generations, and may this be his only punishment. May God have the spirit of compassion, and may forgiveness take hold in the hearts of his victims. "As a man I forgive you for the jail and chains you gave me, but as an Argentinean I cannot forgive the crimes against my nation." As a man I do forgive you for all of my suffering and misfortune, but as the Ramón I am, I can never forgive the injury you gave to my nation. Be alert, there are even tyrants of tyrants, and some are more ferocious than others.

MONDAY, 31 MAY

It is four o'clock in the afternoon, and I am alone in my room. My window is open, and from here I can see everything that happens in Stockton right now when it is busiest. My window looks out upon the lake and affords one of the most lovely vistas you can find in Stockton. There are four steamships spewing out smoke, and the sound of the bells chiming together reminds me of All Saints' Day at four in the afternoon in my own country. The sound of that eternal ringing of four churches whose bells each have a different sound is somehow like the bells of the four steamships ringing all together but each one different from the others. I can also see two sailboats coming up, dancing on the lake almost as though they were flirting with each other, as well as the boats of the fishermen and the young people walking almost beneath my window. The wharf is filled with wagons and thousands of men on their way to embark or accompanying friends who are embarking. The levee and the commercial street are both crawling with people going back and forth. This scene is repeated every day right in front of me, and it is always just as enthralling. How I shall remember in the future my easy chair near the window, reclining with a book in my hands, while the curtains of the window move with the breeze and I play with the heavy cords and the azure tassels that adorn the drapery. With no family or fortune any longer here with me, this is the way I will think of myself as fortunate and happy in the future. There is no doubt that I may well be very happy in a certain sense right now.

STOCKTON, TUESDAY, 1 JUNE 1852

Tomorrow I am going off to Sonora and from there who knows where. I tire of remaining here in Stockton, and I want to spend the two or three months it will take for Samuel's letters to arrive moving and traveling around. I might go to Baja California as a kind of side trip and to see if I can get back the 2,500 pesos two persons there owe me. Before leaving I am going to make an inventory of all my belongings and the things that fill my rooms and leave it here until I return. Ten years from now all of the furniture and even the most insignificant of my possessions will end up being of great interest for me, and since I hope that by then I will be someone in this world, I am going to draw up the inventory as follows:

My closet and all of its old clothes:

1 burgundy cape
1 blue tail coat
1 black tail coat
1 cashmere frock coat
1 sky-blue long summer frock coat
1 suede summer frock coat with mother-of-pearl buttons
2 pair of black satin woolen trousers
1 pair of sky-blue satin woolen trousers for summer
1 pair of violet satin woolen trousers
2 pair of olive-green satin woolen trousers
1 pair of gray satin woolen trousers with white stripes
1 pair of green French cashmere trousers
1 pair of trousers with a stain of her blood on them![140]
1 satin black vest
1 white velvet vest with sky-blue trim
1 suede-colored vest with sky-blue trim
1 gray cashmere vest with dark green trim
4 white piqué vests
1 purple silk vest with sea-green flowers
1 beige winter overcoat trimmed with cloth of the same color. A gift of my
      friend A. Enyart from New York.
3 dozen white shirts
3 silk shirts
1 dozen sets of drill underwear
1 dozen sheets
18 towels or washcloths

6 pairs of covers (the same ones Mother gave me)
2 sets of window curtains or drapes
6 ties of different colors

Furniture, utensils, jewelry, etc., etc.:

1 chest of mahogany drawers with an accompanying bookshelf $40
1 bronze cot $125
Portraits of Pablo and Virginia $20
1 machine for copying letters $20
1 desk covered with blue velvet with secret drawers, etc. $32
2 chests with secret compartments for travel items $32
1 pair of Manton pistols, first class, four shots $32
One-half dozen wicker chairs and an easy chair $22
2 tables lined with oil cloth $14
4 candelabras of imitation German silver $8
1 guitar (the best one ever made, with its case, keys, and clamps for putting
    it together, with 6 boxes of strings, etc.). Its factory price was $150.
1 gold watch with gold dial and numbers $208
1 new gold watch chain with a locket on one end $32
1 gold pencil and a gold pen, mounted with an agate stone $30
Another pencil with pen, this one mounted with an azure stone $16
1 ring of California gold, mounted with a red stone $32
1 double-weight ring of Calaveras gold I took out myself, in a secret locket
    with my initials $30
1 gold nugget resembling a teaspoon $30
Several other small gold flakes, samples $16
Several samples of gold taken by myself from different places $50
1 seal with my cipher chiseled in San Francisco $12
1 very fine penknife $8
1 case for the guitar, once it is put together $10
1 pair of fine mother-of-pearl tweezers $3

Now I will make an inventory of my books. I will not attribute any monetary
value to them, just as I didn't with my clothes. Should I ever fall into poverty,
I would prefer to burn both kinds of possession rather than to have them
pass into the hands of someone else.

Bound books in English:[141]

1 English dictionary   2 Vols.
1 work on astronomy edited by Olmsteds   1

1 complete encyclopaedia   13
The Mysteries of Romanismo   1
1 English grammar by Vreullu   1
1 grammar book by Zenteno and Velasquez   1
1 grammar book edited by Velasquez and Simone   1
The True Religion by Christine Abbot   1

Bound books in French:

1 French-Spanish dictionary   2 Vols.
1 *Histoire des hommes utiles with plates*   1
Leçons de littérature française   1
Les arts et les offices   5
Histoire française by Lavalette   4
Les milles et un nuits   4
Don Quixotte in French   4
L'Alemagne by Madame de Staël   1
Han d'Island by Victor Hugo   1
Les orientales by Victor Hugo (poetry)   1
Les voix intérieures by Victor Hugo (poetry)   1
Valentine by George Sand   1
Variétés by George Sand   1
La reine Margot by Alexandre Dumas   4
La dame de Monsoreau by Alexandre Dumas   4
2 large works on skills and crafts with plates   2
1 map in French   1

Bound books in Spanish:

1 Spanish dictionary by Arnao   2 Vols.
Curso de Geografía   1
Geografía Universal   2
1 book on bookkeeping   1
1 *Arte de la correspondencia*   1
1 *Etimología elemental*   1
1 Italian grammar book by Bruneti   1

Novels in English:

Adventures of a Marquis by Alexandre Dumas   2 Vols.
The Two Dianas by Alexandre Dumas   1

Six Years Later or the Taking by Alexandre Dumas   2
Chevalier of Maison Rouge by Alexandre Dumas   2
Genevieve or the Reign of Terror by Alexandre Dumas   1
The Duke of Burgundy by Alexandre Dumas   1
Cecilie or the Woman's Love by Alexandre Dumas   1
Edmond Dantès', sequel to *Monte Cristo* by Alexandre Dumas   1
The Queen's Necklace by Alexandre Dumas   1
The Friend's Hand by Alexandre Dumas   1
Thousand and One Phantoms by Alexandre Dumas   1
The Young Chevalier by Alexandre Dumas
The Son of Athos, sequel to *Three Guardsmen* by Alexandre Dumas   1
The Viscount of Bragelonne by Alexandre Dumas   1
The Friend's Mask by Alexandre Dumas   1
Luise de la Valiere by Alexandre Dumas   1
Diana of Meridor by Alexandre Dumas   1
The Children of Love by Eugène Sue   1
The Mysteries of the People by Eugène Sue   1
Fair Isabelle by Eugène Sue   1
Temptation by Eugène Sue   1
Pride . . . by Eugène Sue   1
The Mysteries of the Court of London by Reynolds   3
Rose Foster, sequel to . . . by Reynolds   3
Miss Treloney by Reynolds   3
Mysteries of the Court of Naples by Reynolds   1
The Black Tulip by Alexandre Dumas   1
The Fallen Angel or Fernanda by Alexandre Dumas   1
The Stone Mansion of Saint Point by Lamartine   1
David Copperfield by Charles Dickens   1
Comfort by George Sand   1
The Comtesse of Rudolstadt, sequel to . . . by George Sand   1
Caroline of Brunswick by Reynolds   3

STOCKTON, SUNDAY, 6 JUNE

"Either the machine of this world is being destroyed or the Maker of all of nature is ill." Right now, I can say much the same as St. Dionysius Areopagite did.[142] Either the complex machinery of our friendship is breaking down, or my friend is ill. Right now I feel terrible anxiety, as I have seldom felt in my life, at the uncertainty and the mystery surrounding me. If this time my patience does not run out and the string does not break, I will be able to say that I am wiser than Solomon and more patient and prudent than Job. This is what is happening.

I have just received a letter from one of my best friends, Agustín, with the following words: "My friend, it is my duty to ask you what your ideas are and what is the object of your many visits? Please excuse the language of your friend *Q.L.M.B.*"[143] My answer is: "I have many ideas (on politics I have some, on the slavery of Negro people I have others, on commerce I have others, on society and its different aspects I have still others). I do not know which ideas you want to discuss with me. The object of my visits, if there is one, is that of an honorable gentleman who visits the home of his friend." What is he getting at with his singular letter and the comical questions? Are they perhaps circular questions that he has passed around to others who visit his home? Yet in that case they would surely have excepted me, because in friendship I am almost one of the family. Since I am really on the private council of the family, an honor that I am most grateful for, I do not know what to attribute his letter to. At the bottom of the letter in a postscript I added: "For further particulars, come to see me and spend an hour or two with your friend." I am writing this note while trying to figure this all out.

What have I done that might have caused this? Nothing at all, nothing with any duplicity or twisted intent! I did receive from the countess [Lola Ainza] last night a letter and a kiss, but what has that to do with anything? Is she not free, and am I not free? Do we not love each other with tenderness and honorability so much that she places her confidence in me as I do mine in her? He might have found that the marked and complete preference that both sisters show for me was going to be an obstacle for their future marriages with Americans of good standing.[144] If that is so, he would be sacrificing his friends for the well-being and happiness of the girls. In other words, he might be attempting to give me reason to cut off the relationship with them. But he is not capable of that, no matter how much the happiness of his family should come before everything else and even if I am an obstacle, but no, no. OH! An idea just came to me. Maybe this all comes from Neleb [Belén Ainza]. Yet that would be terrible. I had thought that she had gotten over that madness about being in love with me and that her love for me had changed into fraternal friendship. This was especially so, given the correctness and even stubbornness of my behavior with her so as not to give her the slightest reason to believe that I loved her. Perhaps she has induced her brother Agustín to ask me these questions by letter, and maybe that way she can take some revenge on her poor younger sister. That would be horrible! We will have to wait and see what happens, though I am very much suffering from the anxiety and the uncertainty of this entire affair.

MONDAY, 7 JUNE

It is six o'clock in the afternoon, and I just received a second letter from Agustín, in which he says, "Before setting up a meeting with you, my friend, I request that you answer the questions I put to you yesterday." My answer: "I believe that I did answer you yesterday. I can say everything else to you at our encounter." He wrote me a third letter, a pretty stubborn one almost threatening to cut off our relationship. The Navarro and Ocampo in me got to my head, and I answer stubbornly. I concluded my letter with the following words: "If you do not want a relationship with me and my friendship, you can just forget about it. But remember, I never beg anyone." It is looking like our relationship is going to be severed for good. I know that the girls know nothing about this, especially the countess, and they are continually asking my uncle what is going on between Agustín and me. I am increasingly persuaded that this is the work of Neleb in all of her desperation. Whatever the cause of it is, my heart is heavy with pain. Many things are coming together to make me suffer.

TUESDAY, 8 JUNE

The sacrifice is ready! I shall bid the countess farewell forever. "If you see me again some day, it will be when you are free and when the fortune and glory of my name is double that of your family. If by then you belong to another and besides are happy, so much the better for you. I hope you are happy, though it may be at the price of my eternal misfortune!" Yes, the sacrifice is ready, and I have made up my mind. *I am leaving for Chile and from there on to the Argentine Republic.*[145] The decision has been made, and there is no undoing it now. Why have I been given an iron will, if not to take advantage of it no matter how much my soul hurts? "Any apologies they might want to offer me will be too late," I say in my letter, "and if you are unhappy because of your brother and sister, I cannot help it. They may regret having interfered with your happiness and may want to make amends some day, but it will be too late. Farewell."

WEDNESDAY, 9 JUNE

I was not mistaken. Belén, in her desperation, made her brother write the letter I have referred to. She must have thought that I would say something in her favor. But my letters of yesterday have already answered enough. I spoke to her as I would speak to a beloved sister and nothing else. This last blow was a hard one for her, because even though I did not reciprocate her love, she thought that at least I did not love anyone else and, if forced to choose, I would choose her. . . . Poor Belén, without thinking about what she was doing, she has ended up hurting her sister and myself.

SATURDAY, 12 JUNE

It is four o'clock in the afternoon, and I am about to embark for San Francisco. Nobody knows the object of my trip. I am going to book my passage to Chile. I cannot help but admire my resolution, especially considering all the ties linking me to Stockton. Despite the ties, my pride has helped me make up my mind. I have said "I am going," and I am truly leaving. Even my poor old Uncle Rodríguez, who loves me so much, cannot get me to tell him why I am going to San Francisco, nor can the Quirogas.

Two or three days ago an American merchant came here to ask me to give music lessons to a young lady who had just arrived from New York. I told him that I did not make playing a musical instrument a profession. He offered me anything I wanted for a lesson a day, but of course I refused. Finally he begged me to at least go with him so that the young lady, who likes music very much, could hear me play. That I could not refuse. He came to get me three times, and finally I went yesterday afternoon. To my surprise, I realized that the lady in question was the same beauty that I always see gazing out the window when I cross the plains in the morning and the afternoon to go to my famous rose forest, which at this time of year is filled with roses. She has also seen me. She was delighted to hear me play and says that she has never in her life heard an instrument played better. Since I am tired of hearing these compliments, I just shrugged it off. She is very pretty, and the English she speaks is very refined. "Will we meet again?" Yes and no, I answered.

It is eleven o'clock at night, and I am in the great ballroom of the American steamship *Eagle,* together with Dr. Ward, a friend of his, and his friend's wife. The lady plays the guitar and has a very good one with her aboard the ship. I was listening to her play from afar without saying anything when Dr. Ward asked me to play something from an opera. I agreed, and the young lady was delighted to listen to me. The night is very lovely, and we are navigating with a full moon as we watch the trees on both sides of the San Joaquin River.

SACRAMENTO, TUESDAY, 15 JUNE

I reached Sacramento at half past five in the morning. The journey was as beautiful and as comfortable as can be. I saw two American friends from Sonora, and we spent some very pleasant time together during the sailing. One of these friends is Osmer, the one who set up the great raffle in Sonora and who also changed my watch chain. The Sacramento River is running at its loveliest, with the luxuriant trees on both banks making a sight beautiful enough to please even the most demanding of passengers. At 2 o'clock in the afternoon, the *New World* made a stop at Benicia to drop off some passengers. The steamship came right up to the hotel, where passengers were to embark and disembark. We were able to see many very interesting things there. An hour later we came upon the steamship *Senator,* which is more than three stories high and looked more like a hotel than a steamship going upriver. Last night we also passed other steamships, such as the *Confidence* and the *Antelope.* The most amazing part of the trip is the speed of the steamships and the way they pass so close to each other that the passengers can almost touch hands. Steamships going that fast in the middle of the night with their thousands of windows all lit up are truly an amazing spectacle.

After disembarking, it was still dark when I entered my old room at the Sutter Hotel. The idea of being in the same city as Mariquita, perhaps during the same hours when she was thinking of me, made it practically impossible to sleep. I arose at seven, got dressed, and went to her house at S. G. 10th Street. It is nine o'clock, and I have just returned from seeing Mariquita. My heart is palpitating under the double weight of the impression of having seen her and how happy I felt. An English servant answered the door, and, without telling him my name, I asked him to tell Madame Mix that a young man from Stockton wanted to speak to her for a moment. A few minutes later she came down and fell into my arms, quite beside herself. It would be hard to portray the great impression that seeing me so unexpectedly made upon her or to portray my happiness at seeing her and having her in my arms when it had all seemed so far away. . . . When she came down this morning, she was wearing a green satin Chinese robe with a blue bib made of the same material, with large buttons from her chest all the way to the floor. How could somebody be so beautiful after having been roused from bed? "And why don't you ask for your treasures, you bad man? Do you not want them any more? Is it that you do not want them like you did back there in Stockton?" Only he who understands the holy mystery of the words "your treasures" will be able to understand how ecstatic I was. What is going to happen to this angel when she finds out I am going to Chile and I must leave her here behind, maybe forever . . . ? Just writing this makes me tremble, and maybe she will indeed never see me again. In any case, I had to do it, and so I told her. This poor creature! She looked like the most unhappy person in the world. . . . Her soul is shattered with sorrow, and she does not know what will become of her after today. Yet her Ramón told her to accept this and to wait for him to return. Her Ramón would not possibly ill advise her, and so she accepts.

SACRAMENTO, WEDNESDAY, 16 JUNE

Yesterday, after my first visit to María, I returned to Sacramento and took a room at the New Orleans Hotel. After lunch I visited the entire town. Despite the floods of March, the city appears to have lost little, and it looks more beautiful and lavish than ever to me. They have built some immense brick buildings, including public buildings such as the city hall and the courthouse. The streets are cared for by the police, who water them down and sweep them twice a day to avoid the dirtiness caused by the wind in the summertime. There is as much noise and movement as in San Francisco and more cars and stagecoaches than anyplace else in California. The steamships and stagecoaches bound for nearby Nevada and Marysville are also lavishly adorned. I only have a few minutes left in Sacramento, and I am writing this in my book of memories while waiting for the stagecoach to return me by land to Stockton. I have decided on a beautiful coach of a small enterprise that is competing with the great company on this route.

When I returned yesterday at noon, I found María in the living room, dressed with a lovely suede-colored dress, the very dress that has so many memories and mysteries for the both of us. We were together until four. "Now you see, my Ramón," she said, "that I am wearing the dress you like most, the one that brings the most memories for both of us." I have never seen María more beautiful. Her hair was done in the Marie Antoinette style, which so becomes her. My Lord, how much happiness there was, even in our moments of farewell! There were times yesterday when she seemed to forget that this was her last day of happiness. With her arms around my neck she made me laugh at the thousand and one memories she had of her Stockton days. It will be difficult for me to ever forget our last encounter. . . . We were alone in the salon, and only the garden surrounding the house, six yards wide, separated us from the street. In the madness of our joy, we only had thoughts for ourselves. It would have seemed like a sacrilege in those moments of tears and of pleasure, of madness and of solemnity, to have noticed anything other than our mutual caresses. There was nothing more holy and sacred for us during those last hours. Now, sitting here alone, I can just imagine the risk we ran there, and I shudder to think of it! My Lord, ours was passion and temerity. . . . Yet we would have been willing to challenge the entire world and risk our own future rather than to have allowed anything at all to disturb that moment. In an empty room nearby there were two ladies, but we were thinking about as much of them as we were of the king of Russia. There is nothing like a love of this kind to make valiant youths reach the heights of heroism and even temerity. "I fear nothing at all in this world, my Ramón, when I am with you."

STOCKTON, THURSDAY, 17 JUNE

I reached Stockton at 2 o'clock in the afternoon and started to get my luggage together right away. My lovely and elegant rooms now have no curtains, no paintings, no bronze bed, no tassels, no library, and no decoration. The only thing left apart from my memories is the rug, which would have been an annoyance to bring with me. Lola wrote last night, bidding me farewell and including a lock of her hair in the letter.

It is 4 o'clock in the afternoon, and I am embarking aboard the steamship *Sophia,* bound for San Francisco. I am leaving Stockton forever. I was moved by my farewell with the Quirogas and my uncle. Adela's was especially moving because she made confessions and declarations to me that I did not expect. She is very unhappy with her husband. . . . My God, why did she marry him if she did not love him? She says she thought I loved her as she did me. . . . This is the last time I am going to see her and can give her what she wants. . . . And who would believe it, but I only asked for an embrace and a fleeting kiss in farewell. Nothing else!

SAN FRANCISCO, FRIDAY, 18 JUNE

We reached San Francisco at 2 o'clock in the morning. The hotels are all still open, but I decided to stay aboard until seven. I took all my luggage straight to the frigate *Godeffroy,* which is tied up at Cunningham Wharf. I have one of the two cabins toward the bow of the ship and am set up like a true prince. Later I went to my Mrs. Eugenia's house, where I am right now. We might leave for Valparaíso the day after tomorrow, but the captain has already made me wait two days. He demanded that I be here aboard his ship at 8 o'clock in the morning, and I complied even though I would have much preferred to spend an extra day with her. He will never know all the happiness he has deprived me of. But there isn't much I can do about it, so I guess I will just have to put up with the inconvenience.

SATURDAY, 19 JUNE

It is now sure that we are not going to leave today either, and who knows whether or not we will be leaving tomorrow. The captain is awaiting a family coming from Monterey to go on our ship to Valparaíso. Who knows if they will arrive tomorrow by steamship. I am staying at the Caddis's house, and my Mrs. Eugenia is taking care of me like a mother, lavishing all the affection and attention in the world on me. She invited Emilia today because I had not seen her on my previous trip. When she immediately noticed my watch with her chain and her tie around my neck, the ones she had given to me, she blushed and said, "You want to make me think that you have thought of me, when I know all about those goings-on of yours in Stockton that show me that you don't think of me at all." It was not difficult for me to get out of that situation, and so I told her not to pay any attention to stories and gossip like that. After our visit, Rosas's niece Emilia and I were again the best of friends, just like the day she gave me the tie and the chain.

SUNDAY, 20 JUNE

Word just reached us that Sonora has been reduced to ashes. My friends Perkins, Enyart, and Theall have been ruined. As I have said before, it is as though the devil was behind all of this misfortune.

MONDAY, 21 JUNE

We will not leave today either because that damned family still has not arrived. It has been a long time since I suffered setbacks of this kind on the steamships here in California. I guess there is nothing I can do except be patient. All of these days that I am fretting here I could have been in her arms. Poor María, every day I love you more and more, and your memory only sweetens the bitter hours of my existence right now. I bless the moments of pleasure I owe to you, and I will pray for your happiness for the rest of my life.

SAN FRANCISCO, WEDNESDAY, 23 JUNE

It looks like we won't be leaving San Francisco today either because the *Ohio* has not arrived yet with its passengers from Monterey. I have been aboard now for two or three days, but it doesn't look like we are leaving any time soon. We may leave tomorrow, even if the Basquez family does not arrive.

I received letters from Isidro and my uncle Rodríguez. I have suffered much by reading them because of the recollections they brought to me of Stockton, where I lived so intensely. I also received letters from Samuel sent from Lima, where he is a little behind schedule. Leguisamont is responsible for the fact that today I have suffered like few others in my life. He has left unpaid a $60 bill of exchange I sent against him as partial repayment for the $300 he owes me. I have only just found out that this bill, which was sent more than three months ago, went unpaid. Now it has been paid, but it makes my heart bleed to be humiliated in this way by a Rosas supporter, who in fact should have been humiliated by me.

THURSDAY, 24 JUNE

It is seven o'clock in the morning, and we are leaving the port of San Francisco, bound for Chile. Last night at nine, Mr. Arcos arrived along with his wife, Javiera Ugalde. They seem like pretty good people. They are also bound for Valparaíso and from there on to Santiago. The pilot has been aboard since five o'clock this morning, when we weighed the anchor. I have been on deck since much earlier to say my final farewell to California. San Francisco is still pretty quiet, and you can only see supply wagons on some of her streets. You can still see the smoke coming from the smokestacks of the steamships that have come in from Stockton and Sacramento. Who knows if perhaps one of them is bearing letters for me from Mariquita in Sacramento or from Lola, Belén, my uncle, or Isidro in Stockton. But there is no longer any time for anything. Farewell to all of you! As we are leaving you can also see the *Brigantine Copiapó,* bound for Mazatlán, and the frigate *Cape Breton,* also going to Valparaíso like us. The *Ohio* never arrived, and we are going to go by Monterey to pick up the Basque family. It would be quite a frustration were we to miss them.

MONTEREY, FRIDAY, 25 JUNE

We saw Monterey this morning but could not go in because the fog was very thick, as it normally is at this time of year all along the coast of Mexico and California. We only entered the harbor at three o'clock in the afternoon. I have never seen a lovelier and more picturesque harbor in my life. The Spaniards were right to make it the capital of Alta California. From two miles out you can see the very high mountains and their tall pine trees that surround the town. It is hard to paint a picture of a richer and more varied vegetation. The houses are all built in the Spanish style, most of them are low, and the architecture is not very outstanding. Yet the streets are straight and well laid out. We let out nine cannon shots upon entry. It almost looked like we were trying to assault the town. The steamship *Ohio* left yesterday for San Francisco, taking with it the family we had come to pick up here. What a shame, especially since their luggage is aboard with us. The harbor master has just come aboard with two assistants to look over the ship and its cargo.

SATURDAY, 26 JUNE

It is eight o'clock in the morning, and we have a magnificent wind blowing. Yesterday we lost sight of the beaches of California just when it was getting dark. With the last rays of sunshine we lost sight of the golden land of California, the country of marvels, the country of the thousand and one nights, the country that was the scene of so much happiness and so much suffering of mine. The last hills of Monterey with their beautiful pine trees disappeared with yesterday's last light of day. Today there is nothing to see but the sky and the water, and we have left the coast behind with a good tailwind. The *Copiapó* separated from us yesterday with a cannon shot for a salute. We also left behind the *Cape Breton,* but who knows which of us will make it to Valparaíso first. That will be told by the winds and the good fortune of our trip. . . .

Epilogue: Personal thoughts about my diary

My diary has grown along with me and is, for me, a fair witness of my vibrant life, of my conscience, of my open heart. . . .[146] In every page, as my writing and my ideas have changed, you can see how, slowly but surely, I was in the process of becoming a man. Anyone who opens my diary in 1845 and then again in 1846 will be able to see exactly how my life changed. My diary, then, is the mirror of my life, in which you can see, one by one, the things that have happened to me. In my first sufferings, in the first travails of my soul, instead of seeking comfort in my mother or in the friendship of a friend or a brother or in the frankness of a confidant, I instinctively looked for it in my diary, and that is where I have found a universal balm for my soul. Whenever my heart has been filled with sorrow, I have opened my diary and felt its powers of comfort. . . . Whenever I have experienced intimate pain and suffering, I have written entire pages, and every word has helped alleviate the anguish my heart has felt. Only my diary knows when and how I have been most offended in life, and it will keep my secret better than any friend ever could. . . .

My diary, then, is both my prosecutor and my accuser, it is my reliquary, my source of comfort, my bible that helps show me what I have been, what I am, and what I will be if I continue along this path in life, happy at times, unhappy others, at times singing, and at others crying. In sum, my diary helps me bring things down here to earth the way they should be: without getting drunk on happiness or prosperity and without succumbing in the face of misfortune. . . . My diary has also helped me fill the empty hours of my life. . . . All of the things I have contemplated with my avid eyes and imagination I have done so just so as to be able to think about them and to write my impressions of them in my diary. On those long nights of solitude, those eternal winter nights when it rained as though some sort of new biblical flood was being unleashed, that was when I would take my diary and write in it, to the monotonous sound of the falling rain. . . .

Since I am not an angel, nor even a virtuous man, I have not always opened my diary with pleasure and anticipation, because I did not always have a conscience as white as snow to show it. Just like the person who kneels before the minister of God to confess his sins, this is the sort of respect and veneration I would feel when, at the end of some day, I would write in it an account of some incorrect action of mine, some impetuous show of my temper, or some peccadillo that I blame my heart for more than myself. Thus my diary contains both my good and my bad actions, and in this way it has helped me many times to think twice about many actions of mine that, were it not for the severity of this tribunal, would never have come from me in such an honest form.

I have never thought for even a moment that anyone could ever see the pages of my diary, and the proof of this is that I have never kept from confiding in it my weaknesses and shortcomings, which only have it as their confidant. I have written in it always knowing that I was the only one who would ever read it. I have written without rules, in my own way, as I pleased, but I have not hidden from it even the most insignificant secret of my life. It has been my written conscience ever since I had the use of reason. . . . These pages contain fits of passion, confessions of my soul, the venting of my heart, traits of my pride and arrogance that might seem ridiculous for others but not for me. It contains humble petitions, fervent praise, tender farewells, loads of tears, moments of happiness, and good fortune. Yet it is all meant for me alone. These pages are written without intent, without vanity, without presumption; and, like the leaves of my life, they will only be read by me and later reduced to the ashes and to the nothingness from whence they came.

Appendix 1
A Chronology of the Life
of Ramón Gil Navarro

17 FEBRUARY 1827. Birth in La Rioja, Argentina.

1831. Navarro is present in Tucumán during the battle of Ciudadela fought by Juan Facundo Quiroga, the famous caudillo from La Rioja. Young Ramón remembers the encounter he had with Quiroga.

1834. Navarro enters the school of Mrs. Paula Vera, where only reading and writing are taught.

1835–45. CATAMARCA. In the School of San Francisco he studies writing and arithmetic. At the age of nine he studies Latin and Castilian grammar. In 1842, during the period of Rosas's terror, he is witness to the entry of Colonel Maza into Catamarca and the death of many of its inhabitants, including that of Governor Cubas, whose heads were stuck on pikes and exhibited in the main plaza in town. (In Calaveras, he writes a long account of these events, which have not been included in this selection.) His father, president at the time of the legislature of Catamarca, was able to save his own life by fleeing to Chile. His school examinations, carried out in public in church and in the presence of his teachers and the Jesuits, were the cause of great celebration. In the reception after the examination, his mother dared to serve a Mistela wine that had a green color. Navarro tells us that, since this color was strictly prohibited at the time because it was the symbol of hope, it became the cause of the decree signed by the governor in September 1845 giving his family twenty-four hours to leave town.

6 SEPTEMBER 1845. At the age of eighteen, Navarro begins his diary upon his departure from Catamarca with other members of his family for an exile in Concepción, Chile, where his father and his two older brothers, Samuel (23) and Mardoqueo (21), had been in residence since 1842. At this time, his family is made up of his mother, Doña Rosa Ocampo y Herrera, and seven of her children: Ramón Gil (18), Elisea (17), Darío (14), Emilia (13), Parmenia (11), Aurelia (8), and Aníbal (6). The family arrives in San Juan, where they reside for some months in the home of kin, awaiting the proper time to cross the Andes to Chile.

13 MARCH 1846. The family departs from Argentina, crossing the range at the Uspallata Pass, bound for Valparaiso. From there they embark for the port of Talcahuano and the city of Concepción. The family is reunited on 23 April.

9 DECEMBER 1846. Ramón Gil moves to the town of Chillán, where he takes over a business his father had set up. On 12 December his sister Elisea dies.

APRIL 1848. Navarro sells the store in Chillán and returns to his father's home.

MARCH 1849. Navarro departs for California.

24 JUNE 1852. Navarro returns to Chile after the dictator Rosas falls from power in February of this year. There he joins the Club Constitucional Argentino. In October of this year he meets with General Flores, the former president of Ecuador, in the Hacienda de San Juan near Santiago, Chile, and takes note of the correspondence between Flores and General Simón Bolívar. In Concepción in December he is appointed correspondent of the *Mercurio*, a newspaper from Valparaiso.

1853. In Concepción he publishes several installments of his study, "Los Chilenos en California," in the *Correo del Sur*.

1854. His study of Fray Mamerto Esquiú and the sermons he gave in 1853 supporting the constitution are published. (At present, a case for Esquiú's beatification is being prepared in Rome.)

1855. On 13 January he returns to Argentina. On 8 April he is elected representative to the legislative congress of the Argentine Confederation for the Province of La Rioja.

1856. He is appointed envoy of the national government on a mission to the governor of the Province of La Rioja. He is elected national representative for Catamarca in the congress of Paraná. At this point, his diary ends.

1857. He is appointed minister general of Governor Don Manuel Vicente Bustos. He oversees the installation of a government printing press, used to print *La Patria,* the first newspaper of La Rioja. President Urquiza proposes him as a candidate for governor or, if not, as minister of the government of La Rioja.

1858. Paraná. He publishes different reports in the newspaper *El Nacional,* including "Comercio de Chile con la Conerederación por Copiapó" and "La visita a los Departamentos. Visita a Villa Argentina (Chilecito)." In September he publishes another report about agriculture and cotton and tobacco farming in Catamarca. In July of this year he participates in the drafting of a law that organizes the federal system of justice.

1859. La Rioja. He is minister of Governor Manuel Vicente Bustos and emissary of the future President Derqui.

1860. On 3 March he is appointed commissioner before the governor of La Rioja by President Urquiza and President-elect Derqui. In December 1860 he marries his second cousin, Doña Malvina Ocampo y Argüello, who resides in Córdoba. General Urquiza, the first constitutional president of Argentina, is his best man and is represented at the wedding ceremony by Dr. Manuel Lucero. They will have six children, but only four survive childhood: Ramón (1861), Mercedes (1869), Carlos (1872), and Maria (1875), all of whom eventually have children of their own.

1861. Paraná. He is a member of the commission that writes up the Law of

Differential Rights, promulgated in July, breaking the trade hegemony of Buenos Aires, which had not yet joined the other provinces in forming the Argentine Republic.

1862. He is made prisoner in Catamarca by Colonel José Miguel Arredondo, who is working for the future President Mitre. While in the jail of Machigasta, he writes the following text on the prison walls: "Hay penas que van pasando poco a poco sin sentir; lastiman, pero no matan; duelen, pero tienen fin" (There are sufferings that pass little by little; they may injure us, but they do not kill us; they hurt, but at least they end). At the end of this year, he writes about these events in a book entitled *Actor, Testigo y Mártir* (Actor, witness, martyr), an impassioned defense of provincial autonomy against the power of Buenos Aires. (This manuscript was found in the 1970s in a church in the northern part of the Province of Córdoba among the personal papers of the priest.)

1863. Córdoba. He writes a tract, published in Rosario, on the political prisoners of the dictator of Paraguay, Dr. Francia. This was subsequently republished in 1901 in the *Revista del Instituto Paraguayo*.

1866. Córdoba. He is elected representative for the period 1866–67.

1867. Córdoba. The newspaper *El Progreso* is founded by Navarro on 7 September 1867, thanks to economic support from former President Urquiza. This newspaper will exist until Navarro's death. Its editorial line is strongly liberal, leading to numerous confrontations with the traditional clerical political positions of part of the Córdoba establishment.

29 MAY 1868. Córdoba. Ten masked men assault the offices of the newspaper, ransacking it and throwing the printer cases and all the typographical equipment into the street. He is not murdered because he is not in at the time.

1870–83. Navarro holds a series of political offices: national representative from the Province of La Rioja (1870); appointed representative of the governor of Santiago del Estero before President Sarmiento (1870); national representative of Catamarca in the national congress (1871); provincial senator of Cordoba (1871–75); reelected for 1876–80 but renounces upon being elected national representative in the congress in Buenos Aires (1878); provincial senator in Cordoba (1882); and national senator representing Córdoba in the national congress (1883).

1879. He publishes the book *Limites de la Provincia de Córdoba con Buenos Aires, Santa, Fe, San Luis, Santiago, La Rioja y Catamarca—Arbitraje del Gobernador Viso en la cuestión de límites entre Santiago y Catamarca* in Córdoba.

1880. As representative in Buenos Aires, he accompanies President Avellaneda to the village of Belgrano, where the congress is set up. From the pages of his newspaper *El Progreso*, he promotes the candidacy of General Roca to the presidency of the nation.

26 JULY 1883. Navarro dies in Córdoba of pneumonia at age fifty-six.

Appendix 2
A Glossary of Key Persons Mentioned in the Text

Abel. *See* Quiroga, Abel

Adela. Daughter of the commander of Stockton. As Navarro suggests in a letter to Perkins (2 June 1851), at first her father opposed her wedding, though he eventually consented to it. Navarro's diary shows that later she complains bitterly about her husband. As Navarro suggests in a letter to his brother Samuel (13 September 1851), she was also quite adept at dressing up as a Turk and doing certain "oriental dances," to the delight of Mix and Navarro, but less so to that of Mariquita.

Adelaida. *See* Morales, Adelaida

Adolfo. *See* Rondizoni, Adolfo

Aguado. Dionisio Aguado y García, Spanish composer, 1785–1849.

Agustín. *See* Ainza, Agustín

Ainza, Ainzas, or Ainsas. Mexican family in Stockton. In his journal from April 1852, William Perkins refers to this family: "I remained in Stockton that night and, accompanied by Ramon Navarro, paid some farewell visits, the last of which was to the family of the Ainsas, very respectable people from the Department of Sonora in Mexico, and the only decent Mexican family I have met in California. The girls stitched my new *Zarape* which had just arrived from Mazatlán" (Morgan and Scobie, p. 334). The family originally hailed from Hermosilla (Sonora, Mexico), according to the marriage certificates of two other daughters, Maria Ampara and Philomena (both in 1853), who are not mentioned in the diary. See *Gold Rush Days. Vital Statistics,* p. 19.

Ainza, Agustín. Member of a Mexican family from Sonora. In the 1850 census enumeration in Stockton, he is registered at dwelling no. 407 as A. Ainza, age twenty-five, merchant, born in Mexico. In the same house, M. Ainza, age twenty-three, also resides.

Ainza, Belén. One of the young members of the Ainza family who ends up developing an infatuation for Navarro that is not reciprocated.

Ainza, Francisco. Mexican from Sonora. Also called Don Pancho.

Ainza, Lola. Another of the Ainza daughters who maintains an apparently amorous or flirtatious relationship with Navarro. She was fifteen years old at the time.

Ainza, Manuel. Mexican. In the census enumeration of 1850, he is registered as living at the same residence as A. Ainza and others. An announcement exists dated 18 February 1851 of an auction in Hermosillo, Mexico, of "the urban and rural property, a very stylish carriage, an excellent piano, several pieces of household furnishing, and two horses belonging to Manuel Ainza to be held on 15 March 1851 at his residence" (see Ainza).

Aldunate. Surname of a prominent Chilean family.

Alex. *See* Enyart, David Alexander

Arana. This is Felipe Arana (1789–1865), Argentinean jurist, born in Buenos Aires. He was the minister of foreign affairs under Rosas from 1835 until the fall of the tyrant in 1852.

Araoz. Probably a member of the distinguished Chilean family Araoz Otarola. For more on this family, see Cuadra Gormaz, p. 18.

Arnau, Arnaud, or Arnault. Jesuit priest. William Perkins writes of him in his journal: "A young friend, Ramon Navarro, an Argentino—much to my gratification, for the times are mighty dull—came up today accompanied by a Reverend French Abbé; the latter to cleanse the consciences of the sinners about here, and, a secondary object, to make a collection for the purpose of building a Catholic church in Stockton. He appears to be a jolly old Abbé, with a good, open, honest face that wins a man's sympathy at once" (Morgan and Scobie, p. 210). According to the editors of Perkins's journal, "Perkins' 'French abbe', would seem to have been Abbé Reynaud, who with a party of French emigrants sailed for California from Le Havre in the ship Grétry on February 27, 1850. The phonetic similarity suggests that Abbé Reynaud was the Father 'Arnault' said by Herbert O. Lang to have ministered in Sonora during 1850–51. Father Henry Alric was assigned to the Sonora pastorate in May, 1851, and remained until 1856" (Morgan and Scobie, p.210 n.2). In Bonta (p. 285), there is a marriage certificate of Don Agustin Mix and Dona Maria Conception Craig in which "L'abbé Renaud" is present as well as Samuel Navarro and others.

Bárcena. This is Don Manuel Bárcena from the city of Córdoba, Argentina. Son of Don José Antonio de la Bárcena from Jujuy, Argentina, and of Doña María Ignacia de Allende from Córdoba. In 1840 Don Manuel married Doña Teresa Funes y Allende, the daughter of Don Ambrosio Funes, governor of Córdoba and member of an illustrious Córdoba family. Famous for his cruelty, he was also known by the nickname " *Tuerto* (one-eyed) *Bárcena*."

Belén. *See* Ainza, Belén

Belt, G. One of the Stockton prefects who signed the order to arrest the American miners in December 1849. According to an entry in Navarro's diary after his return to Chile (16 October 1852), Belt, or his brother, was a native Californian and was successfully working for President Flores of Ecuador (1830–35). According to family testimony, Belt was evidently married to a Chilean woman.

Benavidez. This was probably Emilio Benavidez, a Chilean.

Besançon, Lorenzo A. According to the journal of William Perkins, he was the tax collector for Tuolumne County, "a lawyer of New York birth, more recently from Louisiana. The *Stockton Times* printed the text of the new law on April 27, 1850, alerting the Sonora community to what was in the wind, but it was not until two weeks later that Besançon prepared to license the miners." On 28 May 1850, the *Alta California* commented that there was a rumor that "General Besançon, one of the collectors, was murdered in the endeavour to perform his duty," though this subsequently proved to be false. On this point, see Morgan and Scobie, pp. 36–37.

Camaño, Marcelo. A peon, probably from Chile, in the original mining company. He returns to Chile in September 1849.

Casimiro, Don. *See* Rodríguez, Casimiro

Chateaubriand. French writer, 1768–1848

Clements, Louise (Madame Clemens). The bridesmaid for the marriage between María Craig and Alfred Mix, where she is listed as a witness to the wedding along with Jos Baran Clements (Bonta, p. 285). She has a young son and may be the wife of Dr. Clements, a doctor mentioned by William Perkins in his diary in November 1849 in Stockton: "The doctor in whose company Perkins found himself was Dr. J. B. Clements, who, with Dr. Jno. W. Reins, was a proprietor of the Stockton Drug Store, advertised in the *Stockton Journal*, November 6, 1850" (Morgan and Scobie, p. 195 n.2). In the Stockton census enumeration of 13 November 1850, in dwelling no. 296 there is one J. B. Clemant, age thirty-four, physician from Maryland. On 23 November 1850 in dwelling no. 479 there is an F. Clemments, age thirty, physician from Louisiana, together with L. Clemments, female, age twenty-two, and a Joseph B. F., age two. J. B. Clements was coroner of San Joaquin County in 1850. See *History of San Joaquin County, California,* pp. 25, 31.

Coll, Manuel. Argentinean from the Province of San Juan. It could be Don Manuel Coll y Andino, married to Doña Agustina Correas. If so, he had a son, Ventura, who was born in Santa Fe, Argentina, on 18 September 1854 (Cutolo).

Collier, W. Judge of Double Spring. According to Ayers (p. 47), Judge Collier, of Virginia, was "a venerable gentleman of distinguished presence, of large experience, and of positive character backed by unflinching nerve." He may also be the Collier who was gunned down by Judge Smith of Calaveras County in a personal confrontation in 1852 (Huntley, p. 32). Navarro refers to Collier as Coller in later articles.

Coronel, Issac. Argentinean, probably from the Province of San Juan. The last entry in the diary about this person, from 18 September 1849, says he leaves Calaveras "ill and tired."

Correas, Saturnino. A friend of Navarro since his days in Concepción, Chile. He is probably the son of Don Francisco Correas and Doña Catalina Olivares, married in Talca (Cuadra Gormaz, p. 99). He has business interests in flour and lumber.

Craig, A. (Agustín). Brother of María Craig. Also referred to by Navarro as "Judas."

Craig, James S. In the 1850 census enumeration he is registered as a physician, age forty-eight, from Kentucky, residing in dwelling no. 613 belonging to Alfred Mix. There is also record of a letter from Dr. James S. Craig, formerly of Little Rock, Arkansas, dated Santa Fé, New Mexico, January 2, 1831, to Col. Robert Bean: "We have been politely favored with the perusal of a letter from Dr. James S. Craig, formerly of this town, to a gentleman of this vicinity, and permitted to take the following extract from it. Dr. Craig went out with a hunting and trapping company which left the Arkansas in the early part of last year, under the command of Col. Robert Bean, of Crawford County, and expected to be absent two or three years" (*Arkansas Gazette,* 8 June 1831, v. 12, no. 24, whole no. 596, p. 3, col. 1). He is also listed in the marriage record of his daughter, María Concepción (12 December 1850, ASJCR, Book M of Marriages, 1:4 [cited in Bonta, p. 285]).

Craig, María (or Mariquita). Daughter of James S. Craig and wife of Alfred Mix. In the Stockton census enumeration of 1850 she is listed as age fifteen, from Mexico, living in dwelling no. 614 belonging to Benjamin G. Wair, justice of the peace, age forty-eight, from Virginia.

Cupertino. *See* Ocampo, Cupertino

Daza, Román. Probably Chilean. Peon of Navarro.

Dickerson, G. According to the Stockton census enumeration of 1850, G. Dickerson lives in dwelling no. 384, age forty-four, speculator from Virginia. He is accompanied by his wife, Isabella, age forty, and several offspring, ages 21, 20, 19, 18, 11, and 14, identified as males in the census but whose names are indicated only by initials. In the diary, Navarro also mentions Dickson, Digson, Digsons, and Dinckinson, which may well refer to the same person. A. G. Dickenson is mentioned as one of the businessmen of Stockton who signed a petition to Charles Weber, asking him to remove any vessels he might own that were blocking the channel, which was detrimental to navigation. See *History of San Joaquin County, California,* p. 25.

Dorotea. *See* Rivera, Dorotea

Dreyfous, F. E. Friend of Navarro and of William Perkins, who mentions him on 25 April 1852 in Sonora at a farewell party given for him on the occasion of his departure from California. See Morgan and Scobie, p. 330, 332.

Elisea. *See* Navarro, Elisea

Elordi, Luis. Argentinean military officer, 1818–95, originally from Dolores, in the Province of Buenos Aires. Son of Martín Elordi and Doña Juana Maza and grandson of Don Manuel Vicente Maza, who was assassinated in the legislature in 1839 during the Rosas tyranny. Elordi had a long political career that began with his participation in the uprising, called "Alzamiento de los libres del Sur," against Rosas. Imprisoned in 1839, he later became a political refugee in Montevideo, Uruguay. He participated in several battles on Argentinean soil as a member of the troops of General Lavalle, where he was accompanied by his brother José Celidonio Elordi. He took part in the battle of Angaco in the western part of Argentina, one of the bloodiest in the history of the country, where he was injured in both legs. He went into exile in Chile in 1842. There he undertook several different activities together with Vicente Piñero, another exile. While he was working as a waiter at a banquet at the house of Mme. Herrera de Toro, a well-known Chilean woman, he was recognized by Sarmiento, who made him sit at the table with him. Later he went to Peru and sailed for California from the Peruvian port of Callao. In Sonora, California, he was arrested, along with Francisco Madero, another compatriot from Dolores. They were about to be lynched, because they had been confused with some Mexican horse thieves, but were saved by an American who recognized them (Vilgré La Madrid, p. 12). According to Navarro, in Sonora, Elordi had a hotel at the placer called the Sonora. In Perkins's diary, he is mentioned as "a gentleman from Buenos Aires," with a house in Sonora where people gathered on different occasions. "Almost every Argentine I know plays the guitar and sings; and every night, the large room belonging to Elordí, a young man from Buenos Aires, and in which they congregate, and where no *Chileno* or *Peruano* is ever seen, resounds with the sweet mournful music of the Argentine Republic" (Morgan and Scobie, p. 285). In 1856 he went to New York, London, and Paris. He finally returned to Argentina after an absence of seventeen years. In March 1857 he was appointed the assistant administrator of the Western Railway, and in 1858 the same company commissioned him to go to London. In 1859 he was appointed captain and assistant of the war ministry, where he worked until 1861. He died in Lomas de Zamora, Argentina, on 28 January 1895. The day after his death, the newspaper *La Nación* recalled the services he had rendered to his country, both in the military and as a civilian. His portrait hangs in the Museum of Luján in memory of his work on the railways. He was married to Doña Felisa Muro. For more on Elordi, see Cutolo; Gesualdo, p. 44; Udaondo; and Vilgré La Madrid.

Emilia. *See* Sutton Mansilla, Emilia

Emilio. *See* Quevedo, Emilio

Enyart, David Alexander. American. Member of the congress and treasury in Sonora. In his journal, Perkins says that he was from Cincinnati, that they came to California together, and that he considered him a brother. In January 1851 he had to return home because of news he received, though he returned in May of the same year, much to Perkins's delight.

Estuardo, Francisco. Chilean, probably from Concepción. He traveled to Chile with Navarro.

Fabio. *See* Zañartu, Fabio

Fernández, Borjas. Probably Chilean. One of the early directors of the mining company founded to prospect for gold in California. He traveled to California aboard the *Carmen* along with Navarro.

Galu. Pedro Pablo Galup. Argentinean. According to Gesualdo (p. 48), he was a *"porteño* [from Buenos Aires] familiar with the southern revolutionaries in 1839. He emigrated to Chile in 1845 and to California in 1849. He set up residence in San Joaquín, not far from Sonora, and was one of the few Argentineans who became rich during the gold fever. He generously placed his fortune at the disposal of his more unfortunate compatriots and paid the return trip for many of them."

Green, Henrique. Perhaps Argentinean, left Chile for California in 1849. En route he was marooned on the Galapagos Islands for three months. According to subsequent accounts of R. G. Navarro (1853), during the confrontations between the Chileans and the Americans he was about to be hanged twice. The first time he was saved because of some gold he had, and the second time he was liberated by force, thanks to the generosity of some honorable Americans.

Gregoire, Madame (also Madame Gremière). This character did not escape the attention of another traveler, who, when speaking of the French participants in the gold rush, described her in the following manner: "In the former, grisettes were to be found, women of middle age, one of whom, and it must be admitted the youngest, took the pleasure in walking about in a short jacket and pantaloons and sporting a felt hat clapped jauntily on the side of her head, in order to attract the attention of the western pioneers who, newly arrived from their forests, could not understand why a woman could have the notion to garb herself in men's clothes" (Gerstäcker 1942, p. 38). In Sonora, Perkins talked of the arrival of a certain Madame Bremaire and also described a woman who dressed as a man: "On the other side of us, for about half a mile, it is open country, with a few tents under the oak trees. A Frenchman and his wife live in the nearest tent, and they dig gold together. She dresses exactly like her husband—red shirt and pants and hat" (Morgan and Scobie, p. 251). It is uncertain whether or not he is referring to the same person.

Herrera, Pedro (also Herreras). Chilean, returns to Chile in September 1849. It may be Don Pedro José de Herrera y Araigada, from Concepción, who was married originally to Doña Paula Cuadros y Bárcena and later, in Osorno in 1860, to Doña María Petrona Barrientos Oyarzún (see Guarda, p. 468). In "Los Chilenos en California," Navarro mentions Herrera's mining company as one of those founded in Concepción with the intention of prospecting for gold in California.

Herz, Heinrich. Austrian pianist and composer, 1806–88. Author of a method for piano still known today. According to Upham (pp. 291–92), "Henri Herz, the celebrated composer and pianist, who arrived in San Francisco on the 1st of April, gave the first of a series of three concerts in Sacramento City, on the evening of the 16th of the same month, at the New Hall, corner of M and Front Streets. . . . The piano used on the occasion, the only one in the city, contained only six octaves, which somewhat cramped the genius of the great master, but he gave an admirable entertainment, nevertheless, and the audience was delighted." Regarding the tour of Herz in America between 1845 and 1851, see MacMinn, p. 366–69, and Hutton, p. 38.

Isaac. *See* Quiroga, Isaac

Isidro. *See* Quiroga, Isidro

Jara. Joaquín Jara, a Chilean from Concepción.

Jesus. José Jesus, Indian chieftain, successor to Chief Estanislao, married to the Indian Manuela. According to the journal of William Perkins, his ranch "was in the vicinity of Knights Ferry on the Stanislaus" (Morgan and Scobie, p. 108 n.2). For more on José Jesus, see Bancroft, pp. 75–76.

Jims. This is probably Jim Bauz.

Juan. *See* Ocampo, Juan

Juan Crisóstomo. *See* Quiroga, Juan Crisóstomo

Juan de Dios. *See* Sánchez, Juan de Dios

Lacombe, Madame. Professor of piano. Navarro met her in Concepción, where she taught a number of his women friends.

Lacourt, Dr. Acquaintance the author had met in 1847 in Concepción.

Lasvignes. Physician. According to Perkins in Sonora in 1851, "Among the late arrivals in town is a jolly little French surgeon, by the name of Lasvignes, a great friend of the Navarros. He has all the characteristics of the *Quartier Latin,* noisy, fond of good living, impertinent, intelligent, and good hearted" (Morgan and Scobie, p. 246). According to the census enumeration of 1850, L. Lasvignes, age twenty-nine, physician, from France, resided in dwelling no. 380 along with another physician, H. H. Radcliff, age thirty, from England. Navarro and Lasvignes evidently ended up on bad terms, as suggested by the entry in Navarro's diary dated 14 April 1852: "While I was returning to Stockton, that scoundrel of a doctor was embarking for Mazatlán. It is better that way." In a letter, dated 15 April 1852, to Samuel, who by then was already in Chile, he repeats the news and adds, "Stockton has finally gotten rid of that animal, who had nearly been forgotten by me and by the rest of the world, after he was sentenced and condemned to perpetual banishment from the state and society of California."

Le Coq, Louis. According to the U.S. census enumeration in Sonora (20 May 1851), Louis Le Coq, age twenty-five, and Louis Ville [i.e., Vielle], age forty-five, both born in France, were tavern keepers in dwelling no. 1026 (Morgan and Scobie, p. 200).

Leguisamont, Mariano. Argentinean physician from the Province of Salta. He set up an emergency hospital for Latin Americans near Mission Dolores in San Francisco. See Gesualdo, p. 48.

Lemon, Frank. According to one miner, Lemon came to California as a mail agent (Pierce, Friday the 4th). Others say he came with the Stevenson Regiment (Newmark, p. 51), though in the list of this regiment, the only Lemon is George F. Lemon (Davis, p. 382). He is also mentioned by Ayers (pp. 51–52):

"We pushed forward until we struck the main road to Stockton. When we got to Frank Lemon's tent at the lower crossing of the Calaveras we were allowed to get some coffee and food." Lemon's place along the Calaveras River seems to appear (as "H. Lemmon") on the map of the gold country published by Wm. A. Jackson (*Carte du District Aurifère du San Joaquin*) and reproduced in Nasatir.

Lippincot, Charles. In William Perkins's journal he is identified as follows: "This young man was Charles Lippincot, brother to the Senator of that name, a highly respectable man from New Jersey, and one of my earliest friends in California" (Morgan and Scobie, p. 232). The editors of his journal make the following qualification: "The reference [to Charles's brother] evidently is to Benjamin S. Lippincot, a New Yorker who came to California overland in 1846, was a member of the constitutional convention of 1849, represented the San Joaquin district as a senator in the first two sessions of the California legislature, and died at Red Bank, New Jersey, on November 25, 1870" (Morgan and Scobie, p. 232 n.3). In the 1850 census there are several Lippincots residing in Stockton but none by the name of Charles.

Lola. *See* Ainza, Lola

Luco. Surname of a prominent Chilean family. According to Pérez Rosales (p. 281), Manuel and Leandro Luco were in Marysville to set up the first charity hospital for poor and crippled Chileans, in a ship they owned called the *Natalia*. He also states that the *Natalia* was the first large ship to navigate without a guide to the port of Sacramento. According to Navarro's diary on 23 May 1849 (in a selection not included in this publication), the *Natalia* ran aground three days later on the San Joaquin River with 100 passengers aboard. He adds: "This is all the fault of its owner, Luco, who could have hired a skilled pilot for $500, but instead preferred a bad one for $300. And now the ship is grounded along the river." Juan Manuel Luco was the owner of the *Natalia* that arrived in San Francisco in 1848 (Davis, p. 408).

MacKay, Juan. Physician and industrialist. Born in Fort Williams, Scotland, 18 February 1819. He came to Chile in 1839, where he graduated in medicine from the Universidad de Santiago in 1840. In 1841 he was appointed physician at the hospital in Concepción. He discovered the coal deposits at Las Vegas de Talcahuano in 1852. After this, he dedicated his efforts to mining activities. He was the founder of the English Club of Concepción. He died on 23 March 1901 during a mining expedition (Figueroa).

Mansilla. *See* Sutton Mansilla, Emilia

Manuela. Indian wife of the chieftain José Jesus.

Mardoqueo. *See* Navarro, Mardoqueo

María or Mariquita. *See* Craig, María

Mármol, José. Journalist and poet, 1818–71, born in Buenos Aires. Author of many different works, among them the famous novel *Amalia,* which was translated into French and English during the Rosas period. He was imprisoned in 1838 and accused of being a "wild unitarian" (an anti-Rosas faction). He emigrated to Brazil and to Montevideo. A famous expression of his summarizes the hatred that the tyrant Rosas inspired in his contemporaries: "America will not even have the dust from your bones" *(Ni el polvo de tus huesos la América tendrá).*

Martínez. Surname of a prominent Chilean family. In his memoirs (p. 277), Pérez Rosales speaks of a young Martínez, age twenty-two, from the south of Chile, who was dying from malaria.

Maza, Manuel Vicente. Argentinean lawyer, 1779–1839, from Buenos Aires. He studied law at the Universidad de Córdoba and was president of the House of Representatives of Buenos Aires when he died. His son, Lieutenant General Ramón Maza, entered into a conspiracy against the tyrant Rosas in June 1839. On the night of 27 June 1839, a group of assassins under the command of Captain Gaetán entered the legislature, where Maza was writing a letter to Rosas on behalf of his son, a prisoner at the time, in which he offered to renounce the presidency of the House. He was stabbed to death. That same day at dawn, his son was executed by a firing squad, and his widow poisoned herself. It has never been proven that Rosas actually ordered the death of Maza. Nevertheless, some historians categorically affirm that Maza was killed on the order of the dictator. See Yabén, pp. 184–88.

Mezzara, Amelia. French woman, age twenty-two, married to Pietro Mezzara. She was educated by her godmother, the wife of the king of France, and was a very good amateur singer. Both she and her husband lived in the Navarro household in Stockton. Her mother must have been Madame Foulon, who lived in Le Havre. She is also mentioned in San Francisco by Levy, p. 92.

Mezzara, Pietro. Husband of Amelia. After her departure for France, Pietro worked in a mine owned by Navarro and other partners.

Milnes. In March 1850, D. B. Milnes was in Sacramento and took part in the organization of the Democratic Party in that city (Upham, p. 279).

Mix, Alfred. American notary public, married Mariquita Craig in Stockton on 12 December 1850. In the Stockton census enumeration of 1850, he is listed as Alfred A. Mix, age twenty-five, county recorder, from Louisiana, living in dwelling no. 613 along with James S. Craig, age forty-eight, physician from Kentucky. In dwelling no. 816 there is another Mix (M. A.), age twenty-seven, trader from Louisiana, probably Alfred's brother. In 1850, Mix was county recorder for San Joaquin County and received an extra $2,000 per year for duties as auditor (see *History of San Joaquin County,* pp. 25, 31). According to the deed whereby he sold his Stockton property to one B. Walker Baurs, in 1854 Mix was living in Shasta County with his wife, Mariquita, and his father-in-law, James Craig. See *San Joaquin County Records,* Book A of Deeds, vol. 5, p. 225, 19 April 1854 ("Lots five and seven in block no. twenty-three E of Center Street").

Moerenhout, Jacques Antoine. 1796–1879, French consul in Monterey in 1848. He reports his trip to the gold fields north of Sacramento in 1848 as well as later developments in the *Gold Rush, 1848–1850*, published later as *The Inside Story of the Gold Rush*. According to Moerenhout, the name of the dead man in Calaveras mentioned by Navarro in his diary entry of 26 July 1849 was Siniac, a carpenter from Le Chateau Briant.

Montes, Lola. Scottish dancer Maria Dolores Rosana Gilbert. She was the lover of Louis of Bavaria, who gave her the title of the countess of Landsfeld. Later she was exiled and died in New York. She owned a house in California.

Morales, Adelaida. Chilean, daughter of Morales and Doña Teresita. She lived in Calaveras with her parents.

Moyano. Argentinean from the Province of San Juan.

Munita. Chilean from Santiago.

Murphy, Miss. This is "Ellen Murphy, daughter of Martin, who came with her father to California in 1844 and in 1850 married Charles María Weber founder of Stockton." See Hutton, p. 38. This marriage is mentioned by an English traveler, who called her father "Grandpa Murphy" (Brown, chap. 1).

Navarro, Elisea. 1828–1847, sister of Ramón Gil, born in Catamarca, emigrated to Chile in 1845 with her mother and her brothers. In 1847 she married her uncle Dr. Domingo Ocampo (1804–77), also an émigré and widower of Doña Encarnación Palma of Chile. Upon Elisea's death, Don Domingo married for the third time, this time with Doña Emilia Navarro, the sister of his second wife (Serrano Redonnet, p. 31). The Navarro brothers gave her name to the ship they bought in California.

Navarro, Mardoqueo. 1824–1882, brother of Ramón Gil. Born in Catamarca, emigrated to Chile around 1842 with his father. He was a member of the Constitutional Club of Valparaiso, founded in August 1852 in order to support the ideas of Juan Bautista Alberdi, author of the book *Bases y puntos de partida para la organización política de la República Argentina* (The foundations and points of departure for the political organization of the Argentine Republic). In Entre Ríos in 1858, he was trustee of President Urquiza, who had called him back from his Chilean exile. He worked with him on different projects until 1862, when he left the management of the salt factory Santa Cándida due to disagreements with Urquiza. He is the author of a curious book called *El General Urquiza y el ciudadano Mardoqueo Navarro. Protector y protegido o sea explotador y explotado,"* printed in Buenos Aires in 1872 (Bosch, p. 734). He died a bachelor in Buenos Aires. The correspondence between Mardoqueo and Alejo Peyret, administrator of the Colonia San José in Entre Ríos (an agricultural colony set up to attract immigrants from Switzerland and Savoy), still exists (Macchi, p. 267).

Navarro, Samuel. Another Navarro brother, born in Catamarca in July 1822. He emigrated to Chile with his father around 1842. He departed for California before his brother Ramón Gil, returning to Chile in February 1852. In Argentina he was general commissary of immigration in 1876, inspector of customs for Alto Uruguay in 1876, and founder of the Colonia Rusa Tudesca in Diamante (an agricultural colony set up to attract immigrants from Russia and Germany) in 1878. In Chile he married his aunt Doña Tomasita Ocampo in November 1852. He had female heirs. In Stockton in 1850 he is listed as residing in dwelling no. 133, together with Sparrow and others, age twenty-eight, merchant from Buenos Aires.

Ocampo, Cupertino. Second cousin of Navarro. Born in Córdoba in 1826, son of Don Andrés Nicolás Ocampo from La Rioja and of Doña Gregoria Ocampo Dulon, his father's first cousin. He emigrated to Chile during the Rosas period and left for California before Navarro. Upon his return to Chile in 1856, he entered into litigation over the Mayorazgo (the entailed estate) at Totox in Córdoba, one of four existing in Argentina at the time. The litigation lasted several years and was carried out under the supervision of Navarro. During that period, two beautiful maps were drawn up, perhaps the best existing today in the Archivo Histórico de Córdoba. Cupertino, who aspired to be the sixth lord of the Mayorazgo, worked as a card dealer at the poker tables in California, causing his cousin great sadness when he saw him this way, having no honor and belittling the illustrious name of the Ocampo family. He was the grandson of the first Argentinean general, Don Francisco Antonio Ortiz de Ocampo. He was also police magistrate in Famatina, La Rioja, where he died a bachelor. See Serrano Redonnet, p. 23, and "Documentos," *Revista de la Junta de Historia y Letras de la Rioja,* 1944, p. 74.

Ocampo, Juan. Relative and friend of Navarro in Concepción.

Oribe, Manuel. Uruguayan general, 1792–1857, born in Montevideo. He took part in the battle of Ituzaingó in the campaign against Brazil. He was president of the Eastern Republic of Uruguay in 1835. At the head of Rosas's army, in 1840 he defeated the liberation army at Quebracho Herrado and again in 1841 at Famaillá. In 1843 he laid siege to Montevideo. He died in November 1857 and was buried with high honors in Uruguay.

Pancho. *See* Ainza, Francisco

Perkins, William. Born on 17 April 1827 in Toronto, Canada (see Newton). He traveled to California in 1849 at twenty-one years of age, where he lived in Sonora. He left California in May 1852, bound for New Orleans. In 1856 in Chile, he married Doña Parmenia Navarro Ocampo, Ramón Gil's sister. According to family tradition, he fell in love with her from the portraits he saw of her in California. In 1861 he took up residence in the city of Rosario, Argentina. There he was a journalist and also presided over the Advisory Board in 1874. He was superintendent of the land department and secretary of the immigration commission. In 1869, President Sarmiento asked him to organize a campaign to attract migrants to set up colonies in the Argentinean Provinces of Santa Fe and Córdoba. In 1870 on the occasion of the national exposition in Córdoba, he received a gold medal and diploma in recognition of his services in favor of immigration and colonization during the period. In

1865 he was designated a member of the Royal Geographic Society of London. He died in Rosario in 1893 at the age of sixty-six. For more on Perkins, see Gschwind.

Polo. Indian chief. A traveler renders the following account of Polo: "The entire mountain district, above the Upper Bar (about four miles from the Lower Bar)—and particularly at the Forks of the Mokelumne—was overrun with Indians, some of whom were of the tribe of the old chief, Polo, and others of a tribe lately made hostile to the Americans by an affray at the Volcano. Polo, it was rumored, had been shot; but I gave no credit to the report. He was much too cautious and cunning to be entrapped. To the miners about that region, he was as much of a will-o'-the-wisp as Abdel-Kader was to the French. More than once he visited the diggings in disguise, and no small company, prospecting above the Forks, was safe from having a brush with his braves" (Taylor, p. 240).

Quevedo, Emilio. Argentinean from Buenos Aires. He left California for Chile in July 1850.

Quiroga, Abel. Argentinean from the Province of San Juan, baptized on 20 September 1829. Son of Don Juan Crisóstomo de Quiroga y Carril and of Doña Cruz de la Rosa. His brothers were Isaac, Isidro, and Juan Crisóstomo. He was married in Argentina to Doña Regis Godoy Quiroga (Calvo, p. 241). According to the 1850 census enumeration of Stockton, he is listed as a merchant, age twenty-eight, from Buenos Aires, living in dwelling no. 135, together with his brothers Isidro (age twenty-five) and Juan Crisóstomo (age twenty-three). According to the San Joaquin county records, while in Stockton the Quiroga brothers were involved in a number of property transactions.

Quiroga, Isaac. Brother of Abel Quiroga. He married twice in Argentina, the first time in 1861 to Doña Concepción Godoy and the second time in 1865 to Doña Aurelia Nieva. For more information, see Morales Guiñazú, p. 265.

Quiroga, Isidro. 1824–1904, another brother of Abel Quiroga. He was married twice, first in 1856 to Doña Emilia Alvarado and later to Doña Andrea Alvarado, her sister. He had heirs by both women. His primary education took place in the Escuela de la Patria in San Juan, continuing his studies later in the school of the Franciscans in Catamarca. He emigrated to Chile during the Rosas period, finishing his studies in Santiago. He went to California along with his three brothers. Upon his return to his country, he occupied a number of different public posts. He was president of the local legislature and then, between 1868 and 1872, was elected as a national representative. In 1874 he was the manager of the Banco de la Nación in San Juan and in 1879 was a member of the Commission for the Reform of the Provincial Constitution. He died in San Juan on 28 February 1904. For more information, see Morales Guiñazú and Udaondo.

Quiroga, Juan Crisóstomo. Another of the Quiroga brothers. He married Adelaida Ovejero. For more information, see Morales Guiñazú.

Radcliff, Dr. The editors of the diary of William Perkins mention a Dr. Henry H. Radcliff, who participated in the publication of the first newspaper in Sonora (Morgan and Scobie, p. 169 n.4). In the Stockton census enumeration of 1850, he is listed in dwelling no. 380, age thirty, physician from England, co-resident with L. Lasvignes.

Rioseco, Domingo. Chilean from Concepción, brother of Tomás. He returns to Chile in October 1849.

Rioseco, Tomás. Chilean, brother of Domingo. He was one of the four original directors of the company formed to prospect for gold in California. He returned to Chile in October 1849.

Rivera, Dorotea. Chilean, daughter of Don Juan de Dios Rivera y Doña Rosario Serrano. She was Navarro's girlfriend in Concepción.

Rivera, Juan de Dios. Chilean, a general during the War of Chilean Independence. Married to Doña Rosario Serrano, they were parents of Dorotea, Matilde, and Urusula, among others (Cuadra Gormaz, p. 438).

Rivero. Probably refers to Demetrio Rivero, Argentinean violinist (1822–89), son of Roque Rivera and author of the "Lid Argentina," the hymn of the followers of General Lavalle. Demetrio was forced into exile during the Rosas dictatorship. He was in Montevideo and in Rio de Janeiro. In California he was a frequent visitor to Elordi's house in Sonora. In 1855, he premiered an opera in two acts in Rio de Janeiro called *El Primo de California*. See Gesualdo, p. 46.

Rodríguez, Casimiro. 1801–70, uncle of Navarro. Military officer, born in Cochabamba, Bolivia, son of Don Miguel Rodríguez and of Doña Patricia Rojas. His long and notable military career began in 1814 as a cadet in battles for independence at Florida and in 1815 at Sipe-Sipe. Later he fought at the orders of General Güemes. In 1827 he fought in the battle of Ituzaingó against Brazil. In the Argentinean civil wars he participated under the command of General Paz as his aide-de-camp (see Paz, p. 355). In 1831 he was promoted to colonel. Due to subsequent events, he retired to Catamarca after abandoning the military service. In 1840 he was appointed commander general of the Catamarca army and fought the *montoneros* in Santiago del Estero. In 1841 he was appointed commander general of Salta. Later he emigrated to Bolivia and only returned to his country after the fall of Rosas, after which he continued to render his services in Catamarca, where he died on 20 October 1870. See Yaben, pp. 184–88, and Cutolo. There is abundant evidence in Navarro's diary (not included in the present selection) that this illustrious figure was indeed his uncle. Examples of this can be seen in Navarro's recollections of Casimiro Rodríguez's being in Córdoba at the orders of General Paz or the fact that Navarro loaned him one thousand pesos upon his return to Argentina. Rodríguez was married in Catamarca in 1835 to Doña Juana Herrera, who was probably the cousin of Navarro's mother, Rosa Ocampo y Herrera. Together they had surviving heirs. It is interesting to note that none of his biographers mention his stay in California.

Rojo, Rudecindo. Argentinean from the Province of San Juan. Son of Don José Rudecindo Rojo and Doña Jacinta Angulo. He married Martina Godoy in San Juan.

Rondizoni, Adolfo. Probably the son of Don José Rondizzoni Canepa, who was born in Parma around 1788 and took part in the Napoleonic Wars. He subsequently went to the United States and from there to Buenos Aires, along with Don José Miguel Carreras. He went to Chile with the Army of Liberation in 1817. In 1852 he was the intendant of Concepción, and he died in 1864. He was married twice, once to Doña Rosario de la Cuadra and then to Doña Dominga de La Cotera (Cuadra Gormaz, 458–59). Adolfo returned to Chile in July 1850. In the original diary, Navarro frequently spells his name as "Rondisoni."

Rosas, Juan Manuel. Argentinean dictator, 1793–1879, born in Buenos Aires. He was appointed governor of Buenos Aires in 1829, took part in the desert campaign of 1833, and finally took power in 1835, when he was appointed governor once again. During his rule, the country was divided between the Federales, his followers, and the Unitarios, his opponents. His favorite motto, which appears on all public documents of the period, was *"¡Viva la Santa Federación! Mueran los salvajes Unitarios!"* (Long live the Holy Federation! Death to the Unitarian Savages!). It was during the "period of terror" in the 1840s that the Navarro family, together with many others, was obliged to take refuge in neighboring countries in order to save their lives. After the battle of Caseros, Rosas was thrown from power in 1852 by General Justo José de Urquiza, the governor of Entre Ríos. Rosas fled to England, accompanied by his daughter Manuelita. He was buried in Southampton, where his remains stayed until 1992, when they were brought back to Argentina by President Menem. After his death, the country was reorganized and the 1853 constitution was drawn up, based on the ideas of Juan Bautista Alberdi contained in his famous book *Bases y puntos de partida para la organización política de la República Argentina* (The foundations and points of departure for the political organization of the Argentine Republic; Valparaíso, Imprenta del Mercurio, 1852). For more on Rosas, see Lynch, *Argentine Dictator*.

Rufino, Leandro. Argentinean from the Province of San Juan. He is probably the son of Laureano Rufino, born in San Juan toward the end of the eighteenth century and deceased in 1853. In the Stockton census enumeration of 1850 he is listed in dwelling no. 22, age twenty-two, merchant from Buenos Aires.

Samuel. *See* Navarro, Samuel

Sánchez, Juan de Dios. Argentinean from the Province of San Juan. His tent was in Calaveras.

Sanfuentes, Valentín. Chilean, partner of the Navarros in a mine. He was probably the son of don Salvador Sanfuentes Urtetegui and of Doña Mercedes Torres

Velasco and the uncle of Don Juan Luis Sanfuentes, who became president of Chile in 1915. See Cuadra Gormaz, p. 479.

Santos, José. Indian chieftain. His name coincides with that of another Indian chieftain, José Jesus, who was the successor of Estanislao. It may be the same person.

Saravia, Federico. Born in Salta, Argentina, and deceased in San Francisco at the end of November 1849. In his diary from 29 November 1849, Navarro says, "I forget to tell my diary of the tragedy that overtook two of my friends it already knows. On Sunday the 18th I was in Stockton when the steamship from San Francisco came in, bearing with it the news of the death of Federico Saravia to the consternation of both Samuel and myself! Only a few days ago this young man had left for San Francisco with no ill omens at all. My poor friend! We lived together for two months in Stockton as though we were brothers, and I know all about his life just as he does mine. He always told me, in tears, about the tragic death of his older brother in the mines with no shelter or other help than that which he was able to render himself. A few days before departing, he received the news of the death in Salta of the only two siblings he had left in the world. He bravely accepted the news of this new blow, aware as he was of the fact that his mother was now alone in the world, with her only remaining son so far away from her! I think he went to San Francisco with the idea of leaving immediately for Salta, and that is where death overtook him at 22 years of age, only four months after the death of all of his siblings!"

Saturnino. *See* Correas, Saturnino

Scollen, John (also Scollan). Scollen appears to have come to California in the Stevenson Regiment. He was appointed alcalde of Calaveras and died in Santa Barbara in 1892. See Ayers, p. 51, and Navarro, "Los Chilenos en California en 1849 y 50."

Smith, Perciford. General, military governor of California. The editors of the diary of William Perkins emphasize the nationalistic feelings of this general, who, having been "sent to California early in 1849 to assume military command, seems to have been infected by this sentiment (strong nativist political sentiment), for in a proclamation issued at Panama in February, he declared that he would check the influx of foreigners into the gold region" (Morgan and Scobie, p. 29).

Soruco. Refers to Camilo and Santiago Soruco, who were brothers from Chile. Camilo died in Panama from cholera in September or October 1851. According to Monaghan (p. 249), the Soruco brothers had a "counting-room" that was destroyed in the San Francisco fire of 1849.

Sparrow. A partner of the Navarro brothers in different business ventures. He set up a merchant house or a warehouse in Stockton together with Samuel Navarro. In the census enumeration of 1850, in dwelling no. 133 there is a M. T. Sparrow, age forty-three, merchant from Maryland, registered together with the Navarros and others. An E. Sparrow is mentioned as one of the businessmen of Stockton who signed a petition to Charles Weber, asking him to remove any vessels he might own that were blocking the channel. See *History of San Joaquin County, California,* p. 25.

Sutton Mansilla, Emilia. Daughter of Richard Sutton (American) and of Mauricia Mansilla Ortiz de Rosas (Argentinean), married in 1828. Her mother was the daughter of the sister of the dictator Juan Manuel Rosas. Emilia married a surgeon named Jacob M. Tucksbury, who was the first physician to use chloroform in Buenos Aires. Her uncle General Lucio V. Mansilla recalls her in his memoirs: "She was married with a doctor and dental surgeon who was passing through Buenos Aires and had his moment of fame. California absorbed Emilia and her husband. I do now know what has become of them. Emilia came twice to Buenos Aires and visited my mother who had always stayed in touch with her by mail, exchanging photographs" (Mansilla, p. 156). For more on Emilia, see Gesualdo, p. 39, and Calvo, p. 87. Dr. J. M. Tucksbury's arrival in San Francisco in 1849 is recorded in Soule, Gihon, and Nisbet.

Taboureux, Regine. Frenchwoman who lived in Concepción before leaving for California.

Terán. Chilean from Nacimiento who was executed in Mokelumne. There are other accounts of his activities in which he is called *Tirante.* See Ayers, chap. 5.

Theall, Hiram Washington. A friend in Sonora who ran a company with William Perkins. The editors of Perkins's journal state, "Hiram Washington Theall had come to California in 1847 as a second lieutenant in Company D. of the New York Regiment, commanded by Colonel Jonathan Drake Stevenson. He was stationed through much of 1848 at San José in Baja California, but by November was at Monterey, as shown by letters in the papers of Henry M. Naglee in the Bancroft Library. Theall briefly succeeded Fraser as *alcalde* at Sonora, was Perkins' partner at least into 1852, and apparently was living at Sonora as late as 1854. By November 6, 1855, as shown by another letter in the Naglee Papers, he had moved to Forest City in Sierra County as the representative of a gold-buying concern. He died at Hamilton, White Pine County, Nevada, about 1869. A street in Sonora is named after him" (Morgan and Scobie, p. 98). Theall had evidently come to Yerba Buena between 1840 and 1841 from Mazatlán: "Teal (sic) brought on a vessel about twenty thousand dollars' worth of Mexican goods; such as silk and cotton rebozos, serapes, ponchos, mangos, costly and ordinary; silver mounted and gilt spurs, saddles, ornamented and ordinary, *armas de pelo,* or riding robes for protecting the legs and body up to the waist; silver headstalls for horses, bridle reins, and other fancy and ornamental goods; an assortment of Mexican products. Teal (sic) opened a store and sold these goods to the hacendados principally. Many were sold to Captain Sutter, who paid for them in land, otter and beaver skins. Teal (sic) was here about two years dispensing of his merchandise, and he made probably $30,000 out of the venture; and had also bought some of Limantour's goods, which he sold with his own. . . . He was fond of chess and also made frequently one of a party at whist, playing chess in the daytime with Rae, and whist in the evening. After selling his goods here, Teal (sic) returned to New Mexico. Both he and Titcomb were originally from New England" (Davis, p. 163–64).

Tomás. *See* Rioseco, Tomás

Tucksbury. *See* Sutton Mansilla, Emilia

Varela, Juan Cruz. Argentinean journalist and poet, 1794–1839, born in Buenos Aires. He studied at the Universidad de Córdoba, Argentina, and was the founder of several newspapers. In 1828 he emigrated to Montevideo for political reasons and was subsequently exiled by General Oribe, an ally of Rosas. He returned to Montevideo after the fall of Oribe and died shortly thereafter.

Virgine. According to Perkins, this woman presided over one of the gambling tables at the Le Coq saloon in Sonora (Morgan and Scobie, pp. 248, 251, 260).

Ward Smith. Commercial firm in California made up by Frank Ward and William M. Smith. Smith, who was from Georgia, was an excellent marksman and had been a circus rider in Mexico. He built his residence in Martínez and eventually committed suicide there in 1854 (Davis, p. 180). Frank Ward, his partner, arrived in California in July 1846. The death of his young wife and business losses led him to attempt to commit suicide, as told by W. R. Hutton in a letter dated 18 April 1850: "Frank Ward, who shot himself in the head about two or three weeks ago, will probably recover. He has spoiled one eye and the ball is still in his nose" (Hutton, p. 38).

Weber, Charles M. Weber is frequently present in the memoirs of the travelers of the period who came through Stockton. According to one Chilean, Stockton "owes its existence to the adventurer Weber who, as one of the protected foreigners who received land from the Mexican Government, also was among the first to abandon the plow for the sword and to serve under the command of Commodore Stockton, whose name he gave to the village of his endearment" (Pérez Rosales, p. 265). He founded, and was chief partner of, the Stockton Mining Company, which prospected around Weber Creek, founded Dry Diggins (later Placerville), and enlisted the help of the Indians under José Jesus in his mining activities in the area around Stanislaus, where the company became concentrated until it broke up. For more on Weber and the Stockton Mining Company, see Bancroft, pp. 74–78, and Morgan and Scobie, p. 14. In April 1850 Weber had a hotel in Stockton, as shown by the account of one traveler: "We refreshed ourselves at a German hotel, the best in town, which a certain Mr. Weber kept, under the proud title of 'Stockton Restaurant'" (Gerstäcker, *Gerstäcker's Travels,* p. 30). He evidently had arrived from New Orleans in 1836 and had been a friend of Sutter (Lienhard, p. 22). Weber was married to Ellen Murphy. In the Stockton census enumeration of 1850, he is listed as follows: dwelling no. 1, Weber, age thirty-six, merchant from Germany. There is also a Weaver mentioned in the diary, who appears to be the same person.

William. *See* Perkins, William

Zañartu, Fabio. Chilean from well-to-do family in Concepción.

Notes

Introduction

1. See Serrano Redonnet, p. 3.

2. Fernando Allende Navarro to María del Carmen Ferreyra, 26 November 1976. Letter in the possession of María del Carmen Ferreyra.

3. See Morgan and Scobie, pp. 202, 222, 285.

4. R. G. Navarro to Don Manuel José Navarro, Valparaiso, 20 September 1952. Ramón Gil Navarro Papers, The Bancroft Library, University of California, Berkeley.

5. These projects are set out in the letters he sent to his cousin José Manuel Navarro in 1853.

6. The authors would like to thank Dolores Martín for her suggested wording of this final paragraph.

7. Joaquín V. González, in the weekly *El Periódico,* Córdoba, 22 August 1883.

8. The bibliography on the California gold rush is vast. The descriptive bibliography of the period recently published by Gary Kurutz is a very useful guide to the existing literature. For a major recent contribution to the field, see Rohrbough, *Days of Gold: The California Gold Rush and the American Nation.*

9. The only exception to this was a series of newspaper articles concerning the fights between the North Americans and the Chileans at Chili Gulch.

10. For a rather unflattering portrait of Navarro as a dandy and a ladies' man, based entirely on hearsay many years after his death, see Reyes, p. 168 n.2.

11. What follows is the complete citation at the Bancroft Library: Navarro, Ramón Gil. 1828–1883, Ramón Gil Navarro papers, 24 March 1845–8 June 1883. 1 box, 4 vols.—Vol. 1: Diary, March 24, 1845–October 16, 1852; Vol. 2: Diary, November 1, 1852–July 11, 1857; Vol. 3: Commonplace book, 1846–December 12 [1854?]; Vol. 4: Letterpress copy book, April 17, 1851–June 8, 1883 (most letters written from Stockton prior to Navarro's return to Chile in 1852), and related papers. The call number is BANC MSS 81/159c.

12. These notebooks are 12.5 x 8.3 cm (4.88 x 3.24 in.).

13. San Felipe is located in the Aconcagua Valley in north-central Chile.

The Diary of Ramón Gil Navarro

1. Navarro is referring to the Vallis Josaphat, mentioned in the prophecies of Joel (3:2), where Yahweh will gather all of his people to be judged once Judah and Jerusalem have been restored.

2. There are eight reales in a peso. Throughout much of the text, the author appears to use the peso and the dollar almost indistinctly.

3. An arroba is an old Spanish unit of weight equal to about twenty-five pounds.

4. Samuel Navarro is Ramón Gil Navarro's older brother.

5. This merchant company, originally from Valparaiso, was established in San Francisco in 1848 (Davis, p. 214).

6. "Therefore it is true, he does not want to work for the company and is only interested in his own business. . . ." The text is in Latin and French in the original.

7. A league is a unit of distance that is the equivalent of approximately 5.5 km (3.4 miles).

8. The California missions were established by the Franciscans.

9. Here the author is referring to Juan Ocampo, Mardoqueo Navarro (his brother), and Fabio Zañartu.

10. This is the name given to the islands of Hawaii by Capt. James Cook in 1778.

11. San Benito of Palermo was an African.

12. May 25 is the anniversary of the revolution of 1810 in Argentina against Spanish domination.

13. The town was originally laid out in the spring of 1849, resurveyed by Major R. P. Hammond, and named after Commodore R. F. Stockton. In the appendix to his *Map of the Mining District of California,* William A. Jackson remarked that, as of December 1849, "Stockton is situated on a slough of the same name, three miles from San Joaquin River, and seventy miles from New-York of the Pacific. The slough is navigable for steamers and barges of four hundred tons. The location is excellent, embracing the peninsula between the two principal sloughs, and extends south to Mormon Slough. Population about 3,000. It contains some good buildings, and presents the appearance of considerable business activity. It is the great depot for the southern mining region, and is destined to be a place of much importance" (cited in Morgan and Scobie, p. 92).

14. Cuyo is a region and Catamarca is a town in west-central Argentina.

15. San Juan is a town in west-central Argentina.

16. *Sacatados* means "basted" or "interlaced."

17. Rosas is the Argentinean dictator.

18. Navarro appears to be referring to poison ivy.

19. Navarro is referring to one's private parts.

20. A *huaso* is a Chilean peasant.

21. According to Navarro's article "Los Chilenos en California," published in the *Correo del Sur* on 4 January 1853, this eating house was called Lucien.

22. This story is included in the 1 April 1853 issue of the *Correo del Sur*.

23. According to Gerstäcker (*Gerstäcker's Travels*, p. 143), the price of laundry was so exorbitant that the only way to get clothes washed in California during those days was to send them to China, and it took seven or eight months to get them back.

24. It is unclear here whether they are going to send for goods to be brought from Chile or from San Francisco.

25. Here Navarro appears to be referring to Commodore Robert Field Stockton (1795–1866), who set up a civil government in California independent of Mexico in 1846 and formally annexed it to the United States.

26. A quintal is approximately equal to one hundredweight.

27. The author is probably referring here to Sonora Camp.

28. The author appears to be referring to Helen of Troy.

29. This is a traditional Argentinean fight song.

30. Here Navarro is playing on the name Placer de las Calaveras, which, while meaning the "placer along the Calaveras River," can be translated into Spanish as the "Pleasure of Skulls."

31. According to family tradition, Navarro actually made his wedding ring from the gold he brought from California.

32. Mokelumne Hill is also called Mokelumne or Big Bar.

33. The consul was Jacques Antoine Moerenhout, who relates the same incident from a very different perspective. See Moerenhout, p. 69.

34. The Spanish term *vara* (a measure of length of about 33 inches) has been translated as "yard" in English.

35. For more on Scollen, see Ayers, chapter 5.

36. Here Navarro appears to be referring to a placer along the San Antonio Creek, a tributary of the south fork of the Calaveras River, between Angels Camp and San Andreas, about ten miles east of the Fourth Crossing (see Gudde, p. 304). Also known as San Antone or San Antone Camp, it was probably originally a Mexican camp, dating from 1848 or 1849.

37. The Areopagus was the earliest aristocratic council of ancient Athens and held wide legal authority.

38. An alcalde is the chief administrative and judicial officer in Hispanic towns.

39. San Gil (St. Gilles) was a French cenobite from the sixth century who lived in a forest along the Rhone near Marseilles. King Childebert ordered a monastery built with Gilles as its abbot. His saint's day is 1 September.

40. This is also known as Murphy Camp, named after John M. Murphy, one of the partners of the Stockton Mining Company, founded by Charles Weber. See Bancroft, p. 76.

41. The phrase "the full rights of conquest" is underlined in the original diary.

42. This placer is also called "Sullivan's Mud Canyon," "Mud Placer," or "Sullivan's Diggins." According to Moerenhout (p. 67), the Stanislaus placer mines

extend for several leagues from north to south. The most important for size and richness are those called *del Barro,* or "Sullivan's Diggins."

43. The word "wagonload" is underlined in the original diary.

44. The author is referring to Frank Lemon, who lived on the road to Stockton "at the lower crossing of the Calaveras." For additional information, see Ayers, pp. 51–52.

45. The author is referring to the Stockton Slough.

46. The author appears to be referring to the El Dorado Street Bridge, which connects Weber Point and the south bank of the Stockton Slough.

47. Navarro published an account of the entire affair between the Chileans and the Americans in several issues of the newspaper *El Correo del Sur,* which appeared on the following dates in January 1853: 8, 11, 15, 18, 20, 22, 25, and 26. In these articles, he identifies the following Chilean companies operating in California: Hermosilla, Orangüi, Terán, Ruiz y Lada, Herrera, Montiel, Pérez de Oyarson, B. Gutiérrez, D. Sisterna, Maturano, and J. Concha. There is also an English-language version of Navarro's account in Beilharz and Lopez, pp. 101–47. For more on this affair, see Ayers, chapter 5.

48. In the original diary, Navarro refers to Chili Gulch as the *"cañada de los niños chilenos."*

49. The author is referring to the inhabitants of Saragossa, Spain, who resisted the troops of Napoleon during the War of Spanish Independence (1808–12).

50. Nacimiento is a town in southern Chile.

51. The author is referring to Judge B. Collier.

52. Mate is a traditional Argentinean and Paraguayan drink similar to tea made from the leaves of a plant native to Paraguay.

53. According to a later account of this incident published in the *Correo del Sur* (18 January 1853), Navarro translated for the Chileans the arrest warrant against the Americans issued by W. Dickenson and G. Belt on 22 December 1849. In it, Concha and Maturano were authorized to apprehend, peacefully or by force, those who had ignored the authority of the subprefect and who had recognized the authority of Collier. Mr. Scollen was the judge charged with seeing that the order was carried out. The rebels were to be taken to Stockton to be tried. Navarro's exact transcription of the order, printed in "Los Chilenos en California" and translated in Beilharz and Lopez (p. 125), reads as follows: "On the 26th of December the Chileans returned from Stockton to the house of Judge Scollen [Scollan], with the said order and arrest warrant against the Americans. I translated this order in the presence of Judge Scollen and, according to my notes, it reads as follows: 'By these present, Mssrs. Concha and Maturano are authorized to arrest and bring to Stockton, either freely or by force, all of the individuals residing in Calaveras who have defied the legal authority of this subprefecturate and who have recognized Mr. Coller [Collier] as a judge. They are authorized likewise to arrest and bring to Stockton all individuals who took part in the robbery, violence, and expulsion carried out against the aliens living in Chili Gulch. By this same order, judges and

all of the loyal citizens of Calaveras are required to give to the aforesaid Mssrs. Concha and Maturano whatever help they need to effect the arrest of the rebels. The lawful judge of Calaveras, Mr. Scollen, will authorize the execution of this order by his presence. The rebels will be brought to Stockton for trial by a jury with competent authority. Given in Stockton, December 22, 1849. W. Dickenson, G. Belt.' " (Navarro, 1853).

54. In the article "Los Chilenos en California" (8 January 1853), Navarro states that W. Collier was the judge appointed ad hoc by the Americans to replace the titled judge, B. Scollen. In another article (11 January 1853), Navarro describes Collier as a man with an irreproachable name and a tidy fortune and says he was the judge of Double Spring.

55. This news turns out to be erroneous. Rosas ends up dying in England in 1877.

56. "To your health, Madame."

57. "You see, sometimes it is necessary for someone like me to disguise myself as a boy and to trick men, despite all of my good intentions. That is the way things are here in California. For two months now I have been wearing the clothes you see, but tomorrow morning I shall have the honor of introducing myself to you as I really am, as Madame Gregoire."

58. In the original diary, Navarro refers to Angels Camp as Los Angeles.

59. Quiroga was a nineteenth-century Argentinean political leader.

60. Empanadas are meat pies, a delicacy of traditional Argentine cuisine.

61. A *batea* is a bowl used for washing gold.

62. The author is referring to the events of 28 December, not 28 November.

63. "Here is Madame Gremière, who is dressed up as a boy."

64. The author is referring to Pittsburgh, founded in 1849 as New York of the Pacific and later called New York Landing. In 1911 its name was changed to Pittsburgh.

65. The author appears to be referring to Telegraph Hill.

66. By the name "Juan," the author is referring to Juan Ocampo, his cousin who lives in Concepción, Chile. The person to whom he is referring as "beloved beauty" is Regine Tabourex, a woman friend of Juan Ocampo.

67. A jarabe is a popular Mexican dance, probably derived from the Spanish zapateado. The *sambacueca* is a combination of two traditional creole dances: the *zamba* from Argentina and the *cueca* from Chile.

68. "I beg your pardon, miss, but I believe that I am bothering you." "Not at all, sir."

69. William Perkins has further details on these events. See Morgan and Scobie, pp. 36–44, 153–156.

70. In the diary, Navarro spells his name as "Visansou," though it appears to be Besançon.

71. Here the author is referring to the events of 25 May 1810, in which the revolution against Spanish rule took place in Buenos Aires.

72. Elisea Navarro was the sister of Ramón Gil and Samuel.

73. The author appears to be referring to the Argentinean authors Rivera Indarte and Santiago Calzadilla.

74. This is the first mention in the diary of María (or Mariquita) Craig, who will subsequently become a central figure in Navarro's tale. According to the Stockton census enumeration of 1850, Dr. Craig was from Kentucky, and his daughter María, age fifteen, was from Mexico.

75. Sonora was originally called Sonora Camp, partly after the first diggers from Sonora, Mexico, who camped there and partly to distinguish it from nearby Jamestown and Wood Creek, or the American camps. It was made the county seat in May 1850 and incorporated as a city a year later. See Bancroft, pp. 469–70.

76. Navarro actually refers to the authorities as the *Comisión de muertos.*

77. Putiphar was an Egyptian dignitary whose wife falsely accused Joseph of having attempted to seduce her.

78. Formally the *Californian,* in June 1849 this newspaper appeared as the *Alta California,* a weekly. See Bancroft, p. 166.

79. These two paragraphs are in English in the diary. There are many spelling errors, which have been eliminated from the present publication.

80. In the diary, this text in italics is in French.

81. In the diary, this text in italics is in English. Spelling and grammar have been modernized and corrected, as the original text has numerous mistakes.

82. In the diary, except for the first sentence, this entire paragraph is written in French.

83. This sentence is in French in the original diary.

84. These two sentences are in English.

85. In "Los Chilenos en California" (6 January 1853), Navarro identifies the two men as a Chilean and a Peruvian.

86. The author appears to be referring to Chili Gulch.

87. This paragraph is in English in the original diary.

88. The text here is in French. Navarro is referring to Dr. Craig's daughter, María, or Mariquita.

89. In the original diary, Navarro spells the surname as Twesbury.

90. He is referring to Father Arnau.

91. For more on the Robinson warehouse, see Davis, pp. 243–44.

92. For more on this incident, see Massey, p. 162.

93. This is an exact transcription of the original French text. In English it reads: "I am going to speak as if your cousin Navarro were not here, and I would like to say that he seems perfectly nice to me and especially that he is a very good-looking young man, upon my word."

94. "Ten cents" is written in English in the diary.

95. The presence of this group was also registered by another traveler in California, though, unlike Navarro, he calls it the *Guard de Noble of Paris* and attributes far greater importance to it: "There are Eight thousand French in the

mines who were sent by the French government to work here, they were the *Guard de Noble of Paris* and for their services were sent a[t] the expense of the government. The Americans do not like it and in Mokelomie [Mokelumne] Co. they have given them (the Frenche) notice to leave or fight. At San an Dres [Andreas] one mile from here, there are a[s] many and I think there will be trouble soon between us. They are all well armed and live and travel in military style having their officers Music Flags . . . with them. Its a shame that our government will allow themselves to be run over by the off scourings of all Gods creation who are taking the bread out of the Americans miners mouths, or the Gold which is the same. Both Americans and Naturalized foreigners are greatly dissatisfied about it. I think that all foreigners who had declared their intentions previous to the admission of this state are all who should be allowed to dig a dollar and I hope Congress will pass such a law" (Fairchild, pp. 99–100). For more on the Mobile Guard of Paris, see Levy, pp. 71–72.

96. For more on this marriage, see Brown, chap. 1.

97. In the diary, most of this sentence is in French.

98. According to Bonta (p. 285), the marriage record reads as follows: "Mr. Agustin A. Mix and Miss María Conception Craig have come before the under-signed with the declared intention of getting married. Mr. Agustin Mix has formally declared that he takes María Conception Craig for his lawful wife, and afterwards Miss María Conception Craig declared likewise that she takes Mr. Agustin A. Mix for her lawful husband. As witness to this, those undersigned have signed this marriage register. Stockton, 12 December 1850. Signed: L'abbé Renaud, Samuel Navarro, Louisa Clements, Jos Baran Clements, B. W. Bours, Benjamin G. Weir, W. W. Stevenson, James S. Craig."

99. The word "fiancée" is *"novia"* in Spanish.

100. The word "ceremoniously" is underlined in the original diary.

101. This dialogue is in French in the diary.

102. This sentence is written in English in the original diary.

103. *Negra,* or *negro,* is a term of endearment used in much of Latin America, quite independent of the color of a person's skin.

104. Chillán is a town in Chile where Navarro worked for a time in 1848.

105. This text is underlined in the diary.

106. The author is referring to Amelia Mezzara, whom he had met some months before in Sonora.

107. French Camp is located just south of Stockton.

108. The passage in italics is also underlined in the original diary.

109. The author is referring to Agustín Ainza.

110. "There is no sorrow like mine, and there is no one who can comfort me."

111. Throughout this entire affair, the entries in the diary, which normally occur almost daily, become less frequent yet often longer. Clearly the affair has altered Navarro's attitude toward his diary. A number of details of Navarro's life during

this period can be found in the many letters he wrote, the contents of which have been extracted and will be included, in part, along with the diary.

112. Both "fellow" and "fire" are in English in the diary.

113. From this point on in the diary, the editors have decided to include extracts of some letters written by the author. These letters were taken from Navarro's letter copier and are located in the Bancroft Library of Berkeley. There are no extant letters from earlier dates. For the most part, the letters explain more of his economic activities in California and Chile and provide a glimpse of certain aspects of his personality that are less apparent in the original diary, such as his sense of irony.

114. Navarro appears to be referring to the Digger Indians. For more on this subject, see Upham, p. 240.

115. For more on Sonora, see Perkins's journal in Morgan and Scobie, p. 219.

116. For more on this event, see Perkins's journal in Morgan and Scobie, p. 221.

117. The journal of William Perkins contains a description of the activities of this group toward the end of 1850: "We have finished a large and handsome Masonic Hall, and St. John's day was celebrated in a very creditable style. The procession numbered over five hundred, in which there were not a few Royal Arches and Knights Templars in their rich regalia. I was chosen Orator for the occasion, and delivered the first Masonic discourse in the Southern Mines. The Order is highly respectable here; surprisingly so, when we consider the state of society. There is more care taken to exclude unworthy men than I have remarked in the United States and Canada" (Morgan and Scobie, p. 183).

118. Earlier in the day, at a 4th of July picnic out of town, Navarro and Agustín had been forced to jump off a carriage because of a wild, unbridled horse.

119. Navarro often Hispanicizes Alfred Mix's name to Alfredo.

120. "You love me still, Mariquita." The Latin spelling is only an approximation.

121. Lansquenets is a card game of German origin that was very popular in France.

122. For more on the misfortunes of Sutter, see Bancroft, pp. 97–107.

123. In his diary, Navarro refers to the Golden Star mine by its Spanish name, *Estrella de Oro*. This mine was probably located near the border of Calaveras and Toulumne Counties.

124. The text in italics is in English in the original.

125. The quoted words are in French in the original diary. The news of Mariquita's pregnancy subsequently proves to be unfounded.

126. This book was published in 1849.

127. "My soul."

128. The text in italics is underlined in the original diary.

129. The text in italics is in French in the original diary. It can be translated as " . . . pregnant . . . Might it be possible that we might just end it all with . . . But that would be impossible!!!"

130. This account coincides partially with that of William Perkins: "The two

horse thieves hanged at Stockton on November 28, as described in the *San Joaquin Republican* the following day, were James Wilson, alias Mountain Jim, and Frederick Salkmar" (Morgan and Scobie, p. 277).

131. "Airam" is the name he uses to refer to Mariquita. It is "María" spelled backward.

132. "Neleb" is a term of affection used for sixteen-year-old Belén Ainza, one of the two Ainza sisters. It is "Belén" spelled backward.

133. "The countess of Landsfeld" is the affectionate term used for fourteen-year-old Lola Ainza, Belén Ainza's younger sister.

134. The entire text in italics is in French in the original diary.

135. This sentence in italics is in English in the original diary.

136. Coronel is a seaport, 17 miles south of Concepción, Chile. The Bío-Bío River runs through southern Chile from the Andes to the sea at Concepción.

137. Damon and Pitnias are Greek philosophers of the school of Pythagoras. For more on Planel's theater, see Perkins's journal in Morgan and Scobie, pp. 300, 302, 304, 306.

138. The jota is a traditional dance from Aragon, a region of northeastern Spain.

139. The author is referring to the Argentine dictator, Rosas.

140. This phrase is in French in the original diary.

141. The titles of the following books are not always given in the language in which the book was written, and the spelling is often imprecise.

142. St. Dionysius Areopagite was a first-century saint converted by St. Paul at Athens.

143. *Q.L.M.B.* stands for "*Que la mano besa,*" which means "who kisses your hand."

144. For some months now, there has been a flirtatious relationship going on with both Lola and Belén Ainza. Much of it transpired more or less in the presence of Mariquita and was, at least apparently, quite innocent. Since the texts on this matter are somewhat repetitive, most of them have not been included in the present selection of the diary.

145. This text is underlined in the original diary.

146. These paragraphs have been selected from a set of loose-leaf pages entitled "My Diary" that were placed inside the diary. They are first mentioned in the entry dated 13 October 1851 and appear to have been written sometime toward the end of Navarro's stay in California.

Bibliography

Works by Ramón Gil Navarro

Actor, Testigo y Mártir: El sitio de la Rioja o sea la intervención de las Fuerzas de Buenos Aires, en las Provincias de Catamarca y La Rioja. Córdoba: Editorial Lerner, 1985.

"Los Chilenos en California en 1849 y 50." *El Correo del Sur* (Concepción, Chile), 1, 4, 6, 8, 11, 15, 18, 20, 22, 25, 27 January 1853. Microfilm No. PCH 259. Santiago, Chile: Biblioteca Nacional, Sección Periódicos y Microformatos. Also published in Beilharz and Lopez, pp. 101–47.

"Comercio de Chile con la Conferederación por Copiapó." *El Nacional* (Paraná), March 1858.

Limites de la Provincia de Córdoba con Buenos Aires, Santa, Fe, San Luis, Santiago, La Rioja y Catamarca—Arbitraje del Gobernador Viso en la cuestión de límites entre Santiago y Catamarca. Córdoba, 1879.

"El padre Esquiú: La Religión y el Estado." *El Correo del Sur* (Concepción, Chile), 12, 14, 16, 21, 23, 26, 28 September, and 3, 4, 5 October 1854.

La Provincia (de Catamarca) y la portentosa riqueza de sus minas. Valparaíso, Chile, 1855.

Veinte años en un Calabozo ó sea La Desgraciada Historia de veinte y tantos argentinos muertos o envejecidos en los Calabozos del Paraguay. Rosario: Imprenta del Ferrocarril, 1863. Reprinted, with a prologue by Manuel Dominguez, Asunción, September 1902.

"La visita a los Departamentos. Visita a Villa Argentina (Chilecito)." *El Nacional* (Paraná), March 1858.

Works about Ramón Gil Navarro

Bazán, Raul A. "Ramón Gil Navarro: Guerra y Política después de Pavón." *La Voz del Interior* (Córdoba), Sunday, 18 August 1985.

Bischoff, Efraín U. "Ramón Gil Navarro, un hombre del Interior." *Revista de la Junta de Historia de Catamarca.* Reproduced in *La Unión* (Catamarca), 9 November 1969.

Garriga, Nilda Correa de. "Ramón Gil Navarro: Su labor parlamentaria y la defensa de los derechos diferenciales." *Boletín de la Junta de Estudios Históricos de Catmarca* 12 (1995–96), pp. 51–73. Catamarca, 1997.

González, Joaquín V. "Ramón Gil Navarro." *El Periódico* (Córdoba), 22 August 1883.

López Urrutia, Carlos. *Episodios Chilenos en California 1849–1860.* Ediciones Universitarias de Valparaíso. Valparaíso, Chile: Universidad Católica de Valparaíso, 1975.

Luque Colombres, Carlos. "El diario el Progreso y la candidatura presidencial de Roca." In *IV Congreso Nacional y Regional de Historia Argentina, Mendoza y San Juan,* 7–9 November 1977, 2:165–79. Buenos Aires: Academia Nacional de la Historia, 1983.

"El mejor algodón del mundo." *Tiempo de Córdoba,* Sunday, 6 August 1978, sección economía. Includes a brief comment on the articles published by Navarro in *El Nacional* (Paraná) in 1858.

Sánchez, Nazario F. "Ramon Gil Navarro: En el Centenario de su Natalicio." In *Hombres y Episodios de Córdoba,* pp. 161–68. Córdoba, 1928. Reproduced in *Los Principios* (Córdoba), 17 January 1928.

Other Sources Consulted

Ainza, Manuel. *Aviso.* Ures, Mexico: Imp. del Gobierno, 1851.

Ayers, Col. James J. *Gold and Sunshine: Reminiscenses of Early California.* Boston: R. G. Badger, 1922.

Bancroft, Hubert Howe. *The History of California.* Vol. 6, *1848–1859.* Vol. 23 of *The Works.* San Francisco: History Company, 1888; printed in facsimile from the First American Edition, Santa Barbara: Wallace Hebberd, 1970.

Bazán, Armando Raúl. *Historia del Noreste Argentino.* Buenos Aires: Plus Ultra, 1995.

Beilharz, Edwin A., and Carlos U. Lopez, eds. and trans. *We Were 49ers! Chilean Accounts of the California Gold Rush.* Pasadena CA: Ward Ritchie Press, 1976.

Bonta, Robert Eugene. *The Cross in the Valley: The History of the Establishment of the Catholic Church in the Northern San Joaquin Valley of California up to 1863.* Stockton CA: Academy of California Church History, 1963.

Bosch, Beatriz. *Urquiza y su tiempo.* Buenos Aires: Eudeba, 1971.

Brown, John Henry. *Reminiscences and Incidents of "The Early Days" of San Francisco by John H. Brown; Actual Experience of an Eye-witness, from 1845 to 1850.* San Francisco: Mission Journal Publishing, [1886]; San Francisco: Grabhorn Press, 1933.

Bunster, Enrique. *Chilenos en California.* Santiago, Chile: Editorial del Pacífico, 1954.

Calvo, Carlos. *Nobiliario del Antiguo Virreynato del Río de la Plata.* Vol. 6. Buenos Aires: Editorial La Facultad, 1943.

Cuadra Gormaz, Guillermo de la. *Familias Chilenas.* 2 vols. Santiago, Chile: Zamorano y Caperan, 1982.

Cutolo, Vicente Osvaldo. *Nuevo diccionario biográfico Argentino (1750–1930).* Buenos Aires: Editorial Elche, 1968–1985.

Davis, William Heath. *Seventy-five Years in California; a History of Events and Life in California: Personal, Political and Military.* . . . Edited and with a historical foreword and index by Douglas S. Watson. San Francisco: J. Howell, 1929.

Fairchild, Lucius. *California Letters of Lucius Fairchild.* Edited with notes and an introduction by Joseph Schafer. Madison: State Historical Society of Wisconsin, 1931.

Figueroa, Pedro Pablo. *Diccionario biográfico de extranjeros en Chile.* Santiago, Chile: Imprenta moderna, 1900.

Gerstäcker, Friedrich Wilhelm Christian. *Gerstäcker's Travels: Rio de Janeiro— Buenos Aires—Ride through the Pampas—Winter Journey across the Cordilleras —Chili—Valparaiso—California and the Gold Fields.* Translated by George Cosgrave. London: T. Nelson and Sons, 1854.

———. *Scenes of Life in California.* San Francisco: Grabhorn Press, 1942.

Gesualdo, Vicente. "Argentinos y otros latinoamericanos en la 'fiebre del oro.' " *Historia* 17, pp. 35–60, n. 66. Buenos Aires, June-August 1997.

Gold Rush Days. Vital Statistics. Copied from early newspapers of Stockton, California, 1850–55. Compiled and mimeographed by San Joaquin Genealogical Society. Stockton CA, 1958.

Gschwind, Juan Jorge. *Guillermo Perkins: Su contribución al progreso económico argentino.* Rosario: Juan José Casabella, 1936.

Guarda, Gabriel, O.S.B. *La sociedad en Chile austral antes de la colonización alemana, 1645–1850.* Santiago, Chile: Editorial Andres Bello, 1979.

Gudde, Erwin Gustav. *California Gold Camps: A Geographical and Historical Dictionary of Camps, Towns and Localities Where Gold Was Found and Mined, Wayside Stations, and Trading Centers.* Berkeley: University of California Press, 1975.

Hafen, Le Roy Reuben. *Journals of Forty-Niners: Salt Lake to Los Angeles.* Edited with historical comments by Le Roy R. Hafen and Ann W. Hafen. Glendale CA: A. H. Clark, 1960.

History of San Joaquin County, California, with illustrations descriptive of its scenery, residences, public buildings, fine blocks and manufactories. Oakland CA: Thompson & West, 1879.

Huntley, Sir Henry Veel. *California: Its Gold and Its Inhabitants.* London: T. C. Newby, 1856.

Hutton, William Rich. *Glances at California, 1847–1853: Diaries and Letters of William Rich Hutton, with a Brief Memoir and Notes by Willard O. Waters.* San Marino CA: Huntington Library, 1942.

Kowalewski, Michael, ed. *Gold Rush: A Literary Exploration.* Berkeley: Heyday Books, California Council for the Humanities, 1997.

Kurutz, Gary F. *The California Gold Rush: A Descriptive Bibliography of Books and Pamphlets Covering the Years 1848–1853*. San Francisco: Book Club of California, 1997.

Levy, Daniel. *Les Français en Californie*. San Francisco: Grégoire, Tauzy et Cie, Libraires Éditeurs, 1884.

Lienhard, Heinrich. *A Pioneer at Sutter's Fort, 1846–1850: The Adventures of Heinrich Lienhard*. Los Angeles: Calafia Society, 1941.

Lynch, John. "From Independence to National Organization." In *Argentina since Independence*, edited by Leslie Bethell, pp. 1–46. Cambridge: Cambridge University Press, 1993.

———. *Argentine Dictator: Juan Manuel De Rosas, 1829–1852*. Oxford: Clarendon; New York: Oxford University Press, 1981.

Macchi, Manuel E. "La colonia San José en su Centenario." In *Anuario del Instituto de Investigaciones Históricas*. Vol. 2. Rosario: Universidad Nacional del Litoral, 1957.

MacMinn, George R. *The Theater of the Golden Era in California*. Caldwell ID: Caxton Printers, 1941.

Mansilla, Lucio V. *Retratos y recuerdos*. Buenos Aires: Editorial Borocaba, 1953.

Massey, Ernest de. *A Frenchman in the Gold Rush: The Journal of Ernest de Massey, Argonaut of 1849*. Translated by Marguerite Eye Wilbur. San Francisco: California Historical Society, 1927.

Moerenhout, Jacques Antoine. *The Inside Story of the Gold Rush*. Translated and edited by Abraham P. Nasatir, with an introduction and conclusion by George Ezra Dane. San Francisco: California Historical Society, 1935.

Monaghan, Jay. *Chile, Peru, and the California Gold Rush of 1849*. Berkeley: University of California Press, 1973.

Morales Guiñazú, Fernando. *Genealogías de Cuyo*. Mendoza: Best Hermanos, 1939.

Morgan, Dale L., and James R. Scobie. *Three Years in California: William Perkins' Journal of Life at Sonora, 1849–1852*. Berkeley: University of California Press, 1964.

Nasatir, Abraham P. "Chileans in California during the Gold Rush Period and the Establishment of the Chilean Consulate." *California Historical Society Quarterly* 53, no. 1 (spring 1974): 52–70.

Nasatir, Abraham P., ed. *A French Journalist in the California Gold Rush: The Letters of Etienne Derbec*. Georgetown CA: Talisman Press, 1964.

Newmark, Harris. *Sixty Years in Southern California, 1853–1913, Containing the Reminiscences of Harris Newmark*. Edited by Maurice H. Newmark and Marco R. Newmark. New York: Knickerbocker Press, 1916.

Newton, Jorge. *Diccionario biográfico del campo argentino*. Buenos Aires, 1972.

Olmos, Ramón Rosa. "Bibliografías Catamarqueñas." *Boletín de la Junta de Estudios Históricos de Catamarca* 5, nos. 1 and 2, p. 46. Catamarca, 1945.

Owens, Kenneth N., ed. *John Sutter and a Wider West*. Lincoln: University of Nebraska Press, 1994.

Paz, José María. *Memorias.* 4 vols. Buenos Aires: Editorial Schapire S.R.L., 1968.

Pérez Rosales, Vicente. *Recuerdos del Pasado.* Santiago de Chile: Editorial Orbe, 1969.

Perkins, William. *El Campo de los Sonoraenses, Tres años de Residencia en California, 1849–1851.* Buenos Aires: Editorial Tor, 1937.

Pierce, Hiram Dwight. *A Forty Niner Speaks.* Oakland CA: Keystone-Inglett Printing, 1930.

Reyes, Marcelino. *Bosquejo histórico de la Provincia de la Rioja 1543–1867.* Buenos Aires: Talleres Gráficos H. Cattáneo, 1913.

Rohrbough, Malcolm J. *Days of Gold: The California Gold Rush and the American Nation.* Berkeley: University of California Press, 1997.

Sarmiento, Domingo F. *Facundo ó Civilización y Barbarie.* New York: Appleton, 1868.

Serrano Redonnet, Jorge A. "Los Ortiz de Ocampo." *Revista del Centro de Estudios Genealógicos de Buenos Aires* 1, no. 1, pp. 3–62. Buenos Aires, 1979.

Soule, Frank, John H. Gihon, and James Nisbet. *The Annals of San Francisco.* With a new introduction by Herbert Ely Garcia. Berkeley CA: Berkeley Hills Books, 1998.

Taylor, Bayard. *Eldorado, or Adventures in the Path of Empire: Comprising a Voyage to California, via Panama; life in San Francisco and Monterey; Pictures of the Gold Region, and Experiences of Mexican Travel.* New York: G. P. Putnam; London: R. Bentley, 1850.

Udaondo, Enrique. *Diccionario biográfico argentino.* Buenos Aires: Editorial Huarpes, 1945.

Upham, Samuel Curtis. *Notes of a Voyage to California via Cape Horn, together with Scenes in El Dorado, in the Years of 1849–50. With an Appendix Containing Reminiscences . . . together with the Articles of Association and Roll of Members of "The Associated Pioneers of the Territorial Days of California."* Philadelphia, 1878.

Vilgré La Madrid, César. "De Dolores a Buenos Aires." *Perfiles* (February 1969), pp. 12–14. Dolores, Buenos Aires.

Williams, Albert. *A Pioneer Pastorate and Time, Embodying Contemporary Local Transactions and Events, by the Rev. Albert Williams, Founder and First Pastor of the First Presbyterian Church, San Francisco.* San Francisco: Wallace & Hassets, 1879.

Woods, James. *Recollections of Pioneer Work in California.* San Francisco: J. Winterburn, 1878.

Yabén, Jacinto R. *Biografías Argentinas y Sudamericanas.* Vol. 5. Buenos Aires: Editorial Metrópolis, 1940.

Zauner, Ph., and Lou Zauner. *California Gold Rush: A Mini History.* Sonoma CA: Zanel Publications, 1980.

Zorraquín Becú, Ricardo. *Historia del Derecho Argentino.* Vol. 2, 1810–1969. Buenos Aires: Editorial Perrot, 1979.

Index

Abbot, Christine, 241

Aconcagua, xix, 277 n.13

Adams, Captain, 182

Ainza family, 146, 147, 194, 215, 220, 228, 233, 258

Ainza, Agustín, 165, 177, 178, 181, 182, 190, 196, 197, 198, 200, 201, 202, 204, 214, 223, 232, 237, 243, 244, 258, 260, 284 n.118

Ainza, Belén (Neleb), 224, 243, 244, 245, 250, 258, 259, 285 n.132

Ainza, Francisco (Pancho), 181, 182, 258, 261

Ainza, Lola (Countess of Landsfeld), 215, 224, 233, 234, 243, 244, 248, 250, 258, 265, 267, 285 n.133

Ainza, Manuel, 258, 259

Airam. *See* Craig, María (Mariquita)

Alberdi, Juan Bautista, xiv, 267, 271

alcalde, 45, 57, 69, 70, 198, 272, 273

Aldunate family, 7, 259

Alemparte, Juan, 1

Alfredo, Mr., 36, 46, 52, 55, 67, 69, 70, 95

Algeria, 160

Allende, María Ignacia, 259

Allende Navarro, Fernando, viii, xi, 277 n.2

Alta California, 250

Alvarado, Andrea, 269

Alvarado, Emilia, 269

Alvares, José María, 23

Alvares, Mariano, 207, 212

Amalia, 265

America, xiii, xvi, 9, 22, 40, 58, 81, 84, 100, 114, 123, 124, 128, 131, 139, 141, 149, 150, 151, 158, 160, 166, 189, 243, 259, 262, 264, 266; attitudes toward, xiv, 47; attitudes toward South America in, 96; character of, xvii, 140, 148, 160, 188; conflicts with Indians in, 51, 56, 105; deaths in, 23, 25, 36, 54, 198; drinking in, 17, 29, 41, 62, 69, 129; friends of, 40, 130, 210, 245, 263; hostility toward foreigners in, 22, 23, 24, 29, 30, 33, 36, 47, 68–71, 74–80, 82–85, 87–89, 92, 97, 101, 119, 120, 121, 134, 263; immigrants to, 94; ingenuity and efficiency in, 15, 82, 113, 117; justice in, 42; laws of, 195; learning Spanish in, 15, 50; marksmanship in, 96; migrants in, 43; music in, 31, 32, 162, 173, 245; ships of, 43; society in, xiii, 94, 96; violence in, 29, 46, 70, 104, 197; women of, 115, 146, 207

American camps, 282 n.75

American River, 207

American Theater, 107, 206

American(s). *See* America

Americana Inn, 12

amputation, 182

Andalusia, 140

Andes, x, 60, 255, 285 n.136

293

Fairchild, L., 283 n.95
Famatina (La Rioja, Argentina), 268
fandango, 16, 173
Fernández, Borjas, 1, 262
Figueroa, P. P., 265
flood, 69, 85, 228, 229, 247, 252
Flores, Juan José (President of
    Ecuador), 256, 259
Florida, battle of, 270
Fort Sutter, 205
Fort Williams, 265
Foster, Rose, 210
Foulon, Madame, 235, 266
France, 23, 25, 35, 37, 83, 85, 89, 90, 91,
    92, 103, 105, 106, 109, 110, 112, 114,
    115, 119, 120, 121, 127, 128, 134, 138,
    151, 154, 160, 163, 188, 191, 202, 204,
    207, 222, 225, 241, 259, 263, 266, 283
    n.95
France Hotel, 206
Francia, Dr., 257
French. See France
French Camp, 176, 179, 283 n.107
French Revolution, 145
French Theater, 111, 172
Front Street, 263
Funes, Ambrosio, 259
Funes y Allende, Teresa, 259

Galán, 220
Galapagos Islands, 71, 263
Galup, Pedro Pablo, 220, 263
gauchos, 16, 90
Georgia, 274
Germany, 29, 135, 142, 232, 240, 274,
    275
Gerstäcker, F., 263, 274, 279 n.23
Gesualdo, V., 262, 263, 264, 270, 273
Gilles, St., 46, 143, 279 n.39
Giralda, 211
Godoy Quiroga, Regis, 269
Golden Star mine, 210, 221, 222, 223,
    225, 226, 284 n.123

González, Joaquín V., xv
Gorenflot, Friar, 62, 69
Green, Henrique, 71
Gregoire, Madame, 83, 281 n.57
Gremière, Madame, 103, 281 n.63
Gschwind, J. J., 269
Guarda, G., 263
Guard de Noble of Paris. See Mobile
    Guard of Paris
Gudde, E. G., 279 n.36
Güemes, General, 270
guitar, xiii, xv, xviii, 16, 23, 31, 37, 57,
    69, 72, 94, 95, 101, 106, 136, 142, 143,
    172, 173, 187, 197, 216, 223, 230, 237,
    240, 245, 262
Gutiérrez, B., 280 n.47

Hammond, R. P., 278 n.13
hanging (execution), 44, 59, 194, 199,
    201
Happy Valley, 109, 113
Hawaii, 9, 278 n.10
Hermosilla, 280 n.47
Hermosillo (Mexico), 258
Herrera, 50, 280 n.47
Herrera, Agustín, 223
Herrera, Andrés, 205
Herrera, Doña Juana, 270
Herrera, Francisco, 221
Herrera, Pedro, 33, 39, 263
Herrera, Santiago, 70, 76, 82, 83,
    84
Herrera de Toro, Madame, 262
Herrera y Arraigada, Pedro José de, 263
Herrera y Guzmán, x
Herz, Heinrich, 111–12, 113, 114, 263,
    264
huaso, 20, 278 n.20
Hugo, Victor, 241
Huntley, H. V., 260
Hutton, W. R., 264, 267, 274

illness, 138, 139, 140

Treasury of San Francisco, 98
Trejo, 23
Tucksbury, Jacob M., 273
Tucumán (Argentina), 102, 255

Udaondo, E., 262, 269
Ugalde, Javiera, 250
Union Hall, 108
Union Hotel, 136
United States, xiii, 29, 34, 92, 102, 113,
    141, 142, 146, 167, 168, 182, 216, 217,
    271, 284 n.117
United States Hotel, 108, 113, 116, 207,
    212
University of California, vii, xix
Upham, S. C., 263, 266, 284 n.114
Upper Bar, 269
Upper Peru, x
Urquiza, Justo José de (President of
    Argentina), xiv, 256, 257, 267, 271
Uruguay, 261, 268

Valdes, Mr., 228
Vallis [valley of] Josaphat, 3, 278 n.1
Valparaíso (Chile), xiv, 2, 3, 8, 11, 18,
    22, 50, 135, 136, 216, 217, 222, 223,
    226, 228, 249, 250, 251, 255, 256,
    267, 271, 277 n.4, 278 n.5
Varela, Juan Cruz, 12, 237, 274
vaudeville, 172, 186, 232
Velasquez and Simone, 241
Venice, 131
Venus, 101, 147
Veranito Camp, 207, 212
Versailles, 215
Vigilante Committee, 199
Vilgré La Madrid, C., 262
Villafañe, x
Villefort, Mike, 158, 159, 173, 209

Virginia, 260, 261
Vreullu, 241

Wair, Benjamin G., 261
Wakes, Mr., 225
waltz, 163, 223
Ward, Frank, 209, 245, 274
Ward Smith, 274
War Ministry, 262
War of Spanish Independence, 280
    n.49
Washington Street, 117
Weaver. See Weber, Charles
Weaver Club, 136
Weber, Charles, 53, 100, 118, 142, 154,
    162, 168, 170, 216, 261, 267, 273,
    274, 275, 279 n.40
Weber Creek, 274
Weber Point, 280 n.46
Weir, Benjamin G., 283 n.98
wharf, 107, 124, 127, 129, 137, 142, 143,
    185, 199, 204, 205, 238
Williams, 190, 231
Wilson, 221
Wilson, James, 285 n.130
Wood Creek, 282 n.75

Yabén, J. R., 266
Yankee, xiii, xiv, 28, 29, 39, 75, 92, 102,
    163, 218, 233
yellow fever, 39
Yerba Buena, 273

zamba, 281 n.67
Zañartu, Fabio, 9, 275, 278 n.9
zapateado, 281 n.67
Zarabia (Saravia), Federico, 21, 30, 272
Zenteno and Velasquez, 241
Zerrano, Manuel, 1